Ann —
Little steps !
Big Feat
Polly Letson

This book is a fascinating account of
one woman's solo journey around the world.
It is a moving story of resilience and perseverance
that all of us in the real estate business can
draw lessons from – goal setting, adapting,
charity and spirit.
Enjoy!

stewart title

3
MPH

The Adventures of One Woman's
Walk Around the World

Polly Letofsky

Denver, Colorado

3MPH:
The Adventures of One Woman's Walk Around the World

Published by GlobalWalk, Inc™
Denver, CO
720.289.3097

Library of Congress Control Number: 2010919343

Letofsky, Polly
    3mph: The Adventures of One Woman's Walk Around the World /
    Polly Letofsky

ISBN 978 0 9832085-0-1

1. Travel, 2. Memoir, 3. Adventure

Dedicated to

IRV LETOFSKY
1931 – 2007

This book's for you, Dad.
You told me I could and I did.

Author's Note

The events depicted in this book are authentic and all people are real. In most of the incidents the names are real, but in a few cases some names have been changed to protect the guilty.

"Only those who will risk going too far can possibly find out how far one can go."
— T.S. Eliot

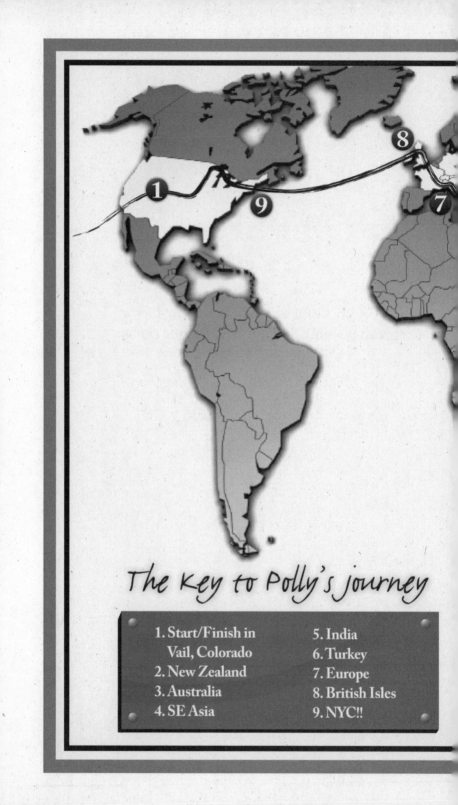

The Key to Polly's journey

1. Start/Finish in
   Vail, Colorado
2. New Zealand
3. Australia
4. SE Asia
5. India
6. Turkey
7. Europe
8. British Isles
9. NYC!!

Prologue

It was March 28, 2002, a typical one-hundred-ten degree day near Kondhali, India, when Shankar, the temporary crew support I'd hired to help me survive the last half of India, pulled up next to me. He said he'd be right back, he was just going to go fill up the car with petrol. "Please, please, don't go," I begged, leaning through his window. "Whenever you leave me, the men harass me and chase me and hassle me. Please don't go!"

"Oh stop, you are being silly. They are very friendly to you. You will be fine. I will be five minutes."

"Hurry!" I yelled after him as he disappeared around the bend.

At that moment, a truck roared around the same corner and headed in my direction. The truck was so overloaded with its cargo of oranges that its burlap tarp was bulging over the sides. When he hit that curve it sent him into a wobble that caught him up on two wheels and sent him careening out of control. I stopped walking and watched as he skidded to the left, to the right, to the left and *SMACK* into a cow. The cow came flyyyyyying through the air right toward me.

Oh good God, I thought. *Please don't let me die like this! How will my parents take the news that I was killed by a flying cow?* I threw my hands over my eyes and ducked.

The cow dropped a few yards ahead of me and bounced on the blacktop.

Dead.

I stood with my mouth agape, unable to move, though grateful that my obituary didn't include farm animals.

Within seconds I watched as the Hindus raced out of the village to the dead cow, weeping, praying, grieving over Her Holiness.

The Muslims were right behind them brandishing butcher knives, and I watched as they tore into the cow, blood pouring into the street. *Don't look, don't look, don't look!* I told myself. But I had to look, and I watched the Muslims lifting slabs of cow onto the backs of their bikes and strapping them down with bungee cords. My stomach came up to my throat and I started gagging.

I tiptoed through the blood puddles dry heaving past the dead cow and made my way into the village. Immediately on my left was a group of women holding down a goat by all four limbs, and I started talking out loud to myself, *Don't look, don't look, don't look!* But I had to look, and at that very moment, a woman cut the throat of the poor goat in what appeared to be a religious sacrificial goat killing.

The shock of it, while still in the throes of hurling from the cow, launched me into another bout of dry heaves, but I didn't have a moment to recover. A group of men had just spotted me and started yelling, "Madam! Madam! One moment, please, Madam!" Now all the men in the village knew there was an unaccompanied woman in their midst and sprang out of the woodwork. I picked up my pace, burst into a sprint, running through the village, gagging, blood on my shoes, the dead cow, the poor goat, *I might faint, oh God, don't let me faint.* I turned around to judge my progress and saw what appeared to be every male in the village—along with a parade of goats, cows, chickens and stray dogs too—running after me, "Madam! Madam! One moment, please, Madam!"

At the far end of the village a truck had just plunged off a bridge. Its two back tires caught the railing, leaving it swinging above the creek below. The men (and ensuing goats, cows, chickens, and stray dogs) immediately changed their focus and ran down to the riverbank to assist the driver as I continued running/heaving/puking out of town and finally slowed to catch my breath.

Within seconds Shankar drove up beside me, "You see?" he said, oblivious. "You are just fine."

Had this happened to me at the very beginning of my five-year journey, I would have cried uncle: "All right! All right! Never mind! I'll take that job back, please, and the condo too!" and would've found a way to live happily beneath the weight of a dream unful-filled. But by that day in March, 2002, I had been on the road for two and a half years. Though I was unaware of it at the time, it was exactly to the mile, (mile 7,062) halfway through my walk around the world, and I had come to accept, even expect, the loony and exasperating demands of the road. Heck, even the good times were demanding. But when people ask, "Did you ever feel like quitting?" I can honestly say no. Not once. Not ever. Not even the time I was nearly killed by a flying cow.

CHAPTER 1
The Seed

It was the summer of 1974. I was a twelve-year-old growing up in Minneapolis, and that was the summer I started to discover the world. Every morning I would go out on the front steps, scoop up The *Minneapolis Tribune*, and spread it across the breakfast table. I read about places called Thailand, Cambodia, India, Turkey, where kids lived an entirely different life than me and my buddies, who spent our summer days climbing trees and playing kickball in the front yard.

One morning I came across a photo of a man in a big, floppy hat, walking down an empty mountain highway in Colorado. The caption read, "David Kunst, walking through Colorado on his way home to Minnesota to become the first man to walk around the world."

Wow, I thought, staring at the photo. *I didn't know you were allowed to think of such a thing if you were from Minnesota.* Fascinated that the simple movement of putting one step in front of the other could transport you through countries, across borders, over mountains, and into various cultures, peoples and ideas, I was inspired. *That's how I want to see the world someday. I'll walk!*

Even then, though, I knew I was thinking way outside the box for a twelve-year-old girl from Minnesota in 1974, so I tucked the idea into the back of my head. The only time I actually mentioned it out loud was years later to a friend when I lived in Boston. We sat side by side on the 6:30 a.m. commuter train to work, surrounded by a sea of corporate executives in beige trench coats, when I suddenly felt compelled to blurt out my secret. "Have I ever told you that my dream is to walk around the world?"

*OK, so I'm not 12 in this photo, but lucky for the world there are no photos of me when I was 12.

14

"Yeah?" she said, her eyes still closed and head nodding off to sleep. "Have I ever mentioned that my dream is to get a job where I can sleep until eleven?"

It was a safe bet that she'd never remember the conversation, let alone hold me to it. In hindsight, it was clearly a journey I'd been subconsciously planning since that summer day when I was twelve.

My first foray into foreign travel came at age nineteen, when I visited the family of a foreign exchange student I had befriended in high school. That summer in Sweden provided a gentle dip of a toe into a new language and foreign culture. But most Swedes know a good spot of English and their climate and food are Minnesota's roots, so it was hardly akin to being thrown off the deep end.

That summer in Sweden whetted my travel appetite. A few months after arriving home, I signed up for a semester of college in Guanajuato, Mexico, a country that bordered my own and differed significantly from Sweden. Mexico gave me my first taste of the third world, and it was shocking. Poverty. Begging. Disease. Lawlessness. One afternoon, while my friends and I happy-houred in a bar, a man was gunned down right there in retaliation for killing the suspect's sister—in retaliation for cheating on a drug deal. That's when I realized I had, indeed, plunged off the deep end. I came home three months later, my nerves so tattered I thought it might be a million years before I'd ever leave the cozy womb of Minnesota again.

Something far short of a million years later, my nerves healed and my eyes aimed for another horizon. I quit my job as a radio announcer and commercial producer and purchased a one-way ticket to London. With twelve hundred dollars in my pocket and an orange daypack over my shoulder, I spent five months traveling through Europe sleeping in parks and train stations, and on occasion showering via a leaky garden hose. It was the beginning of my education on frugal travel and the final test was to survive on $5 a day with only an orange daypack of belongings.

At the end of my traveling-on-a-shoestring adventure, I landed in Boston with an advertising job at a large agency in a downtown high-rise cubicle. But I was the round peg in a square hole. I never wanted the beige trench coat; I wanted walking shoes. For two-and-a-half years, I was torn between what I was supposed to do and what I wanted to do. But I kept trying to make it work. In an effort to find a balance, I ditched the commuter train and opted to slip on my walking shoes at five-thirty in the morning and hike nine miles to get to work by eight.

I finally escaped my high-rise cubicle in Boston before it swallowed me whole, and headed west across the United States taking odd jobs for the sake of comedy. I gathered enough cash from working the chairlifts in Vail, selling hot dogs in San Francisco, and polishing my skills as a coffee runner at ESPN in Los Angeles, to buy a Circle-Pacific airline pass.

Years earlier, I had befriended a New Zealander who extolled his country's great hiking and relative safety for a woman traveling alone. I decided to stop there first. My good-for-a-year ticket, however, didn't quite match the two weeks' worth of cash in my pocket. Regardless, I waved goodbye to Dad at LAX and told him I'd see him sometime between two weeks and a year.

I returned five years later.

It was now 1993 (stay with me here; I know we're moving fast), and I had settled into Vail, Colorado. I lived there a full six years, feeling content and secure; but one thought nagged at me from the catacombs in my head: What about that walk I have always wanted to take?

At that same time, a number of women around me had been diagnosed with breast cancer—friends, colleagues, and two aunts, one of whom died. Let me be clear about one thing: these people lived all over the country, so no need to be concerned about the water in Vail! Nonetheless, it all happened in such a condensed time period that I became nervous and went to the doctor to get a mammogram.

What that doctor told me changed my life.

CHAPTER 2

Ready, Set...
Uh, Oh

"You can't get breast cancer if it doesn't run on your mother's side of the family," the doctor said. "So don't worry about getting a mammogram."

What fantastic news—I couldn't get breast cancer! My Aunt Dolly who had died of it was on my *father's* side. And the medical professional in a white jacket with a stethoscope around his neck had just said I shouldn't even be concerned.

Later that day, a friend called to ask how my mammogram went.

"I didn't have it. I'm one of the lucky ones. I can't get breast cancer."

Dead silence greeted me from the other end of the phone.

"Pretty lucky, huh? Breast cancer doesn't run on my mother's side of the family, so I don't have to worry about it."

"Excuse me? Who told you this?"

"The doctor."

"The *doctor* told you that?" I heard the blood shooting out of her eyes over the phone line. "Well, listen to me, and listen carefully. Every single woman in the world is at risk for getting breast cancer. Eighty percent of those diagnosed with it have no known risk factors. Did you know that?"

Her passion stunned me, but not as much as the realization that I couldn't trust someone dressed in a white jacket with a stethoscope around his neck. "No, I didn't."

"We know very little about what causes breast cancer." She continued her assault on the doctor's words. "In fact, that hereditary link we hear about accounts for only fifteen percent of the cases. It's that sort of bad information that gives women a false sense of security, and this is what we have to put an end to!" I listened intently to her thirty-minute tirade.

Walking home that night, I had my light-bulb moment. *That's it! That's what I'll do the walk for that I've always wanted to do!*

Immediately I loved the idea of a woman walking for women, educating women all over the world about this disease that bonds us all. My head started spinning with a million questions:

Could I walk every day for five years? What countries would I walk through? Would it be safe? How would I protect myself? Should I carry a weapon? Should I take a dog? How could I afford it? I would need sponsors. *How do you get sponsors?* I would need a business plan. *How do you make a business plan?*

During the last mile while walking home that night, I started planning my walk around the world for breast cancer.

It was not only the right idea, but also the right time. I always knew I had to be older and experienced enough to take the inevitable punches the world would throw at me, yet young enough to survive the physical beating. At thirty-four, I owned a condo and had a nice job as Sales Manager at the Antlers at Vail, a condominium/hotel at the base of Vail Mountain. I felt secure, grounded. Paradoxically, I needed to feel settled and secure before committing to a journey of such vulnerability.

That night, I pulled out every world map I could find and spread them all over the floor next to my laptop. I began the process of researching each country and its rules for proper travel documents.

Over the next weeks I also researched who had done this before. A handful of people have actually walked around the word—at last count four men and one other woman. A British woman did her walk in stages; she walked one continent, took a two-year break back in the UK to raise funds for the second continent and then back to the UK, etc. But after she finished, she admitted to catching rides across America, which resulted in her being stripped of "The First Woman to Walk Around the World" title. Despite the skipped thousand miles, I give her enormous kudos. She walked 18,000 miles; I was planning just over 14,000.

The questions continued to bounce back and forth in my head. By the time I got to China, would I have this walking-through-foreign-lands thing down pat or be scared out of my mind? Would I get lonely? Would I starve to death if I didn't find a town where I could replenish supplies?

That night I stayed up until dawn highlighting possible routes, making charts and plans. When the sun came up on the other end of the night, I finally went to bed with my head on fire. I knew I could do this; I could always put one step in front of the other.

It wasn't long before I hit my first hurdle. When I called potential sponsors, I got a big dose of reality.

"Yeah, alone...Yep, yep, that's right...I'm a woman...Five-foot-two, one-hundred pounds...You'll call me back?...Great."

Months went by without a return call. I became so discouraged that I started to question myself. Maybe this, in fact, couldn't be done. Maybe I was just a big fat dreamer.

I'd always been in awe of people who had the vision to make a five- or ten-year plan and see it through. Vail's own local legend Pete Seibert had stood on top of a no-name mountain in 1957 and scribbled a forty-year plan on the back of a napkin to create Vail, the greatest ski mountain in the world. I'd never had a vision for anything—except my walk around the world. It was so clear to me, why couldn't anyone else see it? But if absolutely no one could see this project as clearly as I could, maybe I should listen to them. Maybe I should just let it go. I could aim for the glass ceiling at work, live happily in my condo, and get a couple of cats. I could be happy. Couldn't I?

On the night of that realization, I was at work filing reservations. It was boring, redundant work that allowed ample time for pouting. When amidst the pile of reservations, I came across a slip of paper.

Definition of Commitment
When you find a way over every hurdle in your path
and nothing but success is an option. Commitment.

Where had this come from? I looked around the office. "Is this yours?" I asked a colleague.

He looked at it and handed it back. "No, what do I care about commitment?" Now I'm neither superstitious nor religious, and I suspect that under any other circumstances, I would have tossed that piece of paper. But it had popped up with the right words at the right time. At that moment, the words swept through me like a tidal wave, and I became wholly committed and never again thought about quitting.

When I finally admitted out loud what I was planning, my friends' reactions ranged from smiles and "that's cute" to "the farthest you've ever walked is 210 miles on a backpacking trip and that qualifies you to walk around the world?" Some looked puzzled. "I don't get it. What do you mean *alone*? Who's going with you?" Then there was the old boyfriend who asked, "What are you running from?"

I understood their questions. I was thirty-seven years old. My peers were raising families and/or in the throes of a career path. Why would any reasonable person put that life aside for one of such instability?

But the people who questioned my walk proved to be the exceptions. Most were surprisingly receptive and unalarmed. Those who knew me best knew I could and would do it.

Then I had to break the news to Mom.

Mom had always been supportive of the unconventional routes her kids had taken, even when that support came with a hearty gasp. There was the time my brother, PJ, at age twenty, was hitchhiking around Europe. He called her one morning at three a.m. to tell her he'd made it to Istanbul.

"How did you get to Istanbul?"

"Couple of guys offered us some money to drive a Mercedes from Munich to Turkey."

It was 1979, and the Ayatollah Khomeni had just taken over bordering Iran. Turkey was certainly no place for a young Jewish boy to drive a Mercedes over the border for a couple of strangers. I heard the shriek through the house that morning.

With the same valor, my sister Cara announced she would continue with her scheduled trip to Russia, just days after the Chernobyl Nuclear Power Plant blew up, blanketing the country with lethal radiation.

But telling her I was heading out into the world alone for five years on foot was on a different scale. This wasn't an adolescent traipsing through Europe with an orange daypack. Some people might deem this silly. Unrealistic. Romantic whimsy. I had to break it to her gently.

My chance came when she drove through Vail en route from her winter home in Tucson to her summer home in Wisconsin. I said I had something to tell her, and she sank onto my denim-blue couch and braced herself, I'm sure, for an announcement of either an alternative sexuality or that I now had a parole officer.

"I've had an idea in my head since I was twelve."

"Okay..."

"I've decided now's the time."

She didn't blink.

"I want to walk around the world."

Still no blinking.

"And I plan to leave next year, August 1, 1999."

I explained the plans already in place, the route I had laid out, and the sponsors that had come onboard. Then I waited a moment.

No response.

"I need you to be supportive..."

"No, uh, sure. That's...great. Exciting. It sounds like you've already put a lot of thought into this. Wow. What do you need me to do? Really? Walk? The world?"

I chose to understand this as a full-blown endorsement.

Then I told Dad.

He didn't say anything...for six months.

Getting in shape for a walk around the world didn't mean getting off the couch and getting physical. I'd always been an athlete— running, skiing, hiking, snowshoeing. Training for this trek meant learning about nutrition and first aid, researching cultures. I studied travel regulations and soon discovered that few countries can actually be walked through and most change visa regulations as often as I change outfits.

I read books about people who had attempted endurance events, even inadvertent ones—like the British couple who drifted in a life raft through the South Pacific for five months after a whale capsized their sailboat. They caught sea turtles for food, using dental floss and a safety pin, before being rescued by a passing Korean fishing vessel. It was consoling to know that no matter how bad it got for me, at least I would never have to eat sea turtles on a raft drifting aimlessly in the Pacific.

My biggest logistical question involved how to carry my gear. At a minimum my backpack would be at least fifty pounds, which I'd carried regularly during multi-day backpacking trips. I was concerned, though, that day after day, with an increased water load through deserts and desolate areas, the weight on my back would eventually take its toll on my hundred-pound frame. Another option was to jerry-rig a baby buggy accessorized by bungee cords and mesh straps with strategically placed buckles.

Either way, the picture in my head was to go it alone. There was a brief thought of securing a crew driver but it came and went. Who would I possibly find that would volunteer their time, have money for their own expenses and be able to handle the bumps in the road? To say nothing of having a personality that would blend cohesively with my own. And anyway, how would that ad look?

> *Wanted: Outdoor loving, financially secure individual to volunteer time driving 3 miles per hour around the world. Duties include pitching camp, cooking by campfire, and serving as personal bodyguard if necessary.*

I decided to keep my options open in case someone landed in my lap. Otherwise, I would prepare to go it alone.

I did need someone on the home front to handle website maintenance, sponsorships, proper dispersal of donations followed by thank-you cards, etc. I also needed someone to mail me clothes, shoes, film, and other necessities when needed.

Enter Tabatha.

A friend introduced me to a recent law school grad who had just started a women's sports organization. She was based out of southern California, not too far from Dad. We met her over dinner in Los Angeles and listened, electrified, as she talked with animation and zeal. Charming, bright, and excited about being involved, she told us her mother had died of breast cancer when she was a teenager. That explained her passion for my big adventure.

Tabatha proposed forming a foundation specifically for my project, followed by applying for 501c3 status and assembling a board of directors. She offered to serve as Executive Director, a salaried position paid from corporate sponsorships. Her plan included creation of a sponsorship proposal and acquisition of sponsors to raise funds for the National Breast Cancer Coalition (NBCC). Her ideas sounded terrific. She was exactly what I had hoped to find.

Then that crew support landed conveniently in my lap. My friend Dave, a Mr. Fix-it kind of guy who had moved from Vail back to Missouri, called and asked if I would like crew support. He could pay his own way, and we could use his van. We had worked together and gotten on well, but never spent much time together beyond that. Still, we agreed upon a plan. He'd join me from the beginning through New Zealand—or the first seven months of the walk—and then we'd reevaluate.

My long time dream was progressing steadily toward reality.

Packing up my life at age thirty-seven wasn't the same as doing it at twenty-one, when all I had to do was ship two boxes of belongings to Dad for storage. I had a good job, a mortgage, a 401K, an IRA, a boyfriend. A good life. But slowly I started stripping that life down to its bare bones. In July 1999, I rented a big truck and packed it up with all my household goods: pots, pans, plates, pillows, videos, CDs, and an embarrassingly large closet full of clothes. Then I drove down the mountain to Denver's Mile High Flea Market and sold it all by three that afternoon.

The pieces were falling into place and my To Do list became more immediate.

- Cancel gym membership √
- Cancel People Magazine √
- Forward mail √
- Make doctor appointment for immunizations √
- Make a will √
- Copy of license, passport, credit card to Dad √
- Quit job √

August 1st was closing in.

It was the summer of 1999. JFK Jr. had just gone missing and the world was hanging on through the twenty-four-hour news cycle for any small piece of news. Other than John-John, the world was in pretty good shape. The stock market was on the rise, unemployment was down to four percent, and the war in Kosovo was wrapping up.

My relationship with Tabatha, however, began to display some red flags. She'd been on board for a year, and she still hadn't secured any new sponsors. No marketing plan had been presented, and in each weekly meeting she promised a to-do list that repeatedly had not been *to-do'ed.*

She had, on the other hand, secured 501c3 status for the foundation, appointed herself Executive Director, and was putting together a board of directors. I repeatedly requested that Dad sit on the board to protect my interests, but she declined.

"That seems like a conflict of interest. Besides, *I'm* the one who is in charge of looking out for your best interests."

Dad and I knew an oncologist who would have loved to serve. Tabatha nixed that, too, because, she said, he was too far away. My antennae went straight up, but her ideas and excitement were still infectious and energizing, so I gave her the benefit of the doubt and put the red flags on hold. Besides, I was preoccupied with other preparations.

Then ten days prior to leaving, Dave called hopped up on Vicodin.

"Uh…listen…so…"

Silence.

"Dave? Is that you?"

"Yeah. Sorry. Listen. I'm…in…the…uh…hospital…"

Lost him again.

"Dave? You there?"

"Yeah. I keep…falling…asleep…"

"Did you say you're in the hospital?"

Between naps, Dave explained that the night before he'd t-boned his motorcycle into a turning car that sent him into a double flip over the vehicle. Luckily he was wearing a helmet, but his right leg was shattered. If he didn't lose it altogether, at the very least it would be months of rehabilitation. He was so sorry to disappoint me, but there was no way he could honor his promise to be my crew support.

I called Tabatha, and the two of us launched into a last minute search to find someone else to help me—at least until I could create a system to revert to my original plan and travel solo. In reality, one of the most difficult sections of the entire five-year journey was the very first leg—the sprawling deserts of the American West. If there was any region that required crew support, it was through the high desert plains of Arizona and the Mohave Desert in California.

Within days Tabatha found the perfect person, a woman who loved the outdoors, camping and had no qualms about sleeping in a tent on cold nights in the Rocky Mountains. She liked to cook and would look after me like a mother hen. She could fix the van, too, if it broke down on a lonely mountain road. Her help would be temporary—possibly six weeks—until I got to Arizona. Judy was the mother of Tabatha's boyfriend. Within hours, she called and introduced herself.

"Polly! It's Judy! This is so great! I've heard all about your walk, and I would love, love, love to help you out. Don't you worry about me. I can handle all the weather and the outdoor life. I'm the self-proclaimed mother of mothers, and I promise to take good care of you, protect you, and feed you until you're fat."

"Oh—"

"I know you're concerned that whoever helps you with this crew support job better be ready to be grubby day after day because showers won't be readily available. I'm just fine with that. I'll stay with you as long as I can, but eventually I'll have to get back to my family. I've got two teenage sons at home, and they can't live too long without me. I figure about six weeks. Will that get you halfway through Arizona?"

That was our introduction and apparently sufficient groundwork to spend six weeks together.

Dave didn't need his van for a very long time, if ever again, so he offered to let us use it. Within days, Judy packed her bags and flew to Missouri to retrieve Dave's van, sufficiently outfitted with vanity plate RAC'N DAV.

Judy and I hadn't yet met in person, but as she drove RAC'N DAV back to Colorado, we spoke on the phone regularly. Sharp, sweet natured, with an innate resourcefulness, she was, in fact, the mother of mothers, and I was thrilled to have found her in this eleventh hour.

But I was about to get a glimpse of her other side.

"Polly?"

"Hi, Judy!"

"I'm only an hour away from Vail, but there's been a rockslide in Georgetown. It's closed I-70. They say it might be hours, maybe even morning, before anyone can get through."

"You okay?"

"Yes, I'm fine. I'll find a cheap hotel and get to Vail tomorrow. I just wanted to let you know I'm going to be late."

"Thanks for calling. I'll see you in the morning."

"Okay. Bye."

She sounded lively and animated, hardly inconvenienced. But as I took an extra few seconds to hang up the phone, I heard her ranting to herself and realized she hadn't disconnected on her end: "Oh, sure, Polly! Like you give a shit how I feel! Here I am stuck in this God-forsaken rat hole of a town in these damn rockslides, and all you have to say is 'I'm sorry, see you in the morning.' Yeah, right, you couldn't give a crap about anyone but yourself, you stupid bitch…"

A hot sweat poured through me and I held the phone long after it fell into a dial tone. Oh, good God, I thought in a panic. *Who is this woman? Is she mentally stable? Am I safe on the road with her?*

With the phone still in my hand, I paced the living room. What could I do? I was leaving in three days! Is this what the bride feels like on her way to the chapel when she just found out her groom had cheated on her? I continued to pace while weighing my choices:

1. Tell her I heard her freakish rant and that she should turn around and drive RAC'N DAV right back to Missouri? Then I would go on my own with my fifty-pound backpack.
2. Cross my fingers, pretend everything was fine, and hope we could work through freakishness?

In an emotional state close to numbness, I chose option two; essentially opting to drive to the chapel and marry the cheating man hoping he would change.

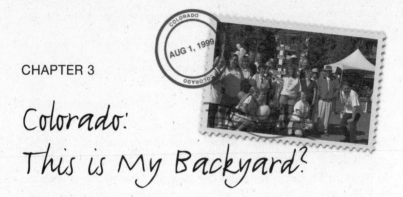

CHAPTER 3

Colorado: This is My Backyard?

Polly's Journal, August 1, 1999

I leapt out of bed at 5:30 a.m. crept through the living room where friends were scattered about on the floor and the couch and the balcony. I made my way to the bathroom for my last morning in this apartment.

My starting line was in Lionshead Village, two hundred yards from my Antlers apartment. My friends and I made our way over to where a bustling crowd was setting up the stage for speeches and a table to sell tee shirts from our foundation for fundraising. A local bagel shop joined the spirit by giving away bagels and juice for the walkers joining me.

For a full hour I made my way through Lionshead Village, saying hello and goodbye. One by one, my friends pulled me aside, looked me straight in the eyes, and gave me their best, wisest, and most heartfelt advice.

"Be smart. Don't take unnecessary chances. Listen to what your body needs. Don't forget to drink LOTS of water. Watch the traffic. Don't trust anyone—there are loonies out there. Walk early; catch the cool weather. Don't forget to take days off! Call me if you need anything, anywhere, anytime!" I spun around Lionshead Village, hugging, thanking, breathing.

Then I heard, "Polly, are you ready?" The emcee gathered everyone around the stage and introduced some key speakers before the grand send-off.

Ironically, the rep from the National Breast Cancer Coalition couldn't make it due to a third and aggressive bout with her own breast cancer.

Mom was next and started with an apropos, "Now I know how Columbus' mother felt." She turned and spoke to me directly. "I know you're traveling light, but there are a few things you should take along. Take patience. You will need it on long, desolate stretches and busy border crossings. Take an open mind to let in new and strange experiences and see the good, the amusing, and the beautiful there. Include a good supply of courage. You'll be walking for all those women who are summoning their own courage to face the specter of breast cancer in their lives at home. And don't forget wisdom. Strap it to the top of your pack. You'll need it every day."

It was then, with a hundred friends and family by my side, that I took my first steps westbound down the Gore Creek recreation trail.

I'm on my way, with all the anticipation and possibilities. Will I discover how the world ticks as I desire? Or will I discover the world is really flat and fall right off the edge?

People had repeatedly asked if this was going to be a Guinness record. I've never given two hoots about the Guinness record, but so many people kept on me that I thought it was best to at least understand the Guinness rules. At the off chance that someday I might give a rip, I'd hate to be omitted on a technicality. Here's what they told me:

To say you've walked around the world you need to
1. *start and finish in the same place;*
2. *walk at least 14,000 miles;*
3. *walk across at least four continents;*
4. *fly to the next continent when you reach the end of one;*
5. *have a witness sign your records every day to confirm that you walked that portion. Save photos and newspaper articles to prove you were on the road. These documentations serve as additional proof for a Guinness record.*

I also established some ground rules of my own. If someone offered me a ride back to a hotel or home, I could accept as long as I was dropped back at the exact same spot to carry on the following morning. I also decided that I wouldn't have such tunnel vision toward this goal that it would make me stupid. Let's say, God forbid, a war was to break out along my route, I wouldn't plow right through the middle of it. I had to remain loyal to my goal to walk every step, yet realize that the world could throw me a curve ball that might warrant a tough decision along the way.

For the first two nights Judy and I stayed with friends. The roads were familiar, friends were still in local calling range, and they'd drive by to see how I was doing or take me to lunch.

By the third day I was in a rhythm and it felt natural. I knew I could do this. I could get up every morning and put one step in front of the other.

On the third night we didn't have a friend to stay with. We were forty-five miles from the starting line and on our own for the first time. At the end of the day, Judy drove up and said, "Hop in, I have great news!"

I hadn't spent much time alone with Judy. Family and friends had surrounded me during the kick-off hoopla, but by the time we reached Dotsero, it was just Judy and I. So far, she had been helpful and cheery, positively positive with hardly a hint of the psychotic phone rant. Maybe I was wrong about—

"You'll never believe what Jesus did for you today!"

"Jesus?"

"Yes, our Lord and Savior, Jesus Christ. You won't believe what he just did for you."

"What did, er, Jesus, do for me?"

"He got you two-way radios for easy communication through the mountains, a free campground and look," she said, handing me a gift certificate.

"Jesus got me dinner for two at the Outback?"

She explained that she'd spoken with a local Radio Shack about borrowing two-way radios for the three months it would take me to walk to the Pacific Coast. Cell-phone service was sketchy through the mountains and the desolate high-desert plains of Arizona and California, so Judy, Radio Shack, and Jesus himself decided that two-way radios were the ideal solution.

"Wow, thank you!"

Which was the real Judy? The aggravated person I heard when she didn't know I was listening, or the Samaritan who praised the Lord and all he did for us? The jury was still out.

On the way to dinner at the Outback Steakhouse, I confirmed plans for the next day. "I think we can make it all the way to Glenwood tomorrow. It's seventeen miles, but if I get an early start—"

"I haven't had sex in six years."

Hmm. "After another seventeen-mile day, I'll need to rest. That's a good pace, don't you think? Walk five days, take a day off?"

"Six years, can you believe it? My husband refuses to have sex with me. He spends his weekends with the guys, late evenings, vacations, too, and he won't touch me. I told him I feel unattractive when he doesn't look at me, doesn't touch me. He said if I'm feeling unattractive, he'd pay for lipo on my hips and thighs."

"Maybe six days of walking and one day off—"

"So off I go to the lipo doctor to suck the fat out of my hips and thighs and stomach, too, and my husband still won't touch me. Let me tell you about lipo. Fucking scam. My stomach still has a pouch and my thighs grew back. All that pain and money and I still have fat thighs and a husband who won't touch me."

Judy didn't have anything near fat thighs. She was a beautiful woman. She had a short, stylish bob of blonde hair with natural highlights. Petite and toned, she dressed with a unique sense of style. Even while camping lakeside and driving a broken-down van through the mountains, she fashioned herself in a stylish cobalt-blue off-the-shoulder sundress with Bandolino slides and bauble earrings.

She was also a natural flirt that spread good cheer. Men were immediately attracted to her. At corner stores, truck stops and rural cafes they'd nudge each other and say, "Wow, get a load of *that*! She's *hot*!"

During the forty miles from Glenwood Springs to Aspen, Judy told me her story: She had three sons by three different husbands, each marriage ending in divorce because of domestic violence. Her father had beaten her, too. After husband number three did the same, she left with her three sons in tow. Alone and homeless on a rainy, empty road, the Lord came to her in a beam of light and told her to move to Lake Elsinore. There she met husband number four. He was a successful businessman living in a McMansion in southern California with a state-of-the-art kitchen and dewdrop-shaped backyard pool. He promised to take care of her, even put her boys through college. They'd been married six years. But she soon discovered that he was an alcoholic, verbally abusive, and she believed he married her to be his trophy wife while he continued living on the down low as a closeted gay man.

That was a lot of raw guts exposed on the road to Aspen and I was conflicted. I wanted to be empathetic and understanding, but my head was at the starting line of my five-year walk and I had a lot to figure out. There was a great deal of work to do between media interviews, fundraising each night and trying to help Tabatha get contacts for sponsorships. I wasn't in the frame of mind to offer her the sort of friendship and counsel she seemed to need.

On the other hand, Judy was a dynamo at being crew support. From town to town she persuaded campgrounds, hotels, and restaurants to donate services in exchange for being featured on our website Supporters page and holding local press interviews on their property. She gathered bystanders at truck stops and parks where she sold our foundation tee shirts and collected donations. Tirelessly and fearlessly, she talked to local bar owners about holding small fundraisers. So, the jury was in; Judy was undoubtedly troubled, but she was also a whimsical eccentric with a fierce work ethic whose ideas helped set the pace for what would become ongoing standards for the next five years.

Two weeks of walking equaled a two-hour drive by car, well within driving range from Vail. My friends, Beth and Randi, came to walk with me from Aspen to Crested Butte via the Maroon Bells, the premier hiking trail in Colorado, particularly in mid-August. I was tickled to have two good friends to share Aspen's panoramic views and mountain peaks for the fifteen-mile trek because I knew once I left U.S. shores, I wouldn't have any visitors, or even see a familiar face for years. Each step we took together bloomed with wildflowers that swept across the terrain like a box of Crayola Crayons.

They got a taste of the steadfast support I was getting every day from strangers when people treated us to lunch and invited us into their homes. They also witnessed what I noticed after only a few days on the road: at every truck stop and convenience store, at every restaurant and mountain road, we ran into women who were directly affected by breast cancer.

Beth and Randi were exceedingly impressed with Judy. Who wouldn't be? On nights we didn't camp, she found us a hotel—donated—and continued to organize impromptu fundraising events at local bars and restaurants. But they didn't see her outbursts, her tears, her anger at the world; or hear about her lipo and her husband not touching her. They didn't see that she could be jovial and high-spirited one moment and paranoid the next. They didn't know she accused me of tapping her cell phone to hear conversations with her husband. They only saw her positive, bubbly self who loved life and Jesus, her savior.

I first heard about Lake City, Colorado, when reading the book, *Walk Across America*, by Peter Jenkins. The town lies in a valley surrounded by six 14,000-foot mountain peaks. Harsh winters with eighty-three inches of snowfall and an average temperature of two degrees don't seem to faze the three hundred people who live there year round. That number triples in the summer when people with summer homes arrive for fishing, hiking, four-wheel driving, and eating.

Anyone would be hard pressed to find a more beautiful town in the world, and I wanted to walk through Lake City on my route from Vail to the Four Corners. Beth had returned home, but Randi was still walking with me. We turned south down Highway 149 and were almost there when in true Colorado form, the sunny weather slowly started to change. To the east a thunderstorm was brewing; to the west, dark clouds threatened to drench us in a downpour of rain.

We laughed at our good luck as the hot sun poked through the clouds shining directly down on us. For miles we kept our eyes on the impending storms, but whatever turn the road took, our single ray of sun continued to keep us in its beam. Eleven miles, twelve miles, thirteen miles, the sun hovered over us.

At fourteen miles our luck changed. Lightning shot out of the west within a half mile of us. "That was pretty close!" Randi exclaimed.

"Let's go!"

We walked fast, then faster. Another bolt struck directly ahead. We tucked our heads down and tried to outrun Mother Nature for the last mile into Lake City.

Despite the pummeling rain, Lake City lived up to its reputation as a beautiful place, the epitome of an old western town with buildings painted vibrant colors and the hundred-year old General Store presiding over Main Street like a patriarch, hovering above the Cannibal Grill and the Mocha Moose Coffee Shop.

Debi Linker and her husband Jim found us catching our breath on the porch of the Lake City General Store.

"Are you Polly, the one walking for breast cancer?"

"Yes, how did you know?"

"We'd heard you were on your way into Lake City. Seeing your soggy backpacks, we made a good guess."

Debi and Jim invited us to their home for dinner, where we enjoyed a wonderful evening and heard her story about breast cancer. She had been diagnosed fifteen months before, going through the gamut of lumpectomy, chemo, and radiation.

Her sister, Ann, had also had breast cancer, twice. Her niece, Teresa, was diagnosed at age twenty-nine and died of related complications at age thirty-seven.

Debi was still recovering from eighteen months of tough treatments. Even so, all summer, she had been training for the Avon three-day walk from Santa Barbara to Malibu and had been trying to talk someone into hiking the two-day trek with her over Cinnamon Pass to Silverton. That's exactly the way we were headed, and she barely blinked an eye when I suggested she join us. She worried about her ability to handle the elevation gain up and over the 12,260-foot Cinnamon Pass with a portion of one lung missing, but jumped at the idea regardless.

The rule of thumb for hiking in the Colorado mountains is to be up and over the Pass and back down the other side to the tree line (11,000 feet) by noon. That's the hour when gray clouds roll over and, like a piñata, drop whatever is inside: rain, hail, lightning. Climbing sixteen miles over 12,260-foot Cinnamon Pass demanded an early start. At five a.m., the high-pitched beep of Randi's watch alarm sounded, and we all hopped into action.

Cinnamon Pass Road provided a beautiful climb. A layer of mist hovered above the valley, and deer darted across the road. A busy beaver tended his pond; even a couple of marmots poked their noses above the rocks to say hello. Four miles into the morning, we stopped to stretch our legs and saw a couple of guys racing down the mountain toward us. They introduced themselves as Rick and

Dave from Minnesota. Dave told us that they had made it to the top of Redcloud Peak, a fourteen-thousand foot peak nearby. When he called his mother to share the feat, she broke the news that she had just been diagnosed with breast cancer.

Outrageous! The only two men we met on this remote hiking trail in the middle of the San Juans at six a.m. had an immediate connection with breast cancer. Let me say outrageous again!

Six hours into the day the trail rose above 12,000 feet in elevation. Randi and I arrived at the summit as strong as a couple of mountain goats. Debi, however, had fallen behind, which was no problem unless dark clouds rolled in.

My watch struck noon, and the dark clouds arrived with military precision. Debi was having a bear of a time with the last mile, but she was almost there. Randi and I cheered her on from the summit. We watched the sky grow darker and louder and looked down at Debi struggling up the trail. Our heads shifted back and forth as though we were watching a tennis match. Dark clouds. Debi. Dark clouds. Debi. *Be patient.* She's missing a chunk of her lung. Clouds. Debi. *Be nervous. This peak is a dangerous place to be. Be patient. Be nervous.* Clouds. Debi. *Hurry. Hurry.*

At 12:30 she made her final crawl to the summit, and on cue, the dark clouds started drizzling. "Oh, good God!" she said, throwing herself over the summit sign that confirmed our 12,260-feet elevation. "That was worse than chemo!"

But there was no time to let her rest. We were far above the tree line and prime targets for a lightning bolt. "Let's move!" we shouted in unison.

We grabbed our packs and high-tailed it down the west side of Cinnamon Pass just as the piñata burst and hail began to pound down. Lightning bolts struck all around us. The skies cracked open with a flood of rain—painful, loud, wet, piercing sheets of rain. The tempest raged so heavy and loud we couldn't talk to each other, nor could we see more than a shadow of each other although we were mere feet apart. We shifted our pace into fourth gear.

Hailstorms usually last five minutes, a bad one maybe ten. Thirty minutes into our downhill dash, the pellets still pierced us and flooded the trail with inches of hail and water, blinding us to our footing on the rocky trail. I peeked out of my hood at the horizon, looking for some sort of shelter, but all I could see were sheets of hail. There was no place to hide. We had no option but to keep running.

Wait! What's that? Another peek out of the slit in my hood caught a faint shadow of a building down the mountain. I got closer to Randi and yelled, "I see shelter! Let's aim for that!"

The shelter turned out to be the old ghost town of Animas Forks. As a ghost town geek, I knew about Animas Forks, but never envisioned I'd see it this way—as shelter from a fierce summer hail storm. And it wasn't as close as it looked. It took another half-hour before the three of us dashed into a sturdy looking cabin, tumbling all over each other in exhausted giggles.

We panted breathlessly, then picked ourselves up, peeled off our wet jackets and rain pants, hung our soaking socks over a beam, and continued giggling, just giggling. No one said a word. We didn't have to.

From my seat on a dry piece of floor I peered out the windows into the old ghost town. There were half a dozen abandoned buildings in Animas Forks, and though decrepit, they served as the perfect shelter in which to take cover from hail storms.

This town used to be a lively mining community of 450 people. The buildings that are only shells now used to be a bustling hotel, a general store, a raucous saloon, and an entire neighborhood of log cabins. Slight snag though; the town was built in a 11,200 foot Valley—prime conditions for avalanches. The town regularly got pummeled by snow, burying the locals. By the 1920s, its mining days neared their end, and Animas Forks became a ghost town. Thankfully for us.

After two hours the rain and hail lifted, and a couple vacationing from Connecticut arrived from Silverton. They drove a rented two-wheel drive Ford Focus—not a vehicle, they realized, that would get them over a flooded, sloppy Cinnamon Pass, and were happy to drive us back into Silverton. Judy would drive us back the next morning so we could carry on.

We dragged ourselves out of the cabin, shivering, stiff, limping, moving no faster than a half-mile an hour. When we reached the car, Debi introduced me to the couple, "This is Polly. She's the girl that's walking around the world."

In Silverton at the front desk of the Grand Imperial Hotel, stood a petite, thin older woman with a pixie hairdo and a retainer in her mouth that gave her a lisp. Her name was Sally Sanders, or as she said, "Thally Thanders."

Since Judy had to return to her family soon, everyone involved in my walk kept an open ear for someone to replace her as my crew support. If I could get help through the Mohave Desert to Los Angeles, I could go on my own from New Zealand. During small talk at the front desk with Judy, Sally leapt at the idea to be my crew support.

That made me nervous. A strange woman jumping at the idea of accompanying me around the world with hardly a second thought made me question her judgment—and it happened numerous times. People had a romantic view of the open road, expecting barrels of fun wrapped up in good moods and sunny days. The reality was bugs, bad weather, hard work, hard ground. It's like people who want children "to hear the pitter patter of little feet" but forget they come with sleepless nights, colic, and half-digested hot dogs thrown-up about the place. When Judy told me Sally was interested, I went down to the front desk to give her a dose of reality.

She told me that she had traveled a lot, particularly through South Asia, and was fully aware of the trials. "There's no greater trial though, than what I've just been through."

"What's that?" I asked.

"My husband of twenty-two years just left me for another woman, a much younger woman. He cheated on me many times, but because he was a prominent doctor in our little town in Texas, no one would believe me. I got a small settlement in the divorce, but not before he and his lawyer trashed me in the newspapers. I escaped Texas and landed here in Silverton to get my head back on straight."

"Why Silverton?"

"I heard it was a nice little town, and I wanted to go where no one knew me. I sold most of my belongings, drove here with whatever fit in my car and rented a house around the corner."

"Could you join me for six weeks from the middle of Arizona to the coast of L.A.?" I asked, not wanting to rule her out.

"Oh, I was thinking I could join you for the whole trip," she said.

"What do you mean the whole trip?" My concern returned.

"You know, the whole trip, the whole five years. I would love to help you."

"I can't pay you. You realize that?"

"That's okay. The settlement from my ex will support me."

She seemed lovely. It sounded like a good deal. But I didn't know this woman. What if she was jovial one minute and accusing me of tapping her cell phone the next? Though she did seem to understand what she was getting herself into. "I want you to think long and hard and realistically about this," I said. "I'll do the same. Maybe you could join Judy and me on the road a couple of days next week to see what it's like. Then we'll talk again."

She agreed, and I limped up to my room.

From Silverton, Randi and Debi returned home, but both promised to meet me in Los Angeles for the dash into the Pacific Ocean that would mark the end of my first leg. So it was back to being alone on the road with Judy. Sally stayed in touch regularly. Although she couldn't join me full-time until I arrived at the western border of Arizona in a month, she joined us for a day as crew support with Judy to see if she liked it.

After that lone day, I wondered if she would pack her bags and head right back to the abuse in Texas.

The day Sally joined us happened to be the day we were invited to an Indian sweat lodge. None of us realized what that entailed, but we were thrilled. We only knew it was a sacred, spiritual event among the Ute people and involved a lot of sweating.

Our invitation came at a Mexican cafe in Silverton where we met Della. A graceful, petite native Ute woman who treasured her culture and heritage, she wanted us to have an opportunity to experience it. She particularly loved the idea that her family would have the opportunity to pray for my safety as I walked around Mother Earth.

Della met the three of us when we arrived in Durango after the day's walk. She led us on a thirty-minute drive through the winding back country to her little white house. The sweat lodge sat in her back yard and represented the womb of Mother Earth. It was an unremarkable brown canvas dome, ten feet wide, six feet high, with a pit in the center for the searing rocks.

Her mother Gail greeted us at the door and introduced us to Junior, who would be leading the sweat. He was an older Ute man with skin like soft leather and a mop of thick gray hair.

Gail led us to a back room where we changed into thin cotton dresses similar to hospital gowns. After a briefing on what we might expect, she showed us how we should sit on our knees and always keep them covered. Gail explained the sweat would last about ninety minutes, and if we started to feel claustrophobic, we should put our faces to the earth because it was cooler there. Otherwise, we should note what everyone else was doing and follow suit.

Night fell and thunder growled as Gail led us barefoot across the backyard toward the sweat lodge. Sally, Judy, and I ducked through the small canvas door and entered clockwise around the rocks, each of us taking a seat on a square piece of carpet.

"How are you doing?" Gail asked me.

"Fine so far." It was warm, but nothing I couldn't handle.

Della took a seat next to me, and three men followed forming a full circle around the rocks. Junior entered last and thanked everyone for coming. He threw water on the rocks, which made them hiss. Then he threw sage on top. At that, one of the men rose and closed the canvas flap to the outside world, and the nine of us were alone in the womb of Mother Earth.

It was pitch black. Not so much as a glow from the rocks. Within seconds, the heat swelled through the dome, sucking all the oxygen out of the tent. I started to panic. The darkness. The heat. The thunder. Junior started chanting, filling the last bit of air left in the womb. My panic overwhelmed me.

I've gotta get out of here! My God, I can't take this for ten seconds. How will I survive an hour and a half! Oh, God, help me! Where is the air? I can't breathe! How can I gracefully hurdle over Junior, avoid the thousand-degree rocks and bound through the exit without causing a scene? No! I would insult their culture, their sacred circle, and they would undoubtedly never stop talking about the white girl who couldn't take a sweat for more than ten seconds.

My choice was clear: either insult my hosts or die in this sweat lodge.

I chose death.

I laid my face down to the earth where it was cooler. *Yeah, this is okay, a little oxygen.* I took a couple of deep breaths. Maybe I would live.

I listened to the chanting. Everyone joined in, and the voices filled the enclosure. With my mouth firmly planted on Mother Earth, I absorbed the sounds of their native tongue while sweat poured out of me like I'd never known: down my face, over my nose, down my back. Suddenly, I heard myself chanting with them. But with my face hugging Mother Earth, no one could hear me.

For twenty minutes, the voices chanted through the heat. Then Junior gave the order to open the flap and a glorious rush of cool air swept into the lodge.

Air! Glorious air!

I peeled myself off the ground and glanced up at Sally and Judy. Sally looked nearly as bad as I felt, but Judy was happy as a clam. She loved exploring various religions—and sweating in saunas—so was well into the depths of her happy place.

In short time it was time for round two. The flap went down and the lodge filled with heat. My panic started again, but I quickly put my head to the ground. This round was for prayers and thanks. Our hosts prayed that we be given strength and good health. They prayed for the women currently fighting breast cancer. They prayed for my safety on my great journey around the earth.

With no warning humility overcame me, and I started to cry. I cried and cried and cried. Add the chanting, the heat, the darkness, the thunder. I was clearly in a place I'd never been before.

When the flap lifted for the third round, the men got up to restock. One by one they put new hot rocks into the pit, while Sally and I watched dazed and sweaty with big eyes, refusing to believe it could get any hotter. One more twenty-minute round to go. They closed the flap, and I wondered if I would live to see it open again. Within seconds I could tell Sally was having a difficult time, and although she was right next to me, I had to feel around for her. I found her shoulder and whispered, "Put your mouth to the ground, it's cooler there." She dropped.

But this round was scorching, and the mouth-to-the-earth trick didn't work anymore. I started feeling dizzy. Oh, God, don't let me pass out! Twenty minutes, just twenty more minutes! Focus!

I discovered that if I put my whole body on the ground, instead of just my knees and face, I managed to catch more air. I curled into a fetal position and wondered if this was how they would find my body.

After twenty minutes that I barely recall, the flap opened for the last time. Darkness had come, and we could barely see each other. Judy was smiling with her arms raised high toward the Gods, Sally was rocking back and forth, crying, "Daddy! Daddy!" I was curled up on the ground in a fetal position, covered in sweat and left for dead.

"Junior," I managed to gurgle as he stepped over me, "Could… you get me…some…water?"

"See, Della," I heard him whisper, "now you know why this could never become a tourist attraction."

CHAPTER 4

Quake and Bake

Sally survived her inadvertent hazing, and we agreed that she would join me as soon as she could pack up her life back in Silverton. She left the sweat lodge sucking down a 64 oz water bottle and went to give her notice at the Grand Imperial Hotel. I would see her in a month on the west end of Arizona.

From Durango I turned right onto Highway 160, and after a month on the road I walked out of Colorado into Arizona. The welcome sign read "You are now entering Navajo Reservation Territory. Please enjoy the scenery." The scenery was a stretch of road filled with an eternal sea of rocky sand, remarkable in its tedium.

The majority of northern Arizona is Navajo Indian Reservation and, because they don't allow camping on their land, Judy picked me up at the end of each day, and we marked my spot with a pile of rocks in front of a recognizable milepost.

Each day the plan was to find a nearby parking lot and sleep in the van or drive all the way back to Cortez, Colorado, to find a hotel that would donate a night. Then each morning Judy would drive me back to the pile of rocks.

Of the entire five-year journey the stretch across northern Arizona was where I most wanted someone within earshot. This desolate area of road had its share of snakes, ugly bugs, and drunk drivers. So Judy and I put a plan together. Because cell phone service was sketchy at best, we wore our two-way radios on our hips. Judy remained within sight (no more than a half mile away). Every time a vehicle stopped, I got on the two-way and described it—which was usually followed by, "Everything's okay. They heard about what we're doing and gave us twenty dollars."

The terrain didn't change much over the two hundred miles from Cortez to the left turn to Flagstaff. Every morning Judy dropped me off at my milepost and I'd plod through the exact same view as the day before. Old rundown Navajo jewelry booths dotted the desert road, and I used them as picnic tables while I ate my apple and peanut butter-and-jelly sandwich.

Once in a while a red sandstone butte popped up on the horizon to entertain me. Sometimes a simple curve in the road did the trick. I regularly set up my big old-fashioned Canon SLR camera on an old beer bottle and ran across the desert, jumped on a rickety eroded jewelry booth, and waited for the self-timer to click.

The generally deserted road did, on occasion, provide a honk and a wave. Once I came across a Navajo man setting up a fruit stand in the middle of nowhere.

"What are you doing out here?" I asked him, genuinely curious.

"I'm setting up a fruit stand."

"People buy fruit out here in the middle of nowhere?"

"No, not really."

Intriguing.

I bought an orange for thirty-five cents, providing him with much of his income for the day.

About three times a day someone pulled over to Judy's RAC'N DAV and bought a tee shirt to add to our fundraising. Once in a while, Navajo children bounded out of a packed truck, screeching, "Are you the girl walking around the world?" Then they dug through their pockets to gather together a dollar. "We heard you on our school radio station, and we want to give you a donation. How long have you been walking?"

When I told them I'd been walking for a month, they tilted their heads and looked disappointed. So, like a kid quoting his age, I found myself stretching it as far as I could with the likes of "thirty-five-and-a-half days" and couldn't wait for the day when I could answer that question using "months" and "years."

Judy continued to be a dynamo, fundraising at truck stops and pullouts on the desert road. Then the next day she'd cry with paranoia that Jesus didn't understand her needs. She was creative and amusing, the sort of woman who could walk into a restaurant and, within the hour, rally all the patrons to link arms and sing show tunes. But she scared me, too. We'd developed a closeness over those six weeks, the kind you only get when you travel with someone. When the time came to give her back to her husband and kids, I was both relieved and heartbroken. I knew we would stay in touch, but I also knew we could never be close friends.

Sally couldn't join me for another couple of weeks, so for the intervening days Tabatha found a neighbor of hers who wanted to help. I said goodbye to Judy and hello to Courtney.

Twenty-nine-year-old Courtney hailed from Southern California. What Tabatha failed to mention is that Courtney had never been out of Temecula and, far more disturbing, had a paralyzing fear of toilets.

On our first day together we stopped at a gas station in Tuba City to fill up the van. I returned from the restroom to find her hunched over the front seat, pounding on the seat chanting to herself, "You can do this. You can do this."

"Are you okay?" I asked quietly, so as not to startle her.

"Yeah, yeah," she said, rocking back and forth. "It's just…It's just…"

"What is it?"

"I have to go the bathroom!"

"Oh, is that all? There's a nice clean one in this Conoco Station. It's in the back next to the Big Gulp."

"I can't use that bathroom."

Being someone who could now pee quite comfortably in any situation, I wondered what that meant, but didn't want to appear insensitive. "There's a McDonald's next door. They have great bathrooms."

"No! No!" she cried, hitting her fist on the dashboard. "You don't understand!"

Courtney lasted three days.

As it turned out, she didn't have a driver's license either, but, hey, details.

And there I was in Cameron, Arizona, population 978, with a beat up van and no crew support.

Sensitive to the fact that she had sent me someone afraid of toilets, Tabatha jumped on a bus from Los Angeles to help me get to Flagstaff, a four-day walk away.

My apprehensions concerning Tabatha continued to escalate. A major concern remained her ongoing determination to bar Dad from any planning or decision-making on my behalf. She refused his help with press, PR, or gathering items for a silent auction she wanted to hold. At one point, she emailed him and said, "Will you please stop emailing me."

My dad, Irv Letofsky, was well connected to the media scene in Los Angeles and around the country. *Why didn't she want him involved?* I wondered. Dad, however, took it in stride. He laughed at her blatant rudeness, and it didn't stop him from developing his own FOP (Friends of Polly) newsletter.

Mom, too, expressed concern. She regularly emailed Tabatha, asking for a list of friends and family who had made donations so she could send them personal thank-you cards. Tabatha ignored all her emails and phone calls.

Both Mom and Dad urged me to find a way to continue on my own, but I had to be prepared first. I decided that accepting Tabatha's offer to help get me to Flagstaff would be an opportunity to get to know her on a more personal level.

I was right. Our four days together went surprisingly well. She was very likable and charming, so much so that I started to question why I struggled with her. But then red flags reappeared, and I couldn't ignore them. Before I discovered Courtney's toilet-phobia, Dad had called Tabatha to find out about Courtney for a newsletter he was writing to supporters, donors and sponsors. "You don't need to know anything about Courtney," Tabatha replied.

I questioned her about it, and she said, "I know about her, and that should be good enough for your father."

A bit disconcerting.

When I asked to see a list of donors, she told me I didn't need to bother myself with that information. She and the board of directors had everything under control.

"Who did you finally line up as board members?"

"They're all good people."

"Did you get anyone in the medical field?"

"No, we don't need that."

"So who are they? What do we know about them?"

"They're my roommates."

At that point I knew my relationship with Tabatha could not continue, and I started working on Plan B. Dad still took Tabatha in stride, but he worried about her being involved with me. Mom always worried.

Between Tabatha's four days on the road and Sally's joining me in two weeks, I had a ten-day hole to fill—and I had a plan.

Mom and her husband John visited me for a couple of days on their way from Wisconsin to Tucson. Over dinner I filled them in on the ever-changing drama of crew support.

"Is that something I could help with?" she asked.

"Yes, yes!"

She agreed without a second thought, and Crew Mama was born.

Two months of road were behind me now (and reveled at every chance to use the word months). Minus the odd dramas, my spirits ran high, and my Walk was everything I wanted it to be—physically challenging, but doable. I still found a thrill in getting up every day and walking down a new road. The fundraising along the way continued to go well. Even walking the most desolate roads we met breast cancer survivors on a daily basis.

Mom met me in Flagstaff for her ten-day stint, and we slogged our way down old Route 66. Once known as Main Street America, it cuts right through Flagstaff. Old motels displayed neon signs from the sixties, touting, "We have color TV!" or "A bathroom in every room!" Interstate 40 replaced a good portion of Route 66 with a fancy four-lane highway and wide medians, leaving many towns deserted. But in recent years, several segments of old Route 66 had been listed on the National Register of Historic Places, spurring a revival. For the most part, I could stick to old Route 66, but through some stretches, Interstate 40 was my only option.

For ten days we carried on down Route 66 through the near-forgotten towns of Bellemont, Ash Fork and Seligman. Some merchants had proven their spirit by renovating their Main Street strips into 1950s Route 66 themes—like the old Chevy that adorned a parking lot, or the malts and root beer floats that appeared on every menu.

Mom took great care of me as temperatures climbed up near hundred degrees, insisting that I drink unprecedented amounts of water. "But Mom, I already drank 120 ounces! If I drink anymore, I'll be watering every sage bush from here to Kingman."

"That's the objective. You need at least 160 ounces a day through this desert."

Drinking 160 ounces of water a day is an infinite cycle of filling bottles, chilling them in the cooler, drinking every few minutes, and peeing just as often. Filling, chilling, drinking, peeing. It was a full-time job.

Crew Mama survived, even thrived, and I realized what a special treat it was to spend ten days on the road with my mom. Since I was just a month from leaving U.S. shores with no plan to come back for at least three-and-a-half years, I treasured our adventure together even more. Knowing that she now understood exactly what my journey would be like put us both at ease.

But all too soon the time came to pass the crew baton to Sally. She was joining me at the beginning of what promised to be one of the most difficult stretches of my entire trip—California's barren Mohave Desert. No towns, no hotels, no food, no water, no breeze, no shade.

I said goodbye to my mama, hugging her tight at gate C-24 as she headed back to Tucson. It would be a very long time before I saw her again.

For four weeks Sally and I slogged across the California border and through the Mohave Desert. (It's either Mojave or Mohave, depending on whether it's the desert, the county, a building, an Indian, in California, Nevada or Arizona. To avoid my brain from swelling, I'm using the "H" version for everything.)

We seamlessly settled into a routine and got to know each other. I found her easygoing, flexible, and capable, and she laughed at my jokes even when they weren't funny. All the characteristics you want in a crew support. She took over Mom's water goading and Judy's great skills without the emotional spikes. We became fast friends trudging and laughing through the stark inhospitable Mohave with an H.

Radio stations from Laughlin, Bullhead City, and Lake Havasu came in loud and clear, giving me an audio glimpse of the region's culture. The DJ said, "Currently we've got no breeze and 105 degrees." I walked and drank and walked and drank, consuming over two gallons (260 ounces!) of water each day. Crew Mama would've been proud. There was no break from the sun, not a cloud, not a whimper of wind.

Drab and forbidding surroundings peppered the forgotten stretches of Route 66. I entertained myself by waving to truckers, who rewarded me with a toot. Every couple of hours the Santa Fe Railway chugged by. I passed a church billboard that asked, "So, you think this is hot?—God."

Sometimes I took the radio out of my ears and listened to the silence, punctuated only by the sound of my feet hitting the road, step after step after step after step, in what very well could be one of the quietest, loneliest places on Earth. Once in a great while I'd pass an old abandoned hotel or the cracked concrete foundations of yesteryear's houses. A faded old sign that read "Cold Drinks Served Here!" lay sunburned on the side of the road. I imagined how it once welcomed traveling families in the glory days.

When Route 66 was displaced by the creation of Interstate 40, these communities went belly up, left to the sands of the tough desert climate. The tiny town of Amboy is one of the ghostly survivors of the glory days, barely.

"Population is seven, not twenty as the welcome sign says," Janet, the Postmaster, said. "During the heyday of Route 66, the town's population peaked at 700."

Janet added that, if there was any such thing as a thriving business in Amboy, it'd be Roy's Motel. If you were to see Roy's almost anywhere in the world, you would run and hide.

A decrepit run-down motel sitting amidst the sage brush; its towering neon arrow points to the registration office all but shouting Boo! when you pass by. The endless emptiness and dull whistle of wind make for the perfect movie set. In fact, Roy's makes an exceedingly comfortable income from Hollywood commercials and B movies starring the Boogie Man.

As Sally and I left the Amboy Post Office, we saw a Hollywood film crew pull into Roy's Motel. They were sold out night after night, so we marked our spot (Roy's) and drove ahead to the Best Western at Joshua Tree National Park. Little did we know it would be ten times scarier than Roy's Motel.

At 2:46 in the morning Sally and I were hurled from our sleep by violent shaking. A hundred thoughts raced through my head in seconds. *Oh good Lord, the room is possessed! Is the hotel falling apart?! A tornado! We're having a tornado! There's a tornado in the desert!*

I glanced over at Sally and saw her bouncing from one side of her bed to the other. Above the roar, she quite calmly said, "I think we're having an earthquake."

An earthquake! "Are we supposed to go hide under a doorway?!" I screamed back over the noise, gripping both sides of my bed.

She tried to get out of bed to take refuge under the door jam, but couldn't catch her footing.

"I don't see anything that could fall on us!" I yelled to her, noting no shelves above the beds.

"There is the second floor!"

A solid argument.

I'd experienced a handful of tremors during my bouts in L.A., and this was no tremor. It was a powerful, chucking-people-out-of-their-sleep convulsion.

After what seemed like fifteen minutes—all right, forty-five seconds—the rocking settled into a wave. We immediately turned on the TV to get an update, but the electricity was out. Our only contact with the outside world was a muffled conversation we heard through the walls of the Best Western.

We didn't know what to do after an earthquake when you can't watch CNN, call anyone, or go outside and talk about the drama with your neighbors. So we went back to bed.

But aftershocks persisted the rest of the night, and the big rumble right before dawn shook us out of bed for good.

"We may as well get up," I said, slipping on my walking shorts. "We're going to get thrown out of bed anyway."

"Can you imagine how powerful it must have been at the epi-center, if we got this big a jolt out here?"

At 6:30 a.m. the electricity popped on, and we quickly flipped through the channels in search of CNN. Breaking News scrolled across the bottom in bright red letters: "*7.0 Earthquake Hits Joshua Tree, California.*"

"We're *in* Joshua Tree, California!" said Sally as my mouth fell open.

The reporter continued. "There are no reported injuries. Fortunately the quake's epicenter was a very sparsely populated area of the Mohave Desert…"

"That's us all right."

CNN reported that the earthquake had lasted forty-five seconds and had jolted residents throughout Southern California, Nevada, and Arizona. It had derailed an Amtrak train just north of us in Ludlow, California. They showed aerial footage of the expansive high-desert plains that had been my home for weeks and explained that, due to the location, it was a rare and lucky occurrence that an earthquake of this magnitude could transpire with virtually no damage or injuries.

Highway Patrol and Los Angeles media roamed the Amboy desert road throughout the day, looking for visual damage: shattered windows, products rocked off retail shelves—anything for a good picture. One photo shown over and over revealed a massive crevasse in the earth just north of Amboy.

We continued watching the coverage while getting ready to walk. I wanted this desert behind me and was prepared to crank out as much mileage as I could while keeping a sharp eye out for any crevasses that might suck me into Mother Earth.

It was October 30, International Breast Cancer month, as I walked to the Pacific coast. Two friends from Vail, Stephanie and Randi, flew out to walk the last five miles with me. My sister, Cara, flew in from Minneapolis. Friends I had met on the road also showed up: Vicki, a breast cancer survivor I met in Glenwood Springs, Colorado, on day six; and Debi and Jim Linker from Lake City, who owned a winter home in nearby Palm Springs, plus friends Flora, Lisa and Judy from southern California.

Throughout the morning people walked together in twos as though they'd always known each other. Debi and Randi walked together a bit, Stephanie and Cara wandered off ahead, Sally ran around trying to get video footage. Judy was everywhere. Jim and Lisa brought up the rear. Vicki stayed with me. They all then slowly migrated to other walking partners and the chatting continued.

When I topped the last hill and glimpsed the blue water for the first time, everyone was well ahead of me. I couldn't see the ocean clearly yet, but it was there. I could smell the salt in the air.

I was at my emotional peak, and even more people came to meet us: Dad and Brian Ann, Tabatha, and Judy's family. After all the greetings and introductions, we kicked off our shoes and socks, joined hands in a human chain, and together we ran across the thick warm sand into the Pacific Ocean at Capistrano Beach.

Three months after leaving Vail the numbers read 1,102 miles, twelve lightning storms, three hailstorms, forty-two blisters, seven weeks of desert, a high of 105 degrees, and one earthquake.

I had done it. I had completed the first leg of my global trek. Sure, there had been a handful of hiccups, but nothing I couldn't handle. It was only three months in a five-year journey, but it was the farthest I'd ever walked, and I'd proven to myself I could do it.

But was I ready to leave U.S. shores? Moreover, could my relationship with Tabatha be healed, or would it implode?

CHAPTER 5

New Zealand: Green Hills and Red Flags

The twelve-hour flight over the Pacific gave me quiet time to reflect back on my personal history with New Zealand.

It started in April 1989. I had arrived at the Auckland Airport that April morning and hitchhiked to the nearest youth hostel. Not having much money, I immediately noticed a job listing on the bulletin board that said simply, "Fruit pickers wanted in Kaukapakapa. Lodging supplied." I had a clumsy time with the big red phone, to say nothing of the proper pronunciation of Kaukapakapa, but they gave me the job.

After two days bent over pulling orange-horned melons from the earth, they yanked me out of the field and said I would be much more useful on the production line sticking labels on the fruit. The melons raced down the conveyer belt at a furious pace, leaving me frantically sticking labels between the sharp orange horns while trying not to shred my fingertips.

That started a year traveling through New Zealand and Australia, moving from orange-horned melons to a variety of under-the-table odd jobs from picking kiwi fruit to filling shampoo bottles. My most impressive job was working at the post office distributing staff uniforms. My most lucrative job was taking inventory at a computer warehouse. The most humiliating job was wearing a sandwich board over my shoulders walking up and down Auckland's Queen Street promoting the weekend sales blitz at Dr. Shoe.

When I got enough money in my pocket to continue traveling, I moved on to the next town for hiking, caving, bungee-jumping, rafting, etc. I racked up thirty-two jobs that year, nearly earning me a chapter in the *Lonely Planet Guide Book* on how to work your way around the world.

After a year New Zealand Immigration granted me the cherished Residence Permit, and my life took a turn. I said goodbye to jobs that required stuffing, picking and frying and said hello to the New Zealand domestic travel industry—the job that introduced me to my two dear friends, Rachel and Sarah. This glorious time provided an unbridled opportunity to explore every crevice of New Zealand.

Five years later it was time to return to the United States. Rachel had already packed up and was well on her way gallivanting through Asia and Europe. So it was Sarah and I who sat at the airport, crying, and laughing and saying goodbye.

From the moment Sarah and I met we were joined at the hip. She had a mind of her own and a mouth like a truck driver. She was a gifted singer, professionally trained in opera, but Janis Joplin was her preference. If she had so much as one beer, she would be on top of a table belting out "Me and Bobby McGee" with a voice that filled the room.

Three years after I left New Zealand, a mutual friend came to visit me in Colorado. "I have some news about Sarah," he said.

"What about Sarah?" I asked eagerly, expecting news that she'd been touring Europe singing opera with Kiri Te Kanawa. But instead, a bomb.

"She's been sick for months," he said. "The doctors kept misdiagnosing her, and when they finally pinpointed it as leukemia, she had to be whisked right off for a blood transfusion. She's not in good shape."

I froze.

"She wanted someone to get hold of you and have you call her," he said, and handed me her phone number. (This was *right* before email swept the planet.)

I took a deep breath. Everything would be okay. Sarah was young, strong and sassy, she was my friend. My friends don't die.

Within a week I was on a flight to Auckland to spend time with Sarah while she struggled with the whys, hows, and whats.

For nearly two years Sarah was in remission. She felt good enough to accept a part-time job, get her own flat in Auckland, take on a couple of boyfriends and was accepted for vocal training by the premier opera coach in New Zealand. She had a future again, and to celebrate she started making plans for her "Invincible Summer" party.

Then back home in Colorado one cold snowy night, I got an email from her.

4 November, 1997

Pol—You know how I've moved to Waiheke and life is great and I'm celebrating my wellness. Well, two days before my Invincible Summer Party (1 Nov), I found that within one week, my leukemia had literally exploded and I have been given less than a month to finish my fabulous life. The cancer is so aggressive they can't even give me palliative care that just prolongs things anyway.

I feel I have done everything I can to fight this persistent bastard and, although I am having some pretty sad moments, I am in a good place, physically and spiritually. Whatever happens will be very quick. No one will be roughly trying to keep me alive. They will let me have as much morphine as I need and that is a great relief. I still feel quite well. A little bone ache and a large spleen have been a bit uncomfortable and will probably get worse, but nothing a Panadol can't fix.

Yesterday I went for a swim in the sea at Onetangi Beach. I looked gorgeous. I have a great tan and rosy cheeks, a #2 hairstyle, thick eyelashes and beautiful bushy eyebrows. I think I'm beautiful, and although I don't have any regrets, it would have been nice to realize that throughout my teens. Life could have been much easier.

> Anyway, Polly, I don't want you rushing over in a panic again, but I'd love the opportunity for a chat.
>
> I love you, you big, bad, buff groover!
> Sarah

I set my alarm for the middle of the night to catch Sarah at a decent hour down under. She sounded tired but her sense of humor was very much intact. We giggled, we gossiped, we reminisced, we talked about where she might be going. I told her I felt ripped off that she was being taken from me so early, and that, when I die, she'd better be there to greet me so we can carry on. She promised that if she could she would protect me and keep an eye on me. She expressed that she was in a good place spiritually, but next time she wants a body that will keep up with her. The most painful thing about it, she said, is seeing the pain in the eyes of her family.

Two days later at her home on Waiheke Island, my dear friend, Sarah Alley, passed away. The month they gave her lasted two weeks.

Sarah had a great love for New Zealand. She treasured the land, embraced the Maori culture and bragged about the natural beauty. She loved the idea that I chose to do my walk for breast cancer— being that it was related to the disease she fought, but more directed toward women, as all women's issues were passions of hers.

Although she'd been gone for two years, I was sure she'd be with me every step of the way.

Landing in Auckland, I glanced out the window at the lush green farmland surrounding the airport, and memories of Aotearoa (the Maori name for New Zealand) came flooding back. I had returned to the land of 3.8 million people and 40 million sheep, the land that invented bungee jumping, jet-boating, and black-water rafting. They add u's to words like colour, flavour, and tumour and turn letters around in theatre, centre, and metre. They pronounce the "h" in *herb*. "*Cuppa?*" means "Would you like some tea?" "Would you like some tea?" means "Would you like some dinner?" If you order lemonade, you get a 7-Up. The steering wheel is on the right side of the car; driving is on the left side of the road. When you turn on the blinker, the windshield wipers go on. Thank God the brakes are in the same place.

Sally and my friend Rachel greeted me when I stumbled through the gate, wrestling with two luggage carts. Rachel and I had been friends since working in the travel industry together in Auckland's backpacker market. She's one of those people I describe as an old soul, clearly ahead of her time. Her smile attracted men from around the globe (we kept track), and after a string of amusing flings, which included guys from Australia to Zaire, she met Adrian, an English traveler. They'd now been married for two years, and baby Lucy was nine-months old.

Before my arrival Rachel had carted Sally around to get us organized; get a cell phone, open a bank account, arrange a rental car. She even volunteered to teach Sally the death defying feat of driving on the left-hand side of the road while sitting in the right-hand side of the car.

Ace Rental Car donated a four-door Nissan hatchback for two months, and for the other two months they charged only a nominal fee and threw in insurance for the duration. They were so generous that Sally half expected they'd come along as our local guide.

After a relaxing couple of days in Auckland, poking at Lucy's cheeks, Sally and I climbed into our Nissan wagon for the five-hour drive to New Zealand's northern tip at Cape Reinga.

According to Maori mythology, the spirits of the dead depart Aotearoa for their homeland Hawaiki at Cape Reinga. Although one may not feel the spirituality there because of the 50,000 visitors each year, that morning proved different.

Sally and I met Waireti Walters, a highly regarded advocate for Maori Health Care Services. Waireti had heard about our walk and wanted to get Maori women involved. The toughest part of her job, she explained, was encouraging Maori women to get regular mammograms. "An uphill battle," she admitted. "When Maori women get breast cancer, they accept it as God's will, so they often don't fight it at all." Determined to change that perception, she asked me to help as I walked through the Maori communities.

Moody clouds filled the breezy morning sky, allowing only a single ray of sunshine to poke through. Over the rocky cliffs, we could see the point where the Tasman Sea and the Pacific meet and their waves slap up against each other. Waireti had arranged a Maori ceremony to send Sally and me off down the North Cape and throughout New Zealand.

Puti, a Maori minister small in stature, became tall and eloquent when she spoke. Her long gray hair coiled on top of her head, and I imagined that behind every wrinkle on her face resided a great story.

Three elder Maori men and a dozen Maori women from the North Cape area gathered around. Waireti stood at my shoulder, interpreting as Puti spoke to me in her native tongue. "She's giving you a blessing to keep you and Sally safe while you walk the roads of New Zealand," Waireti told me.

She had explained earlier that it was an honor to have an elder man speak, so when a man named Charlie asked if he could say a few words, I straightened up and listened as though I understood what he was saying. Listening to him speak in his native language, I envied the Maori people their spirituality and how they have a solid grip on their heritage and commitment to each other. Charlie looked about sixty, with a head of thick gray hair, a warm round face and easy manner. He addressed me personally in English, welcoming me to the tip of the Aupouri Peninsula and thanking me for dedicating my walk to women's health.

Waireti told me that whenever I address a group of Maori people I should always start with my name, where I'm from, my age, and where I fall in the birthing order of my family. Then I should speak from the heart rather than present facts. So I spoke of my lifelong dream to walk around the world and how it had evolved into an opportunity to do something for women everywhere. I ended by telling them how Sarah had loved this land and how honored I felt to walk through New Zealand with the Maori people's blessing and support.

As the ceremony wrapped up, an elder named Graham asked if he could present me with some soil from Cape Reinga. A gift of soil from the Maori is considered a very special honor, and because he hadn't planned it, Graham scrambled to find a container for the soil.

"I have a Ziplock baggie," Sally offered.

Charlie scooped some rich soil into the bag and instructed that when I reached Bluff, the southern point of the South Island, I should sprinkle some of the soil back into the Foveaux Strait to give thanks and keep me blessed.

The ceremony ended as a trickle of rain began. Everyone watched me slip on my yellow rain coat, then waved goodbye and ran for the shelter of their cars. Sally drove away to meet our hosts for the night, and after weeks of pomp and hoopla, I found myself walking alone down the back roads of New Zealand.

I looked around and caught a glimpse of the Tasman Sea to my right, the Pacific on my left. Wet skies and round, green hills welcomed me. Cows watched cautiously. Sheep paid no mind. Nary a note of music filled my ears, but I danced. At last, I was walking in New Zealand.

It was November, early spring in New Zealand, and as I walked down the North Cape I quickly discovered that the trickiest thing about walking in New Zealand proved to be hospitality overload.

The people took great care of us, spoiling us with warm beds and homemade meals straight off the farm out back. It occurred to me, had we traveled through New Zealand with no schedule, we wouldn't have gotten anywhere. It was difficult enough to stay on pace, to say, "No, thank you, we can't move in and stay a while," and "No, thank you, three helpings are enough."

Families directly affected by breast cancer heard about Sally and me and came to find us. "G'day, girls, how are you? If you don't have any plans to stay anywhere tonight, my wife and I would love to have you stay with us." Maori nurses took a break from their clinics to walk with me. Breast-cancer organizations and town mayors invited us for luncheons and speeches and gathered to walk me through their towns. All sorts of farmers invited us for dinner, from pig breeders to orange farmers to avocado aficionados.

That's not a typo. A couple named Jim and Gillian, who lived just north of Kaitaia, were avocado enthusiasts, buffs, fanatics— their lives ruled and fueled by a seemingly simple, but odd-shaped green crop. Jim and Gillian heard we were coming down their road, and without debate prepared rooms for us, ready to stop us at their fence post and invite us in.

Over dinner we learned of Jim's passion. "You think there's not much to know about an avocado? Think again. The avocado is a very sexy fruit."

The avocado is sexy?

Jim spoke with passion. "It doesn't ripen on the tree. It's got to be *plucked* off the tree, not yanked, and held in just the right climate to survive the twenty-five day journey from our orchard to your grocery store in Colorado."

The avocado is a fruit?

"The exporting-importing business can be tricky," Jim continued, "because the avocado has to be under proper refrigeration on the ship overseas. Sometimes the temperature has to be tweaked by a couple of degrees, so they don't start to ripen before hitting the shelves. That would be tragic."

Avocado *and* tragic *in the same sentence?*

"Don't even get me going on the proper respiration of the avocado!"

On our way out the next morning, Jim filled our Nissan wagon with a crate of ripe avocados and made us promise, cross our hearts, to spread the word on the special attributes of the avocado as we traveled the globe. "Don't let the avocado be the world's best kept secret!"

The breast cancer community in New Zealand also took my walk to heart. Only months before I arrived, the government had implemented a nationwide program called the Free Breast Screening Programme, offering an annual mammogram for women ages fifty-five to sixty-four. At Waireti's request, I enthusiastically promoted the program as I hiked through the country. Local newspapers, national radio and television stations, women's magazines, even the family cable channel regularly found me along the road, and we'd make our way to an adjacent cow paddock for a quiet interview. I averaged four interviews a day. Reporters listed the toll-free number for the Free Breast Screening Programme, and their volume of phone calls skyrocketed. As a side benefit, the news stories kept the locals informed as to why this strange American with a cell phone in her ear was walking through their town and napping in their cow paddocks.

Sally often went ahead of me to meet with host families or she ran errands like grocery shopping or met with the local breast cancer organization to prepare for a press visit. Together we etched a groove down Highway 1 toward Auckland.

The narrow roads had no shoulders, but lots of hairpin turns and blind hills. Drivers entertained me with a toot and a wave. On a safe pullout, someone might stop to ask if my car broke down and if I needed a ride. One man pulled over near Waipu and explained that he was an engineer who worked for an insurance company testing cars for collision-safety measures. "You should take note," he said, standing on the wrong side of a blind turn, "if you get hit by a car, try to hit it head-on, because the car is designed in such a manner that would have you survive a crash up to 50K an hour. If it hits you from the front bumper, the impact would bounce you into the windshield and over the hood of the car, but you should be fine."

"Duly noted," I said and skedaddled to the safety of the straightaway.

I never would have met these characters had I traveled any other way than on foot. I had lived in New Zealand for five years and traveled the North Cape area a number of times, but always in a car or with a tour. I had never captured the country before at this most intimate level. And the best was right around the corner.

The marae is a sacred place to the Maori people. It's a meetinghouse in the community where Maori people go for celebrations, meetings and greetings. The Waimanoni Marae, near Kaitaia, invited Sally and me to spend the night—an honor, to be sure, but frightening. Their culture is so chockfull of rituals and protocol that chances were ripe for a yahoo like me to inadvertently insult their customs.

It was Waireti's marae. She met us in town for a cold drink before we made our way down the country roads, allowing us a quiet opportunity to get up to speed on marae protocol.

"The night will start with a ceremony. Just do what I do; I'll lead you through it."

"Is there any possibility of embarrassing myself during the welcome ceremony?"

"First thing you have to do is take off your shoes when you enter the marae."

"Got it," I said, scribbling furiously. That was an easy one.

"Never step over a man's legs, never touch a woman's head, and never ever sit on a pillow. They consider the head a 'giver of life'. Sitting on a pillow shows the same disrespect as sitting on someone's head."

I couldn't imagine ever being in a position to step over a man's legs or touch a woman's head or, for that matter, sit on a pillow. But I made a note just in case I was suddenly lured by some enticing temptation.

"Oh, and be prepared to sing a song in front of the whole marae."

"Sing?!"

"Yes," Waireti said, noting my panic. "Each guest who arrives in the marae is given a blessing, and in order to accept that blessing, you need to sing a song in response. Just sing something from the heart. You're from Colorado; sing a John Denver song."

"I don't know all the words to any John Denver song!"

"Oh, just make them up. Nobody will notice. How about that Rocky Mountain High song? They'd love that."

I mentally shuffled through my very limited song library. All John Denver's songs covered a two-octave range, a danger to me as well as the audience. I settled on a different song and tucked it into the back of my head as we made our way ten kilometers to the marae.

From the outside the sizable building was unremarkable—twenty-feet high, built with unadorned wood siding. Sally and I parked behind Waireti and awaited her cue. Three women from the front of the marae motioned us into the "threshold of the building," and the ceremony began as we exited our car.

With Waireti on my left and Sally on my right, we walked side-by-side, inching slowly along a laid-out carpet into the heart of the sacred ceremony.

A group of twenty smiling women and men silently greeted us inside the building. There was no music, no handshaking. We were led to chairs in the center of the room, and one of the men officially welcomed us into their marae in his native tongue. Once, everyone burst out laughing, and I whispered to Waireti, "What did he say?"

"He says you don't look big enough to be able to walk around the world."

Waireti rose and spoke about the importance of women's health in the Maori community and emphasized how they wholly supported my project. Other guests spoke as well, and not one of them sang afterwards, so I thought I must have misunderstood Waireti.

Finally, it was my turn to speak.

Surrounded by honor and spirituality like the night in the Ute Sweat Lodge, I spoke with passion from the heart, from the gut. I finished and returned to my seat next to Waireti.

But she nudged me back to the center floor. "Polly wants to sing a song from her homeland of Colorado, something from John Denver."

I took a gulp. "Are you sure you want me to do this?"

"Go on."

The marae had particularly good acoustics, and I was expected to sing a song to symbolize thanks for their blessing.

"Yes, I am from Colorado," I said, "but I don't think anyone here wants me to attempt John Denver. Instead, I would like to sing a song that was special to a dear friend of mine who recently passed away. Her name was Sarah and she was from New Zealand. One of her favorite singers was Sarah McLachlan, and one particular song reminds me of her. It's called, 'I Will Remember You.'" I dug deep and went for it.

I hit the high note, bringing the first verse to an end. Then I stopped before everyone tore out of the room, leaping over men's legs and touching women's heads while holding pillows to their ears.

From the hills of Auckland's busy north shore, I caught an occasional glimpse of the downtown skyline surrounded by beaches and sailboats bobbing in the startling sunshine. North shore roads were getting busier, more crowded. I walked past road construction workers laying tar on a hot day, a businessman walking his dog, a gray-haired woman in pajamas picking up her mail. School children festooned in sky-blue uniforms skipped and chased each other, and traffic started to pile up. I was almost there.

"You can't walk into Auckland."

It was a woman named Faye Gardner, a breast cancer survivor from Auckland. She emailed me after reading about my walk in the New Zealand Herald to let me know that the Auckland Harbour Bridge is the only road into Auckland, and pedestrians are not allowed. You'd think I'd known that, having lived in Auckland for five years. Then again, why would I? I'd never wanted to walk over the Auckland Harbour Bridge.

"But I have an idea," Faye continued.

Devenport is a suburban seaside village on the north side of Auckland Harbour, as close as I could get to the city without driving over the harbor bridge—barring swimming. While Sally drove over the bridge to meet us on the other side, the Busting with Life Dragon Boat team met me on the shores of Devenport and rowed me across the harbor.

The Busting with Life team uniform was pink, of course, and pink smothered the Bayswater Marina that Saturday morning—pink shirts, pink socks, pink hats, pink head ribbons, pink signs. They were just a pom-pom shy of a pep fest as they shouted their team's cheer in unison: "Feel it, find it, fix it!"

Apart from me, everyone wearing pink that day had a very personal, very different story to tell. Every one of those women had endured breast cancer. Every one of them knew the emotional roller coaster of symptoms, diagnosis, treatment, and, of course, financial and family dynamics thrown into turmoil. Graham, the coach, placed me in the drummer seat on the floor of the boat, while the other women paired up on every bench. Another cheer: "Feel it, find it, fix it!" and we pushed off from shore to the cheers of friends on the north end of the harbour. The women in pink were busting with life. I was in good hands.

In one hour Graham steered the boat straight into the docks of Auckland's viaduct to welcoming squeals of delight. I'd entered Auckland many times in past years, but never experienced anything like that greeting. The woman who heads up the Polynesian Breast Cancer Support Services of New Zealand helped me out of the boat. "Welcome to Auckland," she said, putting a handmade lei over my head. "We're so honored to have you."

We arrived at the part of the viaduct that had been temporarily transformed into "The America's Cup Village," a sort of Olympic Village built for the America's Cup sailing regatta that Auckland hosted that summer. American Express donated their seaside suite for our party, and within minutes of our arrival, the suite over-flowed with pink.

Hors d'oeuvres, adrenaline, and laughter were the fare at the America's Cup Village that late morning. I would have treasured that fabulous moment longer had I known how bad things were about to get.

Four months into my walk, I could count the start of the five-year journey a success. The Free Breast Cancer Programme and the extraordinary reception from so many breast cancer groups and survivors in New Zealand particularly made this so. However, my relationship with Tabatha continued to grow progressively worse. With each passing day Mom and Dad indicated they, too, were feeling the frustration.

> P—Tabatha's silent auction to raise funds for the foundation was being held last night. I put a number of calls into her to volunteer my services. I've even collected a few items for her, but she never returned my calls. Has she been in touch with you?
> –Dad

> Poodle—I've been trying to get in touch with Tabatha, but she's not answering my calls or emails. Do you know of another way to get in touch with her?
> –Mom

I experienced my own disquieting episodes. She rarely returned my emails or phone calls. She was supposed to send me a new pair of walking shoes from our sponsor every two weeks, but week after week we arrived at the designated post office to find no shoes.

We (my parents and concerned friends) tried regularly to find out how much money we were raising, but we got no response.

Friends and family who had made donations hadn't received their receipts for tax deductions, or for that matter, any acknowledgment of their donation. When I'd relay the information, Tabatha became defensive, accusing me of being unreasonable, all but sending our relationship into a nosedive.

I'm not suggesting she was doing anything dodgy. She was sloppy at worst, maybe in over her head. Regardless, this was certainly not the partnership that I wanted—that I *needed*. My spirits began to sink. Sally felt it too and knew I considered going on without

Tabatha, even though I never mentioned it. She assured me that no matter what happened, she wanted to continue with me.

I liked Sally. She was a woman with a good heart and good intentions. She was sweet and honest and had a catchy laugh—but she had no business being on a road trip like this. It's my dime store analogy that she took on this journey because it provided perfect therapy after a nasty divorce that understandably left her lost and angry. Inevitably, while we were on the road, more than a few skeletons came tumbling out.

She mentioned early on that she had a past alcohol problem but told me not to worry; she'd kicked it. As we'd continued south through the North Island, I discovered hidden half empty wine bottles in the Nissan wagon. Part of me wanted to be the girlfriend— to talk her through the demons that threatened to destroy her life, but the topics of alcohol addiction and nasty divorces were way out of my league. Alarmed by legal and logistical problems these issues might cause, I knew we couldn't continue together. What if she got pulled over for drunk driving? What if she hurt someone? She was so kind, so genuine, how could I tell her she had to go home?

With a heavy heart, I continued plodding southbound through the South Island toward Bluff; but the journey was tearing me down.

I communicated with Mom and Dad via email, devising a plan to continue the walk on my own. Meanwhile, I tried to enjoy the rest of New Zealand under the worst of situations, and made sure Sally enjoyed it, too.

I knew Sally really wanted to see other parts of New Zealand, so knowing she wasn't going to continue with me, I urged her to go play for ten days. We talked about getting someone to take her place, and I knew the perfect person.

Pat Montgomery was a three-year breast-cancer survivor from the northland and had been my primary source of support for press, contacts, education, and fundraising. She enthusiastically agreed to help, flying to Christchurch on the South Island within days to meet me.

While Sally ventured off to the tourist sites of the South Island's West Coast, Pat and I went for a plate of linguini and talked like girls do. About guys. She had been married for thirty-two years and had two grown girls.

"Wow, thirty-two years. Congratulations."

"Yeah, congratulations are in order, that's for sure."

Her tone warranted the obvious follow up. "Not all been good years?"

"Well, my marriage is fine. I'm actually struggling with the heartbreak over Robin, the local Anglican priest. I've been having an affair with her for the past thirteen years, and we've just broken up."

Slight pause.

"My husband knows. They've met. In fact, we've gone on vacations together. They like each other. No one says anything, and my husband's reputation as a high-powered attorney in our little town isn't in jeopardy."

Pat waited for a response. But I was busy kicking myself under the table for abandoning my rule: Don't ask the question if you can't handle the answer.

"Are you okay with that? Are you okay that I'm a bisexual?"

"Sure. I have no problem with that." Puzzled, maybe, that she offered so much personal information over a plate of linguini to someone she hardly knew, but not disturbed.

Pat explained that between her breast cancer, mastectomy, and now her break-up with Robin, she'd fallen into a sexual identity crisis. "With my new body, I don't know if I'm attractive to women anymore. Could I even attract a man again?"

I knew that breast cancer affects women in many ways, but this was a new angle.

We made our way back to the cancer center that offered us a room and moved beyond the awkward conversation about Pat's sex life onto something much more amusing—the front page of the *Christchurch Press*. A seven-hundred-pound, fully grown New Zealand fur seal had made his way out of the water, across a campground, and settled in a sunbeam on the roof of a three-week old

Mitsubishi Gallant. We laughed over the pressing issues in rural New Zealand, then retreated to our separate beds and turned out the light.

And then:

"Why aren't you married?"

"I've had great relationships in my life," I answered. "I've just never been in a place where I wanted to get married. Add to that the fact I knew I wanted to do this walk, and it wouldn't be fair to someone. I'm sure I'll be more open to that part of my life after this walk is finished."

"I don't think you want to get married," Pat said bluntly.

"Why would you say that?"

"I think you're gay."

"Hmm."

"Everyone wants to get married. I'm bisexual, and I wanted to be married to a man."

I rolled my eyes in the safety of the darkness. No one should ever have to defend her marital choices, but I did feel compelled to stick up for myself.

"Well, I know very well who I am," I said, "and while I haven't met anyone I want to marry yet, I have been in love—with men. So my response to you is, no, I'm not gay." Then added quickly a *Seinfeldian*, "Not that there's anything wrong with that."

An uncomfortable silence hung in the air, and I wondered if we could get back to the antics of the sun-seeking fur seal.

"You're quite sure you're not gay?"

"Quite sure."

"Well, everyone is at least a little bisexual. How bisexual would you say you are?"

"Close to zero." To emphasize the point, I added, "It seems to me you're trying to make me into something I'm not in order to accept your own identity."

There it was again, that thick silence.

Then she leapt out of bed, turned on the light and whipped off her shirt. And there she was kneeling on her bed, displaying her mastectomy in all its glory. "You ever see a mastectomy?"

My eyes popped wide open. I was shocked. And nervous. But mostly nervous. And shocked.

"No."

"Would you like to touch it?"

Oh, my. Oh, my. Oh, my. A number of thoughts raced through my mind, not least among them, *Why didn't I do this walk for prostate cancer?* If I just flat out say *No!* —complete with an exclamation point—would I throw her deeper into the abyss of a sexual identity crisis? Maybe I could say a softer *no*, with no exclamation point. Clear but firm.

"I'm uncomfortable with that," I squeaked.

She put her shirt back on, turned off the light and threw the covers over herself. "I think you're the one with the identity crisis."

That was day one with Pat.

The following morning was uncomfortable, as were the ensuing ten…whole…days. *Where's Sally? Bright, cheerful, alcoholic Sally?*

Insulted that I hadn't returned her affections, Pat retaliated by making me uncomfortable for the sake of her own amusement. When we stayed with families, she'd say, "Polly and I don't mind sharing a bed. Really. Don't go to the trouble of making up two rooms." Then she'd look at me sideways and I half expected an evil laugh to crescendo in the background. *Maybe I could call Sally and say, please please, pleeease come back. I don't care if you drink and smoke and snort crack cocaine!*

But then I played the game right back and said to our hosts, "That couch really looks cozy. If you don't mind, I would love to sleep out here tonight." Then I'd give Pat a sideways look of my own.

Despite Pat's craziness, she was nearly as good as Judy at PR, fundraising and networking. While I walked for the day she talked to farmers, butchers, road workers, truckers, doctors. Nearly everyone she talked to personally knew someone affected by breast cancer. Pat listened and gave advice, serving as a wealth of information for women and families weighed down with their new diagnoses. This was her passion, her life's work. She was an educator, an activist, an advisor. And loony as a lark.

Sally returned after ten days, wondering, I'm sure, why I was hugging her so much. Pat asked me not to tell Sally about her bisexuality and her affair with the Anglican priest. I don't know why I agreed because I didn't give a rip, but I went ahead and promised. Finally, Pat flew back to her northland home, and I was free of her forever.

Or so I thought.

I had one week left to walk in New Zealand, and my spirits were lifted by the news that my friend Vicki was flying in from Denver to walk the final days to Bluff.

I met Vicki on day six of my walk. She worked for the Colorado Breast Cancer Coalition and wanted to come and meet me before I was too far out of reach. So she drove from Denver and met me at a park in Glenwood Springs. We set off to walk toward Aspen together that morning, and she told me about her bout with stage three breast cancer at the age of forty. She fought it hard with high-dose chemotherapy and a bone marrow transplant, followed by radiation therapy and five years of tamoxifen. After nine miles we became the best of friends.

Vicki knew I was having a tough time in New Zealand, but didn't know the details. Having someone around I trusted implicitly lifted my waning spirit.

Meanwhile, Pat was calling incessantly. Because Sally dropped her phone in the ocean while leaning over the boat looking at dolphins, the only phone between us was mine, and she had it throughout the day. At the end of her first day back, she gave me a dumbfounded look. "Pat has called about a million times trying to find you. She sounds really uptight, almost crazy. She wouldn't leave a message, just insisted she has to talk to you."

She handed me the phone, but I never made the call. The next day, Pat called again and again. And again. She screamed at Sally. "Just go out on the road and find her, you dumb cow! How hard can it be to find a woman walking along the side of the road? Why aren't you having her call me back? Do you know how to give someone a message?"

By the time Sally found me, tears streamed down her face. "How did you survive ten days with her?" she sniffled.

My brilliant strategic plan was to ignore Pat until she went away. But so far that was making everything worse. With all the books I read preparing for this walk, not once did I read a single piece of advice on this topic; so I made a note for writing my book, "The Complete Idiot's Guide to Walking Around the World," to include a chapter on how to evade lunatic stalkers.

Vicki was exhausted after her two-day flight, but nonetheless, got up to walk with me the next day. Immediately, she got a taste of New Zealand's hospitality as locals pulled over and gave me supportive words or invited us to their homes for lunch. She walked right behind me in single file as we caught up, starting with a simple question. "What's going on with Tabatha?"

"What do you mean?"

"She seems disorganized. Remember that contest she held where whoever raised the most funds would win a trip to Mexico? I raised the most, and I can't get her on the phone."

I stopped walking and hung my head low. I turned around to look at her, and tears welled up in my eyes. Everything that had been building up came pouring out. I hadn't just imagined those red flags! Now someone completely independent of my immediate circle had seen the obvious—loud and clear.

Vicki was taken aback by my outburst. Poor passersby had to wonder about the two women on the side of road—one hyperventilating in tears, one consoling with a question mark on her face.

"How did I get myself surrounded by these crazy people?" I sobbed.

"Don't tell me. Sally, too."

"You've been here twelve hours, and you see that?"

"Well, yeah. Is she drunk?"

Sobbing, I nodded. "Tabatha has essentially abandoned all her responsibilities. Turns out the board she put together for the foundation is—get this—her roommates! And she's been generally unresponsive. Sally's lovely but has an obvious drinking problem, and now I have a stalker…"

"Listen to me," Vicki said. "This can be fixed. Trust me. You've handled it better than anyone could. I've been here twelve hours, and I know I couldn't take the drunken woman or the multiple phone calls from that nutty Pat. Tabatha is bad news, so moving on is a good thing. You'll be all right. We'll get you back on track without all these crazy people around you."

Blubbering and laughing at the same time, I said, "Someday, we'll be able to laugh about this, right?"

"Right." She said, soothing me between sobs.

One supportive person made all the difference, and I finished the day with a lighter step.

Our local host in Bluff, Rata, had arranged for a Maori ceremony at the tip of the country to celebrate my safe passage. The Maori people who came to celebrate didn't know anything about the collapse of my relationship with Tabatha or that my crew support had an alcohol problem or that I had a crazy stalker. They only knew I was safe and that the campaign for the Free Breast Screening Programme was enormously successful.

For the last miles, breast-cancer survivors met us at an old school where we had stopped the day before, and for three hours we all meandered down Highway One sharing stories, taking photos, and posing for the local media that came out to help promote the importance of early detection.

And there it was. After 1,346 miles—2,448 from Vail—we stood at the tip of New Zealand. Land's End. One giant step from the South Pole. We'd made it.

The people involved in the Maori ceremony greeted me beneath the bluff and cheered me on as I gingerly made my way across the slippery rocks to the farthest southern point possible while dodging the pummeling waves. The Maori began singing and praying in their native tongue, and it was with that magical background that I sprinkled a pinch of the special Northland soil into the Foveaux Strait. Symbolically, it kept the Maori in the north connected to those in the south. For me, it officially ended my walk through New Zealand.

Thank God.

I couldn't wait to hit the redo button. I needed to get this walk back on track. As Vicki, Sally, and I flew back to Auckland, my mind boiled with the details I had to work out in order to move forward. But Tabatha beat me to the punch!

Back at Rachel's place that very evening, I read an email from Tabatha, informing me that she was officially ending our association. However, she intended to retain the rights to every-thing concerning *my* walk—including the foundation itself, my journals, my website—*even my own likeness.*

*What, you crazy nut job? I **hired** you to run the foundation!*

While I was out, Tabatha spoke to Sally and told her to get a flight back to the U.S. pronto. I didn't even have a chance to say goodbye. If it's possible to be stunned and relieved at the same time, I was. I read Tabatha's email over and over again, my head spinning with the realities and possibilities. What I would have to do to fight for the rights to my own writings, photos, and likeness. I got up from the computer to answer Rachel's front door. What was on the other side was an even bigger shock.

"Look who's here!" I yelled, so Vicki and Rachel would hear me from the living room. "It's Pat! Pat Montgomery!"

"There you are!" Pat bellowed. "Why haven't you returned any of my calls or emails?"

I stood in a dramatic pause. What could I say?

Vicki and Rachel had only heard of Pat, but when she pushed herself past me into the living room, they quickly discovered that I had not exaggerated.

"I've been worried sick," Pat wailed. "I kept picturing you out on the road by yourself. God knows that Sally wasn't going to save you from any crazy people. You could've been hurt in a ditch somewhere!"

I turned to my friends and introduced her. "I want you to meet Rachel and Vicki."

They both smiled and nodded, more stunned than I was.

"Do you guys know how to take care of Polly? I brought you some things that will help." She pulled the first item out of her bag. "You can't go on to Australia without a snakebite kit. And figure out how to use it *before* you need it…it's worthless if you don't know how to use it. Where's Sally? She's not here? How can she take care of Polly when she's not even here? Is she going to learn how to use a snakebite kit?"

I didn't mention that Sally was on her way back to the States or that I wouldn't be moving on to Australia until I got myself reorganized.

Pat pulled the second item out of her bag. "You'll need Vitamin C energy drinks. These are just powder, so they won't expire for years. Just add water when you're out in the middle of that Aussie heat. It will help you replenish those lost electrolytes."

We all sat stunned as Pat continued through her Polly Care Kit, including a vitamin jar full of B6, B12, and magnesium, "Someone has to help Polly maintain her normal muscle and nerve function. The proper magnesium levels will keep her heart rhythm steady and support a healthy immune system. Where's Sally? She has to know this!" Pat paused for a moment. "I have one more thing, but it's out in my car. I'll be one moment."

When Pat left the room, I whispered to Vicki and Rachel, "Do you think Pat could be dangerous?"

"Yes," they replied in unison.

Pat returned holding a necklace with a silver pendent. "I want you to have this."

I read the engraved silver pendent in the shape of a heart. It said, "*I love you.*"

That did it. This was officially the worst day of my life.

Eventually Pat left, but that wasn't the end of her. For weeks, she called Rachel demanding to know where I was. When she heard through the grapevine that I had stopped and headed back to L.A., she repeatedly called my dad's house and hung up. In emails she copied the entire New Zealand breast cancer community with which I had worked so closely to say I was a quitter, a loser, a disappointment to all women fighting breast cancer. It was clear I needed a better plan than ignoring her hoping she would go away. I consulted a friend, who, ironically, had endured a similar stalking experience. She explained that I needed to contact Pat, but only once. I needed to be blunt. Frank. To the point. Don't leave an ounce of wiggle room for her to see what she wanted to see.

I did just that. It was hardly a single line. "Under no circumstances should you ever contact me, or anyone I know, ever again. Period."

And she never did.

Reaching the end of New Zealand marked seven months on the road. The perfect storm had imploded, and the obvious hit me: this wasn't as much a physical journey as an emotional one. It was about connecting with many different kinds of people and trusting my judgment of character.

Society tells us, "Don't judge a book by its cover." But we're also told, "Trust your first instinct." We're told, "Don't talk to strangers." But we're also told, "Strangers are friends we haven't met yet." We're told "If you want something done, do it yourself." But we're also told "Delegate!" Good grief, it's no wonder we get into trouble.

After my dramas in New Zealand, I made a promise to myself that I would never ever ignore those intuitions again. They are our instincts, our inbred alarm clock telling us when something is wrong. I made a promise to myself that I would trust my instincts implicitly from then on, even when it might not make sense at the time. I would be tough about those with whom I could and could not get involved. I would learn how to say no and how to fight for myself. I would listen to my head, not my heart. And I would trust that I could do this journey on my own as I had always envisioned.

CHAPTER 6

Hit the Reset Button

I headed back to the U.S. daunted, but not defeated. God bless him, Dad invited me back to his place. He lived in the heart of L.A.'s Wilshire District with his wife Brian Ann and their two cats, Katie and Joanie. So I landed in the City of Angels. Hollywood. La La Land. A town humming with 16-lane highways, high-protein diets and perfect hair days. A town where people actually say, "Have your people call my people" and are taken seriously.

The silver lining of this unwanted hiatus was that it gave me an opportunity to spend quality time with Dad. We'd always been close, but mostly via phone. Mom and Dad had an amicable split when I was twelve. Two years later, he was offered a dream job combining his two loves, writing and show business, as editor of the *L.A. Times* popular Sunday entertainment section "The Calendar."

Now semi-retired, he did freelance writing for the *Hollywood Reporter* and other trade magazines, reviewing television and movies.

At Dad's for the summer, I planted myself in front of the computer and phone. I had decided not to fight Tabatha because that would have cost a lot of money and probably years of time and aggravation. With a large, deep breath, I decided the best revenge would be success, and I let it go.

Then I changed the name of my walk to GlobalWalk for Breast Cancer and found Hans Dickel with Arkware, who donated his hard work to develop my new website. I chose not to create a foundation. Instead, I decided to work with a breast cancer organization in each country, leaving each financially responsible for incoming funds and tax deduction notices to donors. I would work with them to spread the word they wanted spread—which differed from country to country. Each country in which fundraising was viable (not all were) would retain the funds collected. I asked only that the funds be directed to breast cancer educational campaigns.

Slowly but steadily, I found sponsors. I put an All Points Bulletin out to all friends and friends of friends, asking for contacts with certain products and services that would help me as I attempted my trek alone. I found myself on the phone with the founder of DHL, the delivery service: "Sure, we'd be happy to provide you with shipping services." A friend of a friend of a friend got me in front of Best Western and Agfa film and the greatest travel guide of all time, *Lonely Planet Guidebooks*. They provided not only their priceless guidebooks, but also maps and language handbooks.

After years of trying various shoes, I discovered that the best shoe for my feet was New Balance. I contacted New Balance via their Sponsorship Department, promotions division, fundraising sector, and the president himself. What I got was a collection of one paragraph rejection letters saying, "We don't sponsor one-person events, and we already give to breast cancer, but best of luck." Regardless of their lack of support, I still wore New Balance shoes. I contacted the regional sales rep to ask if he would consider selling them to me at cost throughout the course of my walk. He agreed and sent my first three pair.

My friend, Stephanie, a pilot for United Airlines, offered me two flights back to Melbourne, one for me and one for Vicki, who would attend my Melbourne kickoff.

I also needed someone to help me from the home front to maintain updates for the website, to send me proper clothes during seasonal changes, keep records, keep sponsors up-to-date, field phone calls and interviews, and to send out monthly newsletters. One afternoon Dad and I walked down the block to his mailbox— the furthest he cared to walk, he often reminded me—and he said, "You know you can depend on me for whatever you need. I want to see you succeed in this, if only because I see you're so driven to do it. Lord knows where you get the want or wherewithal to do such a thing, but I would love to be your main support."

Then Mom called. "I've been thinking," she said. "I would like to volunteer to maintain your website."

"Wow," I said with maybe a hint of hesitation, "I didn't realize you knew anything about websites."

"Well, I don't. But there's a course at the local college, and I really think I could do it and have fun with it!"

I never would have asked either Mom or Dad for help to the extent they offered, but after they both stepped up, I realized how perfect it was to have them involved. I trusted them both and could depend on them because they always had my best interest at heart. My plans fell into place and my spirits rose from the abyss.

Debi and Jim Linker from Lake City, Colorado, invited me to their other home in Morro Bay, halfway between Los Angeles and San Francisco. Debi asked how I was going to carry my gear.

"I'm going to get a baby buggy, like one of those off-road sports utility strollers made with off-road tires. They seem pretty tough. I'll strap down my gear with bungee cords and jerry rig it with water-bottle holders and map pockets. I'll be the envy of all home-less people."

"Have you called B.O.B.?"

"Who's Bob?"

"B.O.B. They make the sports utility strollers you're talking about. I'll bet they'd make a special buggy just for your needs."

Yeah, right, I thought sarcastically, *it's tough enough just to get someone on the phone. I'm sure they're going to leap at the chance to create a specially made product just for me and my little walk.*

"B.O.B. is just up the road in San Luis Obispo. My son knows those guys. He works across the lot from them. I'll bet he could make an introduction for you. Let me give him a call."

Within minutes, we were on our way to the neighboring town of San Luis Obispo to meet Phil Novotny, founder of B.O.B.

When I walked into the warehouse, I discovered that B.O.B. is an acronym for Beast of Burden. The warehouse was filled with bike trailers and knobby tired baby strollers decked with shock absorbers, hand brakes, and bright colors. Phil loved the idea of my using a B.O.B. stroller onward through Australia.

"We should get my buddy John Cutter involved with this. It's exactly the sort of project he loves."

"What does John Cutter do?"

"John designs bikes for pro racers. He also designs tents and backpacks for North Face. He especially loves designing gear for mountaineering expeditions and one-of-a-kind adventures. Let me give him a call."

Within another few minutes, we were standing at John Cutter's drafting board, discussing my needs for maps, water bottles, and weight distribution while he drew up blueprints for a special one-of-a-kind backpack on wheels.

My shattered walk was taking shape again, but there was one more hurdle I needed to clear—money. Tabatha refused to return the thousands of dollars of my own money I had given her to start the foundation, even though she signed a contract agreeing to pay it back. Again, though, to take her to court would have cost even more money. So I took a larger, deeper breath and let that go, too. Then I did what the newly arrived and hopeful do in L.A.—I registered with Central Casting.

Central Casting hires extras, the background actors in TV sitcoms, movies, and videos. It's freelance work that you accept at will, which was perfect for my situation. Every morning, I called their recorded registry that listed the character inventory they needed for the day. They might need, "One woman fifty pounds overweight to walk across the street on *Ally McBeal*," or "One-hundred teenage girls and boys in purple and silver prom attire for a music video." Sometimes they'd have a cattle call, which means they're trying to fill a stadium, and it doesn't matter what you wear or how fat you are.

Over the months I qualified for a series of work assignments, including the sitcom *Titus*, in which I played a delirious patient with a broken arm who wandered through the hospital. On *Nikki*, I portrayed a waitress in the background and had to mime order-taking and pouring drinks. I was a crowd person, applauding on cue for *Judge Judy*, *Battle Dome*, *Power of Attorney*, and *Family Feud*, to name a few. My most lucrative gig was when I was a guest on *To Tell the Truth*. That's the game show where three contestants all claim to be the same person. If the panelists guess incorrectly, the contestants win money. I had to claim to be an expert on all things Spam. I won $665.00.

One morning, in a change of events, Central Casting called me. An agent told me the new film version of *Planet of the Apes* was being directed by the rowdy Tim Burton, and he needed mother apes who were about five-foot-two and athletic.

"According to your Central Casting registration," the agent said, "you're about five-foot-two. Is that still the case?"

"Yes, I'm still five-foot-two."

"Are you relatively agile?"

"Define agile."

"We need our mother apes to jump on tables and chairs on occasion."

"Yes, I'm agile. I used to be a gymnast."

"Wow, a gymnast," he marveled. "That's perfect."

I wanted to tell him that had been in high school twenty years ago but didn't want him to stop marveling at my agility.

He hired me on the spot and directed me to a week of training at Ape School on the Sony film lot. My fifty fellow mother apes and I spent seven hours a day learning how to walk like apes—shoulders back, knees out, feet turned under, arms swinging freely. We had costume fittings and makeup sessions until we were comfortable as apes, until we felt like apes.

In September I got my long-awaited call from John Cutter. My custom-made baby stroller was ready. With all the pieces of my walk back in place, I couldn't wait to hit the road again. However, filming of *Planet of the Apes* had been pushed back and back, and it seemed unreasonable to fly back from Australia for a few weeks of shooting in December, then boomerang back to Australia. With regret, I handed in my custom-made ape outfit and with it, my career as a movie star.

I bolted up to San Luis Obispo to pick up the last piece of the puzzle. John Cutter led me down the backyard path to his workplace and introduced me to my new crew support. He wasn't bipolar; he didn't have a problem using toilets. Neither did he over-imbibe nor have a sexual identity crisis.

He rolled into the world at 23 pounds, 28" in length with 16" solid rubber, off-road tires. He was teal colored and outfitted with multiple pockets for maps, food, toiletries and water bottles. It was love at first sight. His name was Bob.

CHAPTER 7

Australia: Living with Lions

O ur seats were in their upright positions and tray tables locked as Vicki and I prepared for touchdown in the Land of Oz. From my middle seat I tried to catch a glimpse of the place that would be home for the next eight months, and a small lump lodged in my throat at the realization that I had made it work. It had taken seven months to get myself reorganized, but my walk would now be the way I had always envisioned.

The going, however, would be a little different. In New Zealand, they very considerately staggered their towns some 15 miles apart. In Australia, towns are 50, 75, and 150 miles apart, even on the populated east coast. Also, unlike in the U.S. and New Zealand, where I had built-in support systems, in Australia I was completely on my own—destined to camp on roadside for days at a time with only a radio, a low-signal mobile phone, and my teal buggy Bob to keep me company.

The good news, particularly for directionally challenged people like me, is that very few roads run through Australia. One main highway skirts the edge of the continent, except from Melbourne to Sydney, where multiple routes exist. After a short review, my walking plan became clear: North to Cowra Road to Sydney—for no better reason than it would lead me through towns named Wagga Wagga, Dookie and Butty Head.

For four days, Vicki helped me tackle my to-do list, which included meeting with Lyn Swinburne, founder and CEO of Breast Cancer Network Australia. It's the premier organization in the country, working to ensure Australians diagnosed with breast cancer receive the very best information, treatment, care, and support possible.

"We're right behind you all the way," Lyn assured me. She offered to put a story in the BCNA Newsletter to spread word across the country that if anyone saw me on the road, to please put me up and feed me.

My role for Breast Cancer Network Australia was to promote their services. Funds raised would benefit an educational campaign they were preparing to launch. My goal was to raise AU $10,000 during my eight months in Australia, primarily through media accounts and perhaps an occasional fundraising event in major cities, if I could find the support. It was a lofty goal, considering I had no support system and knew no one.

The morning of the kick-off, Vicki and I met the BCNA management team at the dock in St. Kilda Pier, a neighborhood south of Melbourne on the shores of Port Philips Bay. It's the sort of coastal village that bustles with artsy folks selling crafts, and families who pause to listen to street musicians while they're out exercising the dog. Walking to the official starting point at the end of the dock, I began to hear the lowdown on how to survive the lonely roads of the land down under.

"You ready for the snakes?" one woman asked. "Don't forget, Australia is home to the ten deadliest snakes in the world!"

"She's right!" another chimed in. "You have a snakebite kit? You'd hate to get bit by a snake and while the venom is racing to your heart, you're digging to the bottom of Bob trying to find the instructions!"

"And beware! Those cheeky buggars love to hang out in the tall grass. So when you're walking down those long lonely desolate stretches, never ever pee in the tall grass! One nip in that naked bum, you'll drop dead and we'll never find the body!"

"Spiders too! We're home to the seven deadliest spiders in the whole world! Those little buggers love hanging out in dark moist places, so always check your shoes before putting them on! Can't tell you how many times we hear of a farmer losing a foot or a whole darn leg because he put on his boots without a good shake."

"Got it," I said, making mental notes complete with exclamation points. The animated advice continued through the group with hardly a breath, and I quickly learned that Australians actually took pride in the deadliness of their country's natural habitat.

"Now listen carefully. When you're up in Queensland, never ever go swimming in May. It's high season for Jellyfish and those little buggers will wrap themselves around you and squeeze the life out of you given half a chance…Mosquitoes, too! Good Lord, those mosquitoes up in Queensland will give you malaria, dysentery, typhoid, kidney stones…"

"And if they don't get you, the crocodiles will!"

"All right, that's enough."

I heeded the dire warnings from the Death Squad, and with Melbourne's skyline in the foreground, I was finally able to take Bob by the handle bars and put one step in front of the other. We strolled up the pier and north into the land that wanted to kill me.

Vicki walked with me for a week as I headed north out of Melbourne. Well, she walked half way through the day then turned around to either hitchhike or walk back to her rental car. In the meantime, Bob and I got acquainted. His solid rubber tires could roll over glass on the roadside without popping. He had no steering mechanism on the front wheel so when I needed to make a sharp turn I had to pop a wheelie on his two back wheels. Even with fifty pounds of gear, he was effortless to push. He sported a slot to hold my current map, water bottle holders on both sides, and a bright yellow rain-coat so the truckers could see us during a rainstorm. Women who had had breast cancer signed their names and wrote messages on Bob, constantly reminding me why I was out there. People along the road, in cafes, and at stoplights were attracted to Bob, sort of like when you take your Shih Tzu puppy for a walk and people stop to coo and tickle him on the belly. "Oh, he's so cute!" "What's his name?" "Does he have good tires?" He was a joy, a pal, the perfect crew support.

For the first few nights north of Melbourne, women from the BCNA put Vicki, Bob, and me up. But my comfort zone ended 123 miles north in the little lakeside town of Nagambie. I had tried to prepare emotionally for the day Vicki would leave and I would be left on the side of the road to tackle the world on my own. I didn't want the day to come. But Bob was working out well and I felt as ready as anyone could be who is going to walk alone into unknown territory.

When the day finally came, I watched her rental car disappear back over the road we'd just traveled. Then I moped back into my donated Lakeside Motel room and did what I imagined Columbus and Magellan had done before they forged into the world. I took a nap.

The TV droned on in the background as I dozed off with thoughts racing around in my sleepy head. Would I be safe? Would I get lonely? Who would know if I disappeared off the face of the earth? Could I get as much awareness work done for breast cancer as Vicki and I had managed together in the first week?

In the midst of my sleepy doze, I heard a television news voice break into scheduled programming. "A body has just been discovered in a river near the tiny town of Nagambie…"

I shot out of my doze. *That's where I am!*

"The body was discovered near the Nagambie campground this morning. The victim had been wanted by the police—"

Aughh! I abruptly changed the channel. *How could this be? The very first day I'm left completely alone there's a dead body found right along my route! Is this a sign? Am I dreaming? What should I do?*

I abruptly opted to put a pillow over my head and went back to bed. If I were oblivious to the dangers, I deduced, I would somehow be immune to them.

Despite that disturbing news, I got up the next morning and pushed Bob out the door. I looked both ways for someone who might be hiding behind the bushes waiting to murder me, then headed north onto High Street.

It was a gorgeous October spring morning in Nagambie, a pretty little resort community. The lake provided the main attraction, but historic wineries and ice cream shops drew their share of tourists.

Scott and Marie at the Bytes and Bites Internet Cafe spotted me walking by and came out to greet me. "Are you that girl walking around the world?" I nodded. "There's a story about you in the paper this morning. Gee, that is unbelievable. Walking around the world all by yourself. You are one brave girl."

I wanted to tell them that the walk from the Lakeside Motel to their front stoop was the first fifty meters I'd walked on my own, but I didn't want them to stop admiring my valor.

"Could we get you a cup of coffee for the road? How about an egg sandwich? Come on in. Have a rest. We'll show you that newspaper."

Well, it *had* been a full fifty meters, and the A39 wouldn't have another appropriate rest stop between here and Murchison, except for tall grass with the spiders and snakes, so I took Scott and Marie up on their offer. An hour later they handed me a bag of cherries, another sandwich for the road, and waved goodbye. Columbus and Magellan would have been envious.

It was eight o'clock when I left the Bytes and Bites and veered onto the A39. The sun was rising high in the sky and people stopped to chat, mostly asking, "Do you and your baby need a ride?" I turned on my little radio hanging from Bob's handlebars, found a station playing Van Morrison and put one step in front of the other on a road I'd never traveled before. I didn't know where it would lead or where I would spend the night. Pumped up with confidence, I was doing it! Was this what people meant by the romance of the road? The lure of open spaces, the sense of freedom, the unpredictable voyage of discovery. Nothing could stop me now.

Except the police.

"'Eh, lady, you can't walk on this road. This is the Dhurringile Prison road!"

And the romance ended.

Murchison, a quaint little town on the banks of the Goulburn River, had modest houses and well-trimmed lawns with golden retrievers chasing sticks. A leading area for growing fruit and exporting tomatoes, its tiny size didn't rate so much as a paragraph in my guide-book. I gleaned that tidbit of information from local billboards.

The only prospect for accommodation looked to be the Murchison Pub Hotel, but even that didn't hold a great deal of promise. In Australia, pubs often double as gathering places for after work male bonding and lodging for weary travelers. Basic accommodation, usually consisting of a fifteen-year-old mattress on a spring cot and a shared basin down the hall. From my earlier years traveling in Australia, I knew that a pub with *hotel* in its name actually meant they had no accommodation. Yet if it was just called a *pub,* without the word *hotel,* a room might be available. It's lodging dyslexia.

"Would you have rooms for a weary traveler?" I asked the bartender at the Murchison Pub Hotel, as all the patrons stopped to eye Bob and me coming through the door.

"Sorry, we don't 'ave rooms 'ere. Only beer. But if yer lookin' for a room, this fella 'ere could help ye out." He pointed to a man who jumped off his bar stool to greet me.

"Lookin' for accommodation, are ye? I just started a backpacker lodge up the street. In fact, you'd be my first guest."

I know, I know, red flags should do more than wave when a strange man jumps off his bar stool and says he just started a back-packer lodge tonight. My subconscious shot to full alert after the murder the night before and the nearby Dhurringile prisoners. But I felt no red flag at the Pub Hotel. The patrons were genuine folk sharing a Fosters, a chinwag and helping promote their friend's new lodge.

Keith's place was only two hundred yards away. He pushed Bob while I briefed him about my walk. I felt delighted, albeit a little guilty, when he offered this very first guest not only a donated night's accommodation, but dinner, breakfast the next morning and a lunch for the road.

I'd seen my share of backpacker lodges in my day, and Keith's place was a joy—clean, roomy and hot showers with water pressure. Murchison was hardly on the traveler's route, he acknowledged, but come tomato season his beds would be filled with seasonal pickers. I set the table while Keith tinkered about his kitchen whipping up a lasagna.

"What made you decide to turn your house into a backpackers' lodge?" I asked.

"Well, it's not a pretty story. See, almost exactly a year ago to the day, I came home to a note from my wife. She said she was leaving me for a younger man and they were off to travel through Australia together. So sorry, take care."

That was a lot more information than I'd expected. Men, particularly Australian men, aren't known for their accomplished communication skills.

"I'd always wanted to renovate this big ol' farm house," he went on, "but my wife was never crazy about the idea. So after a period of heavy grieving, I dove in. My friends here, the ones you met at the pub, have been so supportive. They come by to help me do the plumbing or electric, or just bring me cooked meals to make sure I'm eating. The whole experience, between building this place and watching my friends surround me in a protective circle, has been really good therapy."

I smiled. "It must be. You built this entire place in less than a year!"

"Yeah, I'm getting over her."

"Have you heard from her since?"

"Not a peep."

We sat down to lasagna and salad and soon (as I discovered happens a lot to travelers in Australia) the conversation turned to kangaroos. "Have you seen any kangaroos yet?"

"Only dead ones," I replied. "It's like Roadkill Highway out there. I plug my nose and run past them. There are plenty of signs, though. Lord knows there must be a kangaroo-crossing sign every half mile."

"Come on," he said, standing up from the table in mid-bite. "Get in the car."

I took my plate with me and within minutes, we pulled over in front of a meadow where hundreds of kangaroos were bouncing and hopping with no apparent destination.

"There ya go. Seen your first kangaroos."

I stared into the field. How on earth could millions of kangaroos hide all day? "So it's not just a myth," I said. "Australia really is full of kangaroos."

"Far too many. The reason you haven't seen any is because kangaroos are nocturnal, like most Australian wildlife. The koala bears, too—but a forewarning, they are not the cuddly furry little bear they look like. In fact, they're quite coarse. A big, foolish cuddle of a koala would do you in." I mentally added the koala to my list of Australian wildlife that wanted to kill me.

"Wallabies, possums, cane toads, dingoes, even most snakes, are nocturnal."

"That's why I've seen only dead ones along the side of the road."

"Yeh, most Australian animals are potential meals for another animal, so they work under cover of darkness when those little predatory buggers are asleep. Say a kangaroo is getting some water in the ditch near the side of the highway; a big rig comes flying down the highway and takes him out."

"So after the truckers roar through the roads all night, we walkers have to dodge the aftermath."

"Then the snake comes to feed off the dead kangaroo and ..."

"Another big rig takes *him* out."

"Don't walk at night."

My first day alone on the road was over. I had done it, and minus the detour down the prison road, it could be deemed a complete success. When I walked into little Murchison and saw the little houses and lives ticking along, it occurred to me that every single road in the world is somebody's neighborhood, part of somebody's everyday routine and comfort zone. Why, I then reasoned, couldn't I be perfectly comfortable walking down their road?

Sort of the open road's version of "a stranger is a friend I haven't met yet."

The next morning I thanked Keith profusely, zipped the leftover lasagna into Bob and headed north to test my new theory. The C357 road to Tatura was in *someone's* comfort zone; therefore it could be in mine.

And that's the day that changed the course of this walk.

I rolled Bob into Tatura around four o'clock. On the way into town I passed a couple of ma-and-pa motels and a caravan park, but after my one successful day walking to Murchison I had the confidence to go a step further (so to speak) and camp out. I looked around for a campground or a town park. The chances of a deranged murderer being in both Nagambie and Tatura, I reasoned, were pretty slim.

A woman walked up behind me. "Can I help you with something?"

"Yes," I answered. "Is there a town park in Tatura?"

But she didn't hear my words. She only heard my funny accent. "Well, well, where are you from?"

I told her who I was and what I was doing, and she exclaimed, "Well, I'll be! Fancy that! Let me introduce myself. My name is Margaret, and I'm the President of the local Lions Club. The Lions Clubs have got to get involved with this! You've got to come home with me."

And so I followed Margaret home.

"Have you been in touch with any Lions Clubs?" she asked, as she led me through the streets.

"A handful. I even stayed with the president of the Lions in Kilmore. A month ago I'd never heard of the Lions Clubs, and you're now the fourth person who has mentioned that the Lions should get involved with my walk through Australia."

"After you stay with me tonight," she beamed, "I'll call the Lions Club down the road in Shepparton, and they can call the next one, and so forth. This is exactly the sort of project the Lions of Australia support, and I don't see why it couldn't carry on right up the entire east coast."

Work it, Margaret! I learned that the Lions are an international network of community clubs operating in almost every country. Each club is made up of a band of local volunteers who work to fill the charitable needs of their communities. They started in Chicago in 1917 and quickly spread through American communities then around the world. While they're best known for their international work to end preventable blindness, they also work with local needs projects.

At Margaret's house, she showed me to my room, handed me a towel and, while I was making myself at home, she called all her Tatura Lions Club buddies to meet us at the pub.

Rural Australian pubs, I soon discovered, are gathering places for everything from kids' birthday parties to date nights to guys' night out. Pubs are the town's social life, a community center of sorts—with beer. Nearly everyone in town gathers at the pub on a regular basis, and that's where we headed.

Within five minutes of our arrival Margaret stood on top of a stool, and high above the crowd she announced to the Taturians that I was walking around the world to promote breast cancer awareness. "All the funds raised in Australia stay right here in Australia," she bellowed, "so let's show 'er what us Aussies are made of!"

With that, she plucked the hat off a guy's head, and I watched in awe as the hat weaved its way down the bar, across the restaurant and back through the pool hall. Strangers cheered and raised their glasses, urging everyone to put more in the hat. "Belly up, ye cheap wanker. I saw more bills in that wallet!"

In fifteen minutes the hat made its way back to the barkeeper, who tipped the hat, spilling out a pile of colorful Aussie bills then counted them with nimble precision. He announced to the cheering crowd, "We raised $323 for the Breast Cancer Network!"

The barkeeper then put it in the form of a check and mailed it right then and there to the Breast Cancer Network Australia. All of the pub patrons patted me on the back. "Good on ye', Mate," as if I had anything to do with it. All I did was show up at the right intersection and look oblivious—a strategy that worked exceedingly well.

Day two turned out even better than day one, and I was on my way.

Margaret called the Lions Clubs in Shepparton, which called the Lions Club in Rutherglen, which called the Lions Club in Albury. Every night a group waited for me to stroll up their Main Street, where they would say, "Let's go to the pub!" and I'd say, "Okay!" and we'd make our way down to the Hotel Pub and raffle off a meat tray for the Breast Cancer Network Australia.

The Lions Clubs not only kept me safe by providing a warm place to stay, they also provided hot showers and the Internet access I thought would be so elusive. Moreover, with the press that the Lions Clubs generated across the nation, it was as if the entire country mobilized behind me, ensuring I would make it through their country fat and fine without spending a dime.

If a story was reported in the local media, the regional media picked it up. Then I received phone calls from national women's magazines and radio stations from Adelaide to Perth. My days filled with roadside interviews, where I quickly learned that live radio interviews were the best because they could never misquote me. Newspapers, on the other hand, quoted things that never came out of my mouth (the upshot being that they often made me sound much more articulate than I am).

Often the facts were wildly misrepresented. One reporter wrote that I had walked through 140 countries or that my mother had breast cancer and that's what launched me out the door and around the world. The falsehoods then spread to the next media outlet without fact checking, and I found it next to impossible to put the brakes on a fast-moving story.

After a few weeks in the national media, most people driving the Olympic Highway knew about the girl with her little buggy, Bob. "'ey there! You must be Polly. Heard you were on this road and thought I'd bring you some food. Hope you like banana bread. Just baked you a loaf; it's warm, fresh out of the oven—and a basket of fresh cherries right off the tree. Mangoes, too."

"Oh, thank—"

"Goodness, it's so bloody hot out here I thought you might need some electrolytes. Walkin' 'round the world, I 'magine a little girl like yourself gets low on her electrolytes! Made a stop at the Woolworth's to pick you up some Gatorade."

In short time, I was waving to all the truckers and farmers like I was running for Mayor. Who knew that one stop at a small town intersection would lead to a two thousand mile pub-crawl up the east coast of Australia and national concern over the levels of my electrolytes?

Breast cancer survivors saw me in local newspapers and came to find me on the road to sign their names on Bob. Sometimes they'd walk with me through their town or for the day. The police kept a protective eye on me, too. As temperatures climbed past a hundred degrees, they regularly stopped to let me take breaks in their air-conditioned patrol cars.

Working with the Lions Clubs was one of the great triumphs of my journey, but it wasn't always as simple as it sounds. While I was safe from the dangers of spiders, snakes, and deceivingly cuddly koala bears, I was relentlessly busy organizing my evenings with them. Margaret in Tatura passed me to David in Rutherglen, who passed me to Andrea in Wodonga, who didn't know anyone in Albury. So I hit a dead end. One broken link could end the whole chain and leave me in the tall grass with a snakebite on my bum.

"Maybe you could call and introduce yourself as a Lions member from Wodonga and make an introduction for me?" I suggested to Andrea. "I'll take it from there."

"Oh, that's a bit odd, calling someone you don't know."

So I made cold calls to restore my chain of Lions Clubs. Sometimes the recipient would have heard of me and jump right on board; other times, I got dead air.

"I don't get it," they'd say.

"The Lions Clubs have been assisting me," I would tell them. "They're passing me town to town as I make my way to Sydney, helping me to raise funds for the Breast Cancer Network Australia."

"Well then, why haven't I heard of this before?"

"It's sort of been a day-to-day relay from one town to the next."

"Why haven't I read about it in the paper?"

"In fact, it's been all over the papers. It was in your paper this morning. Did you see it?"

"No, I don't read the paper."

"It's been on the radio, too."

"I don't listen to the radio."

"I spoke at your regional Lions Club last week."

"I don't go to those meetings."

Hmm.

I gave the name of someone in the organization that could vouch for me, and the fragile chain was once again restored.

Once or twice a week a breast cancer survivor would find me on the road and invite me to her house for a survivors' dinner. On those nights, instead of a raffle at the pub, I would speak to local survivors who, in turn, made donations to the BCNA. They then passed me on to a breast cancer survivor in the next town; but when they didn't know anyone in the next town, the breast cancer chain was broken, and I would try to re-connect with the Lions and hear dead air on the phone.

Up the Cowra Road from Melbourne to Sydney, I worked the two networks of people on the phone amidst the roar of trucks and hordes of Aussie black flies fighting to get up my nose. I got used to calling strangers. "Hi. Giles? I met your Lions Club friend, Geoff, in a pub last night, and he suggested you'd be happy to drive thirty miles down Cowra Road to pick me up, take me home, feed me and let me sleep on your couch."

As the tenuous Lions chain reached up the Olympic Highway, I began to see the potential of an official partnership with the Lions Clubs. If I could secure an official sponsorship, it would allow me to plan in advance, thus allowing the clubs more time to get organized and the fundraising would be that much more successful.

As it stood, every morning someone would call the next club and they would respond, "Tonight? She's coming tonight? Sure wish I'd known in advance!" and they would scramble to find me a spare bed and dash to the Woolworth's for a meat tray. I needed the right person in the upper hierarchy of Lions, and they were in Sydney. So until then the fragile chain continued—with hardly cause for complaint.

Cowra Road was the road less taken and put me in the heart of "real" Aussies. Like a relay from town to town, I sat at family dinner tables getting to know the ordinary and the eccentric people who make up this large island nation. They told me about their jobs raising emus, growing cherries, or farming sugar cane and what it really takes to get a pack of sugar from the cane fields to a coffee cup. All day, every day, people stopped on the side of the road and checked on me—like the retired couple named Betty and Barney Rubble (swear to God) who stopped and gave me a box of freshly picked strawberries.

The list of colorful characters grew every day—and night. Like in Cootamundra when I stayed with Maureen and was awakened in the middle of the night by her neighbors' rather ferocious lovers' quarrel. Bellowing accusations of infidelity, she kicked him out. Doors slammed, f-bombs were tossed, sirens roared, cops came. I noted the exact time at 1:17 a.m. in case the police needed me as a witness.

In Woodstock I stayed with Mick, whose life-long collection of matchbox cars filled shelves from floor to ceiling and down the hall-way into the bathroom. His wife, Daisy, claimed her kitchen a matchbox-car free zone, whining that their vows said nothing about matchbox cars.

Meanwhile, Daren and Jenny's house near Mundurama was filled with a collection of grandfather clocks with cuckoos that startled me out of my sleep every hour on the hour.

In Junee, I stayed with Jane, whose two sons, Charles and Warwick, tried to teach me how to play cricket, and with it new terms: "Six and out! Your bowl!" I learned that during cricket season, wives and girlfriends are cricket widows as "tests" go on for five days. Poor girlfriends.

Aussie characters showed up in the most unlikely places. From a mile up the road, the little white general store looked like a perfect stop for a quiet retreat from the incessant black flies that swarm through Australia's back roads. So wasn't I surprised to find fifteen women, all over eighty, whooping it up for their annual Christmas party. They were dressed in party hats with Christmas whistles in their mouths, indulging in chocolate truffles and blueberry cheesecake, and the place was strewn with wrapping paper. Fifteen heads turned in unison as Bob and I walked through the doors of the quiet little country store. "Well, where on earth did you come from?"

"Don't let me interrupt," I said, taking a seat. I removed my hat, revealing a fierce case of hat-head. "I'm just out for a walk and need a cold water."

"Hey!" one of them said, "you're that girl walking 'round the world!"

"Walking?" said her friend. "Oh, stop it, Elsa, now why would anyone be walking around the world, right past the Illabo General Store?"

"I read about her," said another. "That's you, isn't it? Is that Bob? Bob was in the photo! I know that's Bob."

"Who's Bob?"

"That little buggy of hers. He was in the paper yesterday."

"Yes, this is Bob."

They converged on Bob and examined all his signatures, the messages of hope from women who had been through breast cancer.

"That's right!" said one of them. "Your little walk is for breast cancer, isn't that right? Son of a gun. Right here in Illabo General Store. We should make a donation to her breast cancer foundation," she said to her friends. "It stays here in Australia, that right? All right, everyone pitch in. That means you, too, Lily."

Some of the women who had been through their own bouts of breast cancer signed Bob. Others put names of friends and relatives.

"Come on over and join us," invited the fifteen ladies. "We're having a Christmas party!"

After walking fifteen miles in temperatures climbing over a hundred, I really just wanted to read the paper and sit with a glass of cold water, but I couldn't bear the thought of being out-partied by a posse of eighty-year-olds. So I accepted a Christmas whistle and started singing carols.

The reception I received in rural Australia surpassed all expectations. So much so that the BCNA called to ask what on earth I was doing in order to send them a check every other day. The last they'd heard I didn't know anyone in Australia. But I did now, and could hardly believe the turn my walk had taken. Every day was filled with cars and trucks of friends I hadn't met yet who cheered me on, dropped off an ice cream bar or stopped to meet Bob. I felt comfortable enough that, if I were to meet a dodgy character, I could wave down the next passing truck/car/tractor and be swept away to safety. Who needs crew support when an entire country has your back?

The miles piled up behind me and, God bless them, my hosts had no problem whatsoever driving out to pick me up at the end of each day. It had been six weeks since I left Melbourne, and the towns were getting farther and farther apart—fifty, seventy-five, one hundred kilometers. I could no longer walk between them in a day. "If Australian farmers don't drive two hundred miles in a single day," I was told, "it's hardly worth getting out of bed." When my hosts drove thirty-five miles down Cowra Road to find the sprite wee girl with her buggy Bob, they did so with enthusiasm, and always with a scarf or orange tee in the back of their truck to tie to a fencepost to mark my spot for the next morning. They then drove me home, cooked up a dinner of meat and potatoes, escorted me to a pub, raffled off a meat tray, and the next morning drove me back to the orange tee on the fencepost.

The Lions Club chain grew stronger as I neared the Blue Mountains—the mountain range that stood between Sydney and me—so much so that I was able to plan a few days in advance as opposed to the night before. Each morning my host gave me the name and number of my new host up the road. I would contact them, and they would come out to meet me on the road with a cool drink full of electrolytes to save me from the hundred-and-five degree heat. I felt so confident about my future with the Lions' help that I took a leap of faith and shipped my camping gear home to Dad's closet, reducing Bob's load as I inched towards the mountains and the steepest hill in Australia.

For weeks I'd been warned about the climb over the infamous Mt. Victoria. "Steepest hill in all of Australia," they'd say, "but there's no way to avoid it. It's the only road over the Blue Mountains to Sydney."

"I don't even like to go over it in my car," one would say.

And my personal favorite, "If you catch a ride, I won't tell anyone."

Nevertheless, the roads leading me closer to the Blue Mountains got hillier and heftier. The day of the big climb over Mt. Victoria started with a ten-kilometer ascent to its base, sort of like Mt. Everest where you hike for ten days to Base Camp in order to start the real climb.

I rested every chance I could. At the Old Bowenfels petrol station, they cried, "You're walking over Mt. Victoria? Whoa, bloody 'ell, be careful! Honey, this little Sheila 'ere is walking over Mt. Victoria!"

"Tell 'er we'll give 'er and that baby of 'ers a lift if she doesn't mind waiting an hour till I'm done with lunch."

A few miles closer, I dawdled into the cafe in Hentley.

"That road's not meant for walking," they said. "Why don't you take the 2:34 train?"

Just to clarify, hills don't scare me—the Christmas holiday traffic on those twisty mountain roads with blind turns and no shoulders did!

As I neared the base of Mt. Victoria, the road signs turned into bright yellow warning signs, reminding drivers that their brakes should be in working order, and visibility was about to get exceedingly perilous with blind turns and steep grades.

At the last safe turnout before the final ascent, I stood like a rock climber strategizing my route. After downing a bottle of cold water, I grabbed Bob by the handlebars and charged up.

No…wait…this shoulder is running out. I dashed across to the left side. hoops…getting too narrow here…back to the right side…there's no shoulder over here, just a ditch…wait…eye the traffic…back to the left side…the curve is too tight…dash between cars to the right side…left side…watch for the cars… BEEEP…Bob was stuck in the guard rail…oops, here comes a truck from behind…hang off this railing until it passes…HOOOONK, "Get off the road you crazy &*%!!#!"…Oh, bite me. Come on, Bob, get out of the guardrail! "Would you like some fruit?" someone yelled. "Not right now, thank you!"…walking in this ditch is the only option…Doh! Lots of big rocks…and thorns…ouch! *%!! thorns in my leg…I see blood…Come on, Bob, don't get stuck in the ditch!…maneuver around the broken glass…steer around the roadkill…OUCH!! Damn thorns…can't tend to it now…race back to the right side, there's a short shoulder…wave to the police….

Police?!

A police paddy wagon pulled in front of me with lights flashing, backing up traffic on the two-lane mountain road.

The officer rolled down his window. "We got a call about a crazy woman pushing a baby up Mt. Vic, but that doesn't look like a baby in there." He laughed.

"No, officer," I answered meekly. I handed him a brochure while hanging off the railing with Bob to allow space for cars to get by. Between gasps for air, I explained what I was doing and why I had to climb over Mt. Victoria.

"So we can't give you a ride to the top of this pass?"

"I'm afraid not." Then quickly added in a flash of brilliance, "But how would you feel about taking Bob off my hands and driving him to the next town for me?"

"No problem," they said, surprisingly. "Why don't we drop it at the Best Western for you? It's about six kilometers away."

"Thank you! Thank you!" I drooled with gratitude.

They loaded Bob into the back of their paddy wagon and shouted at me as they pulled back into traffic. "If we don't see you there in three hours, we'll worry about you!"

The pass was only two-and-half kilometers long but a 2200-foot elevation climb. Even without Bob I landed in thorn bushes with painful regularity and endured my share of expletives from passing drivers.

After two hours the road leveled off, marking the top. I wobbled into the petrol station and flopped down on a seat like a bleeding boxer retreating to his corner.

"*You walked* up Mt. Victoria? What, are you crazy?"

Yeah, save it.

"You do know there's a nice foot path that parallels the highway? Starts at the base of Mt. Vic and comes out right in back of us here. Peaceful beautiful trail along the mountain ridge."

I didn't have the strength to shoot her a glare. I kept my head down, pulled thorns out of my ankles and wiped off the blood. "Please don't tell me that."

She handed me an ice-cream bar. "I won't say anything. But we do sell topo maps."

From the top of Mt. Victoria, it was all downhill to Sydney—literally—and the investment in the topography map was a lifesaver. With the detailed map I could avoid the twisty mountain highway and walk through the trendy little mountain villages of Wentworth Falls, Lawson, Hazelbrook and Linden on side roads without a thorn or a honk.

In Springwood I stopped at a bench in the town park when a national radio show called me for a live interview. It was *The John Laws Show* from radio station 2UE, and while I didn't know it at the time, his was the most listened to radio show in the country. That simple conversation left me fielding a throng of phone calls the rest of the morning from people around the country who wanted to help—particularly Lions Clubs right up the east coast that offered places to stay and help with fundraising. What a boon.

The sign read, "SYDNEY 50km." I dropped into Penrith to a very sudden change in culture. Penrith is the town at the eastern base of the Blue Mountains. It's growing so fast that even though it's fifty kilometers from Sydney, it resembles your standard suburb with McDonald's, car dealerships, lottery shops, and petrol stations.

Two days later a sign read "SYDNEY 20km" and the two lane roads changed to four lane highways with traffic lights, sprawling shopping malls and drivers on cell phones.

"SYDNEY 10km." I walked past Homebush Bay, home of the Olympic Park where only three months earlier Sydney had taken the world stage. At the top of every hill along Parramatta Road I caught a peek of Sydney's skyline. Closer, clearer. Full city buses passed frequently. Cars filled the streets, the roar of a subway became constant. Buildings grew taller, closer together, modern. Larger crowds filled the walkways with business people dressed in ties and pressed shirts, carrying computers in one hand, cell phones in the other.

The sign now read, "CITY – CIRCULAR QUAY – DARLING HARBOUR."

I had made it to the heart of Sydney. The Hub. City Center. The belly. Where city slickers rub elbows with tourists, where you can get a photo of the Sydney Harbour Bridge, the Opera house and downtown skyline all in one frame.

I parked Bob next to me and settled into a cozy sidewalk cafe to savor my achievement. I put my feet up on him and celebrated by ordering a mochaccino. Between sips, I people watched on a Sydney summer afternoon. Markets were in full swing. The city basked in the afterglow of Australia's gold-medal performance at the Olympics. Without question, it gets my vote as greatest city on earth.

My personal history with Sydney went back ten years when I stopped to find work while traveling as a vagabond backpacker. In the world's backpacking subculture, Sydney is known as the place to find under-the-table work. The city is always humming with travelers from around the globe who stop to replenish their wallets before moving on. Back then I got jobs that lasted one to three days. I got enough work for five months to supplement my trip north to the Great Barrier Reef and into Southeast Asia.

I knew I'd be back someday, but never quite envisioned it like this—that is to say, by foot, from dinner table to dinner table, pub to pub, with more protectors than the National Guard. I could only hope the support would continue. From Sydney my route took me up the busy, populated, tourist-inundated east coast. Would my reception be as uber-friendly as in the rural regions?

Little did I know that it had just begun.

CHAPTER 8

I Am Lion
Hear Me Roar

On January 2, 2001, I plodded north over the Sydney Harbour Bridge into the twenty-first century. Through friends of friends I had made contact with Barry Palmer, the Lions Club International Director, and arranged to meet him on the north side of the bridge in Manly Beach.

Barry waited for me inside a café, and I could only imagine his first impression as he watched me struggle to lock my teal-green buggy to a lamppost. He was an amiable man, if rather low on enthusiasm. Dressed in a navy suit and tie, he looked very much the community leader or CEO of something. But I led the conversation. I summarized how the Lions had adopted me off the streets of Victoria and passed me up the highway to Sydney.

So, I went on, I now saw a larger picture of the Lions' involvement and how an inspiring relationship could be built through the rest of my walk in Australia. An official sponsorship would be mutually beneficial. I could really use the Lions. Likewise, the Lions Clubs had rarely drawn this sort of international attention. With his blessing I could contact clubs well before my arrival in their towns, enabling a more proactive fundraising plan.

He fiddled with his coffee mug, looking unenthused, and who could blame him? He didn't know me, and here I was dressed in my shorts and—

"Sure, why not."

Sure? He said, *Sure*! Oh sure, he said it like, "*Sure*, I'll humor the poor girl," but *sure* is a low-grade form of *yes*, an affirmative, and I *sure* took it!

Barry agreed to send an email to all the District Governors up through my route and ask them to help any way they could. I thanked him profusely and shook his hand with a firm grip to make up for the wimpy looking rest of me.

An official relationship with the Lions Clubs gave me the authority to contact clubs and make plans on my own, and I ran with it. Whenever I passed a library or Internet cafe, I ducked in and sent multiple emails to introduce myself. As a result, District Governors contacted club presidents along my route. I forwarded schedules, photos and press releases, even introduced myself to regional PR officers who took over the task of contacting local press. Having Barry Palmer vouch for me provided an enormous boost that assured a warm reception.

Continuing up the east coast beach towns of Copacabana, Avoca Beach, Terrigal, Toukley, I conducted press interviews during the day, and each night I met with a Lions Club. Sometimes the Lions gave donations directly from their club's coffers; other times they carried me off to local pub or service club where I gave a brief speech and they passed a hat. By the time I arrived into Newcastle a hundred miles north of Sydney, we had far surpassed the original fundraising goal of $10,000 for Australia.

To combat frequent misinformation in the constant, sometimes overwhelming press coverage, I drafted a press release with bullet-pointed facts and most frequently asked questions—but they still got the facts wrong. Lord knows, in the grand scheme of the world, no one gives a hoot that I'd walked through fifty-two pairs of shoes (the press release said eight) or that they reported I was twenty-six years old (sure, why not), but it did make me question everything I read or heard on the news.

Reporters would call and want to know exactly where they could find me at an exact time.

"I don't quite know. Right now, I'm between Swansea and Belmont."

"Well, where should I meet you?"

Since I was walking into a town I'd never visited before, I couldn't name a meeting spot, which exasperated them. However, over the miles I had noticed a McDonald's at the edge of most towns along the main highway. "Is there a McDonald's?"

"Yes."

"Is it on the north side of town or the south side?"

"South side."

"I'll be there between four and four-fifteen." In effect, my walk became a trek from McDonald's to McDonald's up the east coast of Australia.

Lions Club members and breast cancer survivors met me at McDonald's too, often with grand fanfare, banners, flags and donations. Soon, McDonald's management jumped onboard, offering me a Caesar wrap with fries and chocolate shake at every stop, then calling ahead to the next McDonald's to alert them that I was on my way with a press party in tow. The Lions Clubs chain was relatively solid, but I knew now that if I did become stranded between Sydney and Port Douglas, I could make an SOS call to a manager at the nearest McDonald's.

The summer of 2001 was particularly hot and dry in Australia. Fire was a constant danger. Tall grass and scrub were crisp, and the smell of forest fires wafted by on a regular basis as I walked up Highway 1. Campfires were out of the question, but it got so bad, the news reported, that one poor bloke parked his car on the grassy shoulder to go pee, and the heat from his exhaust ignited the dry grass and shot his car up in flames.

Near the town of Yamba, I smelled fire again, but this time it was different, stronger. Within a mile, I came upon a fire blazing on both sides of the highway. I stopped Bob, and my hands shook as I dialed the emergency number 000 (like 911 in America). "Good afternoon, is this an emergency?"

"YES! There's a bush fire on the highway just north of Yamba!"

"Okay, calm down. Are you in any danger?"

"NO!"

"Is there anyone there in any danger?"

"NO!"

"Is the fire near any train tracks?"

"NO!"

"Then why did you call?"

"Uhh…"

"Let me ask you again. Are you in any danger?"

"No."

"Then I want you to just stay away from it and let the fire burn out."

"So…if I see a fire raging along the highway, I shouldn't call you?"

"Only if you're in danger."

"Oh, okay. Sorry."

"No problem."

Well, didn't I feel the fool?

But the fact remained that I had to get to the other side of the fire, which looked to be about two hundred yards long. The highway was wide enough that if I ran down the middle I would be fine, but I had a flashback to an episode on the Discovery Channel regarding fires jumping across highways. I weighed my options and must admit taking a little comfort in the fact that if a fire ball were to jump the highway and into my head, I could call that woman at 000 with a valid emergency. I made my way to the middle of the road, waited until there was barely a whisper of wind, and ran for my life with a fire blazing on both sides.

A week later that same dry, crisp grass was under water. As I inched my way north through the state of New South Wales I paid little mind to the afternoon mist. Rain suddenly exploded out of the sky. I scrambled to get my rain gear on and tuck the radio and mobile phone under Bob's bright yellow rain cover. I heard the mobile phone ringing but didn't answer it. I wouldn't be able to hear anyone anyway. Keeping my eyes on the road, I charged ahead. The road at my feet soon grew to a shallow river, and the rain beat horizontally into my face. Watching for vehicles whose drivers couldn't see any better than I could became increasingly difficult. *Maybe when I'm finished with my walk,* I thought as I dodged hydroplaning cars, *I'll invent glasses with little windshield wipers.* Desperate to find a building, a wall, an old farm—anything to help me get undercover—I scanned the area. Nothing. I had no choice but to continue plodding through the rain with no windshield wipers for my glasses. Wise words from another Discovery Channel documentary kept popping into my head: "Tragedies usually occur after a chain of events have gone awry—not just one." Here I could count four: poor visibility, heavy traffic, no road shoulder, water on the road. If I could stop for the day, I would.

Magically, a general store appeared ahead of me. It looked abandoned and dilapidated, but Praise the Lord, it was open. I charged right for it and burst through the doors to The Promised Land of food and shelter.

"You biking?" a man asked, unalarmed, from behind the counter.

I stood dripping all over his floor, trying to catch my breath. "No, actually I'm walking." I pulled out a brochure from an inside pocket.

He put up his hand like a stop sign. "Not interested."

"Oh. I just—"

"Probably somethin' to do with health. Not interested in health."

The snotty, grumpy, been-walking-in-the-pouring-rain side of me wanted to say, "That's obvious." But I was polite, "What's the veggie burger like?"

My menu choices were deep-fried fish, meat pie or a sausage that had been sitting there since a week ago Thursday. "A bunch of vegetables in a bun."

"I'll have one, please."

While my veggie burger was being prepared I took a seat outside under the veranda and finally got to answer that ringing phone. It was Jenny, my hostess for the night.

"This weather is dreadful," she said. "Would you like a pick up?"

Yes! "Could you drop me off here tomorrow?"

"No worries."

"Then I would love to take you up on that offer!"

"Terrific. I'll see you in just a few minutes."

"Hey, lady, that veggie thing is ready."

Excellent! Famished, I ripped open my meal only to find a deep-fried patty. Not quite what I was hoping for, but I weighed my options—eat or not eat—and hunger won.

"Ewwwwwe!"

It was half hot, half ice, and I couldn't be sure where the vegetable was, but I saw something that resembled a pea buried in the depths of the fried batter. I wrapped it up and tossed it in the bin.

Now let me say that food in Australian cities is out of this world with glorious fare from Japanese to Lebanese, but the British imported their traditional cooking skills to the Outback and now the rule seems to be to fry and overcook everything beyond recognition.

Then there's Vegemite.

One day a Lions Club met me for a luncheon and while I was happily munching on my salad, one woman said to me, "How can Americans eat those horrible breakfasts of pancakes and all that syrup?"

My response drew applause across the table from anyone not originally from Australia, "I refuse to accept a food editorial from anyone who eats Vegemite."

My first experience with Vegemite was years before while living in New Zealand. A "friend" spread some on a piece of toast for me and told me to take a bite. It looked like chocolate. It looked harmless. I took a big bite. It's hard to explain a taste, but consider, please, that Vegemite is made from leftover concentrated brewer's yeast extract. I gagged like a cat with a fur ball.

The rest of the world first heard about Vegemite when the Australian band Men at Work had their top-forty hit back in 1983. "He just smiled and gave me a Vegemite sandwich...." was the line. And people around the world happily hummed the tune without a clue in their heads as to what Vegemite was. Americans traveling in Australia all bring home their own horror stories of their first (and usually only) experience with the stuff. But Australians love it.

It's on every single breakfast table across this country and what mothers feed their babies as a first solid food.

In the little general store that rainy afternoon, my remaining options were Vegemite and a two-week old deep fried meat pie. I wondered how hungry I'd have to be before I ate either one.

Jenny pulled up in her blue Toyota Corolla, and we tossed Bob in back. "We've got to hurry," she said, hardly taking a moment to introduce herself. "We're having a luncheon at my house in fifteen minutes."

"Will there be food?"

"Oh, yeah. Lots of it."

"Let's go!

The Lions Clubs' assistance continued to grow strong up through the state of New South Wales. My days were filled organizing plans, meeting reporters and talking with breast cancer survivors who stopped along the road. I lumbered through the towns of Forster, Port Macquarie, and Coffs Harbour, pushing sixty-pound Bob up hills, around corners, past road kill.

The Lions Clubs up the east coast of Australia had outdone themselves on my behalf. So much so, that by the time I walked into Brisbane, Australia's fourth largest city, the unrelenting schedule was catching up with me. The whirlwind of speaking engagements, interviews, fundraising events into the night—to say nothing of walking sixteen miles in the heat—started to take its toll. My hands were shaking and I felt dizzy, classic symptoms of exhaustion. Besides, in Brisbane we had a flurry of engagements for four days, including big city media interviews and visits with breast cancer clinics. It was a priceless opportunity for PR and fundraising for the Breast Cancer Network Australia, so sleep just had to wait.

The local Lions had appointed a woman named Bella to Polly duty. "I understand you're American," she said during our first phone conversation.

"Yes, I'm from Colorado."

"I hate Americans."

Oh good heavens.

"My son hates them, too. He's going to university there. Calls me once a week to tell me how much he hates it."

A number of thoughts raced through my head, not limited to: Did she volunteer to help me just to spew her hatred? It reminded me of Libya being appointed to set the U.N. agenda on human rights.

A lingering silence hung in the air—the equivalent of a phone stare-down.

"Never met an American I liked."

"I'm not sure what to say to that."

"You don't have to say anything."

And we were back to silence.

"Well," she finally said, "I guess we should make a plan."

She would pick me up the next morning and take me to her Lions Club meeting, where my plan was to latch onto someone else—perhaps someone from Libya.

I spoke to their group, telling the story of how my walk had started and how the Lions had taken me under their wing for the past four months and helped raise over $13,000 for the BCNA. When I finished, club member Dave Evans stood up. "What you're doing is fantastic. I would like to support you by purchasing your next airfare from Cairns, Australia, to Singapore."

Gasps filled the room—the most audible of which came from Bella. It was an offer so generous it left even this group of exceptionally generous people stunned. The entire room rose from their seats to applaud Dave's big heart.

Next came a tour of the Wesley Breast Clinic, and it was there, during the teatime reception, that my lack of sleep caught up with me.

Dizziness swept through me. I grabbed the back of a chair to steady myself when my guide Jen pulled me aside.

"You okay? You look pale."

"I am feeling a bit faint."

"Come with me."

I was grateful that Jen took control because I felt on the verge of tumbling to the floor. She took me into a quiet room and handed me a glass of water. "I'll get you back to the hotel for a lie down."

I sucked down the water and leaned back on the couch for a few minutes, my eyes closed, my head spinning, my legs weak. I felt so ashamed. What a wimp. Many people in this world endured a harder schedule than this. Why couldn't I do it without dropping from exhaustion? I was in pretty good shape. I ate well—minus the odd veggie burger—and I had a great support team, even though they were all strangers. Was there a way to get a better balance? Maybe one day full of fundraising and press interviews, the next day off?

The reality remained, though, that this support wouldn't last forever. In Southeast Asia I would be on my own, and I'd look back at this overabundance of support and kick myself that I didn't keep it up. So I mustered the energy to take whatever was offered.

After a brief rest I finished the tour, and Jen dropped me back at my hotel just as another torrential rain began. I lugged myself up to my donated room, hanging onto the elevator railings to stop from falling over on the way to the fourth floor. It was a gorgeous quiet downtown hotel, and I felt bad that I couldn't enjoy it because I would be sleeping through my entire stay. I drew the shades and crawled into bed with my eyes already closed.

But the rain grew louder. It pounded against the windows and the roof. The wind howled, throwing chairs around the balcony, banging into the railings. Without getting out of bed, I pulled the curtain and saw a sky so dark you would've thought it was the middle of the night instead of four o'clock in the afternoon. I turned on the TV news where a special bulletin was reporting on what was being dubbed a "freakish storm," one of the worst this century, a storm with hurricane strength winds that moved over Brisbane and parked itself above the city. Within four hours over twelve inches of rain fell.

Outside my hotel, cars floated down the streets and tree branches flew past my fourth floor window. The car dealership across the street had eight cars floating around the lot like bumper cars at a carnival ride. The news reported that a mother had lost grip of her twelve-year-old son when a surge of water came ripping through their car, and she watched helplessly as he was swept away by the river.

I propped myself up and watched the news unfold from my nice, dry hotel room, marveling at the enormous stroke of luck that I was not out on the road. When it rained near that little general store a week ago, a mere five inches was enough to leave cars hydroplaning, as well as Bob and me nearly doing the back-stroke up Highway 1. What would I have done if I'd been out there during this "freakish storm of the century"?

The list of Things That Want to Kill Me in Australia was growing exponentially.

What we seldom hear about floods is the disgusting odor they leave behind once the water fades. The flood killed piles of fish in the rivers and left them on the shores, rotting with an eye-watering stench. On the way north from Brisbane little frogs were spread across the road, and I had to watch every step so as not to slip on them.

Spring days grew warmer and muggier up Queensland's Sunshine Coast, and the mosquitoes grew bigger. As the miles passed, I learned to do bug checks before putting shoes on in the morning, to check for spider webs on outdoor dunnies, and when ducking down to the railroad tracks to do my business, to listen first for oncoming passenger trains.

Further north into Queensland, the road kill indicated a change in wildlife, like dead snakes the size of tree trunks. Queenslanders drive trucks with bull bars to prevent doomed animals from flipping through their windshields because of the long dark roads mixed with a heavy nocturnal wildlife. The seventy-five kilometer stretch from Bowen to Gumlu (a three-day walk) was so rampant with road kill that I often broke into a trot at the rotten smell, holding my breath past kangaroos, snakes, and other unidentifiable carcasses.

Through Caloundra, Noosa Heads, Gympie, Hervey Bay, Bundaberg—the Lions Clubs always prepared in advance so I had no days of rest. Nor did I get much sleep. In Tiaro, for instance, Noel and Pat slept peacefully on the other side of their house when a fire alarm outside my room went off. I spent the night searching in the dark for a chair high enough to disable the blasted thing. The next night we took out the batteries, but even without batteries, it shrieked through the night. The next day I walked up to Maryborough and stayed with Kay and Allan, who had a motion detector they couldn't disable. Every time I rolled over in my sleep the alarm went off.

In Avondale I stayed with Diane and Alan, members of the State Emergency Service (SES). Their phone rang at 3:30 a.m. with an emergency regarding a lost boy near Agnes Waters. They launched into a rescue mission from their kitchen—and an endless string of phone calls and trucks humming in and out of their driveway all night. The next night, Bungi, their pet cockatoo, woke us all up at 4:30 a.m. to request a bikkie ("cookie" to us Yanks). When everyone ignored him, he raised his shrill voice and threw in attitude. "*Give Me A Bikkie! Now!*"

At an old pub one night kids were running up and down the hall all night long, laughing and giggling, slamming doors. I came this close to marching to the room next door and shaming those parents for letting their kids comport themselves in such a manner.

The next morning at breakfast, Kerry and Brian, the proprietors who donated a night, asked innocently, "How'd you sleep?"

"Not so great," I grumbled. "That family in the room next door let their loud, obnoxious kids run up and down the hall until the wee hours. Do they have no control over their kids? You might want to check the furniture up there, too; they were moving beds and armoires from room to room and down the hallway all together."

Kerry and Brian looked at each other. A silent moment stretched between them. Maybe I'd said too much. After all, they had donated the room to me. I should've just shut up and kept that—

"There's no one staying here but you." Kerry whimpered, as though she wasn't quite sure what to say.

"No one...?"

They shook their heads.

"...but me?"

They nodded.

"The running? The slamming? The dragging?"

They shrugged.

I thanked them and promptly headed out the door.

The next night, the Raglan Pub offered to put me up for two nights. After a sleepless week, I asked, "Are your fire alarms working?"

"Yes."

"Do you have any motion detectors?"

"Nope."

"Are you members of the SES?"

"No."

"Any bikkie-lovin' cockatoos?"

"Not really."

"Any, er, ghosts?"

"Well..."

There weren't any ghosts—that night anyway. But there was a small family of possums underneath my cabin wreaking havoc until all hours.

With glassy eyes I continued up Highway 1 toward Rockhampton, the base of the infamous Marlborough Stretch, Australia's version of the Bermuda Triangle. Maybe I could get some rest there.

"You're insane! It's boring to drive for four hours. I can't imagine walking it for five weeks!"

The Marlborough Stretch is the affectionate name for the 340-kilometer stretch of highway from Rockhampton to Mackay. It's so desolate that drivers are known to hallucinate at the monotony of eucalyptus trees. Thirty years ago a string of drivers disappeared after heading into the Stretch, never to be seen again. The road has since been rerouted and nothing mysterious has happened for decades—but it still has a reputation.

The Lions Clubs in both Rockhampton and Mackay went all out to help me form contacts for accommodation, food, and safety along that desolate and fearsome road. The HOGs (Harley Owners Group) in Rockhampton agreed to ride northbound for the following four consecutive Sundays to bring me lunch and check up on me. Three thousand U.S. Marines, who were training off the coast nearby, were notified to keep an eye out for me and perhaps bring water if they were heading my way. Farmers in the area came to find me around 5:00 p.m. on designated nights; driving up to 100 kilometers to pluck me off the empty highway and backtrack the next morning to drop me off again.

But the biggest help I got was from the truckers. For weeks prior to the Stretch, a particular red postal truck passed me twice a day—heading south in the mornings, north in the afternoons. He would always give me a toot and wave, but nothing more. One day, Mr. Red Truck finally stopped to see what I was up to.

"You're a woman!"

"Yes," I laughed. "I guess I am."

"Wait until I tell the guys!" He exclaimed, marveling at his discovery. "I've been passing you for months. So have the other truckers. Whenever someone passes you, they get on the CB radio and let us know where the little old man is."

"The truckers think I'm a little old man?"

"Oh, yeah. You're a regular hit on the CB radios up the entire east coast of Australia. We have bets on how far you'll make it through the Marlborough Stretch, ha, ha. So what is it you're doing out here?"

I told my new friend, Brian, about my walk. It seemed a good time to ask for assistance through the infamous Marlborough Stretch.

"I'd love to! I'll get on the CB and tell the guys. They won't believe the little old man is actually an American Sheila walking around the world!"

With Brian's radio introductions, I marched through the Marlborough stretch with HOGS at my front, farmers at my back and an entire fleet of truckers streaming past me. My trucker buddies kept each other up-to-date through their CB radios as to where I was and what I needed. Before they entered the Stretch, they stocked up on water, food and sports drinks, then barreled down the highway on the lookout for the girl with the teal buggy. The tricky part was that due to the nature of a big rig careening at 120 kph down a major highway, they could rarely stop; they could only slow down, shouting quick conversations for needs or wants, and had no choice but to toss things out the window: sandwiches, McDonald's Caesar wraps, large fries, and drinks with those electrolytes.

One day I saw Brian's easy-to-spot bright-red postal truck coming down the road. I readied myself like the catcher at home plate because Brian always brought me something. He slowed and shouted, "My wife made this for you!" and heaved a lasagna out the window. I watched as if in slow motion as this beautiful lasagna flew over my head, bounced off the tar, and landed deep into the tall grass that wanted to kill me. I'd been eating well, but I had been on this Stretch for four long weeks, and homemade lasagna was drool worthy. I stood alone on the desolate Marlborough Stretch looking into the tall grass and weighing my options. Lasagna? Or death?

The lasagna tasted delicious.

Guest Journal from Lion Alan MacKenzie, May 18, 2001

The first news about Polly walking through my hometown of Mackay arrived in an email late January. I crumpled it up and threw it away. Over the next two months, I received at least five updates as to her progress through the country, proving that this Polly thing was not going to go away. And the communication began.

Her goal was rather daunting: She planned to walk from Rockhampton to Mackay, the desolate "Marlborough Stretch." My goal was to change her mind. I told her of the desolate narrow roads, no mobile phone access, speeding traffic, criminal-minded people, and that she'd be better off doing something more conventional than walking on her lonesome with a trolley named Bob. Of course I hadn't met Polly yet. Otherwise, I wouldn't have wasted my time. As a Lions Club, we get lots of requests for assistance and funding, so I wanted to be sure about this Polly girl. I contacted the Breast Cancer Network Australia and asked them to tell me what they could about this Polly and her GlobalWalk. Well, if I read their reply once, I read it ten times. It was what I was looking for, and my admiration and enthusiasm for what was important to Polly now became equally important to me. The planning began.

With our Club President, Peter, and his four-wheel drive loaded with food, sleeping bags, water jugs and our walking shoes, we headed down the Marlborough Stretch toward the hamlet of Clairview—a "town" that consists of the only caravan park in 340 kilometers. Our plan was to shuttle Polly back and forth to the Caravan Park for a couple of days until she was in shuttling range of a farmer again.

To drive down that lonely stretch of road and suddenly come across a sprightly female pushing a trolley is really a stunning sight. Peter and I introduced ourselves, met Bob, marked Polly's spot with an orange tee on a Eucalyptus Tree and motored back to Clairview to settle in for the big game of footy.

Peter decided to "cook" a meal, which consisted of a couple of half pounders of the best rump steak, accompanied by lettuce leaves, a couple of tomatoes cut in half and a slice of white bread. Polly had been trying to cut down on her Aussie BBQ meat, so Peter gave her a bit of extra lettuce.

While Peter and I dove into our hearty meals, as only two hungry Australians could, we looked up to find Polly methodically tearing up her salad ingredients into tiny bite-sized pieces. She then poured on a little Paul Newman ranch dressing that she carried with her, and started blending it all together." What are you doing?" we couldn't help but ask. "Tossing my salad!"

We tried not to look too surprised, suppressed a couple of burps, and waited for the big footy match.

All of the organizing went as planned and Polly's entrance into our Lions District was enormously successful. Events went on for four days in Mackay and together we raised a lot of needed funds for the Breast Cancer Network Australia.

In the meantime there were two related comments made by Polly at differing times regarding her association with Lions that got me thinking. One was that someone in the south had asked her if she would like to be a Lion. The second was after a Lions meeting in Mackay when Polly commented that when she got back to Colorado she was going to join a Lions club. So I went for it. "You don't have to wait until you get back home to join Lions," I said. "You could join our club now and transfer into a club at home when you return. Then we could become sister cities!"

It sounded like a great idea, but I had questions. "How would I become a member if I'm never going to be at the meetings?" Alan explained that he would be my main contact as I traveled around the world. He and other members of the Mackay North Lions Club would help me contact Lions in other countries, and if I got into any kind of desperate situation they would be my support system. He also wanted to lobby their district for The GlobalWalk for Breast Cancer to become a District Project, which meant that thousands of Lions across Australia would continue the help with the Breast Cancer Network Australia even well after I left Aussie shores.

It was an enormously generous offer, and what a boon it would be to have their support all over the world. But my experience had been that a lot of people get caught up in the moment, then the moment fades and so does their enthusiasm. Alan was a spritely and mild mannered man. I had been communicating with him for a couple of months and trusted him, but had he thought this through?

"Are you sure you want to commit to that much?" I asked him. "I have at least three years of walking left, and you're saying you want to commit to being my main contact with Lions around the rest of the world. Do you know what you'd be getting yourself into?"

"I do know. I've been waiting for a project to come along that I could be passionate about, and this is it. Of course the entire club would be helping, but make no mistake, I would be your main contact."

And so, five days later Alan picked me up on the side of the road near the town of Proserpine and stood next to me at the District Officers Training Meeting while I was inducted into the world's largest volunteer organization. With that, my walk took a giant step forward.

Bob and I had six weeks remaining in our walk through Australia. With the help from my Mackay North Lions Club, the logistics flowed more efficiently than ever, and fundraising swelled. Lions all the way up to Port Douglas got advance notice that I was on my way. As I arrived in each new town, they introduced me to local businesses that offered donations. Breast-screening organizations hosted morning teas where locals came to hear me speak.

In addition to planned fundraisers, kids peddled out on their bikes to find me and donate a dollar; truckers threw spare change out their windows when they couldn't stop. When road construction brought traffic to a halt north of Townsville, I strolled past a mile of cars until a trucker who was familiar with my project got out to make a donation. That started an avalanche of donations from car to car and a party started on the A1.

Even the extreme Australian weather started going my way, settling into a calm tropical winter—similar to a Colorado summer—with warm days and cool nights. It was glorious payback for the endless cycle of heat, floods, forest fires, rain, flies, and humidity of the first seven months.

I felt strong and confident plodding on toward Port Douglas, pushing Bob and singing out loud to Shania Twain in my earphones, reveling in my good fortune to have stumbled across the Lions Clubs. When I hit a high note in Shania's "You're Still the One," a sharp sting nipped me in the belly.

I stuck my head in my shirt and, there, tiptoeing across my abdomen was the hairiest, thickest black spider in all of Oz.

"ARGH!!!" I danced and flapped about, flailing and shooing, yanking my shirt off over my head. "OUT! OUT! GET OUT!!! AUUUGH!!"

Poor spider didn't know what to do. So he bit me again.

"Why you &*%$#!!" I was half-naked now, thrashing about on the Bruce Highway in my bra, shrieking colorful expletives that would make my trucker friends cower.

Within hardly a minute, that may as well have been an hour, the spider was gone. I took several deep breaths and paced in circles for some time before I noted the quintessential nightmare—I was out in public in my underwear.

I retrieved my shirt from the middle of the road. Before I put it back on, I turned to get tea tree oil for my new bites. It was right here on the top of Bob....Bob?

Oh, good Lord, Bob was gone. I looked up the highway, down the highway. No Bob.

I looked in the ditch. No Bob. "Where the...."

I slumped at the side of the highway with my hands on my hips, earphones dangling from my neck still blaring Shania Twain. How could Bob just disappear? He's a big teal-colored buggy! It was only seconds.

A car drove up and parked in front of me. "That was sooo funny!" said the driver. "Ha, ha, ha. Oh, oh..." The middle-aged couple rocked back and forth laughing and laughing. They could barely speak for laughing. "We were driving by when you ripped off your shirt and started dancing around in the middle of the road. Bet you're wondering where your buggy is."

"Yes," I said rather clipped, not yet able to see the humor in the situation. These strangers had, after all, just seen me dancing half naked in the middle of the highway, a situation I can't say I've ever developed the social skills to deal with.

"When you were getting rid of that bug inside your shirt, your buggy drifted across the highway and leapt off the embankment. Come on," said the hubby. "Ha, ha. We'll help dig it out."

It took three of us ten minutes to find Bob buried over his top in a pile of old sugar cane waste in a ditch, and as annoyed as I was that these two couldn't stop laughing at my misfortune, I was grateful that someone had seen the whole sorry bout. If not, what would I have done? Call that woman at 000 and report a missing buggy? I imagined how that awkward conversation would've gone.

"G'day, is this an emergency?"

"Yes! I'd like to report a missing buggy!"

"A missing...buggy?"

"Yes, my buggy, Bob!"

"Your buggy...has a name?"

"Yes, and he disappeared very suddenly while I was dancing half naked on the Bruce Highway!"

Silence.

"Didn't you call a few weeks ago from Yamba about the bush fire that wasn't hurting anyone? What are you, some sort of homeless nomad?"

"Well...yes."

Click.

With thirty new Australian friends surrounding me, I entered Port Douglas for my final trek down under. Reflecting on the nine months and 3,800 kilometers (2,346 miles) from Melbourne, it was hard to believe all that had transpired. Despite all the fancy camping gear I not once had to pitch a tent. The amount of awareness work surpassed anything I'd hoped for, and joining forces with the Lions Clubs was a gift beyond measure. With their help, we passed the $30,000 mark.[1]

Not a day passed when strangers didn't stop to offer fresh fruit from their backyard trees, or someone in an RV pulled up beside me on a desolate road to offer me an ice cream bar. New passions surfaced with the discovery of mangoes, orange beach pants, and my new Aussie tennis crush, hunky Pat "hubbahubba" Rafter.

Best of all, when I arrived in this land down under, I knew no one. Eight months later I had two address books bulging with new friends. It was hard to say goodbye to this sun-kissed land.

My next stop was Singapore, where the Lions Club already planned to pick me up at the airport and had begun liaising with the Singapore Breast Cancer Foundation to prepare the Asia kick-off.

Part of me couldn't wait to experience the Asian culture so intimately, but another part knew I'd have many more challenges than stinky road kill and Vegemite. There were multiple languages, religious traditions, and of course, a whole new breed of bugs. And I was ready.

But if the Lions Clubs provided the most stunning twist I could never have predicted, there was an equally stunning turn right around the corner.

---

[1] The number is still climbing because the Mackay North Lions Club made the GlobalWalk for Breast Cancer a continuing district project.

CHAPTER 9

Asia 101

Polly's Journal, Singapore, August 6, 2001

Everyone's cautioning me that I can't spit my gum out on the streets of Singapore, so I spent my last day in Australia spitting wads of Juicy Fruit into the streets of Queensland just to get it out of my system. Then I boarded a seven-hour Garuda flight back to the north side of the equator.

Studying my Southeast Asia guidebook, I'm becoming eager to tackle this strange new land but am bracing myself for sensory overload. If we learn something new every ordinary day, then surely walking through Asia will up that ante to a hundred. Even in Australia, a culture similar to my own, there were days when I got so overwhelmed by all the new tidbits of information I could feel the seams of my brain bursting. In Asia not only will the languages be different, but also the smells, gestures, food, religions.

Reading the Cultural Dos and Don'ts section, I'm quickly surrendering to the fact that it's only a matter of time before I inadvertently insult someone with a western faux pas. "Don't hand things directly to a Buddhist," it warns. "When you hand things to people, be sure to use two hands," "…remove your shoes here…cover your head there…no photos in the temples…don't use the left hand to give or receive…no pointing…and when entering a mosque you mustn't touch the Quran!" I'm only on chapter one and my brain is swelling. (Definitely frowned upon.)

Lion Yeo Soon Keong—or "SK," as he's known because many Chinese people of Singapore and Malaysia go by initials—drove me from the airport into the streets of Singapore. I watched streams of Asian women dressed in the latest fashions standing in line at Starbucks talking on their flip phones. Streets were lined with Planet Hollywood, Denny's, and billboards advertising Singapore's version of "Who Wants to Be a Millionaire?" I could have been in any California city.

Singapore is a city notorious for its ubiquitous behavioral signs, and driving from the airport, I witnessed the first ones, starting with the infamous, "No gum-chewing," followed closely by "No waiting," "No spitting," and the mysterious "No studying." Singaporeans are so well behaved they don't even have a word for "double-parked."

A clean, polite city with great food really gets my blood pumping, and I wondered if this was the place that could finally knock Sydney off its perch as my favorite city. Any city that fines people $1,000 for throwing a cigarette butt on the sidewalk gets a ten from this judge! Getting caught with drugs is grounds for caning, and they're just as tough if you throw litter on the ground. If you don't like it, you are reminded that the border is only a few kilometers away. It was then I realized I was *not* in any California city.

SK took time out of his job as a prosecuting attorney to act as my personal driver/manager/interpreter for the week, shuffling me to radio and newspaper interviews and luncheons with sponsors like DHL and Estee Lauder. With help from his Singapore City Lions Club, SK led fundraising events that raised over $5,000 in the fleeting six days of my stay.

SK also introduced me to Asian food. A brave undertaking as it was well outside the American version in the little white boxes with wire handles.

"Is there anything you're allergic to?" was the extent of SK's food qualifying.

"No."

"So you'll eat anything?"

Trying to settle for a balance between launching into this glorious new Asian fare and not wanting something to arrive staring back at me, I replied, "Anything without eyes and organs."

"Great. Wait here."

SK sat me at a table in the middle of a bustling food market and disappeared amid the food stalls. He would briefly pop out of the crowd to slide a mysterious something in front of me, tell me what it was—which always included at least five syllables—then disappear back into the crowd. I never knew what I was eating, but it was always delicious. I even rejected the fork, courageously opting for chopsticks. But after three attempts landed in my lap, hair, and the neighbor's beehoon soup, I had to admit defeat and ask SK for that fork.

So began my one-year odyssey across Asia. With forty Singapore Lions, Breast Cancer Foundation workers, breast cancer survivors, and even a few members from the American Club, we kicked off under soggy skies from Sentosa Island, continental Asia's south-ernmost point. They guided me through their island nation and over the Causeway, where the Malaysian Lions halted traffic with a welcome banner that spread across three lanes and two countries. And that's where the *real* foreign leg of my GlobalWalk began.

The Malaysian welcome entourage led me through the main door of customs, and on the other side stood a throng of cheering peo-ple 150 strong. I wondered who this crowd could be waiting for and figured I should probably get out of the way when I noticed the signs bouncing over their heads were for me!

An eight-foot banner stretched across the sidewalk that said, "Welcome Miss Polly to Malaysia and her GlobalWalk for Breast Cancer." Local TV stations and newspaper reporters vied for position; people were yelling my name for photos, shaking my hand, and pinning badges and flags all over Bob. My head swirled as I tried to catch up with the size of this unexpected welcome.

"What will you be doing in Malaysia?" the reporters yelled.

I caught my breath and managed to put a sentence together.

"The money raised in Johor Bahru will go to the Breast Cancer Support Group, an organization that travels around your state hosting exhibitions and forums, teaching women how to do self breast exams and educating them about early symptoms."

The crowd started cheering, which gave me a moment to gulp down some water before I continued. "The Breast Cancer Support Group is trying to break through cultural barriers and let women— and men—know that if breast cancer is caught early, it can mean the difference between life and death."

"What will you do first in Malaysia?"

There were so many people, so many microphones in my face. The 100-degree heat and humidity were making me dizzy, and the magnitude of this reception made me wobbly. "…umm…I intend on studying my *Malaysian Phrase Book* so I'm ready for you guys next time."

I turned to Shien Chen, the Lion on Polly duty, and said covering the mic, "How do I say hello in Bahasa?"

He whispered back and I turned to the crowd. "Selamat petang!"

They cheered wildly while I stood upon a makeshift stage, still wondering if they had the right person.

I followed Shien through the crowd, shaking hands, kissing cheeks. I had no idea where we were going, but the mass of people led me into the heart of Johor Bahru for a breast cancer forum hosted by the Johor Bahru Breast Cancer Support Group. There, while everyone else was dressed to the nines, I, their guest of honor, addressed the forum on stage in my shorts, tee shirt and messy mop of hair. I spoke briefly of the whys, how's, and where's of my walk and the fact that the rate of breast cancer in Malaysia is starting to catch up to the western world. I told them that now was the time to start education. I then stood by, feeling self-conscious and possibly smelly, as an interpreter repeated everything I said in Mandarin, then Bahasa, then Tamil for the Indians.

The overwhelming events of the day made me think back to the many conversations I had during the previous year when people insisted I wouldn't be able to talk about breast cancer in Malaysia because of its Muslim culture. "You can't wear shorts or tee shirts," they told me. "Get rid of your blonde hair. Dye it dark or people will paw at you." "They don't like Americans; tell people you're from Australia."

But one thing I'd learned on the road is that people who give advice are usually people who have no business giving advice. So I did what any shorts-lovin', tee shirt-wearin', blonde American woman would do—I asked the Lions.

"Shorts and tee shirts are fine," they assured me. "Your hair is fine, and if people try to paw at you they'll have to answer to us."

They explained that the east coast of Malaysia is still conservative Muslim, but the west coast, where I would be walking, was more liberal and more people spoke English.

Malaysia is a melting pot of Malays, Chinese, Indians and the indigenous Orang Asli. Their religions are just as diverse. Islam is the state religion, but multiple religions are evident when you see Muslim mosques up the block from Buddhist temples, next to Hindu temples, down the road from Christian churches. Nearly everyone knows at least two languages, most know three, and English is common.

After my lost opportunity at the border to greet a new country in their language(s), I launched into a quick study to learn the basics in both Bahasa and Mandarin—salutations, numbers, directions, and a few basic phrases like, "Let's go for a walk!" (Always a hit.)

MK, a woman from the Johor Bahru Lions Club, taught me how to say thank you in Mandarin—"Shay shay" (phonetic spelling only!)—so at the big celebratory kick-off from Johor Bahru the next day in front of fifty local Lions and the Breast Cancer Support Group, I stood above the crowd and shouted a confident, "Shee shee."

The crowd exploded with laughter, and I smiled proudly at their appreciation of my attempt at their language—until, that is, MK whispered in my ear that I had just told everyone to go pee behind a bush.

Augghh! How did I do that?! "Shay Shay!" I yelled quickly, trying to redeem myself. "I meant Shay Shay!"

Good grief, you'd think whoever started this language would allow a bigger buffer for such errors. But I reasoned that with the heat, humidity and ensuing water consumption, "shee shee" may be a very useful phrase in Malaysia.

One passion all the Malaysian races share is love for their exotic tropical fruit. Every two hundred meters there was a family fruit stand decorated with spiny red rambutans hanging from the roof or enormous jackfruits lined across the counter. Then there's the King of Fruit, the durian.

The infamous durian requires the term that Australians use when initiating a first timer to the repugnance of Vegemite: "It's an acquired taste." But when the smell of a fruit compares to that of an open sewer and is forbidden entry into hotels, subways, and public buildings, I, for one, am in no rush to try it. The durian is the size of a watermelon but not nearly as pretty. It's spiky and hard shelled, with a stench so bad that one day I actually found myself looking around for road kill before realizing it was a nearby durian tree. But Malaysians love it and get a morbid kick out of watching a foreigner's face pucker when forced to try it.

The rest of their food was spectacular. Indians eat with their hands, Chinese eat with chopsticks, and Malays eat with a fork-spoon combination in one hand like chopsticks. For the sake of time management, I sided with the Indians on this one. They don't just eat with their hands, but stir everything together with their hands as well. The first time I was invited to knead together rice, sauce, and veggies with my fingers, I plunged in and immediately became infatuated with a culture that finds eating with hands socially acceptable.

Dozens of people joined me every day as I trudged north up the Malay Peninsula. Mostly Lions members, but curious locals also made their way into the crowd, as well as the Hash Harrier running clubs who found it painful to slow down to three miles per hour. Most nights the Lions Club in the new village put me up in a hotel like the five-star Westin Resort, where we held a press conference followed by a massage in their spa. Other times my room held a cot and included an array of geckos on the wall. Shien contacted Lions Clubs through every village on my route, who then arranged breast cancer forums where a doctor spoke to the local women, showed slides of sick breasts, and talked about early symptoms. If we were lucky we heard a local woman's personal journey, proving breast cancer was not a death sentence.

Lion Soo of Simpang Rengam created leaflets in Mandarin on the subject of good breast health and instructions for breast self-exams. He then recruited a group of teenage boys and girls to distribute the leaflets in shopping centers as we walked through the area.

Each of the five languages in Malaysia had a national newspaper, and every one of them covered the progress of my walk an average of three times a week. The thrilling part was that (besides reporting the national news that I'm single and childless at the age of thirty-nine) they covered the breast cancer information thoroughly, complete with lists of early symptoms and local doctors who were familiar with the disease. They encouraged women not to be ashamed for doctors to see their breasts. The reception in Malaysia was staggering; hard to believe that anyone had thought that talking about breast cancer couldn't be done in this Muslim nation.

Lucky for me, the Lions Clubs in Malaysia are enormous and very influential. The reception and support were unprecedented, and every day I was thrilled and grateful. But if I thought the schedule in Australia was exhausting, that was the minor-league of GlobalWalking. Consider an average schedule of three days:

September 2, 2001: Twenty-five kilometers, three interviews, forty people walking, two educational forums translated into three languages, dinner at 9:00 p.m., two more interviews followed.

> *September 3, 2001:* Breakfast with twenty-five people, two interviews before walking, after ten kilometers someone drove by to say, "Reporters are waiting for you in Kajang at 12:30, you have to run." I stepped it up to a full stride for the last eight kilometers through rush hour traffic to three more interviews, lunch with forty people and an educational forum with a hundred people.
>
> *September 4, 2001:* A "day off" started with a press conference at eight—no one showed up until ten. Lunch was scheduled for noon with fifty people ten kilometers away, followed by an educational forum at two, followed by a meet n' greet with local sponsors, a fundraising event at five, dinner at eight.

And so on.

Thirty, forty, eighty people walked with me every day, all day; breakfast, lunch, dinner, well into the night, people, people, people. It was like *Forrest Gump does Malaysia.*

Swarms of people walking with me every day scrutinized my every move. If I had to stop and scratch my leg, the whole crowd came to a halt and asked, "What's wrong with your leg? Should we take you to the doctor? Somebody call a doctor."

One day I had to remove a pebble from my shoe, and the words echoed through the crowd, "Ta de xue you yi li shi tou!" "Ta de xue you yi li shi tou!" Which evidently means "She's got a pebble in her shoe!" When I confided to a woman in the back of the crowd that I had to shee shee, she bellowed the newsflash to the police officer, who threw a flashing siren atop his patrol car, blew his whistle, halted traffic in both directions, and with great urgency split the group like the Red Sea and escorted me across the street to use the loo at the Shell station.

Through Muar, Merlimau, and Malacca, whenever we walked into a new village—upwards of four a day—a new Lions Club took over and choreographed my every move. It sounds fabulous in theory—an enthusiastic, supportive group of professionals organizing your every move in a foreign land. But here's the reality: the new club would welcome us into their village waving flags and banners, posing for photos click – click – click – click. I shook hands with eighty people from the previous club, said "Goodbye, nice to meet you." Shook hands with eighty new people, "Hello, nice to meet you," and we all started walking. Then one by one, people sauntered up next to me and struggled to talk in English. "Why did you do this? Where have you been? Where are you going? How many pairs of shoes have you been through? How do you get across the ocean? You're not married? Why aren't you married? When will you be married?"

They disappeared back into the crowd, and someone else moseyed up with the same questions, "Why did you do this? Where are you going? How many pairs of shoes have you been through? You're not married? Why aren't you married? Do you have a problem with the love between a man and a woman?"

In six more kilometers I was cheered by a new Lions Club waving flags and banners, pose-pose-click-click-click, "Hello, nice to meet you," shake hands with eighty new people. "Goodbye, nice to meet you." Shake hands with eighty more people, flags, banners, march onward, answer questions.

And again.

Mayors welcomed us into each town. They usually served as crew support for a few hours. Their primary duty was to transport a car full of water bottles for the dozens of walkers. Every half mile Mr. Mayor hopped out of his car, popped the trunk and passed out water bottles to those with rosy cheeks and sweaty brows. It was there I witnessed my first real bout of culture shock.

Mounds of litter piled up along the Malaysian roadside. The stench of garbage rotting in the heat made my eyes sting, though no one else seemed to notice. When I asked about the litter problem I was told it's not a problem, no one minds, no big deal.

I watched the other walkers tossing their empty bottles straight into the gutter, and I didn't know what to do. For days I hung onto my empty water bottles waiting for a trashcan, but that was a futile effort. I finally gave in against all my natural reflexes and tossed my empty water bottles into the gutter. It was so unnerving that, within two hundred yards, guilt overcame me and I raced back to pick them up.

I held onto them until I passed the mayor's popped trunk where I put them back in the box. Then I watched, startled, as the mayor himself lifted the empty box out of the trunk and tossed it into the tall grass. Instinctively I walked into the tall grass, retrieved the box and put it back in his trunk then watched as the poor mayor turned around and retreated back a step upon spotting the reappearing box. Bewildered, he lifted it out of the trunk again and with an impressive heave, tossed it high over the tall grass and into the canal below where we both watched it float away south toward Singapore. Clean, tidy, anal Singapore where they'd toss you in the slammer for doing the same thing.

My first month in Asia was a melting pot of experiences and challenges. The languages, food, and overwhelming attention were the obvious. But the biggest challenge was the overabundant Asian hospitality. People wouldn't take no for an answer. I tried. Lord knows I tried. But every night there was a conversation similar to this:

"We pick you up for dinner tonight at eight o'clock."

"Thank you anyway, I'm really tired after thirty kilometers in that ninety-degree heat. I really need to sleep."

"We take you early. We eat early. You sleep later."

"No, thank you. I really need sleep. I've been out late every night for weeks. I'll just eat an apple and go to bed."

"Apple? You want apple? We bring you bucket of apples!"

"No, thank you, I'm all set on apples. I need to sleep."

"We come over and eat apple with you. What kind of apple you like?"

"I have an apple. But let's do breakfast."

"Breakfast, too. But tonight we come by with apples. We be here eight o'clock. Bye bye."

Personal space was not a basic human need in this land that sits ten people around a table for five and seemingly has no translation for the term "elbow room." Ironically, as I planned the trip, I had prepared exhaustively for being alone, for the inevitability of loneliness. What I never even thought about preparing for was the polar opposite—the overwhelming attention, the constant crowds, the pushing, pulling, even lifting on occasion.

Walking alone as a woman, far from being a hindrance, had in fact, turned out to be a boon. At this point I had more help and support than I ever could have imagined, someone at my beck and call for everything from egg whites to visas. Yet I had rarely been so stressed out.

I prescribed spending a day alone.

I arrived in the city of Seremban, desperately anticipating my scheduled two days off, when I was unexpectedly presented with a schedule that kept me busy from 8:00 a.m. to 9:30 p.m. each day. Those on Polly duty had been told up the line to let me rest, but they said no way. In a whisper folks explained that the idea that I would walk through their town without fanfare was unacceptable. It was a matter of Lions Club honor to outdo each other, and if one club put me up in a three-star hotel and threw a fifty-person educational forum, then the next club would strive to put me up in a four-star hotel and have a hundred person forum—with catering—and international press. What that meant for me, however, was an uninterrupted schedule for two solid months.

I looked at the schedule planned for my two days of rest. It started at 6:00 a.m. with two hardboiled eggs and a banana, followed by a meeting with the mayor, then morning tea followed by a breast cancer forum, press conference, and lunch—then sightseeing to the temple, the mosque, the local waterfalls, afternoon tea, followed by more interviews until dinner at nine.

I tried gently to explain that this was all too much—what I really needed was some time alone to rejuvenate. "If you don't mind, I would like to take at least one of these days by myself and wander through town at my own pace."

"That sounds great, I go with you."

"I don't know that you'd be happy going with me," I suggested. "I want to saunter through town and take photos, maybe stop at a cafe and have a mochaccino while reading the newspaper. I might attempt the crossword, then give up and go see a movie and change my mind three times about what I want to see. I might call a couple of friends and not worry about someone waiting for me, then stop at a bookstore and wander through the books looking for nothing in particular. I might sit on a park bench and just watch people without making conversation. I want to be alone to discover, peruse, reflect, ponder, meander, chill."

They all looked at me across the table and nodded with approval. At last I got through to them.

"I want to be alone, too. I go with you."

"Me, too!"

It gave me a newfound respect for politicians and other high profile figures who have endless schedules and have to be *on* all the time. Are they stressed out? Or do they thrive? Doesn't Bill Clinton ever just want to chill in a cafe and do a crossword over a cappuccino? Is it just my personality type that isn't comfortable with this sort of attention?

When I called Dad and mentioned that it was actually annoying to have people pounce on my every need, he gave me words I took to heart. "Let them help you," he urged. "People feel good when they can help. They feel part of something bigger, like they're making a contribution, even if it's just making you hard boiled eggs."

That was a light bulb moment. This walk wasn't about me and my stress level—it was about people, strangers banding together for one cause, and I happened to be the tool. That was driven home a couple of days before I walked into Kuala Lumpur when a member of the Malaysian Parliament, Datuk Napsiah Omar, and one hundred of her colleagues came out to greet me. She organized a ceremony full of pomp and fanfare at a local mall to officially announce the beginning of a breast cancer awareness campaign in her region. And she meant it.

MP Omar immediately started urging the Malaysian government to subsidize an annual mammogram for women aged fifty-five to sixty-four. My stress level was insignificant compared to the effort being made to establish a breast cancer campaign across the country. It made me think of one of my favorite quotes by Dr. Wayne Dyer: "When you change the way you look at things, the things you look at change."

With a renewed mindset I tried to embrace the crowds and the overwhelming support. I would take a deep breath and be patient, let people pounce, over-schedule, even lift on occasion.

That was September 10, 2001.

CHAPTER 10

And Everything Changed

It was a Tuesday night when the local Ampang Lions Club walked me into a nearby hotel. It featured an Internet cafe that offered me a chance to catch up with the current events on CNN. Noting that nothing of a world-changing nature had happened, I called it a night. It was 8:45 p.m. Malaysian time—8:45 a.m. in New York City, September 11, 2001.

The next morning I finished my hardboiled eggs and banana in the hotel restaurant, took my vitamins, and geared up to start another day in the 100-degree heat when my walking buddies started to assemble in the lobby. Lions member Soong walked in and, contrary to the enthusiastic person I had known for the past few days, he looked rather glum. "Did you hear the bad news?" he asked.

There's not a lot of news, good or bad, that Soong and I would have in common, so I assumed it had to do with the weather. "Is it going to rain today?"

"No, no," he said. In his broken English, he recounted the news with key words "hijackers" "crashed into World Trade Center," "buildings collapsed," and "watched CNN all night."

"Excuse me, I don't understand."

Another walking buddy approached us and said that he, too, had had only an hour's sleep, as he sat up all night watching events unfold on CNN.

I didn't understand what they were telling me, but I did understand it was big. The first newspapers of the morning were just arriving at the front desk, and while they were in Bahasa, the photo was clear—New York's landmark World Trade Center was up in flames.

My walking group continued to gather solemnly in the lobby. They asked if I wanted to continue walking that day or did I want to get near TV, phones and Internet? I opted for walking but asked if they could they help me find access to CNN afterwards. They would, and our crowd left the Ampang Hotel and somberly headed north.

In every village throughout this central Malaysian region, people talked about the unthinkable. Villagers who knew no one in New York were shocked, stunned, horrified with the rest of the world. TVs hung in open food stalls where crowds gathered shaking their heads feeling helpless, while the footage looped over and over and over, as if maybe the hundredth time the plane would miss.

My thoughts strayed to home. How were my friends reacting? How would this affect everyday life in Minneapolis and Colorado? The world? My walk?

At the end of the day, Soong found a family for me to stay with that had both CNN and Internet access. Their names were Irene and Radha, managers of a six thousand acre oil palm plantation complete with monkeys. And, ironically for this day, they were Muslim. They call themselves liberal, modern thinking Muslims, as they dress in crisp new western styles and wear no headscarves. Theirs was not an arranged marriage, and they found no shame in enjoying a nice cold beer after a long day's work. They said they were not Muslim by choice but rather by default. When Irene's mother, a Buddhist, married a Muslim man, that obligated her to convert to Islam. In turn their children were born Muslim. Irene then grew up and married Radha, a Hindu from India. In order for them to marry, he had to convert to Islam. They explained that their children have to be Muslim.

"Can't you just not be Muslim?" I asked in my American free-to-be-who-you-want-to-be innocence.

"No. Once a Muslim always a Muslim."

They explained that they had three children, two of whom had already graduated from high school and were attending higher education in Australia, where they felt there was more opportunity.

139

They spoke with their daughter in Sydney earlier in the day to see if she was safe.

"Why wouldn't she be safe in Australia?"

"Because she is Muslim."

"But if she looks Chinese and Indian and doesn't actively practice Islam, how would anyone know?"

"If someone asks if she's Muslim, she would have to say yes, even though she doesn't practice. If she said anything else, it would be an embarrassment to Islam, and her family would lose face."

"But you're her family. Would you lose face?"

"No. Her Muslim family."

If this had been any other couple I wouldn't have asked such bold questions; but they appeared eager to explain their situation. I felt comfortable then telling them about an article I had recently read which explained that in America, a full fifty percent of the population practices a religion other than the one they grew up with. "Let's say your daughter moves to the Australian Outback and doesn't know a soul. Could she start her life entirely over again and choose a different religion? One that she truly believes in and wants to aspire to?"

"No." They both said, looking down into their laps. "Once you're born a Muslim you're always a Muslim. You can't hide from it, even in the Outback of Australia."

Irene and Radha explained that in Malaysia if you're Muslim you have the opportunity to own land. That's not the case if you're Buddhist, Christian or Hindu. If you're Muslim you also have access to free higher education and social welfare, but not so if you're a non-Muslim. They told me that if you go down to the social services office and sign a document that confirms you are changing your religion to Islam, then you have rights different from the Chinese or Indians of the country. "Just sign at the bottom line because once a Muslim always a Muslim." Irene went on, "My relatives on my mother's side, who have been in this country for two hundred years are still considered Chinese. They will never be Malaysians until they sign at the bottom line proclaiming their conversion to Islam."

Instantly, it gave me a whole new respect for America and what the words *freedom of religion* really mean. In America you have the freedom to be born Catholic, marry a Lutheran, raise your kids Jewish, then get divorced and convert to Buddhism and your friends would throw you a party for finding yourself. Or you could choose to practice no religion at all or make up one of your own. And no matter what religion you choose you have equal rights protected by law. My whole life I've heard that in America you can be whatever you want to be, but that never really clicked to my very core until this moment with Irene and Radha.

Their fifteen-year-old son logged me onto the Internet, where I found streams of emails being sent back and forth among my American friends expressing messages of support and profound words to live by. "We can make our actions today part of the answer instead of part of the problem." In one group email promoting "Flags Across America Day," everyone was encouraged to buy flags and display them on their home, car, office, bike, anywhere to show Americans would stick together. Retailers around the country were giving away red, white, and blue ribbons for crafting unity lapel pins.

There were also emails from friends around the world that I'd met over the past two years, expressing their grief at the day's events. One from Rose in Singapore said, "I've tried to call you all day. Please don't walk alone for a couple of weeks."

From New Zealand, "Everybody here is stunned. We're thinking of you."

From Australia, "What has happened in your country is just inconceivable. Although you're alone in Malaysia, you're not alone. Australians cheer you on. God Bless America."

A friend in Minneapolis wrote, "We all need to get up today and sing. Not to ignore the tragedy but rather to demonstrate and experience our own spirit."

From a friend traveling in Jordan, "People here are laughing and rejoicing. I'm completely stunned and feel lost in this land that laughs about the death of thousands of innocent Americans."

Mom emailed from Arizona, "I went to donate blood, and so many people showed up there was a six hour wait!"

And from Randi back in Colorado, exactly where I wanted to be, "We're all just hanging around in front of the TV."

The patriotism and unity flooding through emails made me homesick. It was my first twinge of understanding the tribal nature of human beings, wanting to be among our own people during tragedy. I wanted to go home. I wanted to sit in front of CNN all day and night until it made some sort of sense, until we had all the answers, to be with fellow Americans while this unfolded, to talk, analyze, ask, fuss, cry, bitch and bawl.

But I couldn't. I was on an oil palm plantation in Slim River, Malaysia, miles from home and no closer to answers than anyone else.

I wasn't around when Pearl Harbor was bombed, and I was too young to remember where I was the day JFK was shot. But I'll never forget where I was the day America lost its innocence. I was on an oil palm plantation in Malaysia, grieving with Muslims.

Overnight I became keenly aware that I was no longer a woman walking for women. Clearly now I was an American woman with a Jewish last name walking through a Muslim country during holy jihad, talking about breasts.

Alan called from my Mackay North Lions Club with an urgent tone, "What's your escape plan? Do you have an emergency plane ticket back to the U.S.?"

But there would be no hopping on a plane back to L.A. or Colorado. My immediate reflex was a desperate yearning to be home with friends. But I'd always known there would be tough times; times I could not foresee or prepare for. This was one of them. It had been a pretty good run for the past year since the Tabatha debacle, and it was time to stiffen up my back and step into the painful discomfort zone again. I immediately turned to the words that were permanently tucked in my wallet: "Commitment: when you find a way over every hurdle in your path and nothing but success is an option. Commitment."

In the days immediately following 9/11 I was as well protected as possible; crowds of people were walking with me every day and police escorts accompanied me all the way to the Thai border. The U.S. State Department had issued a warning to all U.S. nationals overseas to keep a low profile. That meant press coverage and breast cancer forums had to be halted immediately.

Malaysia is a peaceful country, but this was no time to put my hands over my eyes pretending no one could see me. I had to take precautions. Lions, Rotary Clubs, even the Hash Harriers Running Club walked beside me every day, and if strangers asked, I said I was from Australia. "From Queensland," I'd say in my best accent, "I teach secondary school maths," thinking the "s" on the end of math was a nice touch.

A few days after 9/11, I crossed the border into the State of Kedah, a state with a ninety percent Muslim population—a more conservative population than the southern state. Since Friday is a holy day in Islam, every two kilometers there was another mosque where streams of Muslims, young and old, made their way to pray, filing into the blue and gold structures with onion-shaped domes. They were dressed in long robes and slip-off sandals, so they could easily enter the mosque in bare feet, prepared for prayer. The women had their heads covered and the men wore white beanie caps.

"What is the significance of the white hat?" I asked Kalai, an Indian man joining us for the day.

"In the past, the white hat meant that they had made the pilgrimage to Mecca, the holy place of Islam," he explained, "but these days everyone wears them. On Friday everyone wears the hat, which tells the world they are Muslim. On other days it's optional."

Of course everyone noticed the odd looking white girl walking down the road in the funny sun hat. Feeling the egg shells under my feet in an uber-sensitive world mood, I gave every passing man a friendly wave and smile as if to say, "See, I'm from the West, and I'm not so bad." They, in turn, gave me friendly waves and nice smiles, too, as if to answer, "See, we're Muslim, and we're not so bad either."

One old man stood at the entrance of his mosque in robe, sandals, and white beanie, and waved me in to join them. Part of me wanted to, of course, but I quickly decided that it was inappropriate. Maybe another time. Almost any other time.

When I reached the cafe in Sungai Limau, my destination for the day, a man in a turban approached me to introduce himself. Not realizing he was with the local Lions Club, I gave him my standard line. "Hi, I'm Polly, from Australia."

He shook my hand and with a laugh introduced himself, "And I'm with the Taliban." Knowing straight away I'd been busted, I burst out laughing.

"Well, my Taliban friend, I suppose you know where Osama is hiding."

"I do!"

"Let's go find him and split the bounty."

"We'll be rich!" he played. "But let's have a drink first."

His name was Singh. We ordered cold drinks and snacks in a nearby Muslim cafe; then I excused myself to use the loo. The owner, dressed in traditional robe and headscarf, pointed me to a dark concrete four-by-four foot dungeon at the front of the cafe right next to a table of five.

The adventures we Westerners have with Asian toilets provide endless fodder for conversation. At some point we've all entered a loo and not been able to put the pieces together. We'd whisper, "Have you figured out what the hose is for?" "What's with the bucket of water?" And for women, "Which way do you face?"

These "tandas" don't come with directions, and like snowflakes or fingerprints, there never seemed to be any two alike. I learned to walk in, peruse the playing field and implement a game plan. Flushing is an entire category in itself. There are knobs, strings, levers, chains, pedals, and sometimes nothing. Options are to push, pull, twist, yank, crank, or on occasion, admit defeat and apologize profusely to the next person in line.

The loo in this Muslim cafe was my greatest challenge yet. I closed the tin door behind me and wrapped the string around the nail to hold it in place. The hole in the roof allowed me a small ray of light. There was a thing on the wall rather like a urinal, but it was four feet off the ground. No woman I've ever met can pee four feet up a wall. But that was it. There was no hole in the ground, no bucket, no squats. I reasoned that they misunderstood me and this couldn't be the loo, so I walked out of the little dungeon back into the cafe.

The patrons and the owner laughed in my direction, knowing I'd been stumped, and without words the owner turned me around and pushed me back in.

"Okay," I shrugged, closing the tin door behind me and again pulled the string over the nail.

I stood in the middle of the dark loo and gave myself a pep talk, "Okay, I'm a resourceful girl, I can figure this out." I looked around and considered my options. "We've got a urinal four feet up the wall, maybe I could…? No. Not possible." Then I noted a small hole in a lower corner of the wall. Like a mouse hole. "Am I supposed to…? Do I…? But what if I'm wrong?" My mind flashed to school kids reading history books twenty years from now. "…and while the world was on pins and needles waiting for U.S. retaliation, an American girl piddled on a Muslim's cafe floor and set off Holy Jihad." I couldn't shoulder that kind of responsibility. With embarrassment and a touch of humiliation, I opened the fragile tin door, and all the patrons of the little cafe smiled in my direction. Maybe later the police could escort me to a Shell Station.

The weeks after 9/11 passed slowly while the world waited nervously for the reaction from the U.S. government. Tourism came to a halt, particularly in Muslim countries like Malaysia. Despite the call by the U.S. State Department for Americans to keep a low profile, the Lions— in an effort with the Malaysian Government to prove their camaraderie with Americans—arranged local mayors, governors, and members of Parliament to usher me into every town with grand fanfare. There were hospital tours and fancy dinners, fundraising events and grand welcomes. But I felt alone.

A characteristic of Asian culture, I discovered, is that while they were warm and welcoming they would never dream of talking about anything resembling thoughts, fears and feelings—the widespread trait among most American women. So during these unprecedented world events, I had no one to talk to. I felt lost, plodding along day after day surrounded by crowds, yet isolated. And every night, with the grand fanfare and national dignitaries, I suddenly found myself caught up in a brand new world of Asian protocol I knew nothing about, operating by the seat of my pants trying desperately not to embarrass myself—and now my country.

Only ninety kilometers to Thailand and I was walking as fast as I could. I had been crossing my fingers that if President Bush and NATO decided to go to war, they would at least hold off until I crossed the border into Buddhist territory.

But no. The first news I heard on the morning of October 7 was that America and Britain had launched strikes into Afghanistan. The Lions and the local Hash Harriers gathered to walk with me that morning, so I briefed them on the latest developments. I suggested again that if anyone along the route asked, to tell them I was Australian. They assured me that no need for that existed because Malaysia was a very peaceful country and meant me no harm.

Yes, Malaysia is a peaceful country. The reports I heard about the far-north, predominantly Muslim area were mixed, however. "Muslims in Malaysia are very friendly; you have nothing to worry about," someone said. Then someone else would whisper, "There are many extremists hiding out up here in the north. You must be very careful." And the next person, "The Muslims here know Bin Laden is a terrorist and cheer on America. They'll stand by you." Then again, "See all these green flags with the white circles in the middle? That means they're extremists, so stay away." I knew better than to believe any of it, but under such unique circumstances, I had to keep my eyes wide open. The Lions went out of their way to ensure my safety by continuing to arrange groups of people to walk with me every day. They also made sure I got safely into my hotel at night.

A fierce twitch in my left eye became so strong I sometimes clocked thirty seconds of fluttering at a shot. During a welcome ceremony at the Kinta Medical Center, people said how sorry they were about what my country was going through, and I burst into tears. I was clearly sinking.

It didn't help when my hosts for the night regularly bombarded me with conspiracy theories about 9/11. "Come now," they said. "You must admit it's a possibility that American and Israeli governments are behind the attacks." Or "You must admit it's a bit fishy that 5,000 Jews work in those buildings, and none were at work at the time." Good grief, they're still pulling unidentified bodies out of the rubble, and they're saying they know none of them are Jewish? Is there some kind of secret phone tree to alert 5,000 Jewish people not to come to work? Do people really believe this stuff? But I couldn't respond. I could only nurse my twitchy eye.

Until one night.

In my hotel room one night, I opened my little computer and spilled all my thoughts into my daily journal. I typed furiously in a stream of consciousness that hardly edited a thought, using entire sentences and ideas my friends had emailed during their rants, too. Then I had an idea. Why don't I send this journal into *The New Straits Times* as a Letter to the Editor?

The New Straits Times is Malaysia's English newspaper, tightly controlled by an anti-American Malaysian government. *The New Straits Times* regularly featured bold headlines declaring "America deserved it." If I only knew about America through their news coverage, I'd hate it, too. Unlike America, which puts their scandals on the front page, you would never find a bad word about the Malaysian government in the newspaper.

So while I knew my journal-turned-letter-to-the-editor would never make it into *The New Straits Times* editorial section, I also realized it was the perfect way to get things off my chest. But I was a foreigner in Malaysia, a fundraiser, advocate, and honored guest, a guest who had been treated extremely well, so it went without saying I couldn't use my own name. Under a name pulled out of thick air—Paul Sinclair—I emailed my rant to the editorial section.

Dear Editor,

"Americans deserved it?" Shame on you. Nearly 5,000[sic] people were killed on 9/11, completely innocent people of all nationalities simply going about their day, working hard.

No one wants to march into Afghanistan and kill innocents, particularly the Americans who, to this day, are the largest suppliers of food and aid going into that country. Contrary to your headlines Americans have only tried to help Muslims. If not for the U.S. led operation into Kosovo, the Serbs would have slaughtered millions of Muslims. How about the U.S.-led Desert Storm that liberated Kuwait—a Muslim country?

Even today I've heard stories in the United States of citizens reaching out to the Muslim communities. In Denver, Colorado, citizens went to a mosque and formed a human circle around it holding hands and singing, assuring the Muslims in Colorado that they were welcome American citizens in this difficult time.

Like it or not, its sheer size, technology, education, and money makes America a leader. Now it has a responsibility to do what is necessary to protect its citizens and the world. Unfortunately your hate for America gives you the luxury of either yelling Isolationists! or Imperialists! at whatever they do.

I can name you five-thousand times when the Americans raced to other countries to help during natural catastrophes, yet every year American towns are wiped out by tornados, earthquakes, mudslides, or hurricanes, and have any of you raced to help the Americans in trouble? No, you haven't.

It's America that started the Peace Corps. Thousands of everyday Americans volunteer years of their time, going into poor countries helping build homes, schools, hospitals, plant crops and teach farming techniques.

I am fed up with the endless anti-American headlines in your newspaper. Shame on you again!

—Paul Sinclair
Kuala Lumpur

Polly's Journal Notes
October 9, 2001

It's 65 kilometers to Thailand. The opposing Muslim political party in Malaysia, PAS, have declared a jihad against the United States and claimed that several Malaysians have already left for Kabul to fight alongside the Taliban.

On the way back to my hotel room, I found a *New Straits Times*. I turned to the editorial page and couldn't believe my eyes. A headline editorial letter by Mr. Paul Sinclair— an entire quarter of the page! Aughhh! I wanted to jump up and down and tell everyone, "Look! Look! My letter is in the paper!" But I had to refrain, no one can know it's me, and I couldn't show emotion. You can't show emotion.

October 10, 2001

Today I got emails from Rachel and Nick from New Zealand. Both had heard that westerners traveling through Malaysia are advised to keep their heads low and their mouths shut. (Well, Rachel added the latter.) I was surprised because the papers here imply the opposite. According to the Malaysian press everything here is peachy keen; westerners here have nothing to worry about. I won't dare tell Rachel that I'm now a published writer—even if it is under an alias.

Only 40 kilometers to Thailand.

October 11, 2001

The New Straits Times editorial section is chockfull of letters rebutting Paul Sinclair's letter. They read: "Mr. Sinclair, if you can name 5,000 times when the Americans raced to help people in trouble, I can name 10,000 times when the Americans have committed crimes against humanity."

October 12, 2001

More and more letters to the editor hit The *New Straits Times* today, rebutting Paul Sinclair's letter, as well as letters rebutting the rebutters!

"I agree with Paul Sinclair's letter. The Taliban was given the chance to hand over Osama and his band. It must now bear the consequences and be responsible for its own fate."

And "No one can prove Osama Bin Laden had anything to do with the events of September 11. It's just a way for the U.S. to have an excuse to invade more Muslim nations."

Paul Sinclair has ignited a rage through the editorial pages and I…ahem, I mean *he*, would love to keep the flames of debate kindled by penning more opines, but "Mr. Sinclair" is closing in on the Thai border.

A dozen people joined me for my last day in the rather desolate region of northern Malaysia, and I had mixed emotions about my two months there. Malaysia was one of the most productive stretches of my walk. It was successful due to the unrelenting work of the Lions Clubs. While the people had heard little about breast cancer when I entered Malaysia, they sure had by the time I walked out two months later. However, due to the unprecedented world events, for me, Malaysia was one of my toughest stretches.

On the other side of the border lay Thailand, a predominantly Buddhist country, where the relationship with America was strong and healthy. But Thailand's southern isthmus was still heavily settled with a Muslim population. It wasn't time yet to put my guard down.

I crossed the border in the nick of time. Muslim extremists had gathered at the U.S. embassy in Kuala Lumpur that afternoon, and violence had escalated out of control.

CHAPTER 11

Land of the smiling Thais

Years ago I read a book by Steve Newman about his walk around the world. He wrote of a nasty brush in the south of Thailand involving bandits, weapons, and a narrow escape, so naturally a nerve-racking seed took sprout in my wild imagination.

But that was twenty-odd years earlier when Muslim separatists scoured the southland region as machete wielding bandits. While they'd since retreated, there was fear they might resurface after the atrocity of 9/11. When I reached the Thailand border, the landscape bloomed with flowers, and the customs officers couldn't have been nicer. There were fifty smiley Thai Lions standing with the press— a far cry from Newman's trek back in the 80s.

The All Thailand Experiences crew also met us at the border. ATE, as it's known, is an eco-cultural tour company owned by three Americans and one Thai woman named Ott. They specialize in custom designed adventure tours for families, groups, and those who have a hankering to walk through the country, apparently. I had contacted them very early in my walk to ask if they would consider being a sponsor for my trek in Thailand, and they replied with a simple, "Yes, we'd love to." After 9/11, Randy, one of ATE's owners, contacted me to say that instead of a driver who would check in with me a few times a day, their driver had been instructed to follow right behind me all day every day at three miles per hour. He said, "Not only do we want to make Thailand the best, easiest, most beautiful, and productive country you walk through, we want to make sure you're safe. We'll have Prayoon, one of our drivers who speaks English, meet you at the Malaysian border."

Randy was right. Thailand quickly became one of the best, easiest, and most beautiful countries on my global trek. But he was wrong about one thing: Prayoon the driver knew no English at all.

Ott, a beautiful, petite Thai woman, who spoke English fluently, reiterated what Randy had said earlier: they had instructed Prayoon to stay right behind me all day as a precaution. It had only been four weeks since 9/11, and there were a number of Muslim villages in the south of Thailand. The war in Afghanistan had just started, and tensions were running high among the Muslim population. If anything happened to me, Thailand would endure a great deal of international embarrassment.

Thailand is known as the land of the Smiling Thais, and it was hard to imagine anyone could possibly want to cause me harm. But I couldn't ignore the realities of a region with a violent history. I agreed that my safety would be best served by keeping Prayoon right behind me every step of the way.

After the welcome party at the border, Ott and Prayoon helped me lift Bob into the back of the van, and we started making our way through the border town of Padang Besa with Prayoon at our tail. The town is hardly a dot on the map, yet flooded with humanity. Massage parlors advertised reflexology for five dollars an hour, and chicken carcasses hung from the rafters at food stalls. Noodle cafes filled the streets with smells of Thai spices my nose had never experienced. A new alphabet left me illiterate. Moreover, the simple step over the border seemed to create a new mood, a freedom, an energy where the norm, even in this small rural village, allowed girls to dress in modern western styles of designer jeans and printed low cut tees. In sharp contrast, other shops, run by Muslim women dressed from headscarf to toe, sold conservative clothes for women. One animated woman stood in her doorway touting Osama bin Laden tee shirts.

"May I take your photo?" I asked with Ott's help.

The woman giggled and shyly ran to the back of the store.

The owner of another storefront wore his Osama bin Laden tee shirt, posing proudly for a photo.

In yet another display of a culture in conflict, a parked Toyota truck proudly displayed an Osama bin Laden bumper sticker.

I wondered if I should be more nervous in Thailand than I had been led to believe. In Malaysia, a proud Muslim country, I never saw a bumper sticker or a tee shirt praising Osama bin Laden, but in Thailand, a Buddhist country, people appeared freer to express themselves. In fact, I was impressed that one of the first articles I read in the English language *Bangkok Post* concerned a call from the Thai Government, urging their citizens to participate more in freedom of speech. Was I experiencing what freedom of speech really means? Or was the mood in southern Thailand dicier than that in conservative northern Malaysia?

For two days walking from the border at Padang Besa to Hat Yai, Ott stayed with Prayoon and me to get us off to a good start. The Lions Clubs met us each night to check us into a hotel and take us to dinner. Their clubs had been contacted right up through Bangkok six weeks away and would be waiting for us. The crowds that nearly overwhelmed me throughout Malaysia had disappeared, and, in turn, it was a relief to have just Ott—the balance of just one person to talk to.

"It doesn't seem like Prayoon knows any English," I said as she prepared to leave.

"He knows English," she insisted. "He's just shy."

But he didn't. We spent our first day alone together in a fierce game of charades and shoulder shrugging. I wondered how on earth we would get through the day, let alone four months together. With my one translation book, I managed to communicate to him that we needed to walk out of Hat Yai via a bookstore. I dashed in and grabbed every version of translation book I could find—English-Thai for me, Thai-English for him, three of each—and piled them in the front seat figuring that somewhere amidst this pile of books would be the words we needed to know to get us by.

We launched into learning our respective new languages trying to communicate the simplest needs from "I'm hungry" to the trickier

"Have you seen my yellow bandana?" We laughed when he couldn't pronounce the English word "thirsty" because there's hardly another language in the world that has our "th" sound. And I couldn't pronounce…well, anything.

Upon entering any new country, I learned to master the top five words or phrases; "Hello," "Goodbye," "Thank you," "Where's the toilet" and "I don't understand." In Thailand, I also had to learn how to say, "Not too spicy, please," "May I take your photo?" and for the near-brutal Thai massage, "Please don't crack my bones."

"Each word can be said four or five different ways," a Malaysian friend told me before I crossed into Thailand. "Each inflection has a different meaning. The word "ma," for example, can mean "dog," "horse," "very" or "come," depending on the inflection. "Try it," he said. "Ma, ma, ma, and ma."

"Ma, ma, ma, ma."

"No. Listen. Ma, ma, ma, ma."

My Midwest American ear didn't hear the slightest difference.

"Ma, ma, ma, ma."

"No. Ma, ma…"

And this conversation went in circles until I was dizzy. "Ma, ma, ma, ma."

"That's it!"

Yeah right. At that point if there were any changes in inflection, I'm betting they were attitudinal.

In the southernmost part of Thailand, no one spoke English. This launched me into a crash course of the Thai language that sent the word north to not be offended by anything I may inadvertently say. Within days, my *Lonely Planet Thai Phrase Book* had gotten a workout. The spine was fully broken in and notes scribbled throughout. I was learning fast. But those darn inflections were tricky little buggers. I cooed—or thought I was cooing—to a cute little three-year old boy, "He's a very nice looking boy." Evidently I cooed, "He's a very handsome horse." The child started crying. I scribbled a note: work on "ma" inflections.

While practicing my numbers one afternoon, my hosts started

giggling when I got to number seven which has an awkward "jy" sound that's tough on western tongues. "Arai na kham?" ("What's so funny?"—a key phrase to learn in any language!) They explained that the way I pronounced the number seven was dangerously close to saying a dirty word, so I noted that I should order six apples, never seven.

Being in a country where the language, even the alphabet, is different is like having your whole world blurry. Road signs, newspapers, menus, people talking, singing, fighting—it's all blurry. Once in a while my eyes or ears would catch a passing glimpse of a word in English and for that single moment my world was in focus, otherwise I rarely knew what was going on around me. For example: a monk was walking down the middle of the road backing up traffic for miles. I couldn't ask why. A fight broke out between two women in a hotel lobby with fists pounding tables, voices shrieking and security guards running. I'll never know why. Three motorcycle police pulled in front of the All Thailand Experiences van and watched over me like a mother hen for five kilometers outside Songkhla. I couldn't ask why.

Prayoon and I inched our way through the language barrier. I was learning Thai as fast as I could, and he studied his Thai-English dictionary as he plodded behind me at six kilometers (3mph) per hour. Like a couple of kids, we developed our own language—sign language, limited vocabulary, and a comical attempt at charades. When he said, "Talk, food, *Bangkok Post*" I knew he was telling me to order with the waitress before I looked for a newspaper. When he said, "Shirt. Osama," that was his way of telling me to put on a long sleeved shirt because we were entering a Muslim village.

Our language skills included no conjunctions, no tenses, no plurals. Pronouns didn't exist. I spoke in Thai; he responded in English, everything was in the third person.

"Polly hungry. Where eat?"

"Okay. Prayoon stop. Polly like noodle?"

"Polly like noodle. Delicious."

"Prayoon cook Polly good noodle."

"Prayoon very good."

It was like Dick and Jane go to Thailand.

For eight to ten hours a day, Prayoon lumbered right behind me in first gear. He helped me with directions, ordered my lunch at cafes, and explained to everyone what I was doing and why. When we came across a pack of stray dogs, Prayoon shooed them away with the big stick he carried in the van. Other times he'd jump out to break up an over-zealous group of people who had surrounded me. In short, he became very protective.

One night when Prayoon and I went to dinner with the Lions, Prayoon launched into a story apparently so funny that some of the Lions were grabbing their sides with laughter. Except for something that sounded uncannily like "Madonna," I couldn't catch a word. I finally asked the English-speaking woman next to me to translate.

"He's telling us that you were walking through a Muslim village today, and there was a group of men walking behind the van. They were yelling at you, but you couldn't hear them because you were listening to Madonna in your earphones."

Proof that ignorance really is bliss. It made me realize that because of our limited communication, even though we were together all day every day, Prayoon and I were having completely different journeys.

One afternoon, six police cars suddenly surrounded me like a protective cocoon, and no one could tell me why. Had they heard that I was in danger? Had there been a threat? They urged me to keep walking, and I didn't know what to do except put Billy Joel in my earphones and carry on. It was a full-on entourage with two cars full of Lions behind me, police cars leading the way and at my side and Prayoon bringing up the rear.

Within a mile I spotted a scruffy looking sort and wondered if I had my answer. The man didn't look particularly threatening, just disheveled. He had no shoes but that's not unusual in Thailand. He had no shirt either, but again, hardly a reason for police protection the likes of royalty. What did stand out, though, were the long thick scars on his face and chest, and hair that defied gravity. It actually grew upwards and bounced while he walked. Clearly he didn't own a comb. The only thing he wore was a pair of shorts, those big, baggy ones that hang only an inch away from dropping to his ankles. His gaze seemed locked on the ground, and he never even glanced at the entourage of police cars or the blonde girl walking toward him. When our paths finally crossed, I smiled and said, "Sawadee ka."

The man acknowledged me by looking up but that slight movement sent his shorts into a slide and he made a disjointed move to catch them. That threw the police into a tizzy, and before I could yell, "Hold your fire!" four policemen leapt out of their cars, guns drawn, and pointed at the man with bouncy hair who was just trying to hold his pants up.

I wondered if all this protection was really necessary, but as I got closer to the Kra Isthmus, very close to the oft-troubled Burmese border, I realized it was probably for the best. In the meantime I steered the whole entourage away from any potentially shady characters—for their protection as much as mine.

Southern Thailand supports a constant flow of people. Old men gathered on front porches invited me up for a drink of whiskey. Old women pushed heaping food carts down the road, dodging trucks and motorbikes. Chickens ran wild in every front yard taunting the family cow that was tethered to a tree. Barefoot children chased each other through the mud and the heaping mounds of garbage that were piled in front of every home. And they were all smiling.

I learned straight away how to say, "May I take your photo?" Excited children would gather in a tight crowd while I showed them the immediate results on my digital camera. They had no such technology, but Instant Messaging has never worked as swiftly as the news on Songkhla Road. Thais of all shapes, sizes, and ages raced to their front yards to wave at this peculiar-looking foreigner with the pale skin and blue eyes. "Hello," the little ones yelled from behind a tree, shyly trying to practice their English. "Hello!" I waved back, sending them running in fits of giggles.

The only white people these rural Thais had ever seen were either on CD covers or, possibly, TV, although I never saw a satellite dish sticking out of one of the shacks.

There are poorer places in the world than Southern Thailand; there was no famine there. But there was little else. And an odd thing was happening; those poor but smiley people ran after us to give donations for starting a breast cancer department in Lampang Regional Hospital in northern Thailand.

Not many statistics on breast cancer are available in Thailand. There wasn't a cancer registry, which, in turn, meant no sufficient statistics, and no statistics imply that breast cancer is not a problem. If it's not a problem, no education exists to fight it. Consequently, women don't go to the doctor until the very last stages, at which point they are told to go home and prepare to die. They go home and die, no records are kept, and the cycle continues. Some cases are caught early, but no one knows what percentage.

My plan was to introduce breast cancer as an issue through the press, hoping they would list the earliest symptoms. It was also imperative to explain that the earlier a woman gets to the doctor with those symptoms, the better her chances of survival because, contrary to popular belief, breast cancer is not a death sentence. This was the very beginning of an awareness campaign in Thailand.

We hadn't made plans to actively pursue fundraising while in the poorest part of country, but the Thais on Songkhla Road ran after Prayoon and me, donating ten, twenty, fifty baht at a time. (Fifty Thai baht was roughly US $1.25, a lot of money for those people.) They didn't know about breast cancer, they didn't know the strange looking foreigner walking through their neighborhood, but they knew they were getting involved. If they didn't have a baht, they gave something.

One morning a woman came running out of her house, yelling at me in Thai to stop because she had something for me. She ran to the road and proudly handed me a fifteen-pound green coconut.

She kept bowing and saying things in Thai I couldn't understand, but she wanted to give me something, and a coconut was all she had.

"Thank you, thank you," was all I could say in Thai.

Every day, all day long, people ran after me to give me things. Store clerks dashed out to give me water: six packs, twelve-packs, water in a bag, water in a glass, which I gulped and handed back. Families stood at the side of the road and waited to give me some of their fried coconut sticks or a bunch of bananas or a bag of oranges from their tree.

Prayoon laughed as I kept piling things into the van: bags of noodles, apples, a purplish oval fruity thing, deep-fried somethings from a family's hawker stand, and numerous fifteen-pound green coconuts that rolled around the van.

I accumulated a handful of tee shirts, two pair of Thai pants, three hats, and a stuffed elephant named Su.

People stared at me so hard it looked painful, their eyes big and round with curiosity. They nudged their buddies and pointed, then together dashed up to the side of the road for a better look. I feared it was only a matter of time before we caused a major accident.

A young boy passed me on his bike and glanced over his shoulder to catch a peek. I smiled and waved, which put a smile on him so big it touched both ears. He kept peddling forward while looking behind and failed to notice the ice cream truck that pulled into his path.

Smack!

Soon afterward, a motorcycle driver who couldn't stop staring, drove into a gully. Another time, a passenger watching me wasn't prepared for take-off and tumbled off the back of a tuk-tuk.

We had banners draped on each side of the van explaining briefly about breast cancer—which was the point—but I needed to find a better balance between the awareness effort and the fact that I had become a road hazard.

Walking the streets of Bangkok is taking one's life in one's hands. Traffic in the city is legendary, where the rule is there are no rules.

There are four lanes but eight rows of traffic; green means go, yellow means go fast, red means go faster.

Prayoon and I both let out a sigh of relief when we saw a small bevy of police waiting for us. Prayoon went to chat with them while I got myself together—sunscreen, Walkman, vitamins, and bandana around a sunburned hand.

Prayoon came back, beaming with excitement, "Policeman, two stars!" he said pointing to the two stars on the policeman's shoulder.

"Two stars good?" I asked.

"Ohh, two stars verrry good!"

I didn't know what two stars on the shoulder meant, but Prayoon's excitement was the cue for me to be sufficiently impressed. I bowed to them—twice. I thanked all the policemen, put "Boston's Greatest Hits" in my ears, and because there was a policeman with two stars on his shoulder, I decided to run. Only a Yankee-too-good would hold up Two Stars with a mundane walk.

Two policemen rode motorbikes on my right, Prayoon was behind me, and Two-Stars-on–his-Shoulder lead the way, blocking out an entire lane of precious real estate on the main highway leading into Bangkok. Busloads of people drove by, waving out the windows, cars stuck in the morning commute gave me a continuous flow of thumbs up, which apparently is the international language for "You go, girl!" I desperately wanted to stop and grab some breakfast, but when Two-Stars-on-his-Shoulder leads you through the chaos of Bangkok, you don't stop for an egg at a hawker stand.

Prayoon knew I was on an empty belly so he handed me nuts, bananas, anything he could find at arm's length in the van, but I didn't dare stop.

The sun was rising over the thick smoggy city skyline, and with the beat of Boston's "More Than a Feeling" in my ears, I was having a glorious moment on the crowded Bangkok highway.

Twenty-five kilometers later the whole entourage crossed the Chao Phraya River into the chaotic belly of Bangkok. Colorful temples stood proudly on hilltops, consuming entire city blocks; larger than life photos of the King dominated every corner. Statues of Buddhas posed at every turn; Buddhas hovered over the city. And no string of adjectives could possibly describe the renowned traffic.

The Lions Clubs of Bangkok caught up with us and, without stopping, led me to the fancy Tai-Pan Hotel in the heart of the city—my host hotel for a ten-day break. Ten days for Prayoon to go home and visit his family and ten days for me to run errands, preparing for India and visiting cancer centers.

When the bellman wheeled Bob to my room and opened the door, I felt like a queen. I had a king-size bed, air-conditioning, and an eleventh-floor view of the city. The TV had BBC World news and HBO for my movie entertainment. I had free Internet service, breakfast every day, the *Bangkok Post* delivered to the door. There was a hot shower, a bath if that was my pleasure, a mini-bar full of chocolate, and Christmas music pumping through the TV, which I thought strange for a country that's ninety-five percent Buddhist. I didn't know what to do first, so I tried it all.

My first morning in Bangkok I left the Tai Pan Hotel with a map and a to-do list:
- Visa extension for Thailand,
- Visa for India,
- Antibiotics for India,
- Long-sleeved tee shirts for India,
- Stock up on peanut butter for India.

But the first stop was a much-needed haircut. The hotel receptionist advised that I take a taxi to the salon even though it was just across the street. In my snotty little head, I thought, *Listen, honey, I walk for a living and won't have any trouble crossing a street in Bangkok, thank you very much.* Instead, I thanked her for the advice and sauntered out the front door to Sukhimvit Avenue.

After forty-five minutes I hailed a taxi. "I'd like to go across the street, please."

To the haircutter on duty, I requested, "an inch off all the way around, please."

She was nine months pregnant, if not more, and every few minutes she would stop cutting and let out a small moan.

"Inch?" she confirmed with her fingers displaying an inch.

"Yes, inch."

I only hoped that she could finish the job before she delivered.

I picked up *Glamour* magazine looking for wisdom in the article "What your man REALLY wants for Christmas."

After a full hour she stood proudly behind me, holding the mirror so I could see her work. She then handed me the mirror and went to lie down.

Where's my hair!

I desperately grabbed the back of my head, frantically looking for my hair, any hair. I had become so beguiled by my *Glamour* magazine article I hadn't realized she thought an inch meant that my hair should be only one inch long!

But it was gone; it was all gone, lying on the floor in a scattered hairy heap. I looked in the mirror hanging onto what hair was left and went through the stages of grief in twenty seconds: shock, denial, anger, acceptance.

"Okay then," I reasoned with a shallow breath, "let's cut the front to match."

"All done," was all she could say, lying on her bench rubbing her belly.

Oh Lord, help me. She had barely touched the front of my hair, while the back of my head could've passed for a number four job in any man's army.

"I don't understand," I said. "Now you cut front of hair?"

But she insisted, "All done." Then she let out a moan that sounded as though the crown was showing.

There's no reasoning with a woman dilated to six centimeters, so I quickly paid my bill and walked down Sukhumvit Avenue looking like a poodle. This was a hair emergency. I needed to find a haircutter who knew English.

I walked into a Paul Mitchell Salon, and they spoke English. Oh, good Lord, I'd been saved! I explained in maybe a bit of a frenzied pace that only half of my hair was cut, and even though I only wanted an inch cut off she only cut half of my head and now it's too late, the whole head has to be cut short, and this is what happens when you read *Glamour* magazine articles. Could they help me look respectable before I tour the cancer centers of Bangkok tomorrow?

They put me in a swivel chair and all the haircutters at Paul Mitchell Salon gathered around my head talking in Thai, but I knew what they were saying: "Poor girl looks like a poodle."

"Miranda must help you. Miranda the best. Miranda study haircutting in Philadelphia two years."

Well, God bless Miranda. Send her over.

Miranda stepped up to the plate like Edward Scissorhands. "Oh, you get very bad haircut, I so sorry. I make you beautiful. Just wait. You read this while I cut hair." She handed me a *Glamour* magazine.

Miranda took great pride in her work. "I cut your hair to flow with natural wave."

After an hour and a half she was nowhere near the finish line, and when I asked why it was taking so long she said, "Each hair has own wave so I must cut a few hairs at a time."

So I continued reading *Glamour* and picked up where I left off in, "You Too Can Have a Happy Marriage with One Bathroom."

By the time Miranda matched up lengths and waves and flows, my hair was oh-so-short that I looked like a little boy, not the thirty-nine-year old woman now well versed in what men REALLY want for Christmas. I put a hat on and made my way across the city to errand number two, the Thai Immigration Office. I made my way across town in order to stand in line to apply for a twenty-one-day visa extension to stay in Thailand.

After two hours waiting in line, I stepped up to the window and handed the clerk my application. "Sir, we need three passport photos."

Sir? Excuse me? Did she just call me Sir? And she wants passport photos that would roam eternally through the halls of this Thailand immigration office with an official record of this haircut?

After two years on the road with no hairstyle other than hat head you'd think I'd be anesthetized to hair vanity, but I drew the line at official government documents.

I decided to stop the day in its tracks and go back to the Tai-Pan Hotel to hide from the world. I'd run a hot bath, eat chocolate bars out of the honor bar, and maybe I could find a copy of *Glamour* with an article on "How to Pamper Yourself after a Bad Haircut."

A big fat myth has woven its way through the world that Asians don't get breast cancer. It must be their diet, people say, so western-ers race to supermarket shelves snapping up soymilk and pig-snout soup, hoping they hold the answers to good health. The fact of the matter is that no one really knows how many people are getting—and dying—of breast cancer or other diseases in Asia due to lack of effi-cient record keeping and an alarmingly low diagnosis rate.

In the U.S., New Zealand, Australia, even Singapore, it's easy to preach about annual mammograms, because facilities are so wide-spread. But in Asia that's not so. The only Mammography machines in Thailand are in Bangkok, and mammograms are expensive. I had to alter my message in every country, and in Thailand it was down-right silly to advocate an annual pilgrimage to Bangkok to prevent a disease they'd never heard about. During my walk through Thailand, all donations benefited the Lampang Regional Cancer Center, which would use the proceeds to create a breast cancer department. I passed out brochures written in Thai that explained early symptoms of breast cancer and how to do breast self-exams. That may seem like a tiny step, but to the women who received those brochures, it might have been a life saving step.

In Thailand, the word cancer still connotes a death sentence, a tough barrier to break through. An American woman based in Bangkok was in the process of creating The Bangkok Breast Cancer Foundation. She had contacted me about organizing a tour of Bangkok's hospitals.

The first one, Bumrungrad Hospital, had a cancer center called *Horizon*, where I met General Manager Mr. Schroeder. "Notice there's no hint of the word 'cancer' anywhere in the title?" he asked. "That's because the people who come here don't know they have cancer. Their families know, but they tell them that they have to come here for a blood condition. That's the only way we can get them in here for chemo treatment. If we told them they had cancer, we would never see them again."

We then went on to visit the government hospital, where I met Dr. Kris, the grand poo-bah of breast cancer in Thailand. He's a rare type, a gentle man with a type-A personality, and yet took time to sit down with me for ten valuable minutes. He realized the resultant problems of not having efficient national records and implemented such a system at the hospitals where he works, although he admitted that's not enough. His next move was to implement the same systems in all the hospitals throughout Thailand and eventually throughout Asia.

The Bangkok Nursing Home Hospital, Samitivej Hospital, and the Bangkok Hospital all gave me a warm reception and an even better education. All gave donations to my effort, realizing the need to get past a tough barrier. Everyone at those facilities understood there's much more behind the big fat myth that women don't get breast cancer in Asia.

My ten days resting in Bangkok were spent visiting with Lions and sightseeing at a leisurely pace. Sightseeing in Bangkok or anywhere in Thailand generally means seeing your share of temples, and temples scare me. Holy sanctuaries of any sort seem to put the fear of God in me, which, I gather, is exactly the point. But Buddhist temples have the additional intimidation of rows and tiers of Buddhas keeping heedful eyes on your every move.

The brochures say "Take off your shoes, wear long-sleeved shirts, dab water on your head and assure at all times that you don't point your feet at anyone." I wondered if your feet aren't always inadvertently pointing at someone but was afraid to ask in front of the rows and tiers of heedful Buddhas.

I was instructed not to pose for photos in front of a Buddha image and certainly not to clamber up on them, and women are not to touch the monks or even hand anything to them. But women are allowed to talk to the monks, so the Dutch woman next to me said to the men in orange, "Hello" and "Sawadee ka," but the monks didn't so much as crack a smile. She whispered to me that she understood why they didn't smile: here was a group of men who couldn't touch women and had to wear orange every day. She said it must be hard being a monk when every time you accidentally bump into a woman crossing a street or standing in a crowded elevator you have to run back to the temple to do a dozen Hail Marys or whatever it is in Buddhism. The whole conversation scared me there in front of all the Buddhas, so I ignored her and kept an eye on my feet to be certain they weren't pointing at anyone.

In Buddhism there's no special day of Sabbath nor is there any sort of liturgy or mass in which a priest presides. Most Buddhists visit their wat (temple) every seventh or eighth day depending on phases of the moon. They can visit wats whenever they feel like it and stay as long or short as their mood and schedule suits. I liked that about Buddhism.

There are over 32,000 temples in Thailand, which in a country that size means you can see a temple from virtually any spot. When in doubt just look up toward the highest mountain, because the Buddhists like to build their temples at the peak of the tallest hills. If there's no mountain the Buddhists will pile together a mountain, climb to the top and start building a temple.

And just like the Australians, who every day for nine months asked if I'd like to go see the kangaroos, my hosts every day in Thailand asked if I'd like to go see the town temple. Of course, I was afraid to say no to visiting a temple—that would bring bad karma. If I were to say, no thank you, I'm up to my eyeballs in temple-seeing, then surely I would drop dead right then and there and return as a stray dog doomed to drift through monasteries begging for food from men dressed in orange.

No, for my remaining few weeks in Thailand I would carry on with a daily dose of God-fearing temple-seeing. I would shyly smile at the rows and tiers of mindful Buddhas and wonder, as I got closer to India, where the Hindus stood on foot-pointing.

Prayoon returned from his ten days at home at 4:00 a.m. and called me to come right down so we could beat traffic out of Bangkok. I wanted to say, "Are you crazy? It's four a.m.!" To my regret, that wasn't in any of my ten translation books.

"Ready five minutes," he requested, leaving me stumbling out of bed longing for the days when we couldn't communicate at all.

A dozen of Bangkok's highest political dignitaries welcomed us into City Hall, along with the Lions District Governors, where we were given a send-off fit for a queen. The vice governor presented me with a "Welcome to Bangkok" medal in a locally made box of tiki wood. Then every person—upwards of thirty—put a flower lei around my neck. When the time came to depart, the vice governor snapped his fingers, and a posse of police appeared to escort us out of the city just as we had arrived, in our very own highway lane.

Prayoon and I continued northbound, and after ten days apart it was nice to have him back, taking care of everything, communicating with the Lions every night, and ordering for me in restaurants. One morning I did try to order by myself and thought I had requested two hard-boiled eggs. However, the waitress brought me pork ear soup. Must've been the inflection. Knowing I was a little shy digging into animal body parts, Prayoon grabbed the soup from under my spellbound eyes and said something to the waitress that resembled, "Get her some vegetables with rice please."

Menus in Asia look like something from an animal autopsy— sautéed pig ears, pig feet marinated in oyster sauce, fish eye soup or deep-fried chicken intestine—although the Thai word for chicken intestine is the same as "homosexual" with a different inflection, so you need to be very careful when you order.

The first time I saw chicken feet soup I was mesmerized by the foot bobbing there in the broth with scaly skin and toe nails. I wondered about the first person who thought that if they were to chop off the chicken's leg at the knee and toss it in a pot that might be a tasty appetizer.

Even the simple chicken is difficult as it comes complete with all the innards. And they're not easy to remove, as there are no knives. Thai's eat with a fork and spoon combo, no knife. And why would they need one? They just pop that chicken into their mouth, tendons, liver and all while I sit at the head of the table as their guest tearing away all the organs with my fork and spoon.

One night the snow peas in my vegetable stir-fry must've been eight inches long, so I asked for a knife.

Everyone talked animatedly amongst themselves so I could only imagine the conversation.

"A knife, she wants a knife."

"What does she want a knife for?"

"I can't imagine, just get the girl a knife."

The cook out back shrugged his shoulders, "A knife? What does she want with a knife? Honey, do we have a knife anywhere. The American wants a knife."

While waiting, I tried cutting my monster snow peas with the spoon/fork combo but that stringy bit that holds the snow pea together was a tough little bugger.

I tried the Thai method of just maneuvering the whole thing in my mouth but it was all such a mess with the oyster sauce hitting me in the nose and the chin, I thought it best for everyone if I simply waited for the knife.

"Don't worry," the Lion next to me assured while handing me a napkin, "They're back there trying to find you a knife."

The cook finally came out with the only knife-related tool in the kitchen—a machete. One of those big square machetes they use to hack up the chickens. There's hardly anything as frightening as a man with a blood stained apron standing over you with a machete asking, "What want cut?"

"Uhhhh...," I said softly looking at the scene above my head, "It's my peas. My peas are a bit big."

He glared at me with a short silence, "Peas big?"

"Yes."

He grabbed my plate, marched back to the kitchen, chop-chop-choppped my peas as if they were trying to escape, and brought them back to me in four-inch pieces.

"Peas okay?"

All eyes were on me and the four-inch peas. They were still too big, and I really would've loved to have them cut into two-inch bits, but I wasn't prepared to die that night.

"Yes, peas okay."

I thought about going out to the van to get my emergency food supply of crackers and peanut butter, but then again, I'd need a knife.

It was January 2002, and the world was on edge. Richard Reid—dubbed the Shoe Bomber—had been thwarted when he attempted to blow up an American Airlines flight to Miami by detonating explosives hidden in his shoes. *Wall Street Journal* reporter Daniel Pearl had just been kidnapped in Pakistan, and John Walker Lind, an American born in DC, was arrested in Afghanistan as an enemy combatant. People were jumpy, and no more so than in Southeast Asia. Thailand regularly hit the news for its alleged loosely organized network of al-Qaida cells and CIA undercover operatives reportedly inundated the region. Every night at the hotels, I'd spot an American and wonder if he was an undercover CIA agent, and if not, did he think I was?

"Good disguise," I imagined him saying to himself. "Why else would she have such an awful hairdo?"

Aside from the headlines, my walk through Thailand was nearly perfect. North of Bangkok, Muslim villages were few and far between. The police no longer arrived out of the blue to escort us.

The disastrous haircut from Bangkok was growing out, which only made it worse. I didn't give two hoots while I walked, of course, but when I spoke and met honored national dignitaries, I didn't want to appear disrespectful with my unkempt hairdo. When we reached the town of Lampang, The Lampang Regional Cancer

Center hosted an official greeting for me at the Municipality. With an hour to kill, I thought I'd race into town and find something that might help camouflage the hideous hairdo—a chic hat, a trendy scarf, a bag.

Coming out of yet another pharmacy with nothing to hide it, I got stuck in the doorway waiting for a passing marching band. They weren't playing, just marching silently down the street with their big drums and sparkly hats, followed by a long line of high school students dressed in purple uniforms.

Nothing in all of Lampang was going to hide the bristle on top of my head, so I could only hope the morning would include few photos. I wrapped my old yellow bandana around my head as chicly as possible and made my way to the Municipality.

No one was there.

Alone in the empty parking lot, Prayoon and I sat on the bumper of the van.

Then Miss Duriya came around the corner. Miss Duriya had been my contact with the Lampang Regional Cancer Center for the past four months. She had been out on the road to meet with us a handful of times and taken us to nice dinners as we got closer to town. To look at all seventy pounds of her with her innocent eyes, you'd never guess she has an armful of fancy degrees with six words each and initials behind them. "We're ready for you. Follow me."

We walked past the marching band and the throngs of high school students dressed in purple when Miss Duriya said, "We're having a parade for you."

"A parade! For me?"

"Yes," she said, leading me past the crowd. She led me up the front steps to the waiting dignitaries—Dr. Suratat, Director of the Lampang Regional Cancer Center; the mayor of Lampang; Ott from All Thailand Experiences; all the Lions from the Lampang club; and Margaret! Margaret is the publisher of *Welcome to Chiang Mai Magazine* and had been helping with press communications in Thailand. She originally hails from Ohio and has a face as white as my own.

Everyone was dressed and pressed so nicely, and there I was, the guest of honor, dressed in baggy traveling clothes complete with holes (albeit clean). I was embarrassed and made a mental note to get one relatively nice outfit when I reached Chiang Mai.

The reception was beautiful. The mayor made a delightful presentation and offered me a key to the city with a personal note expressing a special friendship between our countries.

As the parade began, locals lined the streets. I was directed to the front to lead the way up the main street. School kids and Lions Club members held up banners about breast cancer in both English and Thai. Brochures on the how-tos of breast self-examination were passed out to every woman on the sidewalks—men, too. People flooded out of the shops, offices, and pharmacies to donate every spare baht. I felt like a politician on the campaign trail: waving, shaking hands, posing with babies. I was uncomfortable with all the attention, but I remembered what Dad said, "Let them help you." I was playing a role, and out of respect for that role I didn't want to undermine the importance of it. The GlobalWalk was about something much bigger; I was just the messenger. So I smiled and waved, shook hands, posed with babies.

There was no doubt we made a splash about breast cancer awareness through the streets of Lampang that day. We plugged up the main roadway for nearly two hours, walking the slowest three kilometers in GlobalWalk's 7,000-mile history. And much to my chagrin, we set an unbreakable record for photos taken in one day.

When I contacted the American Embassy in Rangoon about continuing my walk through Burma, they were brief. "Don't even think about it." They explained that with the ongoing civil war and the militia controlled government prohibiting travel to a large portion of the country, it would be impossible. "But good luck, have a nice trip. Thank you very much."

The original plan back in Vail, when I had maps spread across my floor, was to continue north from Thailand through China then west into Kazakhstan and Russia. China was issuing visas, but only for ninety days. It would take me—with no interruptions—at least twelve months to cross China. The Chinese embassy told me that I could apply for extensions every ninety days, but that I would have to leave the country in order to apply, and even at that point, there would be no promises.

Doing the math I added up the fact that I would have to fly in and out of the country three times, apply for a $300 visa four times, to say nothing of the waiting periods between trips, which could go on virtually for months. Moreover, there were still a number of regions that a visitor cannot enter in China, which would have led me thousands of miles out of my way via detours, and I would need crew support, and—well, I was on to Plan B.

Now Burma was no longer an option.

While I was fully aware that the four men who had walked around the world also had to fly over this region, I had always held a sort of Pollyanna attitude of certainty that by the time I got there everything would be hunky dory. The Burmese Junta would welcome me with open arms, maybe even offer complete crew support right across the country and cook for me every night right after the welcome parades. But "don't even think about it" slapped the Pollyanna right out of me.

I moved on to Plan C. India.

Chiang Mai, Thailand, marked the end of the Southeast Asia leg, and for the first time since I started in Vail, I had to skip a portion of the world. I had to fly over Burma and carry on from Kolkata.

Although Chiang Mai doesn't sit right on the border there were many people who thought it the best place to finish. Chiang Mai is home to Margaret and Goson, publishers of *Welcome to Chiang Mai Magazine*, who had become wonderful friends. It was also Prayoon's home.

Randy and Mike from All Thailand Experiences—also from Chiang Mai—suggested the perfect finish line. "But it'll be tough," they warned, "seventeen kilometers up a mountain. And just when you think you're done, there's a set of three hundred steps to climb to the very tiptop. It's as close to heaven as you'll ever be. It's the Jewel of the North, the Doi Suthep Temple."

A cool breeze created a perfect last day. Tour buses full of *farang* (foreigners) passed by, watching through their windows and no doubt wondering why anyone would climb up this big hill when they could take a perfectly lovely air-conditioned bus. Bruce Springsteen sang in my ears, Prayoon followed right behind me in the van, and I felt strong charging up that mountain, pleased that the Colorado mountain goat was still in me.

As we neared the top, my people began to gather. The Lions found us; Miss Duriya and the women from the Lampang Regional Cancer Center came. Television cameras arrived, filmed and went. Many cars beeped and waved, suggesting they'd see us at the top, and that was my cue that it was time to bring this memorable portion of my journey to an end.

Ten of us plodded up the infamous last three hundred steps to the top of Doi Suthep Temple. We climbed ten steps at a time, rested for a whole minute, walked ten more steps, and rested again. Right before the top, we waited for the last stragglers to join us so that we could take the final ten steps to the finish together. I was joined by representatives from all those who made this leg so successful. Miss Duriya climbed in her platform shoes; Ott, manager from All Thailand Experiences, was on my right; the Chiang Mai contingency represented the Lions who helped me all along the way. Margaret took the train up. And Prayoon, who had been my driver, interpreter, chef, manager, and protector since the day I crossed the Malaysian border, was right there by my side.

Together we reached the top and were greeted by American Consul General Eric Rubin and his wife Nicole, whose mother had recently passed away from breast cancer.

During my three and a half months in Thailand, we raised a total of US $2,500 for the Lampang Regional Hospital. That would start a breast cancer department and keep it going for a couple of years. It is particularly touching to note that these funds were raised at the equivalent of twenty-five cents at a time. A few Lions Clubs gave larger donations of US $50, but the majority, by far, came from locals running after us, plunking ten baht in our cup. A cup, I might add, that we had to find in back of the van because we had no idea we would be doing any fundraising at all along the road. The Lions Clubs from my route in Thailand also vowed to carry on the breast cancer advocacy work through fundraising and continuing support for distribution of informational brochures.

The Amari Rincome hotel, one of the fanciest five-star accommodations in Chiang Mai, spoiled me silly, allowing me ample opportunity to relax and prepare my body and mind for India. For five days, I shared lunches and dinners with my new friends at the American Embassy, Lions, and the All Thailand Experience crew. I ran errands, sent emails to India, and studied my Indian guidebooks. I also tried to wean myself from seeing Prayoon every day.

When we walked into Chiang Mai, Prayoon's work with me was finished, and he started new jobs right away—jobs that were, for the most part, one day long, returning him home every night. I'm sure he was thrilled. I know when All Thailand Experiences was looking for a driver to help me, Prayoon accepted the job, even though that meant he had to leave his wife and two teen-age children behind in Chiang Mai for four months. I'm certain at the time he was unaware that it was going to be one of the great challenges of his life: helping some silly American girl walk the length of Thailand to take care of her every need because she knew nothing.

Now it was time to say goodbye.

We met at the Malaysian border where I knew one word in Thai, "hello." He knew the same amount in English. But we started laughing. We laughed when I tried to pronounce Thai words that started with "khh" and ended with six vowels. We laughed when he ended up in the hospital due to tendonitis in his accelerator leg from going only six kilometers per hour all day, and I'm the one that had just passed walking the 10,000 kilometer mark. We laughed when the monkey jumped through the van window and Prayoon tried to defend himself with a roll of toilet paper. We laughed when

I thought I had just gotten a great deal buying a t-shirt from a hawker stand, but he explained that I had just bought a woman's old shirt right off her clothesline.

Miles of laughter saw us from Pedang Besar to Chiang Mai and saying good-bye with a bouquet of flowers or a trinket from the local night bazaar wouldn't cut it, I wanted him to hear me say good-bye in my voice, in his language.

I wrote a letter, found a translator and at the airport, where Prayoon was seeing me off to India, I handed him this letter:

Hello, my friend,

There are not many people in the world that could do what we just did—that is to say, there are not many people that could spontaneously spend four months on a road trip with someone who is their complete opposite. But not only did we do it, we did it in grand style, proving to the world that friendship can transcend the deepest cultural differences, even language.

From now on when people ask that inevitable question, "What is the highlight of your walk?" I'll have an answer. I'll say the friendship of a Thai man who speaks little English, eats fried bugs, beeps at Buddhas, and thinks nothing of eating chilies whole like I'd eat a bag of popcorn.

I'll tell these people how you took care of me every step of the way and I trusted your every instruction—what to eat, when to stop, who to talk to, and who to not. You spoke for me in interviews and answered daily questions, rescued me from crowds of people and pointed me in right directions. You were always on the phone organizing Lions, dinner, or the next event. Taking photos, beating off dogs, helping me find peanut butter, and every night, the Internet. All I had to do was walk.

You've learned my morning routine well enough to order for me: "She'll have two hard boiled eggs—that's HARD boiled, not soft boiled, she likes them boiled for ten minutes. Could you please bring a little salt instead of soy sauce? And a spoon, but not those Chinese spoons, a regular spoon, she can't eat out of those Chinese spoons."

Then you go out to the van to get my peanut butter because you know exactly where I keep it next to my crackers and tuna and other emergency foods.

I could order for you, too. "He'll have two fried eggs with sausages, a bottle of ketchup, cup of coffee, an orange drink, and water. And three pieces of toast on the side smothered with pineapple jam, please."

Of course for lunch and dinner, you'll eat anything from deep-fried chicken feet to pig's blood soup, which is all way out of my league. I'm from Colorado; we think ketchup with eggs is a little dodgy.

It's a strange world where you know someone's routine so well, and you laugh and dance and share a drink, but you can't talk to him. But from now on, when people ask me about the biggest lessons of my walk, I'll say learning that laughter is the universal language. I'll tell them that Thailand has been the jewel of my walk around the world. I'll tell them how I met Prayoon in Padang Besa and could hardly say hello—and four months later in Chiang Mai how difficult it was to say good-bye.

Thank you, my friend.
xxx Polly

In Colorado, Randi, Debi and I at the top of Cinnamon Pass
seconds before the storm unleashed

The Busting with Life dragon boat team of New Zealand, helps me
bypass the no pedestrian bridge into Auckland

Vicki and me celebrating at the southern tip of New Zealand

The women of the Breast Cancer Network Australia send me off
into the Land of the Deadly Bugs!

The Australian Hogs look after me through the infamous
Marlborough Stretch

I needed a sign to tell me this? (Marlborough Stretch, Australia)

The Mackay North Lions Club the night I was inducted as a Lions member. (Alan is to my left)

The Lions of Malaysia welcome Bob and me like rock stars

The Lions of Malaysia always pointed me in the right direction

Always a BIG welcome in Malaysia

The youngest Lions (Leos) help us promote the importance of
early detection in Malaysia

Dancing with the villagers in Thailand –
after handing out Oreo cookies

Prayoon with the All Thailand
Experiences van

There were some proud Osama
fans in the Muslim villages
of Thailand right after 9/11

The city of Lampang, Thailand, threw me a surprise parade

Governor Shri Viren Shah of West Bengal,
walks me out of Kolkata

The Lions of Tamluk, India, went all out
with the breast cancer campaign

Enjoying lunch in a typical Indian cafe

The Lions Club of Istanbul sent me off with
grand fanfare after a month of rest

The villagers of Turkey always greeted me with enthusiasm

The Lions of Great Britain greeted me into town with
fundraising events every night

Lady Liberty greets me back
onto US shores in NYC

Debi Linker helps me with interviews
across Wisconsin.
(See our home in the background.)

The school kids of Watsontown, Pennsylvania, cheered me on

Breast cancer survivors, and longtime friend, Stephanie,
(first row; left) greet me into Minnesota

Four generations of my family meet me for a few steps in
Detroit Lakes, Minnesota.(That's Grandma next to me.)

Friends, old and new, join me for the last mile on July 30, 2004

The end of mile 14,124

CHAPTER 12

Honk if You're in Kolkata

M y bedroom door squeaked open slowly and an old woman dressed in a traditional Indian sari walked in. She looked at me—not so much into my eyes, but rather as if I were a science project she discovered growing in her fridge. She examined me up and down while making her way around the bed toward me.

At 6:30 a.m., propped up on a pillow and still halfway under the covers, I was typing on my little handheld computer, writing about my arrival into Kolkata the night before. The plane had barely touched down when everyone ripped the seat belts from their laps and leapt out of their seats vying to be the first off the plane. There was a Dutch couple sitting in front of me with a look on their faces that mirrored my own—that uh-oh-what-have-I-gotten-myself-into-now look. When the crowd dispersed the three of us emerged, and although we hadn't spoken a word to each other during the flight, they knew exactly what I meant when I said, "Are you ready?"

"Not sure," they laughed.

I said hello as the old woman slowly made her way around my bed, but she didn't reply, didn't blink, didn't look me in the eye. She sat down next to me on the bed, examined the top of my head, noted my fingers on the keyboard, touched my ears, then my earrings, fondling them a bit. She fiddled with my tee shirt and pointed to a stain. She touched my arm, rubbed it a little to feel the skin color, took a handful of hair and felt it between her fingers. I don't know what you're supposed to do when an elderly Indian woman examines you without saying a word, so I kept typing. She straightened out a wrinkle in my shirt then looked me solidly in the eye. "Husband."

All right, here we go. I had been forewarned about this. My guidebook and everyone who'd ever traveled in India had tipped me off about the persistent flow of questions regarding marital status. If you don't have a husband, you're supposed to answer with a polite, "Not yet." If you're asked if you have children, you should never say, "Oh God, no."

From their perspective I was an enigma; Indian people live with the whole family. Seventy-five percent of marriages in India are still arranged, and they marry young—between sixteen and twenty-one. When a couple marries the new wife moves in with the husband's family and now you have the grandparents, parents, kids, and the brother's family, too, all living on top of each other in a three-bedroom bungalow. A thirty-nine-year-old woman with no husband or children—and her own condo—exceeds all enigmas.

Although the old woman wasn't really asking a question, I did respond with a simple "Not yet." She got up and left.

This was Kolkata, the poster child of third world cities. If you travel to Kolkata you are known in backpacking circles as a champion traveler at the top of your game. But I was by no means in that league. I was being escorted and looked after, pampered to the point of embarrassment. Ravi and Ranita Pargawal from the Kolkata Lions Club watched over me in a way that would make my mother sigh with relief.

However, just experiencing the drive from the airport to Ravi and Ranita's house proved that nothing could prepare me for traveling across India by foot, alone, as a woman. Even an all-too-politically-correct blog I read ("Don't be offended when you see peepholes in your hotel room; they're just interested to see what you look like naked.") said India would "test the patience of a saint and even the most experienced travelers find their tempers frayed." Western travelers will tell stories of how they waited three days for the 11:30 train to New Delhi or how they bought a Coca Cola only to find it half filled with tap water, consequently landing them in the emergency room. But there is no greater test of your human spirit than experiencing as little as a single day of it yourself.

And people love it.

Travelers who had traveled the sub-continent said to me, "I just love India!" When I asked why, they said they couldn't explain it, "It's just so…so…different." When I pushed for more, they said, "It's the colors," "The sea of humanity," "The unusual smells."

"Countries have distinct smells?" I asked, urging them to elaborate.

"Oh yes, the air is wafting with spices you've never smelt before." Then they'd hesitate for a second and add, "Oh sure, you get the odd whiff of garbage and, well, human waste, but hey, that's why I love India! It's…different!"

I could never decide if someone who tossed around the word "love" to describe a country that smelled of garbage and human waste was someone I should keep at arm's length or admire deeply. But I knew I wanted to love India. I wanted to be one of those people that bubbles to life and says, I just love India! It's cool to love India, and of course I'm always striving for the cutting edge of cool. So it was with those words ringing in my ears that I arrived ready to fall in love with India.

Ravi and Ranita are upper class. When they drove me from the airport their driver dropped us at the front door of their building, where the doorman swung open the heavy metal door to greet us. The elevator man dressed in gray polyester poked button twenty-three, and when the elevator arrived, he slid open the two-part elevator door and guided us off the platform with a helping hand. The door to their apartment wasn't locked, but when I went to push it open they bellowed, "No, no, no! That's for the houseboy. We must wait." So we stood outside the unlocked door, waiting for the houseboy to race across the garden patio, the kitchen, and the living room, too, so none of us had to exert all that energy pushing the door open.

It didn't take long to notice the different roles in this new culture; it's not just between men and women, and there aren't really many different races in India, so what decides who plays which role?

Social classes. The caste system has been outlawed in India, though its remnants remain in the class system. But it's not my culture, I reminded myself. That's how they do things in India, and it seems to be acceptable to all parties. So I patiently waited outside the unlocked door for the houseboy.

Inside the apartment Ranita snapped her fingers and the cook started to whip up some lentils and curry. I bubbled with anticipation as Indian food sits atop my favorite food categories. Walking across India promised the potential of one big food fiesta. From the very first bite of a curry one late drunken night in London years ago, I was hooked. I loved it and wanted more. But I knew I had to keep the curry eating under control while in India and remain vigilant about eating well and staying healthy. "You can't eat the raw vegetables," people warned me. "Sometimes they'll cut up cucumbers and put them on the side of your dhal, but you have to forego the cucumbers because they've cut them with a knife that's been washed in that water that will kill you. Stay away from meat, too," they'd say. "Most of the country has no refrigeration, so only the Lord himself knows how long that chicken has been hanging on that meat hook. You can eat anything with a peel. Oranges, bananas and hard-boiled eggs are the perfect foods; they have a natural shell that serves as a protector between the vitamins B and C and protein that will keep you strong, and the water that will kill you in a drop."

Fellow travelers repeatedly warned me that every single ounce of water I drink had to be out of a bottle. "Don't even think of drinking that water if you yourself haven't broken the seal. If you don't hear that little 'pop' when you unscrew the lid, don't drink it. Say someone hands you a bottle of water with the lid already taken off, you've got to hand it back and say thank you very much, but don't drink it. If someone offers you a tea, you can't trust that the water was boiled long enough. An unboiled tea could throw you into the fetal position for days, hoping, wishing, praying for death. Don't drink it. You can eat the breads all day long, foods with a natural shell, and anything that's been heated up, but stay away from meat, raw vegetables and water bottles that don't pop."

I had to start on the Indian food slowly or my whole system might implode with all those glorious spices. So after a first night of lentils I had to bring out my personal stash for breakfast: crackers with some peanut butter from the sixty-four ounce jar of Jif that Dad had mailed ahead. One-by-one the people in the house came around the table to sniff at my peanut butter. They would lift up the big jar, peer inside with a curious squint, wiggle their noses with a sniff, then put it down and back away slowly. I urged Ravi to try a little on his fingertip, but he pursed his lips and grimaced as if I asked him to eat a bug. When I finished, I began to wipe up my crumbly cracker bits when the house cook launched out of the kitchen, nearly throwing herself on the table, shrieking, "No, no, no!" and wiped them up herself.

That's the class system, and it was a real mind twister. I experienced a little of it with Prayoon, when people questioned why he stayed in the hotel and not out in the van where he belonged, but it's even more blatant in India than in Thailand. All through Thailand, and even more so in India, I felt uncomfortable watching people fluff my pillow, wipe up my cracker crumbs, or boil water for my tub so I could lounge in the comfort of a hot bath. Drivers slept on concrete floors behind the kitchen just in case Ravi or Ranita needed a ride in the middle of the night. But most of the time drivers slept in the car, and if you needed a ride somewhere early in the morning, you just knocked on the window to wake them up.

My first full day in India, Ravi scheduled interviews for eight consecutive hours with local and national press. The original plan was to hold one press conference at which all the reporters would show up at once. It's a plan I'd cultivated over many months and miles to save my sanity from the onslaught of redundant questions. But that plan fell short when Ravi argued, "They all wanted an exclusive," to which I wanted to counter with the obvious, "Is there such a thing as fourteen exclusives?" Instead, I put on my best face one after another after another, feigning the illusion that I had never before been asked how many pairs of shoes I had walked through.

In India, although their questions are the same, they somehow differ from every other country. Their first question is always, "What does your husband think of this?" When I said I wasn't married, they asked why not?

"I just haven't met the right—"

"Do you have a problem with the love between a man and a woman?"

"No, I think it's wonderful—"

"Why don't you have children? Do you not like God's creatures? When will you have children?"

At first I was taken aback by the personal nature of their questions, but it made me think: if someone doesn't know they're being offensive, do you have the right to be offended? It's offensive in my culture, not theirs. So at once I tried to shift a thought process that's been imbedded in my psyche forever: do not be offended when people ask, "How much money is in your bank account?" "What is your religion?" "How long have your mother and father been married?" "What does your father do for work?" "How much money does he make?" And my personal favorite, "What does your mother cook for you?"

Not only was I fighting the not-offensive-in-this-culture angle, but for someone walking around the world for breast cancer, I was finding their questions entirely irrelevant. So after five interviews, I was tempted to make things up just to entertain myself.

Better yet, I'd shock the wits out of them. I'd tell them the truth.

"I'm not married because I'm still looking for a man who knows how to cook and isn't obsessed with sports on TV, preferably one who has already been through his mid-life crisis. However, I have lived with three different men, one of which only lasted six hours before I sat him down and said, "This just isn't going to work."

I detected a sharp intake of breath.

195

"I've never felt the maternal pull to have children, but I'm only thirty-nine, so I still have a few years to toy with the idea."

Silence.

"My mother and father have been divorced since 1975; both have remarried and are living in different states. I have two sisters and a brother, and only one is married. She just had the first baby in the family at the age of thirty-six, and after two months she went back to work leaving baby Rosie at home in the care of her husband.

"My mother was raised Lutheran, my father was raised Jewish, but we only dabbled in those beliefs while I was growing up, and I am still considering my spiritual options. And the last time my mother cooked for me was when I was fourteen and she left a note saying, 'The pizza is in the freezer next to the Milky Way bars. Help yourself.'"

The air hung in stunned silence. Crickets chirped in the background, and I wondered for a brief moment whether immigration might come and ship me home. The interviewer swiftly regained composure and asked a follow-up question, "So when will you get married, exactly?"

Exhausted by all the interviews, I just wanted to go to bed and hide under the covers. But Ranita insisted that before I hit the open road she should take me into the markets of Kolkata to teach me some crucial haggling skills. She snapped her fingers to the driver and said, "We're ready to go to the markets now; could you hold open the door and call for the elevator boy?"

The markets of Kolkata threw my senses into overdrive, squeezing, bumping, and maneuvering through the sea of humanity like a Walmart at Christmas. Hindi music blared from the shops, women wore colorful saris, and men in cafes ate with their hands, cross-legged on top of the dinner table. Only if I were shipped to Mars would I have been more out of my element. And when you're so removed from your comfort zone, it's impossible to gauge what's normal. Ranita and I walked past an old man carting stacks of caged chickens on his head; another was barefoot, carrying a stack of plastic jugs on his shoulders; a woman walked by with a full grown tree balanced on her head, and Ranita said, "Wow, did you see that man's shoes?"

Hawkers descended upon us, and I watched like a good protégé as Ranita haggled and quibbled then walked away with hawkers in hot pursuit. When they offered her a final price, she wiggled her hand slightly down at her side, and they bolted without a counter offer. Racing to keep up with her, I said in awe, "Wow, you're a real pro."

"Watch and learn. You must let them know who's boss. They are quoting much higher prices than usual because you are with me. They see white skin and think you're rich. 'Here comes a white person with straight teeth—raise that price!' They're unscrupulous." It didn't help that a Lions Club member stopped to talk to us. The Lions in India are held in such high esteem that just being seen with them meant we must be as rich as Croesus himself.

After two hours honing my haggling skills, Ranita was ready to promote me to my next lesson: crossing a street.

There are entire chapters dedicated to the how-tos of crossing a street in Kolkata. I skipped over those chapters pooh-poohing the silliness. Certainly if I was patient enough to wait for the light and take my turn swiftly, I would be just fine. Had I actually read those chapters I would have known there are no lights. Well, maybe a few, but those are broken so the poor policeman has to stand out there in a crush of vehicular anarchy with nothing but a whistle and a prayer.

I hesitate to use the term "traffic" because that might imply some sort of system, and there is none. You don't drive, but rather weave, dodge and maneuver. There are no lanes, no blinkers, no right of way; driving on the left is only a suggestion. And the vehicle in India is nothing without its horn. When someone is in your way you honk the horn. (And with over a billion people, when isn't someone in your way?) When you see the "No Honking" sign, you honk because it's in your way.

The horn in India is used an average of fifteen times per kilometer. Multiply that by the forty-five million horns on the road, and you have a lot of people going deaf or crazy at an early age.

Cars, buses and taxis are only the tip of the congestion iceberg. There are human-motored rickshaws, ox carts, men riding goats and cows crossing the street, but you don't honk at the cow because the cow is holy and you don't beep at Her Holiness.

I saw a taxi bounce—actually bounce—off the back of a bus. There was no stopping, no exchanging of insurance information, just a chuckle and a honk. To use the excuse, "Sorry I'm late; the traffic was just horrific," doesn't fly in Kolkata. It's like those construction companies back home in Colorado that say they would've finished much earlier but "who could've guess there'd be so much doggone snow?"

Ravi and his buddy offered to drive me to an overnight Lions meeting about forty miles away—a two hour drive. The three of us piled into a small red Toyota. Ravi grabbed the steering wheel at ten and two and tore out of the parking place like an Indy driver out of the pit. I hung on for dear life, and my real introduction to Indian roads began.

He bolted around rickshaws, ox carts and cows. He swerved to miss the stray dogs, the family on the bicycle, the chicken crossing the road. He bounced right through a pothole and my head crashed against the roof. *Watch out! Cows on the right! There's a truck! On your left! Woman with a basket of wheat on her head, DOH! Dodge the man carrying bricks on his bicycle.*

Ravi eyed me through the rear view mirror and asked, "How's your insurance?" I managed to squeak over the ceaseless horns that I had a medical evacuation sponsor.

"Good," he replied and accelerated down the straightaway. An ox cart pulled out in his path so he slammed on the brakes launching us into a skid to the left, to the right, to the left, then his phone rang and he answered it because why wouldn't you? You'd think with all the squealing and honking and skidding, people might blink an eye, but it was all perfectly normal to them while I fell into shock and started to weep. But with all the buses laying on their horns, no one heard my cries.

Women in India, like other Asian countries, face breast cancer more often than statistics indicate, because it's so grossly under-diagnosed. Awareness hasn't hit the rural areas at all, so if women have breast cancer they don't know about it until stage four, at which point it's too late. Ravi told me that the Lions Clubs from Kolkata to Mumbai had eagerly jumped on board to take hold of this cause in their communities. He said that Lions Clubs across the country had each arranged crew support through their respective regions, so I should leave Bob packed up in his apartment, and he would ship it to me when I got close to Mumbai (formerly Bombay).

Ravi also organized a press conference with the American Center in Kolkata, which was attended by forty people representing a cross section of doctors, survivors, advocates and reporters. Rex, the American Public Affairs Officer with the Center who had helped arrange the event, introduced me to the audience. After a few words I took questions. First a reporter asked how I planned to spread awareness in rural areas. I explained that with the Lions' commitment and their connections with the local press, we should be able to tap into the rural population so that women from every economic level would hear the message.

Next a doctor raised his hand and I gave him a nod. "How do you plan on spreading awareness in the rural regions?"

Hmm, I thought. *Maybe he was busy doodling while I just answered that.* So I summed it up again, "We'll have a great deal of support from the local press and Lions members throughout the route." Then a breast-cancer survivor raised her hand. "The rural regions have never heard of breast cancer, how will you be able to spread the word?"

I sat perplexed for a moment before Rex tapped me on the shoulder for a private conversation behind the mic. He whispered, "I know you think you're crazy, but trust me, this is a well-known Indian characteristic; entire books have been written on this topic.

We'll talk more later." He took his hand off the mic, put the crowd back on track, and I experienced my first bout with a well-known phenomenon: The Indian Hearing Deficit.

After the press conference Rex explained that the Hearing Deficit is a characteristic that runs deep in Indian culture. He told me of a British businessman who came to assist the Indian government set up radio towers across the country. He would gather all the workers and tell them they needed to dig a ditch three feet wide and six feet deep. He displayed the measurement on the field and confirmed that everyone understood. They did. Later that day when they said they were finished, he went to check their work. The ditch was two feet wide and one foot deep. Not even close. They talked about it again. The workers confirmed that they understood and hours later came back to say they were finished. Now the ditch was two feet wide and three feet deep. Rex said The Hearing Deficit is something you just have to get used to. "Understand quickly that you'll never be able to control anything, or you will never survive here."

It does help explain some other situations that occurred. For nearly six months through an exchange of emails, Ravi told me he had a route and schedule organized from Kolkata to Mumbai, complete with contacts in every village along the way. "They're so excited to help, so don't worry about a thing. India will be very easy for you with crew support, friendship, and love every step from Kolkata to Mumbai." You can imagine my confusion then when he said he would accompany me on my first day so that he could look up the local Lions Club and ask for their help.

"Oh," I said, befuddled, "I thought everyone had been contacted and are waiting for me."

"They are. Don't worry about a thing."

Then he pulled out a generic roadless map and asked which way I would like to go.

I tried to gather all the thoughts racing through my head. "What do you mean, 'which way would I like to go?' I thought you had all my route and contacts arranged. You said they were waiting for me with the friendship, the love, the crew support."

"They are. Don't worry about a thing."

Other travelers had alerted me about the cultural characteristic of Indian people that dissuades them from telling you something you don't want to hear. They want to give you good news *only*, so they make things up. They don't mean it to be malicious, but good grief, how could I work with that? I had no choice but to quickly take the reins.

"Actually, Ravi, if you could help me get a good detailed map I could whip up a route and schedule within an hour. I mean there's only one road to Mumbai, right? It can't be that difficult." I laughed nervously. "I'll take Bob as usual, and if you get me a list of the Lions Club contacts along the way, I'll be happy to give them a call."

"No, no," he said firmly. "I have contacted everyone, you are just fine. Don't worry, everything has been arranged. Now, which way would you like to go? You tell me and I will contact them."

Visions flashed through my head of me sleeping amid the cows in tribal villages with nothing but a duffle bag and a box of water.

Ravi insisted I leave Bob behind, and I felt I had run out of options. I felt caught between two cultures. In this culture women are dominated—men tried to tell me what to do and how to do it. Could I possibly have handled Ravi and the Hearing Deficit any other way? Could I have insisted on taking Bob and the list of Lions Clubs and go alone? Or was that insulting to him because a) I'm a woman, b) I'm a guest, and c) he's my elder? I struggled with the guilt between wanting to respect his position in his own culture and wanting to protect myself. The guidebooks didn't cover that.

The morning of my departure I tucked Bob away behind the couch in the den and invoked a prayer.

Standing over the Hooghly River on the eastern coast of India, I watched masses of people bathing in what looked to be a flowing garbage dump. But it appeared that they were comfortable with their lives, and who are we to say that they aren't happy? It was my observation that we western visitors are too quick to judge their happiness because we put ourselves in their position—bathing as a community in the dirty Hooghly, driving rickshaws barefoot all day long through chaotic traffic, never being able to eat raw vegetables. They farm, they cook, they have families and communities and religions they love. I respected the heck out of that.

What I found particularly curious was the Indian people who had been to cities of the West—clean ones with orderly roads, the rule of law and appliances where you can toss your clothes in to wash, dry, fluff, fold and be ready within the hour smelling of Bounce—and they opted to return because this was what they love. Ravi's friend Adil, said he had been to Hong Kong, and when I asked if he liked it, he sort of shrugged and said, "There's nothing exciting happening."

I watched the people washing themselves in the Hooghly just moments before starting my trek across the Subcontinent and decided my hope for this experience would be to learn to be a fraction as comfortable with this way of life as they were. This promised to be the most challenging portion of my GlobalWalk—probably my life, and despite India being "different," when someone would later ask me how I liked India, my hope was that I could answer with a perky, "I just love India!"

Ravi and the Lions planned a big send-off that started at the Governor's House, where the Governor of the State of West Bengal, Shri Viren J. Shah, officially launched the India leg of GlobalWalk. Experience had taught me that I needed to take a moment for myself before big events. Once they begin, momentum takes over, and there is no stopping to breathe or rest. So I had a private moment before I stepped through the gate and heard the television crew say, "There she is!" And the chaos began.

One TV interview, then another, then another, and I not only got hoarse but also confused about what I had just said. I even wondered if I had just repeated myself, repeated myself.

At the podium in front of two hundred people, I said that when I originally planned my walk I envisioned walking through India alone, "but look at this great group of people seeing me off today. Could somebody take a photo so I can send it to my mother?"

Together, the entire mass of people made its way out the door. Everyone tried to get into the photo, so much so that they squeezed me out entirely, and I landed in the middle of the pack. "Where's Polly? Where's Polly?" Everyone was barking orders about how fast to go, who should pose where, the children should go first, stand next to the children, hold the signs, ready, go, no, wait, you stand over there, show the sign this way, walk slower, wait till the photographer is ready, okay, go, slower please, walk to the right, watch your step, we're losing Polly again, get her up front.

The Governor, His Excellency, finally took the bull by the horns with a concise "I'm going now, have a nice trip." He disappeared, and the crowd walked toward the front gate of his mansion and onto the streets of Kolkata.

Valerie, a breast cancer survivor who came specifically to walk with me the first day, made her way through the crowd to me. She's a British woman who had lived in Kolkata for twenty years and struggled with breast cancer for the past five. Things had been going well until the previous year when she was told the cancer had spread to her lungs, throat, and brain. She was in remission and simply crossed her fingers about tomorrow. I took hold of her hand and yanked her through the crowd. The photographers clicked away while Valerie presented me with a pin. "Mother Theresa gave this to me," she said, "and it's obviously given me good luck because I'm alive today to walk with you. I want you to have it now to continue that good luck as you cross India."

I was overcome, standing right there in the streets of Kolkata touching something that was once touched by Mother Theresa, and even though I was getting jostled around in the crowd while I pinned it on, I didn't give two hoots if I poked myself.

We crossed the city of Kolkata and began my three-month trek to Mumbai. The original crowd of two hundred slowly dispersed, leaving Ravi's friend and Lions Club member, Adil, and me alone for the last few miles. The weeks of anxious anticipation, the emotional tumult of the send-off, and the chaotic road that spread before me as far as I could see, launched my heart to my throat. The toughest journey of my life lay at my feet right here, right now, ready or not.

I returned to Ravi and Ranita's several nights while their driver took me to my starting point every morning and brought me back at the end of the day—a drive that grew at least twenty kilometers daily. Adil had taken a few days off from his travel agency to walk and help get me assimilated. A gentle, agreeable man, he was more than prepared to help me do whatever it was I needed—he was a priceless gift.

The first day walking outside the city, a soft-spoken woman named Gulab joined us. I met her at the kick-off when she expressed interest in joining me for a number of days, to which I agreed. I learned, though, that walking on the roads outside the cities was so filled with chaos it was not suitable for any conversation.

Adil, Gulab and I stepped out of the car at our starting point and began handing out breast cancer brochures to villagers. The sight of a white woman in the village was enough to cause a ruckus, but a white woman handing something out for free created a mob scene. A hundred men surrounded me, and I furiously tried to keep up with the flock of hands reaching just to get something, anything, didn't matter what it was. In one minute all the brochures were gone, and I found myself in the center of a tight circle ten people deep. They were all men, staring, hissing, poking to feel my skin, and asking for more of whatever it was I was passing out. I panicked. How could I escape the mob? I had just come from a Buddhist country where you can't touch a man or that will send them to the temple for days of prayer. I didn't know where the Hindus stood on a woman touching them—even if it was to push them out of the way, so I cowered in the tight circle waiting to be rescued. I faintly heard Adil yelling through layers of people, "Polly! Polly!

I'll get you out!" He pushed himself through the crowd, shoving people off to his left and right, "Excuse me, Pardon me! Beg your pardon!" He grabbed me by the arm and yanked me out in full sprint, "Let's go!"

No one was there to hurt me, I knew that. They were just curious. But the reality was clear: if you are a woman alone in the rural regions, you are fair game. I wouldn't be able to sit in cafes people-watching. I was the *people-watchee*. I wore a long-sleeved light cotton shirt, long cotton pants and a hat that covered my whole head and neck too, so there was hardly an inch of my white skin to be seen. I thought that would make me relatively invisible and enable me to watch Indian culture unfold without the chaos of being the raisin in the sugar bowl (or would that be the sugar cube in the raisin bowl?). However, it seemed no measure of disguise could hide the fact that I was a white girl. When Adil walked beside me, the men of the village only stared, but if he got ahead of me, even by fifty feet, men quickly teamed up to cackle and poke.

I had no alternative other than to hightail it through the villages without lingering for even a moment. When Adil and Gulab got ahead of me and I heard a man yell, "Madam! One moment please, Madam," that was my cue that the men of the village had spotted me, and I had better catch up. Pronto.

Gulab seemed unfazed by all the harassment and commotion. She wanted to have a nice easy chat like girlfriends do, but my head was swiveling from side to side watching the life of India whirl around me. Families cooked outside their grass huts, bathed their babies in muddy rivers, and washed their clothes in the same pond that other villagers peed in. Just ahead a man was peeing by the side of the road. Unschooled in the etiquette of encountering a man peeing beside the road, I waved. He waved back.

The traffic was a maelstrom of buses, rickshaws, bikes, trucks, and streams of people converging from both sides of the road and, seemingly, out of the woodwork. There were potholes to dodge, puddles to jump, cow dung to sidestep. A bus drove by with a man standing on an outside window ledge holding on from the top railing. The bus swerved left and right, speeding around cows like a skier on the slalom, while two dozen men on the roof swayed with every screech. Gulab tried to make conversation when she asked, "What's the most dangerous thing that's ever happened on your walk?"

"*Walking on this road!*" I yelled over the noise.

Gulab, a petite girl, shy and reserved, wore a beautiful red and yellow sari with black walking shoes. "Polly, can I tell you about my dream?"

I leaned in to hear her over the horns, "Of course."

"Since I was a child, I, too, have wanted to walk around the world. That's why I've wanted to come join you. My dream is to walk through every single country on this beautiful planet and promote world peace."

Ironically, my first thought was the demoralizing one so many people had offered me: *Yeah, right.*

Gulab went on to say she thought it would take six years. "I want to leave on September 11—in just eight months, but I don't know how to do it. Will you help me, Polly?"

"I'll do whatever I can," I said, feeling bad about my first thoughts. But I had to break it to her that I was walking through twenty-two countries in five years. Realistically, to walk through every country in the world—at last count 194—across every circle of latitude, would logistically take, oh, two hundred years. A little enthusiastic. I had been relatively clueless when I first started planning my walk, but at that point at least I had traveled extensively, had a route sorted out, and a number of long distance walks under my feet.

Gulab had never been out of West Bengal. She'd never walked more than one day and lived in a culture that made it nearly impossible for her to pursue any life outside the home. She had no support from her husband, and her mother and father said she was crazy for even wanting such a thing. It's not easy to break the teensiest tradition in India, particularly one that meant leaving her family. Such dreams were not considered, especially for a woman. But she insisted on joining me again the next day to try walking two whole days in a row.

Gulab didn't show up. She never answered another email.

Having Adil with me for the first few days was invaluable, sort of like having someone to hang on to while I dabbled my toes in the water. He also gave me my third dose of the infamous Indian Hearing Deficit.

On the drive to our starting spot, we had a long, thorough conversation about the route and schedule of the day. I said we should walk at least twenty-three kilometers to the town of Alampur, which would allow us to finish about 3:00 p.m. He agreed. We discussed points of time and location, how after fourteen kilometers—or three hours—we would stop for lunch, then carry on for another three hours. Imagine my surprise then after one hour of walking he said, "Okay, is that far enough? Are we done? Should I wave down the driver to take us home?"

"But we've just begun," I said. "We'll walk for two more hours, stop for lunch, and then walk another three hours."

He stared at me with a blank look on his face. "Are you sure?"

"Yes. I have to walk at least twenty-three kilometers to Alampur today in order to stay on schedule. Remember, we talked about it on the way here?"

He agreed, and we continued. After another hour he turned around and said, "Okay, I'll wave down the driver now. That should be enough for the day. Is this a good place to stop?"

I reminded Adil again that we had to walk for three hours, stop for lunch, then walk for three more hours. "I need to cover at least twenty-three kilometers today."

It's not a language barrier; most Indians in urban areas know English very well, a gift from the British. In fact, while the Indian constitution is written in twenty-six languages, English is the official language during national gatherings and political functions. The confusing part is that it's not just a characteristic with Adil, no, no, no. It's a national characteristic, which invites the question: How do national characteristics evolve?

Despite The Hearing Deficit, Adil was an amiable fellow, married for eighteen years and father of two daughters, ages fourteen and seventeen. Ten people live in his four-bedroom, one-bathroom apartment in what's called a joint-family. In the West we would call that one bitchy reality show. He asked how many family members live in my house, and I felt like a loser trying to explain that my friends and siblings either live alone or have platonic roommates. Suddenly it seemed like such a waste of space—having one or two people living in each house across America. I tried to explain that in America we move around the country a lot for jobs and school or new opportunities, many times leaving families strewn across five states.

He was astonished. "Wow, so do you feel you can really grow personally and make decisions without consulting parents, brothers, kids, and the extended family next door?"

"You find the right call plan."

I asked if his was an arranged marriage, and he said it was. In fact just the previous night, he said, his seventeen-year-old daughter urged him to start looking for her husband. Arranged marriages absolutely intrigue me. India is modernizing in many ways, producing the largest number of engineers in the world. Bangalore is Asia's answer to Silicon Valley, yet Indians still stick to the tradition of arranged marriages.

It's not such a bad idea. Parents in India look for their child's marriage partner to be of similar socio-economic class, religion, and education level, someone from a good family with similar interests and goals. If they find a good match, they exchange photos and arrange a meeting. Isn't that pretty much an E-Harmony profile?

The intriguing part is that Bollywood has built its movie industry around the boy-meets-girl, star-crossed lovers, love triangle genres; yet the love marriage is fiercely looked down upon. A Bollywood actress would be harshly criticized if she were to indulge in even an onscreen peck on the cheek.

I asked Adil if he romantically loves his wife, and he said, "What do you mean?"

"When you left the house this morning, did you kiss your wife goodbye and say I love you?"

He laughed so hard he had to stop walking and grab his side. "Oh, no! Don't be silly!"

I noted walking through the villages that men can hold men's hands, women can hold women's hands, but men and women can never hold hands. On Valentine's Day there was a story in *The Times of India*, the national newspaper, of protests taking place in front of shops across Mumbai that sell romantic products like love cards, teddy bears with hearts, heart candy, etc. They were picketing against Valentine's Day alleging it's all a conscious attempt by the West to invade their culture with romantic love.

"Did you ever have a crush on a girl when you were a kid? Or flirt?"

"What is this… crush?"

"A crush is when you're attracted to someone from afar and whenever you get near them you get butterflies in your tummy," was the best I could come up with.

"Oh no! No such thing." Again, he laughed, hardly able to control himself. "We don't have this…this crush."

I can't imagine that romance, flirting, blushing-when-you-see-him isn't as normal as puberty itself. Could it even be possible that crushes are a learned, and not an innate behavior? Then he threw me a twist. "But Gulab would put me in a romantic mood."

Aha! I thought silently.

"Oh, she has a wonderful voice, doesn't she?"

"You have a crush on Gulab! That's a crush!"

"Oh no! Ha ha. Don't be silly!" he insisted. "But walking with her again would be most delightful. Maybe I'll call her just to hear her voice. I can show her photos of our first day walking."

And there it is—Cupid's version of The Hearing Deficit. But here's my question, straight from my own Western linear thinking: if marriage is a social contract and has virtually nothing to do with romantic love, is it socially acceptable to have a crush on someone, to flirt with someone, as long as they keep their commitment to the social contract—to their legal spouse? Is that a rude question? Or bona fide curiosity? Who could I ask?

We were six days from Kolkata and Ravi had been in touch with a handful of Lions Clubs, enough to start handing me off like a baton down the NH6. Ravi and Adil dropped me off in Tamluk to the grand fanfare of a dozen Lions Club members, and Ravi reiterated that I had nothing to worry about. He promised that every Lions Club from Tamluk to Mumbai had been contacted and were waiting with organized educational forums, newspaper interviews, a crew driver, a place to stay, and a box of water to hydrate me in the 110-degree heat.

And he did it! For three whole days. With help from local Lions Clubs I walked through the villages of Debra, Balivassa and Bangal and into the new state of Orissa.

But then the chain of contacts ended and no one had ever heard of Polly, her walk, or Ravi from Kolkata.

CHAPTER 13

West Meets East

I was doomed. No Bob, no cell phone, nothing but that haunting vision of sleeping amid the cows in tribal villages with a duffle bag and box of water. For two years on the road I had been the CEO of my walk, the organizer, the decision maker. I'd confirmed plans with clear vision, knowing where I was going and how long it would take. Now, because I wasn't strong enough to stand up to The Hearing Deficit, I was left vulnerable and dependent, completely reliant on someone, anyone, to get the word to the next Lions Club to transfer my gear.

While it was like trying to juggle Jello, I survived day-by-day, step-by-step. The local Lions Club would get word the morning of my pending arrival that I was on the way, and they were fabulous at whipping together an educational forum. That usually included a local doctor and local women and was held in a neighborhood clinic or hospital or, on occasion, an empty parking lot.

Often the villagers gathered near the fence but wouldn't come in—poor women, the underclass, who didn't feel comfortable coming into a room or even a parking lot full of local upper class men and one white woman. But the Lions urged them to join us, and eventually they did, even if just for the novelty of seeing a white woman. A number of people in the central tribal regions of India had never seen a white person before. They couldn't take their eyes off me. Heck, if that's what it took to get them through the gates to hear about breast cancer, I was happy.

Every day the new Lions Club came out to meet me and said, "We didn't know you were coming until this morning. Why hasn't someone let us know sooner?" All I could say was "Gee, I'm so sorry.

It must've fallen through the cracks. But hey, maybe you could help me by calling ahead to some clubs so they know I'm on the way." They said they would, and the next day I had the same conversation with the neighboring club who would bust a move putting together a forum and press coverage.

And every morning the poor Lions Club would say, "You really should've had crew support arranged across the country. That would've made our job a lot easier. Or what would have been perfect is if you had a buggy on wheels to transport your duffle bag!"

Sometimes the Lions put me up in their homes, but more often they put me up in the local Government Guest House, a one room concrete government-owned building usually located on the edge of town. Generally there would be a bed in the middle of a large room and a bathroom with a hole and a bucket. The British built the Government Guest Houses back in the forties as a place for politicians to stay during village elections and other important events that might warrant a visiting VIP. For anyone to stay in a Government Guest House, the local mayor had to grant permission. So after walking for ten hours in 110-degree heat, the Lions took me to stand before the village mayor, where I answered his questions about my marital status and how much money my father makes, patiently awaiting the nod that endorsed my questionable *VIPness.*

If a town was big enough to have a hotel, I stayed there. To check in, the manager pulled out the Red Book, a registration book that I was told the government insisted I fill out thoroughly. When the Red Book opened it spread out three feet long with thirty columns posing the questions that no one finds invasive: What is your husband's name? How much money does your husband make? How long have you been married? How many children do you have? Etc. Then ten people would escort me to my room where I'd spend the rest of the night managing the stream of curiosity seekers.

Knock-knock: "Meet my neighbor's son. Can we take a photo?"

Knock-knock: "Here's my card. I own a faxing store. If you need to fax anything, I'm right down the street serving all your faxing needs."

Knock-knock: "I heard your name is Polly. What is your real name?"

Knock-knock: "I hear your name is Polly. What religion is that?"

Knock-knock: "You didn't fill in your husband's name in the Red Book."

Knock-knock: "Why you don't have children? Don't you like children? When will you have children?"

The Lions Club said they would pick me up at the Guest House and drop me at my starting spot at 7:00 a.m. However, presumably due to The Hearing Deficit, sometimes they showed up at 8:30 a.m., sometimes 10 a.m., sometimes never, and then I would walk into town in search of a rickshaw driver and attempt to translate the fact that I wanted them to follow behind me all day. "No," I would try to explain, "I don't want to be *in* the rickshaw, I want you to *follow me* and transport my duffle bag and box of water."

Every single day grew longer and more aggravating—the sort of aggravation when you look at your watch and think, "Oh good grief, is it *still* February 26?" I was digging, begging, praying for more patience, reaching so deep I started reciting the Serenity Prayer, "God, grant me grace to accept the things I cannot change..." and I didn't even realize I knew it.

People had warned me this was going to be tough, "If you want anything to run smoothly in India then you're likely to go mad," they'd say. "Give in, go with the flow, relax, don't make a schedule." All very good and well if I was on holiday, but I was here on a job. What could I do with no schedule when I couldn't depend on anything? Certainly I wasn't the only one trying to get something done in India. Didn't people have to show up to work on time? If a meeting was scheduled at 8:00 a.m., did people show up at 8:30, 10, or not at all? How did businesses move forward? Or did they? Conversations weren't heard, and decisions were taken from me. Men wanted to control how far I walked, how I walked, and where. And, of course, working within the confines of The Hearing Deficit meant I had to question everything I was told. I had no control over anything.

So big deal. Why was I getting so upset? I should have been an accomplished traveler at this point; these annoyances shouldn't bother me. Why was I so annoyed with the crowding, the staring? There was a lot of staring in Southeast Asia; why was it different in India? Some people have the ability to entirely immerse themselves into all elements of such a different culture, and I was ashamed to admit that I was just not that developed. I wondered if other people would be having such a rough time.

I had to get a grip on this new reality before my eye twitched right out of my head. Each morning I took a deep breath before opening the door to start a new day. Eighty villagers followed me across the street where I was eating breakfast with the Lions Club. They swarmed the table and I smiled in their direction, while out of the corner of my eye I could see the men nudge each other for a better view of the white girl eating her hard-boiled eggs with her eye twitching.

Over the first month the terrain had gradually moved into the heart of rural regions, and I marveled every day at the scene unfolding before me. While the traffic was not as congested as in the villages near Kolkata, it was still categorically manic. Almost no private cars traveled the road, replaced instead by an unrelenting flow of buses and overloaded trucks. Typically thirty percent overloaded, truck sides bulged with product held down with a burlap tarp and canvas straps. When the trucks swerved to avoid a bus or a cow, they would tip up on two wheels, sometimes spewing oranges across the NH6 inviting villagers to an orange gathering free-for-all.

The traffic was so chaotic that on my daily twenty-three mile stretch of road there was an average of eight crashes per day. One day I counted sixteen! The first crash I came upon was a truck that had hit a school bus head on. The two vehicles slammed into each other, throwing the school bus on its side shattering all its windows. By the time I walked by, the kids had all crawled out of the wreckage and stood safely on the side of the road. Crashes were clearly the norm. Trucks regularly smashed head-on into oncoming trucks and sideswiped trees; buses flew off cliffs, over bridges, and into mountainsides. After the horror of seeing my first crash and wailing into a panic at not having a cell phone to call 911, I slowly became impervious. Even starting a tally with a tick on the notepad that hung from my hip. And for my safety, I kept an eye out for every single car, truck and bus that passed within two hundred yards—after all, oranges really can fly.

I moved deeper into the tribal region where languages changed every few miles. No one knows how many languages are actually spoken in India; one study estimates over a thousand. Others say no one will ever know for sure because there are many unknown tribes hidden in the hills that have clung on to their original languages. My people-watching changed when I walked into more primitive tribal areas. I saw people with no shirts dressed in skimpy little dhotis (a sort of loincloth) in lieu of pants. The deeper I got into the tribal region the less aggressive people were toward me. They were still curious, but the people of the tribal region just stopped to look with a half a smile on their faces as if they didn't know how they should look at me. Was it okay to smile? To look? They were too shy to say hello, and there was a very welcome lack of my being chased through villages.

One of the local Lions invited a group of tribesmen over to have their photo taken with me, and when I showed them the photo on the back of my digital camera they marveled as if they'd just witnessed a miracle. Another Lions Club member was walking with me when we came upon a tribal woman who asked if she could give me something. It was unusual for a woman to say anything to me; I had been told the women of the rural regions weren't allowed to talk to women they didn't know. It seemed this tribal region was different. The woman went to a tree and grabbed a handful of long green leaves and started to weave the leaves into a bowl. With a big smile on her face, she continued to weave as she spoke to me in her native tongue—which, of course, I didn't understand. When she finished, she handed the bowl to me. The Lion explained that they weave their own plates and bowls in which they eat their food. "She wants you to have it."

I was thrilled. I loved the tribal region and would've given anything to be able to understand that woman.

One downside of the tribal areas was the limited food options along the roadside. Usually one or more of the local Lions members joined me for the day, and I would follow their lead as to which cafes were safe—although well aware that the guidelines on what was safe for me and what was safe for them were two very different things.

Guidebooks say that if a lot of Indian people are eating at a restaurant it's probably a safe bet. But I couldn't help but note that these are the same Indian people who can drink this water that will kill me in a drop. Was this really a reliable gauge of a safe place to eat?

Throughout the tribal region the only cafes available were the quintessential poster places for where *not* to eat. They often consisted of one cement wall, two wood walls on the sides, a dirt floor and a grass roof, the sort of places that closes for the day by blowing out the fire and walking away. No cleaning, no sweeping, no locking any doors. Yet they all consistently had glorious food.

When the Lions assured me a cafe was perfectly fine, I didn't argue. We sat cross-legged on a hammock, as you do, and I had a moment to look around at my surroundings. A goat had just crawled under my hammock, presumably assuming position in case I dropped a morsel. Two stray dogs rambled in and out of the café, one scratching at her fleas, the other, a puppy, just peed next to the goat. Two hammocks down a man perfected the sport of spitting.

Spitting is a widespread national pastime, I discovered, along with belching and farting, a couple of characteristics that are by no means offensive in their culture. The national acceptance of farting, I must say, I found to be admirable. All day long and well into the night people ate lentils and farted—in elevators, small cars, business meetings; there's no giggling, no begging of pardon, no mischievously pointing to the other guy. This is a free country, free to fart at will as though it were in the Bill of Rights, an innate human liberty.

I thumbed through my guidebook index under "F," but there was nothing that even remotely touched on socially acceptable bodily functions. Perplexed again, I contacted Rex at the American Center. He confirmed, "Yes, you're not crazy. Farting is like breathing here, perfectly acceptable. Frankly," he said wisely, "it's a custom I'd like to integrate into the West, the freedom to fart at will. It's actually quite liberating. You should try it." So, at last, I took note of something I genuinely learned to love about India.

Via an inner strength I had no idea was inside me, I kept getting up every day and putting one foot in front of the other. Every morning I awoke to the 4:00 a.m. call to prayer that wafted through the village, and before I even opened my eyes, I took a quiet moment for myself to visualize what the day might throw at me. It was my first attempt at meditation, a grasp at any means to help me get to Mumbai.

It was imperative to find Internet every day to at least touch base with Mom, Dad, and Alan at my Lions Club. Just seeing messages from them with simple words about normal life moving along somewhere besides these dusty roads gave me strength. I was pushing myself harder each day than I ever had before. The norm had been to cover about 450 kilometers a month. This month I was closing in on 750.

Near the town of Kendujhargarh a doctor from the local hospital kindly escorted me to the Internet cafe in town. He explained that I couldn't possibly go myself because that would disrupt village life, clogging roads and requiring police for crowd control. The doctor picked me up in a rickshaw, and the driver peddled down the busy street toward town with skilled dexterity, dodging potholes and goats and cows, honking his little horn. My eyes darted all over the road trying to keep up with the chaos until I saw something ahead that made me stare. Could that be…? A…a body? A human body? No…could it be?

Oh, good heavens! It was a man lying in the middle of the street! Legs spread eagle, arms above his head, mouth gaping open.

Oh my God, it's a dead man! In the middle of the street! Why isn't anyone doing anything? Isn't someone going to help him? Why doesn't anyone stop? Rickshaws and buses maneuvered around him like a traffic cone, paying no mind whatsoever to the man lying dead in the middle of the street. Our rickshaw driver skirted around him and the doctor didn't blink an eye. "Shouldn't we stop and help that man," I managed to gurgle. "I think he's dead!"

The doctor burst into laughter. "No, no!" he explained. "He's not dead, ha ha." He translated my worry to the driver, which sent him into a fit of laughter too. "Silly American! He's not dead! He's just sleeping! Ha ha ha! Dead? Ha ha, oh, that very, very funny!"

Sleeping? The man was sleeping in the middle of the road at rush hour, and *I'm* silly? I felt pressured to join in the laughter, but it came out fake.

If this man just needed a power nap, it begged the question of what common sense truly is. One dictionary defines common sense as "sound practical judgment independent of specialized knowledge, training, or the like." Could it be that common sense is, in fact, not as defined by us in the West but rather a culturally learned concept? It's a question I struggled with every day in India, every time I saw a truck stopped in the middle of the highway so the driver could take a nap underneath his vehicle. He wasn't pulled off to the side of the road or safely tucked into a parking lot, but parked in the middle of the highway on the wrong side of a blind turn. Every time I walked past farms and saw women in their saris bend over to pick their zucchini, their sari scarf fell forward and they had to flip it back over their shoulder. They would bend over to pick their zucchini again, and the scarf fell forward, and again they would flip it back. That continued all day. In my western linear mind I'm thinking, so, *tie it up.*

I am a woman brought up in a society accustomed to making things happen pronto, naturally programmed to tackle the inefficient in a jiffy. It took quite a paradigm shift to rewire that lifelong thinking process, so—chop, chop—I quickly thought about things in my culture that made no sense to them. Most certainly, my very presence here, a white woman alone, walking, was crazy, when getting a ride from town to town would make more "sense." And what sense did it make to them that I came all this way to talk about breast cancer with tribal women who couldn't read and didn't have water fit to drink?

In fact, I'm sure everyone at home was wondering what *sense* it made for me even to be in India during this tumultuous time in the world. Just a few months after 9/11, tensions were heating up between Muslims and Hindus leaving a trail of riots breaking out in towns and cities around the country, particularly along the road from Kolkata to Mumbai.

The riots in India were making international news, which meant my daily Internet cafe sessions produced emails similar to Dad's:

> "With the turmoil in India at the moment, indeed at every moment, the better part of discretion is to move expeditiously."

And from Rachel:

> "We're watching what you're in the midst of. Run. Just run! You don't even have to be nice to people, just get through there."

But it wasn't as if I could take a detour—there was only one road from Kolkata to Mumbai. When I got closer to the entrance of a town in the midst of riots, the police always directed me inside a nearby hotel or any empty building until curfew was lifted, usually a couple of hours. I emailed back insisting I was fine. But I wasn't convinced that was true.

Raipur is a city that lies in the center of India, and I reveled in the fact that I had made it half way. But I was struggling. I was so wound up I tried to visualize what my frazzled nerves looked like inside my body. But the outside looked worse. My weight had plummeted to ninety-three pounds (from my usual 105-ish), and my nightmare Bangkok hairdo had sprouted out in every direction. I was still nursing that discernible twitch in my left eye. My nerves were cracking. I needed to talk to someone, to hear a familiar voice, a good friend to help lift my exhausted spirits. I wandered aimlessly through the streets of Raipur looking for a place to make a phone call, and when I found a Phone Store I decided Vicki was the one to lift me up. That poor girl.

She answered the phone and said hello, and in that single moment, when I heard a familiar voice, and could picture a familiar place where I felt safe and comfortable, I erupted into tears. Oh, I burst—heaving and convulsing into the ugly cry, the sort of crying where no one could possibly understand the noises spewing out of me.

She waited silently trying to decipher who was on the other end. "…and the men are chasing me…there are…riots…trucks flying off…I've got this twitch…"

She managed to calm me down, and when she finally spoke they were gentle words of encouragement and support. "Tell me slowly what's going on."

I knew my emotional limits were being pushed, but I had no idea I had reached the point that I could no longer form whole sentences. Every time I tried to speak I exploded into blubbers. Then she said gently, "Is there any way you can come home?"

"Huh?…sniffle, sniffle…come home? What do you mean?"

"You can go back to India later, with proper help, and carry on when it's not in such turmoil. God knows we're watching it on the news, and it looks unbearable. Come home. You're probably not safe there. It's just a matter of time before you get hit by one of those trucks or find yourself in the middle of the riots. But for now, why don't you just get a ride to the nearest airport and catch a flight back to Colorado. I'll help you get back on your feet."

Well, she was right. I knew it. I was miserable to be sure, and probably not safe, but go home? Quit? For weeks my brain had been toying with ways to get out of there as fast as possible in as safe a manner as my body could handle, but I had honestly never even thought about going home. Moreover, I was walking for women with breast cancer, women who don't have the liberty to just throw up their arms and say, "Well, I have had it with this cancer nonsense, all this chemo, my hair falling out, the daily throwing up. I think I'll just fly home to my cozy life pre-cancer diagnosis." How could I ever face anyone with breast cancer again? Those women didn't have the option of quitting. Neither did I.

But clearly I needed some help. My fuse had grown so short with the constant harassment, the Hearing Deficit, the riots, and hunting down either a Lions member or a rickshaw driver every morning, that my biggest fear was that I was going to snap. It took every ounce of focus I could muster right down to my toes to remain patient. I would walk amidst the cackles trying desperately to go to my happy place: sitting with Vicki and Rachel at an outdoor cafe over Auckland's harbor, sipping a cappuccino or a blueberry smoothie. I feared what might happen if one of those men who approached me hissing and harassing would provoke a final snap, turning me into a crazed maniac, heaving him up over my head with Herculean strength and throwing him into an oncoming truck. Could little ol' five foot two me be declared a lethal weapon? Every minute of every day, I had to concentrate on my happy place while half ignoring and half accepting the chaos and aggravations. Yes, I needed help.

Walking now twenty-six miles a day, I figured I could polish off the last half of India in six weeks. But twenty-six miles (42 kilometers) was almost twice my daily mileage. Was that too much? Was my desire to get out of there going to grind my health into the ground? Maybe. I also knew if I continued at my normal pace, my health would undoubtedly implode amid the cows. So I asked myself, what do I really need? What would it take to survive the next six weeks, to stop the men from harassing and chasing me through the streets, to protect me from riots, and to help me communicate? I thought about hiring a taxi driver for the six weeks. Maybe a rickshaw driver? Then it struck me: I needed to rent a man.

The harsh reality is that in this culture my life would improve ten-fold if a man were just standing next to me. He wouldn't even have to do anything, just be there. Logistically it was too difficult for a woman alone; every move was a struggle, from eating in a cafe or buying oranges in the market, to standing in front of the mayor to get the nod on a VIP Guest House. If I could rent a man I wouldn't have to depend on the Lions coming to pick me up. I wouldn't have to hunt down a rickshaw driver every morning to transport my duffle bag to the next village.

Great idea, Letofsky! Now how on earth do you rent a man in the tribal regions of central India? Like you find anything else these days—you Google.

My hosts in Raipur agreed to let me stay with them until I got the proper help to carry on all the way to Mumbai, and it was the best town to be in. Raipur was a good-sized city; big enough to have all the major services needed, in particular, plenty of Internet cafes for proper Googling. I walked down the street from my host's house where there was a great Internet cafe—thatched roof, goat under my chair nibbling at my ankles—and Googled "rent-a-man/India."

Well, okay, not exactly. But I did Google tour companies across India and emailed twenty-five of them requesting a driver to accompany me for six weeks. He would have to drive directly behind me at three mph and be at my side 24/7. I got one response.

A tour company from Chennai in south India said they had just the person. His name was Shankaran—Shankar for short. "He knows English and has guided westerners around India before, so understands you very much." He could be in Raipur in three days.

Shankar arrived in Raipur in three days, as promised. Even more astonishing, he was on time for the 5:30 a.m. departure our first morning. It was the first glimmer of light on this very dark road.

CHAPTER 14

What a Riot!

National news was covering the ongoing riots in Akola, the city I would be walking into in a few days, so I kept my eye on the updates as closely as I could. The riots began on Holi day, a spring festival held on a full moon in March, the day when nature starts donning new colors. To celebrate this great Indian kaleidoscope of colors, strangers and friends alike throw paint on each other throughout the day. In Akola, some yahoo splashed paint all over the local mosque; Muslims retaliated by burning down a number of city buildings and houses. Hours later six people lay dead, fifteen were injured, all businesses had to shut down, and a curfew was imposed throughout the city until further notice.

With Shankar right behind me, I walked into the hostile region. People repeatedly stopped to warn us not to enter the city. While I wasn't crazy about being a white woman in an area of such unrest, I couldn't see any other option. Since, again, there was only one road to Mumbai, I couldn't very well walk around the trouble. There was no place to stop anyway—no building, motel, or VIP house—so I just kept putting one foot in front of the other watching the mileposts countdown to the city—5km, 4km, 3km.

On cue, at the 1km mark, the police stopped me and confirmed that I needed to get inside the nearest hotel right away. They pointed to the Greenland Hotel across the street, and when I looked to my left I thought I'd seen the new world. There stood the most stunning hotel I had seen in months, an oasis in the midst of riots and malaria and trucks flying off cliffs.

I thanked the policeman and walked across the street into my new world, a palace complete with air conditioning and indoor plumbing—including a sit-down toilet and a shower with a towel! Most important, cable TV that hosted a lineup of all those mindless American sitcoms that I love: *Seinfeld, Friends* and a marathon of—are you ready—*Three's Company*!

There was a restaurant too. Although it was closed due to the riots, the kitchen remained open. That's right. Can you say *room service*? I called my Lions contact, who conveyed the awful news that I would be confined to the Greenland Hotel until further notice. He told me they knew I was going to arrive there and had organized appropriately. "A room is all set for you and your driver, but we can't come to visit until they lift the curfew, probably three days."

So let me see if I have this straight, I thought. *No one can come and visit me because there is a curfew, and all press interviews and events are on hold. The local police are forcing me to stay in an air-conditioned three-star hotel, where I have nothing better to do than sleep, watch cable TV, take two hot showers a day, and sit down on a toilet—just because I can? And in exchange for this concession, I merely have to put up with religious riots and a* Three's Company *marathon? I'll take it!*

For the next three days my aching muscles healed themselves with rest and hot showers. My mind, on the other hand, slid into numbness from watching seventy-two hours of American sitcoms. Poor Shankar had to put up with my sitcoms for three days—and was kind enough not to offer commentary.

Life outside the walls of the Greenland Hotel and life on the TV couldn't have been more different. I would give anything to know what Shankar was thinking.

Seinfeld, Friends, Three's Company—all shows about dating into your thirties, friends living together, sexual innuendo, one-night stands, talking freely and openly about respective sex lives—were they a new concept for him, or had he been exposed to this kind of culture before?

We caught some Oprah as well. She talked about menstrual cycles and finding your spirit; women spoke of brilliant careers and choosing singledom after a bad marriage or three.

Women in the U.S. are considered equal partners in relationships; tradition does not dictate their lives. One story on the BBC addressed women having children over the age of forty-five. He must have been as confused about our culture as I was with his.

On the third day the Lions member on Polly duty got permission from the police to visit me. An affable fellow, he apologized profusely for holding me up so long in the hotel. It would have been rather insensitive for me to say I thought these riots were the best darn thing that have ever happened to me, so I simply assured him that I was making the best of this most unfortunate situation.

He also announced that due to ongoing fighting the curfew had been extended. The police refused to let me walk through town and insisted instead that in the morning they would drive me four miles through the city and drop me at the west end.

I sat down to get my head around the news. It had been two and a half years without missing a step (except the unavoidable Burma) and now the police insisted I get a ride for four miles. I asked if they could escort Shankar and me through town as opposed to driving me. "We could do it at five in the morning and I could run. It would take me forty-five minutes tops. Maybe thirty!" But he shook his head and said it just was not safe. "They'll pick you up at 5:30 tomorrow morning."

The Akola police drove me through town while the early morning sun peeked over the city buildings. The feeling of peace that blanketed the town astounded me. Nowhere did I see a single soul. Since I had arrived in India there had not been a single moment where I could look around and not see a sea of people. That morning from the backseat of the police car, I looked out on what I imagined to be the quietest, most serene town in all of India. Boarded up shops, closed businesses, deserted streets, not a cow on the horizon. How did the cows know there was a curfew? I was grateful to the Akola police for looking after me, but I wondered if walking through this empty town might have been the safest I'd ever been. And if the Akola police were to see what I had been walking through in the past few months, would they have insisted on driving me all the way to Mumbai?

They dropped me at the western end of town where Shankar took over once again as my sole protector. Stretching on the side of Shankar's car preparing for my first walk in four days, I wondered how to explain in my records why I had to get a ride for four miles. Then I looked up and couldn't believe what I saw: a sign directing me off the main road, "Detour 4 miles."

Mom, Dad, Alan,
The sign reads, "Mumbai, only 179 kilometers!!" Well, I added the exclamation points. And the word "only."

The mileposts are counting down to Mumbai and I thought absolutely nothing could stop me from that finish line, but yesterday, at about the 24th mile, I actually starting to feel nauseous. At first I wondered if it could've been an ice cream cone I ate. (Lesson: don't buy ice cream after the electricity has been out in the village for 7 hours,) But with only 5 days left to Mumbai, I think my body might be rebelling against the torture I've been imposing on it the past three months. It's not just the walking 24 miles a day, but along the way I've been inhaling diesel fuel and enduring incessant cackling from the truck drivers. Add the 110-degree heat, and my body is being thrown into the proverbial wall.

I'm finding it hard to finish every single day.

I'll call when I get to Mumbai.
xxx Polly

I had to depend on the locals to give me directions. Maps in this part of the world were vague at best, and the disconcerting truth was that I am directionally challenged. There had been times during the past two years and nine months on the road that I had inadvertently found myself standing in a sort of flustered bewilderment at the dead end of a rock quarry or seaside gully slowly heading out to some uncharted atoll. (I remind you that most of these countries only have one road, so how I ended up in these predicaments is anyone's guess.)

You can imagine my angst when Shankar announced that he was much too nervous to drive into Mumbai because, as he put it, coming from the roads of southern India, "I've heard there are lanes there and you're meant to stay in them." I quickly launched into groveling. "Please don't leave me. No one will ever find me out there."

But there was no use fighting a paralyzing fear of lanes.

Before Shankar left me, we scoured every shop for a detailed map of Mumbai, but there weren't any. The best one we could find looked something like a cartoon, suggesting that this city of sixteen million people has five roads and can fit on the size of a postcard. A sense of doom swept over me. Shankar dropped me off thirty kilometers north of central Mumbai, we said our goodbyes and off I went, walking to the south. I think.

One day years ago while hiking in Colorado, a friend taught me how I could find south by pointing the hands on the face of my watch to the sun. I was tickled to learn this new skill, and from that day on you could regularly find me outside restaurants, tops of mountains and on busy intersections pointing my watch at the sun dazzling friends with my knowledge of which way south was. Of course they already knew. Everyone knows. Except me.

The first twenty-five kilometers posed no problem. The highway was straight and no clouds were hiding the sun from me and my watch. After five hours my surroundings started getting busier and louder. More shops and people, fewer cows, and, yes, traffic lanes started to appear. I made a mental note to email Shankar and inform him that he should never be afraid of Mumbai again because people pay absolutely no mind to them. I was entering the heart of the city.

The highway stopped being an easy, straight road and became inundated with options. Roads converged sometimes seven, eight, nine at a time, coming at me from every angle. They would curve, bend, circle, and every few meters there was a new intersection offering a dozen more options. The watch-sun trick couldn't help me now. And I don't know why I did it other than force of habit, but I started asking directions.

Indian people mean well, they really do, but they think it's rude to say, "I don't know," so they take a guess. It's up to you to sort out whether it's a knowledgeable answer or a guess. Tricky business, as the wrong answer could send you miles in the wrong direction.

Before doing anything else, I went into a decent-looking hotel and asked if they had a better map of Mumbai than my postcard. They did! I then asked where we were, and he drew a big circle around the suburb of Dharavi. The circle covered a ten-kilometer radius, so I asked if he could be more specific. Could he tell me the street I was on, and dare I ask what cross street.

The man studied the map, flipped it around and upside down, called in a couple of buddies, they held it up between them, spread it out on the desk, chatted some more, called in the neighbors and finally woke me up to say, "We think we're roughly about right here somewhere, we're pretty sure. Yeah, for sure."

I didn't push it any further. "So how many kilometers to Mumbai Central?"

"Twenty-seven kilometers," one of them said convincingly.

Grant you, I am one of the world's worst navigators, but after three years on the road I could assess the exact speed that I walked at every varying pace. Multiply it by the near five hours I had been on the road, minus lunch—and the nap—and unless my watch-sun skill had failed me and I'd been heading north all day, I couldn't have been more than five kilometers away from the Hotel Shalimar, my goal for the day.

As instructed, I turned left out of the hotel, walked for "a few minutes," went "half-left" to the "top of the road" to "carry on" for "a while" to "the other side."

"The other side of what?"

"Just carry on."

I asked a nicely dressed business man, "Which way to the Hotel Shalimar?"

He gave me a sweep of the arm that encompassed at least two roundabouts and seven interchanges.

"That way?" I pointed to a specific street, hoping he would return with a point just as specific. I got the 180 degree sweep again.

You would think now that I had a map I would be well on my way. After all, with the aid of a good map I am a directional whiz able to tackle short cuts across backyard gardens, over fences, and down back allies. But in order to find out where you're going you need to know where you are, and on top of the fact that no one could tell me that, there was the added challenge of having no street signs in all of greater Mumbai.

I asked a storeowner, "Do you know where the Hotel Shalimar is?"

"Not here," he replied. Not particularly helpful, but I found his honesty oddly refreshing.

I feared I was wandering in circles, and it occurred to me that perhaps that man was right when he said I had twenty-seven kilometers to go.

At a mega-tiered-hexagonal-fly-over-intersection, a young man speaking flawless English saw me struggling with my map and asked if he could help. "Yes, thank you," I said letting out a breath of exhaustion I didn't know I was holding. "I'm trying to get to the Hotel Shalimar. Could you tell me where I am on this map?"

He took the map, flipped it around, upside down and said that perhaps we could do this better over lunch and a bottle of wine at his place, "I live right around the corner. Afterwards I'll drive you over to the hotel. I've got a brand new motorcycle. It's red."

As tempting as the offer was to polish off a bottle of wine and race through the streets of Mumbai on a red motorcycle, I needed to find the Hotel Shalimar before sundown, and had to turn down his offer. "Could you tell me which way I'm supposed to go?"

"Go down this street and carry on," he pointed.

Wait! Not a sweep of the arm, but rather a point of the finger? Perhaps I've been too hasty about this man! Maybe I could enjoy a lunch, a red motorcycle ride, and revel in an afternoon of proper directions. But I had to "carry on," "down the road," "for a few minutes," "over the top," "to the other side," and like the final two minutes of a basketball game, my last five kilometers went on for hours.

It finally came to an end when I discovered a Baskin Robbins and decided to take a break with a double scoop. A nice young man overheard me asking for directions and offered to walk me there. He was heading that way himself. "But it's quite far," he warned. "About a kilometer. And there's a hill. Can you walk up hills?"

"Yes, I think I can handle that hill just fine."

As we walked my last kilometer he regularly turned around to ask if I was okay, if I wanted to rest. I didn't bother telling him that I had just walked 2,021 kilometers from Kolkata, not to mention the now 12,470 kilometers from Colorado. "Do you want to catch a taxi? I'll hail you a taxi if you can't go any further."

We rounded a corner and there it was, the elusive Hotel Shalimar! I could feel a smile spread out across my face as the day's exhaustion lifted. The nice young man who led me there had no idea the magnitude of this particular kilometer, the last kilometer of a two-thousand kilometer stretch that would undoubtedly affect me the rest of my life in ways I might not even recognize. The toughest leg of this GlobalWalk was, at this very moment, behind me. I had made it across India. In a few more days I would officially walk to the Arabian Sea three kilometers away, but I would be led by the Lions Clubs of Mumbai, omitting any need for maps, watches, and for that matter, the sun. My Good Samaritan, noticing my delirium, asked again if I was okay and suggested that I go rest now after that tough kilometer up the hill.

But there would be no resting. Not yet. I had plans to meet the folks from the American Embassy for a celebratory beer. When I called for directions they said, "We're really close, just up the hill. But we'll come and get you, we'd hate for you to get lost."

In an effort to de-stress and revive whatever spirit I had left, I had gone to great lengths to hibernate inside my hotel room. The Hotel

Shalimar had Internet, hot shower, and cable TV. I was happy there and couldn't think of a single reason to leave the womb. But every once in a while I felt a twinge of guilt that I was in an international city and all I really knew about it was that Oprah came on twice daily at 6:30 and 10.

Just that morning, while eavesdropping on a conversation between two strangers at the free breakfast buffet, I heard a South African man telling an Australian woman how much he loved India. He repeated his words with emphasis, "…just *love* it!"

I wanted to love India, but maybe it was expecting too much to start in Kolkata and walk alone as a woman and expect to fall in love with this country. But Mumbai was their most Western city, so maybe I could start all over. That was it …I'd start fresh. So it was with the South African man's words ringing in my ears that I left the womb and went out to fall in love with Mumbai.

The nice doorman opened the door for me with a smile and wished me a good morning. "Why, thank you," I said, smiling.

I walked down the three stairs into the parking lot when suddenly a car came screaming out of nowhere—taking no notice of the other two-thousand square meters of empty space—and charged straight at me! A two-ton rocket of steel hurtling at me so fast I barely had time to mutter, "What the—?"

The side of the car skimmed me, sending me whirling into a heap on the ground, so close to becoming road kill that I found myself looking down at my toes to see if they were still attached. The tear in my pants exposed a bloody gash in my knee. I glanced over at the nice doorman, hoping he might send some much needed sympathy my way. He smiled and told me again to have a nice morning.

I brushed myself off and limped out to the street to hail a taxi to the Leopold Cafe in the Colaba neighborhood. It reportedly had great food, a Baskin Robbins around the corner, craft markets up the block and a movie theater nearby. It would be a nice easy day full of good food, ice cream, shopping, and Russell Crowe. If a girl can't find love in that day then she's just not trying!

The driver stopped at the cafe and told me it would be 120 rupees. I told him the meter says fifty-three rupees, "so I will pay you fifty-three rupees." He said no, for me there was a hotel tax and the price was 120 rupees.

"Hotel tax?"

"Yes. I pick you up outside hotel, so you pay hotel tax."

Aware that there was no hotel tax and I had gotten caught in an all-too-typical case of merchant seeing foreigner and jacking up the price, I stuck to my guns. Then I remembered all I had were the bigger notes of a hundred rupees and had to admit I was on the losing end of this rip off. I had no choice but to give him my hundred-rupee note.

I walked into the famed Leopold Cafe and settled on some south Indian food that I had become quite fond of. "I'll have an order of iddly, please, with chutney sauce."

"We're out of iddly."

"Out of iddly?"

"Yes, we're out of rice." Iddly is a sticky rice dish.

I accepted defeat and ordered a bowl of chicken byani even though I had no idea what that was.

"We don't have that."

"No chicken byani?"

"It has rice. We're out of rice."

"How about a cappuccino?"

"We're out of cappuccino."

I asked him if there was a south Indian restaurant in the neighborhood. He pointed me to one just around the corner.

A nice man greeted me at the door, handed me a menu, and sat me down in front of the window for some class-A people watching down one of Mumbai's main thoroughfares. Things were looking up. "What can I get you today?" he asked.

"I would love some iddly, please."

"We only serve iddly after eight o'clock tonight."

"Okay, how about some masala dosa?"

"We only serve masala dosa after eight o'clock tonight."

I changed my approach. "Let's do it this way," I suggested. "Why don't you tell me what food you have available?"

"We don't serve food now," he said. "We open at eight o'clock tonight."

I nearly opened my mouth to ask some obvious questions, most notably, why am I sitting here with a menu? And why are you standing over me with a pad and pen waiting for my order? But I couldn't think of one single answer that would help me begin to understand.

After I stared into space for a short time gathering my thoughts I decided to forego the hunt for a good iddly and go straight for Baskin Robbins. Surely they couldn't be out of ice cream.

And no they weren't! I looked through the glass case drooling, and after a great many taste tests I settled on a double scoop of mint chocolate chip double fudge chunky nut. Maybe some ice cream and a double scoop of Russell Crowe could save the day.

I walked out the door of Baskin Robbins with renewed vigor. Heading for the theater a block away around a blind corner, I found myself accosted by a family of beggars. The mother blocked my path to the front with her hand out, and the seven year old was on my left chanting, "Give it up. Give it up." It was when the three-year old tugged at my right arm so hard that it sent my double scoop lurching to its death that my love affair with Mumbai went into a nosedive. I didn't know if even Russell Crowe could save me now.

Unfortunately, I was spot on. A trip to the movies was merely the final plunge into the abyss of hassles.

I stood in line at one ticket booth only to find that it was the exclusive booth to the Bollywood film, *Lagon*, even though there was no sign saying that. So I went to stand in the next line and they said yes, this was the correct line for *A Beautiful Mind*, but we only sell the floor seats here. That line over there is for the balcony seats. I stood in the third line and splurged a buck fifty on a balcony seat, but that propelled me into a whole new set of challenges. When I asked for directions to the balcony seats, I got that vague sweep of the arm that covers 180 degrees, topped with an even vaguer "over there." After a series of wrong turns that included the popcorn storage, the men's loo, and very nearly a chicken coop on the wrong side of the exit, I ended up on the third floor of a thousand-seat movie cinema. Even though I had assigned seating, I found the balcony empty, so I took a seat front and center. I settled down to enjoy my popcorn, only to find that they put butterscotch sugar on it because there is a national obsession with butterscotch. I sighed and left it in the seat next to me.

Thirty minutes into the movie, the only other two people on the entire planet to buy balcony seats poked me on the shoulder and said, "Excuse us, you're sitting in our seats." The teenage usher, relishing the power bestowed upon him wearing a uniform with stripes and tassels, stirred his flashlight around the seat numbers and faces, "May I see your ticket, please," and confirmed I was indeed in the wrong seat. "Your seat, in fact, is right behind them, so could you please move and sit where God intended." The upshot was that now I didn't feel guilty when I put my feet up on the back of their seats.

I am happy to report that the taxi driver on the way home did not rip me off and was unaware of any hotel tax. I was so excited at his ease and honesty that I rounded out the fifty-three rupee fee with a hundred (from one dollar up to two).

But the day was not over. I was hungry. (Let's recap: no iddly, no chicken byani, no masala dosa, no double scoop mint chocolate chip double fudge chunky nut, no popcorn, and, categorically, no butterscotch.)

Not wanting to go out and fight the elements any longer, I asked the hotel reception if they could give me the number of any restaurant that delivered. They apologized but said they do not allow any outside food onto the premises.

Feeling defeated entirely, and with my eye twitching furiously, I lugged myself up the three flights of stairs. Admittedly I'd never be cool enough to love India. I crawled into bed and threw the covers over me as though they could protect me from the world, and turned on Oprah. Today's topic was just for me: "Has your spirit taken a beating? Spiritual makeovers, next on Oprah."

I didn't feel that I had handled the India segment with any measure of grace. I wished I could've had more patience or more fortitude to be one of those pros who are able to immerse themselves into such a foreign culture, to have fun, go with the flow. I knew that well after the rawness of this experience healed, I'd be asking myself tough questions: Why couldn't I accept this culture? When people ask, "How did you like India?" how would I answer? "Oh, it's different!" followed by a light laugh. It's tricky, in fact, to explain to people who haven't been there; you have to be there to wrap yourself around all the idiosyncrasies and the contradictions, to feel the onslaught on all your senses.

So who are those people who say "I just love India!" Are they just more developed than I am? Perhaps they were there for a week staying at nice hotels with a tour guide to help them every step of the way? Using the word "love" after a one-week stint in India on a tour bus is like using that same word after a lusty one-night stand—and we all know how silly that would be!

I often wonder how other women would have handled this journey. If a hundred women were to walk alone from Kolkata to Mumbai, how would my tolerance have measured among them: Bottom of the barrel? Or lone survivor?

One lesson among many that I learned while walking across India came one morning when a young man ran after me to hand me a note. He had heard I was in his village and stayed up all night writing me a message with the help of a friend who knew some English. He wanted desperately to come to America and asked if I could help. He asked for sponsorship programs, even agreeing to be smuggled in. He just wanted an opportunity that he would never have in his small village. It broke my heart to have to say there was nothing I could do for him when all he wanted was a chance to work hard. In India—and in other countries around the world—the class system means if you're born in the gutter, that's where you stay. You don't hear many great rags to riches stories in those societies.

"The land of opportunity" is only a catchphrase until you see those around the world who aspire to bigger things and simply aren't afforded a chance. I'll never take that for granted again.

I can thank India for that.

> Ravi,
> I want to confirm that you got my message about shipping my trolley, Bob, on to Turkey via my DHL account.
>
> Because of the war in Afghanistan, both Pakistan and Iran aren't allowing any Americans in, so I'm flying onward to Turkey in just four days and haven't received Bob yet.
>
> To reiterate, if you just call DHL, they'll come and pick it up from your house. The good news is that there's a DHL office very close to your home!
>
> Thank you. Polly

CHAPTER 15

A Turkish Delight

One look in the mirror and I knew I needed a break. After a daunting three months crawling through India my clothes were ragged, my nerves were frazzled, my face was hollowed. The reflection warranted surrendering all rights to be offended if anyone were to call me ugly. I warned the Lions in Istanbul (that I needed rest, that is, not that I was ugly).

Five members of the Yesulyurt Lions Club met me at Istanbul's International Airport, and disheveled as I appeared, I was excited to get into this new country I knew little about. A man named Timur was the chosen one, the Lion appointed to Polly duty. He was tall, thick, handsome man with a full head of silver hair. His warm greeting and easy manner at the airport immediately put me at ease.

Dad had sent my Turkey guidebook ahead to Istanbul, so I was arriving blind to everything about this new country. My introduction to the city was the ride from the airport, which put me into nearly as much culture shock as the night I arrived into Kolkata. Lush green landscaping lined the roadside with flowers bursting in reds and purples. Traffic flowed smoothly on the right with designated traffic lanes and stoplights. Commuter traffic buzzed along at a hum—not a honk, not a beep, not a tootle. There was no one peeing in the road, not a single cow dozing in the intersection. Everything you want in a country.

Driving by it looked like a sunny, vibrant city with young people laughing in sidewalk cafes over tea or a spirited game of backgammon. I knew I was in for a surprise as most people are who don't know anything about Turkey other than Alexander the Great and Midnight Express.

Turkey is a country just slightly larger than Texas, and its unique geography—nestled between the Middle East, Europe, Central Europe, and Africa—leaves the Turkish people quick to refute the old cliché about their culture as a society of sultans and harems swinging from carpets. On the contrary, they are a modern, secular, Western-oriented society.

On the drive from the airport Timur told me that only five years ago wearing shorts or tee shirts was frowned upon. Today in Istanbul you'll find women dressed in the latest European fashions sharing a tea with their girlfriends in traditional Muslim headscarves talking about their careers in medicine and law.

Watching this bustling urban landscape was like being in the front row seat of a revolution, and no doubt Kemal Ataturk would be smiling if he were walking through Istanbul today.

Kemal Ataturk is the national hero and virtually synonymous with the Turkish Republic. His face is on every lire bill, every stamp, every coin. He is their hero. Now mine too.

Here's a man who almost single handedly remade Turkish society and is the subject of umpteen books, but as gleaned from my guidebook I'll try to wrap up his biography in a nutshell.

While Turkey teetered on the brink of collapse during the War of Independence (1919-22), a young general named Mustafa Kemal broke through the ranks. He reorganized the armies, focused the soldiers, and like a superhero of blockbuster proportions, saved the day sending the Greeks home with their tails dragging behind them. Mustafa Kemal then led Turkey into becoming a democratic republic by drafting a constitution, Westernizing legal codes, and removing Islam as the state religion; he gave women the right to vote and hold seats in Parliament.

His next step in modernizing the society was asking all Turks to choose a family name. At the time Muslims had only one given name, so he himself was proclaimed Ataturk, or "Father Turk" by the Turkish parliament, and he became Kemal Ataturk.

Among other radical changes, Ataturk engineered the adoption of the Latin alphabet for school curriculum instead of the traditional

Arabic alphabet, recognizing that it took a fraction of the time to learn. Today the country claims a ninety-eight percent literacy rate. What a guy.

He then adopted the alphabet of the West but dumped the "X," the "W," and the "Q," and for this reason alone, he is my personal hero. Although I've never had any personal vendettas against the "W" I have often wondered why we have the letter "X" when half the time it's pronounced like a "Z" and the other half you could easily substitute with an "eks." Example: eksample. And who decided the "Q" could never stand on its own?

The new Turkish government then added a few new letters; among others, they turned our "ch" sound into one letter, and our "sh" sound is an "s" with a loop on the bottom, for an alphabet total of twenty-nine.

The handful of alphabet changes were a drama for us tourists sitting in the internet café because the "ch" letter was where the period normally is on a computer keyboard, and the "sh" was where the "x" usually sits, sending us all into a tizzy of typos.

Who couldn't love a country that boasted three hundred days of sunshine a year, had a love for board games and a government with the guts to ditch its Xs and Qs? I loved Turkey already.

Friends and family were emailing frantic suggestions that with the war in Afghanistan and impending rumble between Iraq and the U.S., I should keep a low profile and not advertise that I'm American. "Turkey is a predominately Muslim country," they'd say. "You probably won't be able to talk about breast cancer openly and freely. Watch yourself, and make a beeline for Europe if you feel threatened."

Nothing could have been further from the truth. As had happened so many times on the road, my timing proved perfect. Just a year earlier in Ankara, Turkey's capital, a prominent doctor lost his wife to breast cancer, which launched him into a rigorous awareness crusade throughout the country. His campaign encouraged men to start talking about breast cancer. He recognized that

Muslim men speaking openly about breast cancer would encourage women to feel comfortable consulting a doctor with the earliest symptoms. By the time I arrived the press, men, and women hungered for information.

There was no breast cancer foundation in Turkey, so the Lions' members in Istanbul teamed with doctors and created a brochure detailing facts and myths of breast cancer and its early symptoms. The brochures were then forwarded to Lions Clubs along my route, where they would be ready to distribute as I walked into their respective towns.

Timur was Chief of the new Hizmet Hospital, which sits on the western edge of Istanbul. His commanding presence makes people stand a little taller and turn on their best behavior when they pass him in the hall. The facility, a one-hundred bed private general hospital specializing in organ transplants and dialysis, was built almost entirely by the efforts of the Istanbul Lions Clubs, an extraordinary feat that made me proud to be involved with the Lions.

Timur arranged for me to stay in one of the hospital rooms through my entire month of R & R—a sparkling clean private room with air conditioning, private bath and the upgraded eastern view of the Burger King across the street. A TV hung high in the corner with access to the BBC and CNN. As if that wasn't perfect enough, they offered three meals a day catered right to my room from the hospital cafeteria.

When I got myself settled in Room 306, Timur came by to ask if everything was okay. I almost purred at all the luxury.

"You're welcome to stay as long as you want. You look like you need a rest. Is there anything else we can get you?"

"Would you happen to have a box of tissues? It seems I have a bit of a sniffle. Probably something I caught on the plane from Mumbai."

Timur snapped his fingers, and in hardly a beat three nurses and a doctor rushed to my door where they surrounded me like an emergency room on full alert.

"Pulse!" One nurse checked my pulse, another was wrapping my arm for blood pressure, and a crowd started to form in the hall ogling at the poor girl who looked so bad she obviously had a critical case of some dreadful disease.

"Say ahhhhhh."

"Really, it's just a little sniff—"

A stick was down my throat, and something of a sharp poking nature penetrated my ears. A third nurse appeared and wedged a thermometer under my armpit. "Sit still, five minutes. Relax. Don't move. Don't worry about a thing. You're in good hands."

In five minutes the doctor rolled up his sleeves and prepared to deliver the grim news. He was clear and precise with his delivery. "I want you to take this drink. I want you to mix it with hot water. It must be hot. Do you understand? I want you to take it three times a day, morning, noon and night, for five days. Don't miss a dose." He scribbled out the prescription and handed it off to the nurse who shot out the door.

Diagnosis: A sniffle.

Prognosis: Good.

Prescription: Tylenol Hot Lemon Drink.

The next morning the nurse came into my room at 7:00 a.m., propped me up, and watched over me like the sniffle police while I downed my Tylenol Hot Lemon Drink. She wiped my face, held the tissue over my nose and urged me to blow. "You have visitor."

Oya, Timur's energetic twenty-something assistant, entered the room and explained in perfect English that she had been assigned to Polly duty—evidently her punishment for knowing my language. Timur directed her to spend the day with me and help orient me to this new culture. "We will have fun. Up! Up! I will meet you in five minutes; we have a lot of work to do."

Oya drove me around the city explaining every facet a tourist should know about Istanbul, from which coin to use on the train to how many zeroes a lira has on the bill. "Right now it's easy to be a millionaire in Turkey because one U.S. Dollar equals 1,650,000 Turkish Lire."

"Does Turkey have a version of 'Who Wants to Be a Millionaire'?"

"Yes, but it is called, 'Who Wants 500-Billion Lire?'"

"Not quite as catchy."

"No. There is talk about changing our currency and dropping six zeros, but until then budget a million lire for a bottle of water and four million for a Big Mac." She laughed and lowered her voice. "Down at the Blue Mosque you can always spot the tourists; they're the ones counting all the zeroes hoping to avoid parting with a ten-million versus the one-million."

She explained that Istanbul is the only city in the world that straddles two continents. Three percent of Turkey is in Europe, and the rest lies in Asia; the Bosphorus Straits divides the two. We found an outdoor cafe overlooking the Bosphorus where Oya took the honors of ordering. She ordered a hot tea she called a cay (pronounced chai) and a snack called gozleme—best described as Turkey's version of a quesadilla, with a classier cheese and flakier tortilla. While enjoying the view, I peppered her with the top ten questions I ask to familiarize myself with any new culture.

Can I wear shorts and tee shirts? (Yes)

Can I drink the water? (It's okay to brush your teeth with it, but you're better off buying bottled water for drinking.)

Are there plenty of ATM machines? (Yes.)

Is English an option on the ATM directions? (Not always. You'd better learn the words "continue," "withdrawal," and "cancel" in Turkish.)

Is tipping the norm? (It's not expected until they learn you're American.)

Are there any English newspapers? (Only in major towns.)

What is the national emergency phone number? (155)

What are the basic salutations? "hello," "good-bye" and "thank you?" ("teshakur edirum," which would take some work.)

For four weeks in Istanbul I perfected the art of relaxation. Each morning at 7:00 a.m. the nurse entered my room, propped up my bed, swung breakfast around on the swivel tray, and my day started the same as every Turkish family: cucumber, feta cheese, tomato, bread and olives. Then I ventured off to explore a new neighborhood, sometimes braving trains and buses, but primarily walking the nine miles into the core of the city to keep my waistline in check after taste testing Turkey's food.

Sometimes I would pop into a cafe and boldly point to a menu item without a clue as to what might land on my table. On occasion the mystery meal was a bust, like the day I ended up with a plate of Albanian liver. But other times I scored, like the time my mystery meal was so good I cried—actually cried. Problem was, I then walked out the door, down the block, and was lost in the maze of the city before I realized I had no idea what I'd ordered. I never found the cafe again.

I also discovered pidé—Turkish pizza—and decided that if I were ever sentenced to Death Row, the Turkish pidé would be my request as a last meal. It's not the round dough with mozzarella like the pizza of the West, but rather a thin flat bread shaped like a canoe and topped with meats, vegetables, caraway seeds and egg, then cooked in a fire oven. The fifteen pounds I lost crossing India were quickly reassembling themselves on my butt, with pleasure.

Ravi-
I have not heard from you and I still have not received my trolley Bob. I start walking in just a few days and I cannot leave without him. Could you PLEASE send Bob as soon as possible? Again, all shipping information is below.

To reiterate, this shipping charge goes onto my DHL account number, so will not cost you anything if that happens to be why it is being held up. DHL will come to pick it up at your house. You just have to call them for pick up. If there is a problem I am not aware of, please tell me.

Thank you for your prompt assistance.
Polly

Four weeks of relaxation and mystery meals provided the quintessential vacation, but my nerves had still not entirely recovered. (Mom thought it was posttraumatic stress from my months crossing India, but I wasn't prepared to compare my experience with, say, our soldiers in Afghanistan.) As fabulous as Turkey was, it wasn't perfect. For example, I could never let my guard down, particularly when it came to unwelcome behavior from men: the hissing, hassling, harassing toward a woman alone.

Petty crime, too, was something tourists were cautioned about throughout the Sultanahmet area, where signs warned of pickpockets and taxi drivers who overcharged those who didn't know the difference between a one million and a ten million lire note. Sultanahmet, the part of town where tourists flock to visit Istanbul's prized Aya Sophia and Blue Mosque, is inundated with touters who stand outside restaurants and shops wrangling in such subtle and masterful ways that you're almost impressed. They might dress in a navy uniform and say, "You're back!" or "Remember me?" Then you say, gee, I don't remem—and next thing you know you're in the store asking for Mustafa's brother for a *very, very good deal on carpet* and your eye is twitching.

After four weeks I was itching to hit the road again, but poor Bob was still holed up behind a couch in Kolkata. Why was Ravi not answering my emails? Why wasn't he shipping Bob? Is it the shipping version of The Hearing Deficit? How could I possibly walk through Turkey without him?

There was no choice but to resort to what I'd become so good at: Begging.

> To Rex Moser
> American Center
> Kolkata, India
>
> Hello Rex,
> I finished India and have since been in Turkey as a tourist,
> fattening up and resting. I feel strong and ready to go again,

CHAPTER 15 – A TURKISH DELIGHT

but I have a problem that I thought I'd run by you to see if you could help.

Normally I travel with my custom-made three-wheeled trolley that I affectionately call Bob. It's how I carry all my gear as I travel along the road. The Lions in Kolkata told me I had no need for Bob in India and that they would take care of me from town to town, urging me to leave him in Kolkata. So I did. They said they would ship him to Mumbai to meet me there. They didn't. I have now sent five emails to my Lions contact, Ravi Pagrawal, and have had no response.

DHL Shipping is a sponsor of GlobalWalk so all charges are covered; it is simply a matter of making a phone call to DHL, who will pick it up. At this point I am preparing to start walking again, but have no Bob to carry my gear.

I am fully aware that this is not your jurisdiction, but at this point I am sort of at my wits end and turning to you for help. I was thinking of a couple of plans:
(a) Could you call Ravi and push him along. Or (and more efficient)
(b) Could you or one of your staff call DHL and go to Ravi's apartment and wait there until DHL comes to pick up the package. (DHL is usually pretty quick and ironically are only 300 meters from Ravi's apartment.)

For the record I am conscious of the fact that American Centers probably have rules about dealing with packages these days so will understand if you can't help me, but as you can appreciate, at this point I have to at least ask.

Thank you for hearing me out,
Polly Letofsky
GlobalWalk for Breast Cancer

Then I boldly turned to Timur and explained my situation. "Would there be any possible way that Lions could transfer my duffle bag from town to town until Bob arrives?"

He agreed to do whatever was necessary to help me get through Turkey, but was terribly sorry he wouldn't meet Bob.

Plan B was set. I was eager to get on the road again, raring to discover Turkey on foot in this most intimate way to explore.

Timur helped me arrange a route down the Aegean Coast from Istanbul to Bodrum and contacted Clubs along the way to ask if they wanted to get involved. The response was enthusiastic. They would be waiting.

It was kick-off day. Timur had rallied a couple dozen Lions to walk across Istanbul, handing out stacks of breast cancer brochures to any woman in our path. We started on the Asian side of the city and crossed the Bosphorus into Europe. They were a lively enthusiastic group, and we whiled away the twelve kilometers chatting and meeting women of every background. It felt familiar. The walking again, the talking, the breast cancer work, the press misquoting me, just like coming home after being at camp for four weeks.

The next day I rode the boat across the Marmaris Strait back into Asia where from the deck I spotted the local Lions of Bandirma waving welcome signs over their heads. I bolted from the crowd to run to them. A man named Ayden, the only one who knew English, greeted me and made me feel comfortable. I clung to him the rest of the morning. A fit, handsome man in his mid-thirties who had never set foot outside of Turkey but spoke flawless English with an American accent. He reviewed my wants and needs for walking from Bandirma to Aksakal, his sixty-kilometer Polly duty zone.

At a nearby hotel, brunch with the group and the local reporter was organized for my arrival. We ate and visited for two hours before the group escorted me to the foot of the road to carry on. Ayden offered to follow behind me in his car, but I assured him I felt perfectly comfortable walking alone. When I showed them the pepper spray hanging off my hip everyone laughed and applauded and waved me down the 36 Road like an old friend. My spirits were soaring again.

The weather was a perfect seventy degrees, warm enough for a long-sleeved shirt, cool enough for a long-sleeved shirt. I put Van Morrison in my ears and basked in my first day walking alone in Turkey. Not a lot went on down these rural side roads—to the untrained eye that is. Muslim women worked hard on the farms picking zucchini and carrots and gathering them into their aprons. When they hit the end of a row they'd dump out their aprons and start down a new row. Once in a while one of them would see me and stop just long enough for a look and a wonder, then lean over and get right back to picking.

If I waved first they'd smile and wave, but they were too shy to wave first. I wondered where all the men were and why they weren't working on the farm bent over zucchini and carrots. A lot of them sat outside the cafes, drinking tea and playing backgammon, but maybe it wasn't what it looked like. I made a note to ask Ayden about the men in the cafes and the women in the fields.

Fruit trees with little white apple-shaped fruit hanging low lined the roads. Part of me wanted to pluck one right off the tree and take a bite, but another part of me remembered watching the Discovery Channel about people who eat strange things in the forest and drop dead. I made a note to ask Ayden what I could eat right off the tree.

Four hours up the road a man appeared out of the bushes. Standing on the side of the road straight ahead of me he yelled into the air about God knows what. I crossed the highway and kept walking in his direction, pepper spray at the ready.

The strange man started yelling in my direction, and while that didn't mean he was talking to me, I shouted that I was sorry but I didn't speak Turkish. Then he moved to my side of the road putting him right behind me, walking, ranting, waving a stick over his head. I walked faster and faster. He walked faster and faster. It started to rain. I started to run. He started to run. It rained harder. I ran faster. He ran faster. I spotted a cafe ahead.

The skies burst open and came crashing down just as I swooped through the front door. I don't know who was more stunned, me for stumbling across an open roadside cafe at my moment of need or the cafe patrons who were playing backgammon and nibbling on gozleme when a foreign girl came bounding in. I paused for a brief moment debating about whether to continue while dripping wet, when the owners leapt up to greet me. Without hesitation they launched into action, taking care of me like a wet puppy, prattling away in Turkish, not pausing for an instant to realize I didn't understand a word. They led me to a seat, got me a dry shirt, a hot cay and a gozleme. All I could say in return was an over abundance of "teshakur edirum." (Thank you.)

I retrieved my Turkish phrase book to look up "crazy" and "man." I pointed outside and down the road, and all the patrons rushed to my side of the cafe to look out the window at the crazy man. After a spirited interchange amongst them, they gave me the international motions for "Don't worry about the crazy man—he's harmless." But I did worry and thought it best to sit inside this cafe with my protectors until he was well into another county.

I stayed put in the little café enjoying broken conversation and laughs as the little old men pounded me at backgammon and taught me how to count to ten in Turkish. The party really got underway when every time I learned to pronounce a new item on the menu, the owners brought out samples unveiling a Turkish feast.

Then Ayden called.

"Hi, Ayden…you guys, stop laughing, okay, sure, one more game…How are you, Ayden?"

"Er—I've been worried about you out there in this rain storm, and I was wondering if you'd like an early pick up?"

"An early pick up would be great…come on, guys, put me down…okay, sure, I'll have another helping of pilaki…Ayden, take your time, no hurry…"

"Oh—okay…"

Polly,
We'd be happy to follow up and help you and Bob get back together. Please send us Ravi's contact information and DHL's and stand by.

Rex Moser
Public Affairs Officer & Director
The American Center
Kolkata, India

With a renewed hop in my step I toddled along through the tiny villages of Aksakal, Gobel, Malaclar, toward Ayvalik on the Aegean Coast. Every afternoon a local Lions member would meet me on the road and lead me to a Guesthouse that had donated a room where my duffle bag awaited me. If no one in the local Lions Club spoke English they would recruit someone in town who did and assign them to Polly duty. There were newspaper interviews, dinner parties, and always a group to share breakfast and wave goodbye in the morning. The Jandarma (police) en route were alerted that I was on their roads and kept an overprotective eye on me. As in Thailand I had no idea how they heard about me; they just magically appeared every morning when I started walking. Sometimes they would drive by every half hour with a wave and a "Merhaba" (hello). Sometimes they'd stop to take photos or invite me into a café for cay and backgammon. Other times they followed behind me at three mph just like Shankar and Prayoon.

Dawdling through ancient towns with cobblestone streets taking photos of the villagers with sunny faces and curious eyes became the daily routine. I dreamt of this exact scenario when I started planning this GlobalWalk. I would talk to villagers with sign language and play snappy games of backgammon with old men. I would fill up on local delicacies with farmers who invited me in for cay and choppy conversation. Big farm families would walk me up to the road to wave goodbye then race back to call the neighbors and forewarn them that I was on the way, so by all means start brewing a pot of cay, invite her in for cay, she loves the cay.

In Turkey I could hardly take three steps down any street without another offer of cay. It's not just a tea, but a national drink. The call of cay is a call of friendship between the Turkish people and their guests and with rare exception is served in a tulip glass. It's not unusual at all to see people walking down the street with an entire tray of cay. You could not possibly accept all the offers. One day, just for kicks, I counted how many times I was offered a cay: twelve. Ten came from complete strangers, two from the Jandarma, and only one in a venue in which I would envision sitting with a cup of tea, i.e., a cafe. The others were a petrol station, a carpet-cleaning warehouse, a strawberry farm, a cherry stand, and a family on the way to Ayvalik with a portable stove for those emergency cay opportunities.

The constant warmth I experienced in Turkey was a far cry from the report about Americans traveling here during this sensitive time in the world. In fact, it seemed as though people got a downright kick out of having an American around. It was such a novelty for them in the rural regions. School kids gathered around me in parks to say "Hello" and "How are you?" and count to ten in English to show me they could. When I said hello in Turkish they burst into giggles and fell all over each other.

In a small village a local man yelled into the air, "She's from America!" and the people of the village swarmed. The children came running, too, but were shy and curious, hiding behind Mama's leg while checking out the strange girl in the big hat who talked funny. The men called a time out from their backgammon game, grabbed their cay and made their way over. Elderly Muslim women in headscarves ran off the farm carrying arms full of fresh carrots and cucumbers for the stranger.

I was a novelty, a new toy, a wind-up doll that spoke on command. "She can speak Turkish, too!"

The ringleader told me to say hello in Turkish, so I turned to the crowd and said, "Merhaba." The entire village erupted into cheers and I felt like a rock star.

They chanted, "More! More!" So I loosened up and gave them my best, "Nasilsiniz." (How are you?) They erupted into cheers, arms waving and cay flowing. Mothers pushed their children toward the house to get Uncle Mustafa and Auntie Gulsa. "Tell them to hurry, hurry, they can't miss the American girl who can say 'Hello, how are you?' in Turkish! And by all means start boiling a pot of cay!"

CHAPTER 16

Mysteries Yet to be solved

> Mom,
>
> Turkey is just fabulous. I'm almost to the Aegean Coast where it will be a bit more touristy than the rural areas, but that has its charms. The upshot is that more people will speak English, so I can have a longer conversation than ordering a gozleme for lunch or asking for a game of backgammon. Turkey is particularly nice because there are loads of stops along the roads, fruit stands conveniently staggered every couple of kilometers, and, of course, millions of olive stands. (I would never hint at the fact that I hate olives. That might be grounds for immediate deportation.)
>
> The hop is back in my step and the twitchy eye is down 50%. xP—

The Lions in Balikesir met me for breakfast—cucumbers, feta, bread and olives, of course—and said they found someone who speaks English to walk with me for the next few days.

I'm afraid I sighed involuntarily. Walking with people through the towns and cities is something I looked forward to, but after the Forrest Gump scene through Malaysia where thirty, forty, eighty people were plodded along with me every single day, I generally put the kibosh on people joining me all day every day. It's about constantly being on, relentlessly entertaining, answering the same questions, having the same conversations.

So Serhat was an exceptional surprise. There were questions all right, but not the standard "How many pairs of shoes? Where have you been? Where are you going? What made you—?" He was entirely uninhibited about answering questions about the life of a young twenty-something Muslim male in today's world.

Serhat, a twenty-two-year-old with boyish charm, possessed Hollywood good looks but didn't know it. He had impeccable manners, a head full of thick black hair, and the body of an athlete—more specifically, a rock climber. Rock climbing was his passion. Serhat and his friends had already climbed every rock in Turkey and recently made a tough trip over the border into Iran to climb mountains there. "But you have to be careful about the gear you use in Iran because they won't let anything American-made over the border. Of course," he added, "all the best rock climbing gear is from America. My fantasy of all fantasies is to climb in Yosemite National Park—El Capitan. Ohh, before I die I must climb El Capitan."

He'd studied English since he was a tyke, not because he had to, but because he felt he could get further in life if he knew English. He was a mathematics teacher, "Not 'math' like in America." Serhat said he'd have to stop teaching in a few months while completing his eighteen-month military service, mandatory for all Turkish men. "But I will figure out a way to get out early because, hey, there's no rock climbing in the army."

He had a bubbling energy that reminded me of a puppy romping in a park. I watched, feeling like an old lady, as he ran to leap over a fence, pick some fruit off a tree, then leap back over to hand it to me. He knew everything about every fruit tree we passed, told me what to eat, what not to eat, and chewed bark right off a tree because he could. He ran ahead to read signs and ran down side roads to try to find a riper piece of fruit. At the end of a day's walk, he was a like the Labrador that goes hiking and does three times the mileage.

I asked him what it was like to be a Muslim man in Turkey these days.

"Me and my friends are not good Muslims," he said with a laugh. "We don't really care about religion."

"Do you pray five times a day?"

"No."

"Do you ever pray?"

"No."

"Do you date?"

"Yes."

"What age do kids start dating in Turkey?"

"Fourteen or fifteen, but at that age they just go to movies together and sit up straight with no hands fiddling around anywhere."

I said that according to my book *Turkey Statistics*, sixty-eight percent of Turks are still married through arranged marriages.

Without a hint of hesitation he said, "How old is that book?"

"It was published in 1998."

He said arranged marriages in Turkey meant that the family simply introduced the couple, but it was always their own decision to marry. "Don't believe what you read anyway, because this generation in Turkey is changing fast, particularly for women. They're becoming more independent than their parents, and that has put a strain on relations between the generations. Girls today are not only going to college, but they are leaving home to do it. They are living on their own with roommates in dorms and apartments. They're becoming more educated, studying subjects that weren't available to their mothers just a generation ago. They're dating, too, and not necessarily dating to marry. They might date one man for a few months, or a year, and be done with it, sort of a tamer, more Muslim version of the American sixties. Their mothers sit home in a village far away and slap their foreheads wondering what they did wrong."

Serhat also knew everything about American basketball, every NBA player and statistic. He told me a lot of men in Turkey know about American basketball because there is a Turkish player on the Sacramento Kings team named Hido Turkoglu, who just made it to the quarterfinal playoffs. "We love the NBA, and it helps me learn my English. It also helps me learn more about America. There sure are a lot of black people that play basketball, aren't there? What do you call the black people of America?"

I said you would call them African-American or black, and that a recent poll found that half of black people (or African-Americans) prefer one, half prefer the other. Some black people are not into the "African-American" title and insist they're just Americans with no hyphen. Others insist on the hyphen.

"But there's another word for the black people of America, what is it?"

I shrugged my shoulders.

"Nigger, isn't that it?"

Whoa, whoa! Whoa! Time out!

I stopped in my tracks. My shoulders stiffened. Even out here on a rural side road in Turkey, I didn't want anyone to use that word. I looked around to see if anyone heard him. "You should never ever say that word. It's a very, *very* bad word."

"I don't understand. I hear it all the time in rap music. Are you sure it's a bad word?"

"Oh, yes, quite."

"No," he argued. "I think you're wrong. Black people call each other ni—"

"No, no, no." I said firmly. "Let me try to explain."

He stopped walking and looked back at me.

I scrambled for an answer. "You know how you could be temporarily mad at your mother and say, 'I hate my mother'?"

"Yes."

"Well, it's understood that while you can say you hate your mother, I could never say I hate your mother, or you would be very upset with me, wouldn't you?"

"Yes."

"It's sort of the same with black Americans. They can call each other…that word, but no one else should. In fact it's sort of an ongoing debate between generations of black people because it is a terribly derogatory term for those who lived through the pre-civil rights era. The post-civil rights generation argues that it's a term of endearment to each other."

He looked at me like I was speaking Chinese. "Just promise me you'll never say that word again."

He looked unconvinced, but agreed, and whether he knew it or not, he just learned a little bit more about America.

For three days Serhat joined me down the D230 Road toward Ayvalik. We walked and talked right through the heavy rains that inexplicably turned into extreme heat, and it didn't seem to bother him a bit. The police drove by on occasion to check in, reporters, too, and because Serhat knew English, they asked him to conduct the interview. With his movie star looks, charm, and composure, he was a natural. All agreed that Serhat just might have a new career ahead of him—as long as TV stations offered rock climbing.

After our third day walking together, I was too far from his hometown for him to keep walking with me. It had been refreshing to have a friend like Serhat, if for even a few days. It made me consider my idea of friendship. I really, *really* value my friends, but I wondered this: If the extent of my friendships for five years was to say "nice to meet you" fifteen times a day, followed by a "please keep in touch" eight hours later, would I get home and be so used to being alone that I'd be incapable of forming any meaningful friendships?

> Polly,
> We went to Ravi's house and retrieved Bob. He is officially shipped and on the way to Istanbul. Please let me know when he arrives.
>
> Best,
>
> Rex
> American Center
> Kolkata, India

The overprotective Jandarma began to follow me nearly every day, all day. Part of me appreciated that they were there for protection, yet another part felt stifled, guilty if I just wanted to take a nap in the park or pluck an apple off a tree.

But one morning they were nowhere in sight. At first I was fine with that, but then realized the alternative was incessant harassment. Truckers hissed and hooted with cattle calls; sometimes they even got out of their trucks and came over to me. I was faced with calling that fine line between wanting to be friendly with a welcoming stranger and realizing that I was in a vulnerable position.

One particular morning there was a man following me—well, see, maybe I shouldn't phrase it like that. He was behind me to be sure, but who knows, the poor guy could've just been walking to the bus stop, and here I was ready to label him a stalker. I had to feel the situation out a little bit before getting hissy, so I crossed to the other side of the road to leave him alone. He crossed over. I crossed back; he crossed back. Now my suspicions were sufficiently raised and I turned to him and yelled from a good twenty yards away. "Durun Orada!" (Stop there!). He stared at me for a moment, then turned around and walked away. If, in fact, he was walking to the bus stop, and I subsequently made him late for work, at the very least he'd have a good story for the boss.

The local Jandarma found me right before lunchtime. I had decided to stop at a nearby cafe—coincidentally, right when the World Cup soccer game was starting. The officers giggled like teenage schoolboys, bounding up the stairs two at a time to watch Turkey vs. Costa Rica. Turkish people, like most people around the world, are soccer fanatics, crazy, wild for their "footy." Since the tournament occurs only every four years, the excitement builds to a frenzy all over the globe. For two Turkish men—Jandarma or not—this was a prized assignment—to sit with the American girl in a cafe during the Turkey vs. Costa Rica game.

Without taking an eye off his TV, the cafe owner slid a cay and gozleme onto my table. The little rural cafe was filled with men, and I sat in a corner by myself eating gozleme trying not to get in anyone's way. I never quite knew what was going on, but I clapped when they clapped, and when everyone's hands covered their foreheads and the room filled with guttural oooh's, I felt their pain.

Soccer moves fast, and I stayed until halftime when Turkey was ahead 1 - 0. If I left, the Jandarma would have to follow—it was their duty—and there are three things in Turkey you don't diss—cay, olives and footy. I tried to tell the Jandarma that I was fine walking alone and to just come check on me when the game was over, but they would have none of it. They followed me out the door and I was laden with guilt, like the wife who drags her husband away from the Super Bowl to go shopping at the mall.

A few hours down the road, the Jandarma pulled up next to me and asked if I wanted to stop for a cup of cay. They led me to a nearby carpet-cleaning warehouse where the owner, Husnu, greeted us at the door in perfect English.

"I lived in Britain for seven years; that's why I can speak English," he explained. "I had an English girlfriend, but we just recently split up. She didn't want to get married and I do. So what's a guy supposed to do? I want to get married, have a house, kids; I want it all."

"Oh." I said, looking around for my cay.

"But she just wanted to be 'good friends.' I told her, 'I have enough good friends, thank you very much.' So I moved back to Turkey and am cleaning carpets while searching for the white picket fence near Ayvalik."

That was a lot of personal information to offer a stranger at the front door of a carpet-cleaning warehouse, but that's what living in Britain—or America—will do to a man. It seems to be a national characteristic of British and American personalities that we can stand in line at the bank or bus stop or whatever and tell the person behind us all about the state of our marriage and our current struggles with the twelve-step program. Personally, I missed it, and was grateful that between Serhat and Husnu I was getting my share of girl talk.

The Jandarma took a seat in the corner watching France vs. Denmark, while Husnu and I shared a cay and a few lively games of backgammon. I always lose at backgammon. Always.

But today the stars were aligned and I was on fire. I needed to roll a six and a two to hit his two open men. Bingo! A six and a two sent Husnu leaping out of his chair with clenched fists punching the air above his head, "Aughh!"

In Turkey they don't just play backgammon; they slam and whirl the dice, then pounce with wrath. The slightest hesitation suggests weakness. You've got to swoop! Roll! Stomp!

The two Jandarma heard the ruckus and realized that while France vs. Denmark was a good footy match, there was a much more physical game going on in this carpet-cleaning warehouse. They peeled themselves away from the World Cup to watch the great board game. I needed a five and a three. Touchdown! A five and a three! Pounced all over his open men. "Aughh!" he yelled again, jumping up and pacing the floor. "Come on, man, concentrate! Get back in the game!" The Jandarma slid their hands over their eyes feeling empathy for their countryman who was taking a beating to his manhood.

What's a bigger threat to a Turkish man, I wondered—being dumped by your British girlfriend, losing a World Cup soccer game, or being beaten at backgammon by an American girl?

Bless them; the Lions Clubs were still transporting my duffle bag from town to town. At night they took me to dinner, and the next morning they walked me out of town and helped me hand out brochures. There was usually a story in the local paper, and I had to hope that they had written the breast cancer information correctly because I couldn't read Turkish. People constantly mentioned that if I had been there even a year earlier, the press wouldn't have been so receptive to printing anything about breast cancer. But today the press was more than welcoming every step of the way. And the Lions came through again, this time in Izmir, holding a very successful press conference and organizing a live TV daytime interview for a full hour.

The city of Bergama also gave us good newspaper coverage, and a public speech outdoors one night was attended by four dozen women. When I walked into Bergama, I found my way to the pidé cafe where I had planned to meet Mustafa, the man assigned to

Polly duty. Mustafa, a man about my age, owned a perfume factory and had a fervent passion for learning English.

"I figured a couple days of Polly duty would allow me the perfect opportunity to practice my English."

"Your English is flawless. You even have an American accent."

"Thank you!" He said, surprisingly proud. "I work hard at it. When you sign up for English classes you can learn Oxford English— the more formal, prissy English that the British speak—or American English. I want to learn English with an American accent and would really love to become fluent in American slang. I thought that while I'm escorting you around Bergama for two days, maybe you could teach me some slang."

His enthusiasm reminded me of Serhat, and since the impending war in Iraq dominated the world's media I took the same gamble. "What's it like being a Muslim male in today's world?"

"Oh, I am not a good Muslim." He sipped on his Efes Pilsen, a Turkish beer. "I don't pray five times a day. Why should I? I don't want to be told what to do. If I want to pray, I'll pray. If I want to go to the mosque, I'll go to the mosque. How dare anyone tell me how to live my life?"

"That's very Western of you," I said. "What's Islam's take on beer? I understand most Muslims don't drink beer."

"Ha, ha, I suppose that's right. According to Islam it should be banned, but Turkey is not so strict. The people are changing their attitudes, especially these past five years. I love beer! Why shouldn't I drink a beer? I don't get drunk and disrespect my family. I just like a cold beer on a hot day." He threw his head back for a long sip as if emphasizing his point.

"Eighty percent of the Turkish population lives within the western quarter of Turkey, and most of them feel free to worship, drink, eat, dress, and behave as they please; they don't feel bound by religion. However, those in the east are still very strict about the rules of Mohammad. The Turks of the east want to break off and become their own country, and the ones in the West want to modernize and become part of the European Union. It's an ongoing debate."

The waiter delivered the most beautiful pidé to our table, and I dove in as though it was my last meal.

"What does 'Yo, Homey' mean?"

I struggled not to choke on my pidé. "I'm sorry—"

"Well, I'm going on a business trip to New York City next month, my first visit ever to the United States, and thought it might be fun to start my presentation by greeting my new colleagues with a little American slang."

I pictured a young Turkish man standing in a New York City skyscraper with a boardroom full of stunned eyeballs. I couldn't let it happen.

"I don't know if 'Yo, Homey' is the best way to do that," I countered.

He asked again what it meant, so I swallowed my bite of pidé, and said, "Well…er…'yo', I guess, means 'hello,' and 'homey' is a slang term for friend."

"So it really means hello, friend?"

I shrugged. "It's sort of urban slang, a greeting that, say, young black kids might say to one another. It's probably never been used in a boardroom in corporate America."

"I don't understand," he said. "If it means 'hello, friend,' why wouldn't that be a nice greeting? Is it offensive?"

There I was, back in the position of trying to explain American vernacular. Slang is a funny thing, I realized. They can be culturally delicate words with complex backgrounds and histories. While slang words sometimes evolve into everyday usage and find prominent spots in the dictionary, at last look Webster's had not embraced either 'yo' or 'homey,' and until then I couldn't recommend that anyone go into a New York City boardroom and greet his new homeys with a yo.

"Then I'm supposed to say, 'wassup?' What does that mean?"

I sighed and wondered what English lessons like this might do to Turkish/American relations. "I guess in the context following, 'Yo, Homey,' it would mean, 'how are you?'"

"So I'm really saying 'hello, friend, how are you?' What's wrong with that?"

"Just don't tell anyone who taught you English."

Just three weeks earlier I had enjoyed cozy days wearing a long-sleeved t-shirt. Now the days were regularly climbing over one hundred degrees. I carried as much water as would fit in my daypack, and if I was lucky a couple of roadside opportunities to pick up a litre or two presented themselves along the way. Otherwise I tried to stay hydrated with water that had been boiling for hours inside my one hundred-ten degree daypack. By ten in the morning it was so hot the tar on the road turned gooey. Big trees offered a moment's shade; the occasional cafes provided a cooling fan.

With rare exception, the local Jandarma continued to find me on the road, looking after me right down the Aegean Coast. They not only protected me from the hissing and harassment, they also served as my translators to reporters and cafe owners. They made a cay run if I was in the mood and sometimes went to get me food if there was no cafe on route. They also kept me on the right road.

In Turkey, as in most parts of Asia, maps were very hard to come by, most times it seemed people had never even seen one. When I was alone on the road and asked someone where I was on the map, they'd take it in their hands with great wonderment, call in the wife so together they could marvel at it, and then say, "We think you're on this side."

I had to wonder if I wouldn't have been better off without a map—at least in Turkey. North always appeared in some improbable corner in the lower left, while major towns and highways were often omitted entirely. So when I was on a long stretch of road one day, I was hardly concerned when the big whopping lake on my left wasn't represented on my map or when the map didn't reveal the river with the enormous bridge or the sign welcoming me to "Bubcusville, Population 11,500."

A police car pulled up next to me, and a smiling officer nattered something out the window. They weren't the police I knew, so right away I held up a finger and said, "Bir dakika." ("One moment, please," a good phrase to know in any language.) I pulled out the letter that had been written in Turkish, explaining my project. I also handed them the letter from the Highway Patrol in Istanbul that gave me the seal of approval to walk on Turkey's highways and byways.

They read everything, passed the note among the three of them and gave me the thumbs up. Then I showed them my map and tried to ask where I was. They pointed to some roadway out in Diddlyville.

If I was in fact way out in Diddlyville as they claimed, then according to the map, I had taken a sharp right turn, something I am reasonably sure I didn't do. So I argued with them—which means a series of charades meaning, "No, I must be over on this road somewhere." They argued back, "No you're on this road." I am paraphrasing here. They actually all prattled away in Turkish while pointing vigorously at Diddlyville on the map.

I tried to explain that I never turned right as the map indicates, but my Turkish argument "walk, walk, walk no right turn…" was not translating. I had to trust them.

The next drama became trying to get back to where I was supposed to be.

By now the policemen were out of the car, the three of them babbling over each other in animated discussion while I stood in the middle trying to catch a single word that might help me understand what on earth they were going on about. I was relieved to see glimmers of smiling and laughing.

I finally called someone for help in translation. Belgin, a French woman I met up in Bergama the previous week, had served as a French diplomat working in South Africa until her husband got transferred up to Bergama, and—voila!—she's living in Turkey serving on Polly duty.

Belgin said, "Don't worry about a thing. Let me talk to the police."

We passed the phone around and around and back and forth until the phone came back to me. Belgin then translated the plan to me: "The police will wave down a taxi and have the driver take you back to the intersection where you took your wrong turn. They'll get you back on the right road. You are in very good hands. *Au revoir, mon amie.*"

I hung up the phone and gave all the Jandarma a thumbs up. They then enthusiastically went out to the middle of the highway to implement the plan.

But something was lost in the translation between French, English, and Turkish. Instead of hailing a taxi, the police waved down the first car that came by. It was a junker of a car, barely huffing and puffing its way up the highway. The characters in the front seat were two of the scabbiest looking creatures I'd seen anywhere—the epitome of guys you never want to get in a car with. Dressed in camouflage vests, they had a series of tattoos on their biceps that included "Anna" (Mother). They had matching shaved heads and earrings, and I was willing to bet good money their names were Rat and Bulldog.

One policeman leaned into the window and launched into a soliloquy that sounded like, "Blah blah blah…American…blah blah blah…Diddlyville…blah blah blah…thank you," then motioned for me to get in the back seat. I stepped back. For all I know they just said, "This girl is traveling alone. She's American, so if you rob her blind and drop the body near Diddlyville, we'll split the bootie. Thank you."

I looked at the three policemen and gave them the international squinty-eyed look for "Are you mad? I'm not getting in that car." But they persisted. They opened the back door and, undoubtedly lacking any more patience with the language barrier, pretty much pushed me in. I fought it like a cat being forced into a kitty-carrier, but shortly gave up and got in.

Huddled in the corner of the backseat, I kept a close eye on my two drivers/hosts/killers in the front seat. They rambled on in

Turkish, then simultaneously looked right at me through the rear-view mirror and laughed.

My only option was to start planning my escape: Spray them in the eyes with pepper spray, and while they're seething in pain club them over the head with my water bottle. Plan set.

Rat and Bulldog drove me ten kilometers back over the route I had just walked. Then they stopped. Right there in the middle of an intersection, they pulled over and motioned for me to get out. They got out, too, and I watched in confusion as they walked out to the middle of the highway to wave down another car. *Good Lord, I would love to know what's going on.* Who in his right mind would stop for two guys who looked like the lead characters on *Turkey's Most Wanted*?

A clean-cut man driving a fancy Nissan SUV became the next unsuspecting player in this relay. After an exchange between the parties, of which I didn't understand a word, they motioned me into the car.

Clean-cut Man tried to talk to me, but all I could do was look at him and give him the international shoulder shrug. The look on his face was something between aggravation and amusement— probably the same as mine. Then he did the oddest thing. Mr. Clean-Cut drove me nearly all the way to my starting point, but two kilometers short of my destination, he stopped. No intersection, no milepost, no reason, just stopped in the middle of the road. Does he think this is my destination, or is a ten-kilometer drive with me enough for any clean-cut man? I didn't know what to do, so I tried the international shoulder shrug in his direction. As it turned out he had an international language of his own and motioned me out of his fancy Nissan. "Me finish. You walk." So with one big blank look on my face, I got out and started my day's walk all over again—plus two kilometers.

Toward the end of a mighty long day I stopped to get some cherries at a roadside fruit stand when horns started honking like crazy. I looked up and down the highway to see if there was an accident, a Buddha, or if I'd taken a wrong turn back to India—

any reason that might warrant excessive honking. Then the fruit vendor said to me, "Turkey 1, Japan 0."

One successful kick inside Japan's soccer net launched Turkey into unprecedented celebration. Turkey had just been propelled into the World Cup quarterfinals for the first time in history. Flags waved from every car. People piled high in the backs of pickup trucks waving flags over their heads, cheering, and screaming in the name of national honor. During the past month I'd caught World Cup fever. Of the eight teams in the quarterfinals, four had never been there before. All the favorites had been dumped, while under-dogs Senegal, USA, Turkey, and South Korea had made it to the quarterfinals. It was enough to get everyone's attention.

The excitement along the road put a spring in my step that lasted the final kilometers of a particularly long day. People were waving flags and high-fiving fellow revelers in passing vehicles. A man approached me from a farm and reached out his hand. I was in the spirit, had the fever, and enthusiastically offered my hand in celebration. I quickly realized though, that this wasn't about a soccer celebration. The man took my arm and jerked me towards him, then started pulling me behind some nearby bushes.

That poor man.

After the months in India, and to a much smaller degree in Turkey, the incessant hissing and ogling from truckers and touters took its toll. One would have to pity the man who messed with me at the wrong time. Unbeknownst to me—and certainly him—this poor fool was the proverbial last straw. With my free hand I grabbed my pepper spray and started yelling so loudly and kicking so furi-ously that he let go of my arm and started running. Like a cartoon roadrunner, he jumped over bushes and fences, leapt over small ponds. I was ranting and raving, so enraged, so tightly wound up after months of harassment that I ran after him!

I ran and ran, bounding like a wild woman screeching at the top of my lungs, "YOU WANT A PIECE OF ME?" In full stride he glanced back to see me hurtling toward him at breakneck speed.

A look of pure terror filled his eyes. Like a grenade that just had its pin pulled, I careened toward him ready to explode. In a hundred yards I got hold of my mind and tried to calm down. My heart was pounding; back straight up like a riled cat.

I scared myself.

I could have seriously hurt that man. It didn't matter that he was twice my size. Like one of those women who lifts a burning two-ton truck to save her child, I felt it—a surge of adrenaline so strong that I could have been declared a lethal weapon.

Breathe, one, two, three…breathe, one, two, three…I got hold of myself and paced around the empty field, hands on hips trying to get my heart rate down. "Yeah! You better run!" I shouted in his general direction, even though he was nowhere to be seen. Passersby saw only a white woman out in an empty field yelling to herself in a foreign language and wisely kept their distance.

I paced the empty field in circles, thoughts churning: How could I get a grip on this harassment crap in a manner that wouldn't land anyone in intensive care? My heart rate came down, and with shaky hands I scribbled on my note pad: Email Mom; ask about meditation.

The mid-Aegean Coast of Turkey is a string of charming little towns—Selcuk, Belevi, Pemucak, Sirince. The road led me down to the coast then veered off into the hills again. Beaches, fruit stands and ancient ruins studded the landscape. Off to the side, you see the crumbled remains of some ancient Roman market— no plaque or ticket booth, just the distant past lying unprotected on the roadside.

My days overflowed with phone calls, interviews, local Lions driving out for a visit and a cay, and constant plan-making for getting my duffle bag from point A to point B—none of which proved an easy task through rough and broken language. My Turkish vocabulary had climbed to upwards of 500 words, including essentials like "Can I play backgammon with you?" "No, thank you,

I don't need a ride," and "No more gozleme, thank you. I'll get fat." They loved that one.

My favorite part of the day came when I spotted a little cafe right about lunchtime, which happened a lot in Turkey. One day a nice old man waved me in for a cay and a rest. I took a seat at the one of colorful tables and pulled out the latest *People Magazine* that Dad sent. The nice old man asked in Turkish if I would like anything, and I knew enough Turkish to reply, "I would like some soup and salad please." The man smiled and brought me a fabulous chicken soup and green salad filled with carrots and cucumbers.

After an hour I packed up my *People Magazine* and thanked him very much. "It was delicious. How much do I owe you?"

"No, no money. I no restaurant, Madam, I furniture store."

That probably happens a lot in Turkey.

The next day the Jandarma followed me into a cafe and took their seats while I went up to the buffet and ordered the fish kebab and cacik.

The cook said no.

"No?" I was confused. "I can't order fish kebab and cacik?"

"No."

He smiled while he said it. It seemed as if he was trying to explain that you can't have those two foods together, and I didn't know what that could possibly mean. Cacik is yogurt mixed with grated cucumber and a hint of mint; I thought it would go well over a white fish kebab. Was eating fish kebab with cacik a toxic combination? Or was today some sort of religious observance when you're not allowed to consume fish with yogurt?

One of the Jandarma leapt out of his seat to solve the problem, and after a brief exchange the cook served me fish kebab with cacik. I shrugged my shoulders to everyone suggesting I don't have a clue what that was all about. That happened a lot (to me) in Turkey. And I simply added the incident to the ever-growing list of Mysteries That Will Never Be Solved.

Rex,

Just received word that Bob has arrived in Bodrum. I will be reunited with him in a couple of days with hugs and kisses, followed by a lengthy get-to-know-you-again crossing of Greece. After a trying separation, we look forward to a long and happy life together. My eternal gratitude goes out to all who made this reunion possible.

Polly and Bob

It had taken me five weeks to walk down the Aegean Coast of Turkey, and I was finishing in the picturesque southern coastal resort town of Bodrum. It wasn't the sort of place you go to for peace and quiet. Oh no, it's a rowdy town with wall-to-wall discos and all-night parties that spill out onto the boardwalk. Sailboats pack the bays, as Bodrum is the jumping off point for sailing trips through the Mediterranean. It would also be my jumping off point to Europe via the Greek Islands.

Getting prepared for Europe put butterflies in my tummy. It felt like a couple of steps toward home, Western society, familiar territory as I'd been there a few times before. I hoped that meant fewer language barriers and less aggressive behavior from men. On the other hand, there was a chance it could become exceedingly more difficult.

For months I'd been trying to get in touch with Lions Clubs across Europe, and had no response. My Lions Club in Mackay, Australia, had also tried to reach them. We sent letters translated into all their respective languages. Timur tried, too. Still no luck.

It wasn't just the Lions Clubs in Europe that hadn't responded to my emails. Neither had any breast cancer foundations or media outlets, which left me befuddled. After years of overwhelming support from both Lions and press, I was finding no interest whatsoever all across Europe. So I gave them the benefit of the doubt—

maybe everyone's on vacation—and made a conscious effort to change my frame of mind. Perhaps this would offer an opportunity to have a go at a different type of experience and go on my own, just Bob and me.

Being on my own might be good for my psyche after three years of walking and talking, entertaining and interviewing. Maybe it would even be healthy retreat from the rigid daily schedule of time and miles, straining to get to the next town by 4:00 p.m. What if I just walked through Europe for a few months and chilled out?

There would clearly be a downside, primarily not doing the breast cancer work. In any case, it looked like I had no choice.

The front desk at my hotel in Bodrum called to say that a big package had arrived: "Very, very big. Please come pick up right away; it is taking much space."

I ran down to the lobby and ripped open the box. And there he was, my buddy, my pal, my long lost teal friend. Amid the wide-eyed wonder of passing guests I popped him together right there in the lobby until he stood like a prince for all to admire. Seeing him again made me realize how much I missed him. The last time I had seen him was in Chiang Mai, Thailand, six months earlier. Even then, I hadn't actually used Bob since Malaysia—over ten months before!

The next morning I rolled Bob out of Bodrum as if we'd never been apart. Arm on handle, alone, buddies off to frolic through Europe.

CHAPTER 17

My Big Fat Greek Tragedy

During three years of planning, three years of walking and a very difficult year crossing Asia, I had envisioned the day I would cross the border into Europe. There would be a big warm welcome sign like "Wilkommen to Europa" where I would party and take photos then send a postcard to Grandma. But there was no sign. There was only the grumpy woman at passport control who corrected my Greek hello. "It's not 'ya soo' it's 'ya shoo!' Next!"

Then there was the grumpy lady in customs who made me strip Bob down to his bare bones while the hashish dealers streamed past her with bongs hanging off their backpacks.

The locals are stressed out, I reasoned, and who could blame them? June, July and August are high season on the Greek islands. Merchants combat dozens of languages, 110-degree heat and thousands of fractionally dressed international twenty-somethings island hopping through Greece to mark their rites of passage. They pack all needed clothes into a baggie and spend their summers frolicking and flirting across Mykonos, the party island; Ios, the party harder island; and Santorini, the you've-got-to-find-a-rich-man-if-you-want-to-party island. I was starting on Kos, the British package-tour island.

Even people who know nothing about Greece know something about Greece. The very name sparks visions of ancient civilizations that dominated the Mediterranean. And thanks to a long history of Greek migration, we English speakers have a naturally healthy vocabulary of Greek, such as *chaos, drama, tragedy, democracy*. My new favorite Greek word quickly became *oreo*, which means delicious, a tasty addition to the American lexicon.

While chatting with locals at an out-of-the-way-cafe, I was surprised to hear that Greeks don't really feel as though they're part of Europe. They're tucked down in the south Mediterranean nestled between the Middle East, North Africa and Europe and haven't quite achieved the development of their Western European counterparts. In fact, their development is so far behind the rest of Europe, they were repeatedly denied membership into the new European Union until they improved their roads, replaced their squat toilets and upgraded other basic amenities that EU members felt would pull them into the twenty-first century.

With the formation of the European Union, the borders across Europe were completely eliminated. On my first trip to Europe as a backpacking twenty-something, my new friends and I enjoyed crossing all the borders, begging the guards dressed in dreary gray uniforms to give us another colorful stamp in our passport. But no more. After the initial port of entry, crossing borders from Greece to Italy to Austria is now no more complicated than hauling through Colorado into Kansas.

At the last minute I made contact with the Lions on my first island of Kos, who met me at the dock and led me to a hotel. I still hadn't made contact with any other Lions in Europe, and I may have gotten my answer as to why. They explained that because it was high travel season across Europe, merchants make seventy percent of their annual earnings over the three summer months. Understandably they wouldn't have time to cater to the moves of an American walker with chaotic hairdos. I took their offer of the next two nights in an air-conditioned hotel and was grateful.

I rose early my first morning on Kos to get a jump start on a full day of errands. Then I learned lesson number one: no one gets up early to do errands in Greece. Breakfast didn't start until 10:00 a.m., while other merchants opened at noon and closed sharply at two for a nap. That didn't stop the promenade from being swarmed by thousands of travelers enjoying early morning window shopping and peering into empty cafes.

Word spread fast among the travelers on the promenade how prices in Greece had increased dramatically since the introduction of the euro six months earlier. They had shot up an average of seventy percent! Having come from Turkey, I found the price differences staggering. For example, Internet access in Turkey was seventy cents an hour; in Greece it was five dollars; meals in Turkey ranged from one to three dollars, while in Greece they were ten to twelve. But what had Greeks themselves up in arms was that a cup of cappuccino had catapulted one hundred and twenty percent! There was such outrage across the country that the locals revolted with a cappuccino boycott.

Walking along the crowded promenade and noting the prices in the windows, I started to stress about my financial situation. Not only did I now have the additional expense of the more costly European currency, but I no longer had the assistance of the Lions Clubs that had always offered a place to stay or invited me in for a meal. My financial plan had rarely extended beyond the if-you-can't-eat-it-you-can't-buy-it budget, but with a full two years left on the road I had to tighten up my finances pronto. From now on there would be no buying maps unless absolutely necessary. Most of these islands only had one road anyway, so I could just wave a car down if I found myself standing at a fork in a road. In Europe showers come with a fee, so they would be budgeted to two a week and/or when I couldn't bear another whiff of myself. Emailing would be cut to once a week, no more postcards home, and I would forego any more bottled water. The water out of the faucet was awful, but it wouldn't make me violently ill (they promised). Moreover, in support of the national revolt, there would be no sipping cappuccinos.

At the far end of the promenade, one lonely corner store had opened its doors and was filled with beach-goers stocking up for the day. I picked up an apple for breakfast and proceeded to checkout. The five people ahead of me and I all watched as the grumpy man at the register berated one person after the next for not having small change. One poor Australian traveler had trouble counting the new currency, and the grumpy man became so impatient he grabbed the money straight out of his hands and counted it for him in elaborate condescension: "This seven euro. You count to seven? You stupid? I tell you what is stupid. Euro stupid. Stupid little coins. Drachma was great currency! Drachma big!"

The poor Dutch girl ahead of me had only a bottle of water and handed him a ten euro note. The rest of us in line looked at each other, silently questioning the consequences of purchasing our sparse groceries while rummaging through our pockets for smaller change. The fact was, though, Greece was a port of entry. We had all just arrived and had only bigger bills.

Grumpy Man's arms flapped above his head, flailing uncontrollably while he addressed everyone in line: "How I all the time to give the change for the pleasurement of everybody? I small store! You bring properly the coins next time or no change for you!"

The Dutch girl calmly suggested, "Well maybe if you know everyone is going to have big bills you should prepare accordingly." And with her words hanging boldly in the air, she retrieved her change and marched out of the little shop leaving me front and center with a twenty euro note, an apple, and a single bead of sweat dripping off my brow.

I hesitated for a moment. Just a moment. Now I'm deemed weak. My heart was pounding. The single bead of sweat dripped onto his counter. Could he wait until I got twenty euros worth of apples?

The people in line nudged me forward.

Three years of hard knocks on the road reared their assertive heads as I watched my arm unwittingly reach out and hand the grumpy man my twenty euro note. He glared at me for a thick moment, plunging the whole store into silence. Without taking an eye off me, Grumpy snatched the money from my fingers, attacked the poor register and mumbled something in Greek I could only interpret as a series of exclamation points. I retrieved my change and strode out of the little store trying to emulate the brave Dutch girl before me. But I don't recall her knees quaking.

I strolled the promenade eating the apple that nearly cost me my life and enjoyed my first views of European shores. Postcards wallpapered the waterfront kiosks depicting Greek island *culture*: girly bums on the sand and a series of postcards entitled *Greek Lovers*, illustrating ancient Greeks in positions I'm quite certain are not found in any high school history book.

A British bloke next to me snickered at the postcards. "Welcome to Southern Europe," he said sarcastically.

Not quite the welcome to Europe I had so anticipated for three years, but one thing was certain: Grandma wouldn't be getting a postcard.

Greece is a country dotted with 1,400 islands, 169 of which are inhabited and divided into six groups. My plan seemed simple in theory: Walk the length of one island, catch a boat to the next, walk to other end; catch the next boat, and so on. But the reality didn't fit the plan: If the island was small enough to walk across in one day then all was relatively simple. I would just take what I needed for the day, do my walk, and when I reached the end of the road, I'd catch a bus or hitchhike back to the boat dock. When a larger island would take multiple days to cross, the logistics became more complex. I would walk for three days to the west end of the island, but the boat left from the east end. So I had to plan accordingly—hunt down a bus schedule, ask if they would take a 70-pound baby buggy, and hope the bus would get back to port on time because, if I missed the boat, the next one didn't leave for three days.

There was another twist: Four shipping companies served the six groups of Greek Isles, and because of a rumored tiff between owners, they refused to talk to each other. A boat might connect two groups of islands only once a week, but you never quite knew when, because no schedules were distributed to the various groups. Additionally, when a fellow traveler passed on information, you couldn't bank on it because schedules changed weekly. So if you're trying to make an island-hopping itinerary from Kos to Athens, you had better prepare, but be darn prepared for those preparations to mean squat. In a word, island hopping across the Greek Islands is not nearly as romantic as it sounds.

From Kos I would be on to Naxos. Naxos had a number of departures onward to Paros, Santorini, Crete, etc. Mind you, I didn't know this because of the schedules at the ticket counters—there weren't any. I soon learned, however, that if I hung out in youth hostels and waterfronts, I would find backpackers exchanging precious information—that would invariably change.

On the way out to walk across Kos, I stopped to purchase my ongoing ticket. The woman at the ticket office was on the phone, so I waited. She leaned back and rocked in her chair, puffed on her cigarette, and laughed with her friend. She saw me, evidently recognized my ability to wait, then turned her chair around to carry on. She laughed and puffed and rocked. I surprised even myself at how the smile stayed on my face without as much as a pouty sigh. Two more people lined up behind me—one from Australia, the other from Britain. "Does she know we're here?" the Aussie asked. I nodded, and her smile confirmed what we didn't have to exchange with words.

Thirty minutes—that's *thirty minutes*—passed. With the phone still balanced between her ear and shoulder and cigarette number three hanging off her lips, she swiveled around to address me. "What you need?"

"I'd like a ticket to Naxos for Wednesday, please."

That was the only communication between us as she multitasked with the phone, the puffing, the laughing. I scooped up my ticket and she swiveled back around in her chair turning her back on the next two in line. I gave the two girls behind me a silent good luck look and left to walk across my first Greek Island.

Before starting out, I went to see George, a Lions Club member I had met at dinner the night before. George owned an enormous cigarette warehouse that successfully kept all the nicotine cravings of Kos satisfied. Ironically there had been a story on the BBC just the night before about the smoking problem in Greece. Actually, it's not a problem for Greeks. They like their habit just fine, thank you very much, and fight the good fight whenever legislators attempt to limit their birthright.

The BBC reported that the Greek government was currently proposing no-smoking sections in restaurants, no smoking in public buildings, no smoking while in the hospital having chemo for lung cancer. That Greece had yet to apply these basic rules was completely out of step with other EU countries. If you were to start in England, the further south you go in Europe, the more smokers you would find. By the time you hit Greece, you'd see a cloud of smoke hovering over the country where an estimated fifty percent of the citizens smoke.

"No," someone argued when I brought that statistic up at dinner with George and his buddies later that night. "We have seventy percent smokers."

Someone else piped in, "Much higher—eighty percent. We love to smoke! Everyone smokes! We have more ashtrays than olive trees!"

They stuck their chests out proudly declaring their title as the world's smoking leader. One man boasted loudly, "In Greece we smoke more than any other country, we drink more than any other country, and we have sex more than any other country."

The BBC piece highlighted one female parliament member who had smoked a hundred cigarettes a day since the age of fifteen. She argued her case in a voice that sounded like Rod Stewart. "How dare the government (cough) tell me how to live (cough, cough) and how to die (puff, puff)?"

George told me that smoking is so ingrained in Greek culture that in the rural areas, locals still measure distance by how many cigarettes it takes to walk, as in, "The dock is a half a pack away."

When I was ready to head out across Kos I asked George what the mileage was to Antimachia, the biggest town half way across the island. He said it's a four-pack island. "Why don't I pick you up this afternoon after a two-pack walk?" In Greek-speak that's twenty kilometers.

A traveler named Yasmin told me the boat to Naxos was delayed until 7:00 p.m. When she said she was from Istanbul I knew she'd be keen on whiling away the five-hour delay at an outdoor cafe playing backgammon. Yasmin quickly pointed out that, while she was from Turkey, she was not Muslim, "Oh no, I am Christian. My family is originally from Armenia, and we are more western than eastern." She rolled the dice and continued to tell me about herself with a change in tone.

"I've been married for sixteen years—sixteen years, can you believe it? We have a son and daughter, fourteen and twelve. Two months ago, out of the blue, my husband comes home and says he doesn't want to be married anymore. It's over. He's done. Just like that—*snap*—my family is broken and I'm a single mother at forty-three."

I wasn't sure what to do with all that personal information spilling onto our backgammon game, so I kept rolling the dice. "It felt like a Mac truck hit me head on," she went on. "I know, I know, it's not easy for anyone, but it's as if I'm stuck between two cultures. In Turkey where divorce is rare, I will be fiercely looked down upon. It's an embarrassment, a disgrace for me and my family." She took a deep breath and sat up a little straighter. "On the other hand, I know I can move forward. I will survive; I am a modern Turkish woman."

After her husband's initial announcement, she explained, he chose to play the sort of game where he would hold on to the relationship, then pull away, hold on, pull away. So she gave him a message of her own: "I'm going on vacation to clear my head. Take care of the kids. I'll be back in a month. When I get back, have your bags packed." So here she was on Kos, on her way to Naxos, trying to make sense of her life caught between two cultures playing backgammon with a stranger on a boat dock.

Yasmin and I searched the dock for a sign that might lead us to the pier reserved for the 7:00 p.m. departure to Naxos. Thousands of young backpackers milled like cattle, searching for any sign of where the boat might dock. We asked several official-looking people if they knew where the boat to Naxos was coming in and got a series of responses, none of which told us what we needed to know.

I spotted a Greek woman dressed in a white sailor suit, so I asked if she happened to know where the boat to Naxos was coming in. "How I supposed to know where the boat to Naxos coming?! All the people all the time asking me where the boat? Where the boat? I don't know where the boat!"

Retreating in defeat, we looked for a corner in which to drag our beaten tails when a small group of backpackers waved at us to join them. "We saw what happened to you," they said as we got closer. "It's happened to all of us." "Look!" We all turned to watch the next innocent fool approach the woman in the white sailor suit. The same loud, scolding rant ensued, sending the poor guy slumping away in shame, and our little group grew.

The boat dock refugee camp was comprised of ten people now, all traveling individually from various countries around the world—Sweden, Australia, Norway, Belgium, New Zealand, and now, the United States and Armenia—all brought together by the common bond of being tongue-lashed by a Greek woman in a white sailor suit. Rob, from Australia, took another sweeping look around. "Crikey! Home to Aristotle, Socrates, and Plato—you'd think they'd learn how to put up a sign."

Just four days in Greece and my morale was starting to droop—like one of those bright spring flowers that starts to wilt after only a few days. I'd arrived fresh and excited, but the easy smile, the patience with no sighs or pouting that had come so easily was already withering. I wondered how an entire national character could devolve into grouchiness. It couldn't all stem from the loss of the drachma. It had to be much deeper than that. I was dying to ask someone about the grumpiness, but who do you ask? I pointed out to Yasmin that my guidebook says Greeks are very hospitable, "one of Europe's most relaxed and friendly countries."

"Yeah," she replied without missing a beat. "It also says they're 'passionate.' I think 'passionate' is the politically correct word for grouchy."

Yasmin, no doubt, had a limited future writing travel guidebooks, but I refused to believe her analysis. Greece has a proud history. How could their national disposition be so cantankerous? Could we just be meeting the wrong people? My welcome to Greece was decidedly not what I had dreamt of, but I was confident it would turn around. It had to.

Email to Alan Mackenzie

Hello my Aussie friend,

Thank you for continuously trying to get hold of any Lions here in Europe. Any assistance would be treasured!

For the past two weeks I've been camping and staying at youth hostels, the past four nights on Santorini where I've been staying in a dorm that sleeps sixty. All of my dorm-mates are about 21 and out living high on the bottle until 3 a.m., then try to climb up into the top bunks in the dark. If I wasn't so tired and hot I would have to laugh.

When I write a travel guidebook I will add these hints for backpacking Europe in the summer:

1) Take earplugs!
2) If it's climbing past 105 degrees, always claim the upper bunk RIGHT under the fan.
3) When camping, don't pitch your tent directly under a tree. That's where the bugs fall. And they crunch loudly under your feet when you have to get up and use the loo in the middle of the night.

There must be close to two thousand backpackers on each boat floating from island to island, and they say that tourism is down 30% due to a combination of 9/11 and the rise of the euro. I can't figure out how the additional 30% would have fit!

Greek people have a different sleep pattern from us. They don't sleep in one eight-hour stretch overnight as we do, but rather two lots of four to five hours. So they work from 10 a.m. to 2 p.m., then sleep until 7. Then they go back to work until 11 p.m., go eat with a posse of friends, rabblerouse, then sleep from about 3 a.m. to 9 a.m. The first invitation I got for dinner was for 11:30 p.m. It was 9 p.m., and I was already fighting to keep my eyes open!

I caught myself ready to say, "Oprah says you shouldn't eat inside three hours of going to sleep…" but couldn't imagine they give a hoot about what Oprah says.

I'll sign off now, I see a McDonald's across the street where I'm going for the air-con!

x Polly

Temperatures continued to climb past 110 degrees while I dawdled across Santorini. It was so hot you could smell the heat bouncing off the road. It's what *thick* smells like. To save money I regularly forfeited a reserved seat on the boat rides opting instead for sleeping on the deck with the engine noise and my arms intertwined around Bob's wheel, because it was another ten euros to lock him up with the other luggage.

Then I hopped over to Crete, Greek's largest island at 260 kilometers long. To beat the heat, I tried to get on the road by 6:00 a. m., but invariably my skin sizzled by eight. There was no hiding from it; not a single tree offered refuge on any of these islands, not even for a second. The most I could ask for was the occasional abandoned car wreck that might serve as a shady haven for a moment's relief. Sometimes I spent the night in a campground, other times I'd luck out with a youth hostel. The toughest nights were when I had to free camp on the side of the road, a last resort as it was worse than sleeping in a haunted house. Once the moon came out every creak, squeak and wisp of wind morphed into space invaders spotting easy prey for their alien abductions. Never a good night's sleep.

When I walked into the village of Sisses, to avoid free camping I hitchhiked back to Iraklio and a lovely youth hostel. That meant the next morning I had to catch a bus back up to Sisses—with Bob—to carry on. The first time I had to shuttle Bob was on Naxos. I got there early to claim the first place in line assuring easy access to load Bob. The driver lifted the doors and a swarm of people launched past me shoving, pulling, lifting, producing a mob scene the likes of an Elvis sighting—pushing me to the end of "the line," doomed to catch the next bus four hours later.

So on this morning, waiting to catch the bus back to Sisses, I stood smack in front of the luggage doors, elbows and attitude ready to rumble. When the driver opened the doors the mob swarmed around me. I was trying to pick up all seventy pounds of Bob, but he's bulky and awkward to lift with no wheels. The driver stood over me yelling in Greek like a drill sergeant. I asked for help, but he kept barking. My window of opportunity was slipping away as backpacks were piling up fast, and I tried desperately to shove Bob on by lifting one end at a time. The bus driver was leaning into me now, yelling louder. As I gave Bob a final shove into the luggage compartment I mumbled under my breath, "Geez, I'm going as fast as I can, you don't have to be so grumpy."

Then I heard behind me—in perfect English, "Grrumpy! You call me grrrumpy?"

He pushed me out of the way, grabbed Bob out of luggage compartment with one easy swoop, and threw him onto the tarmac. "If I grrrumpy, you catch next bus!"

Bob skidded across the loading zone and landed upside down with his loose wheels twirling around the otherwise empty lot. A number of retorts raced through my head, most notably: "Oh sure, now you can lift my buggy."

I decided that this shuttling routine was not worth the black eyes and bruised ribs. Free camping on the side of the road with the possibility of getting abducted by space aliens might be safer after all.

"I'll take three nights, please!" Rethymno's youth hostel included free hot showers, a perfect place to rest my bones and spirit for a couple of days. The unspoiled village on the west side of Crete had charming cobblestone streets that wound around boutique shops and pretzel vendors. Warm rains sprinkled sporadically, and with a budget pared down to nothing but apples and showers, my main entertainment became people watching, like the pretzel man who dashed in and out and in and out at every threat of a sprinkle. The best entertainment, though, was at the youth hostel.

The downside of staying in youth hostels in Europe was being drawn into conversations about U.S. foreign policy. With the war raging in Afghanistan and rumbles beginning for a war in Iraq, it was a difficult time to be an American in Europe. So I kept to myself under a shady tree eating hard-boiled eggs and reading an old *Newsweek*.

A man holding a chair was looking around for a piece of shade, so I motioned him over to share my tree. He said his name was Leonard and that he was from Iraq, but really Iraqi-American, as he had lived in Chicago for eighteen years.

Thirty minutes later a man sporting a small goatee and dread-locks came and shook hands with Leonard. They babbled in Arabic, gesturing broadly with their arms, and Leonard told me this was Ravu from Morocco. "I am from Morocco but I've been traveling for fifteen years," he said, grabbing a chair. We shifted around to make room for him beneath the shady tree.

Within an hour, a colorful group gathered in the shade of the solitary tree. Peter, the Greek-Australian, worked in a mine in Tasmania. He said he felt the pull toward his Greek ancestry and finally made his way to Greece to find himself.

Jane and Gareth were from Belfast, Northern Ireland. "But we don't really think of ourselves as Irish. We don't want to be associated with the Irish, and we certainly don't want to be associated with the English. We carry a British passport, but it's as if we're a people with no identity."

Paul said he was Greek-Canadian, "But I hate everything Canadian. My friends call me Buddha. Buddha the Greek."

He rubbed his big belly; there was no question why his friends called him Buddha.

Selia, the Belgradian-now-living-in-Italy, asked, "Why do you hate everything Canadian?"

"Because they agree with everything the Americans do, and no one should agree with everything the Americans do. The Canadians have no mind of their own. If you ask me, there's something fishy going on there."

Francesca, who was Italian-English suggested, "Maybe they agree with the Americans." Everyone keeled over laughing.

Another couple came by. There was no more room under the shady tree, so they took a seat on the first flight of stairs. "Where are you guys from?" someone asked.

"Holland."

"Just Holland?"

"Just Holland."

"No mixture of ancestry?"

"No, Holland, period."

"Where have you traveled in Greece?"

"We've just come from Pella, home of Alexander the Great."

Buddha the Greek said, "I hate Alexander the Great."

Ev, the Croatian-now-living-in-Athens took the bait.

"Why do you hate Alexander the Great?"

"Alexander the Great is the moron who introduced the Jews to Greece."

Peter the Greek-Aussie shifted around in his chair. "Aye, mate, you don't know what you're goin' on about."

"Ask anyone," Buddha argued. "He brought Jews into this country, they multiplied like Hindus and spread all over Europe. The downfall of Europe, those damn Jews. They're trying to economically rule the world, and those damned Americans have no idea what Jews have done, protecting them like a mother hen. Damned Americans. Fucking Jews. I hate Alexander the Great."

During the past few years Europe had seen a substantial rise in the number of anti-Semitic incidents everywhere from Greece to Sweden. Not only had there been an escalation in violent attacks against Jews, but also an explosion of Holocaust deniers. My friend Chris in Colorado emailed me to say I'll never find a more racist place than Europe, and that when Europeans start talking bad about Jews I'm supposed to get them all riled up by saying that Jews wouldn't be economically taking over the world if the rest of the world wasn't so dumb and lazy. He said it's funny; just watch how it gets them going. Of course I would never say such a thing; I just sat in my shady little chair and cocked a quiet eyebrow.

Peter got his back up. "Listen, Zorba the Greek or Buddha the Greek, or whatever your name is, you're talking a load of nonsense. You need to go back and read your history, mate. Alexander the Great could not have brought Jews into Greece because he never made it back to Greece. He led his troops across Persia and died on the way home. I don't mind having a good wee hash there, Buddha boy, but you need to go home and check your facts."

Buddha the Greek changed the subject fast. "And those Albanians! Aye yah! I hate those Albanians! They have ruined this country. The Albanian government just opens the gates of Albanian prisons and leads them over the border. 'Run!' they say, 'Go on to a new life pillaging Greece!' Damn Albanians, the cause of all the crime in Greece. Have you ever seen them eat? Aye! They eat like pigs!"

Listening to Buddha go on about Jews and Americans and Albanians caused Peter the Greek-Aussie to twitch in his chair. I smirked behind my hand and stayed silent, annoyed and entertained at the same time. Under this tree sat people with pierced noses, lips, and tongues, some scantily clad in bikinis and colorful stripes in their hair. This was the West and God bless it. I'd just come from a year in a very tradition-locked Asia, so I appreciated opinions and freedoms more than ever, even when I disagreed with them. I couldn't help but wonder about the reaction of a woman from say, Afghanistan, if she were deposited into this youth hostel and this conversation at this moment with this medley of people and opinions and fashion and social mobility. The mere thought of it brought a smile to my face.

Peter the Greek-Aussie told us about Alexander the Great. "He led his forty-thousand troops across Persia encouraging them to marry women along the way. He wanted to rule the world and was determined to spread the Hellenistic seed, so to speak."

"So he and his troops marched across Persia just conquering and pro-creating? That's creative genocide."

"Yes, but all that seed spreading killed him. He died quite suddenly in modern day Iraq. Historians have reason to believe he died of syphilis."

Buddha the Greek wondered if Osama bin Laden should use the same strategy for conquering America today. "Just give those American women a little attention and they're yours. Trust me, I know. And once a Muslim, always a Muslim. Can't go back."

Leonard the Iraqi-American said it'd never happen because Osama bin Laden works for the CIA.

My eyes shot to the back of my head and I sighed louder than intended.

"Oh come on," he bellowed in my direction. "The American military has satellites that can distinguish every move a tiny ant makes on the ground, but they can't find Osama bin Laden? Please!" He chortled. "Americans."

Buddha asked, "Polly, where did you say you were from?"

"I'm from Colorado."

"No, *really* from."

"I'm really from Minnesota."

"No, where are you really, really from?"

Apparently they were digging for a hyphen. "Regarding my ancestry, my mother's family hails from Scandinavia and England, and my father's side comes from a Belarusian village." Then I went for it. "They were Russian-Jews."

A heavy moment of silence.

Leonard said, "Letofsky isn't a Jewish name."

I said, "Yes it is."

He said, "No it's not. It comes from Poland. You're from Poland. You don't even look Jewish. You're not Jewish. You're Polish."

My back got a little straighter in my chair. "Danish-English-Russian-hyphen-Jewish."

I went to my dorm that night wondering how traveling in Europe got so racist. It had come a long way from when I was in Europe as a twenty-three-year-old backpacker and our daily objective was to gather new friends from around the world, find a cheap box of wine and frolic topless on Mediterranean beaches.

I climbed up to my top bunk directly under the fan thinking about the enormous power and responsibility that comes with freedom of speech and the people around the world who will never know it. I wondered if the people of the world would ever understand each other. I wondered if Alexander the Great's Hellenistic seed could have possibly spread all the way north to the villages of Belarus. And while the French-Canadians, the Croatian-Italians, and the Holland-Periods started to snore, I dozed off plotting how to secure a position with the U.N. and internationally abolish the hyphen.

The small boat pulled into the dock of Kefalonia. It's a much different island than the Cyclades, Crete and Kos, which are volcanic and arid. Kefalonia is a green, mountainous island with a harbor that resembles a quaint New England fishing village. Kefalonia was a one-day island and one step further north from the equator—with any luck, making the heat a little less extreme. It had been so sizzling hot that I was drinking three hundred ounces of water per day. My head constantly throbbed, which was the cue that I was dehydrated and should drink more, but it was just not possible to drink one more ounce. Could the same headache warning me that I was dehydrated also indicate that I was drinking too much? That would be one silly irony, like the same word in Thailand that means both 'near' and 'far.' The good news was that there were trees on Kefalonia that helped filter the heat of the sun.

As it turned out, though, those glorious trees were also a haven for lunatics.

There was a man yelling from the hills. I took my earphones off and looked around but saw nothing but an abundance of trees, so I put Van Morrison back in my ears and carried on.

There it was again. I turned around and watched a youngish man bounding down the hill out of the forest. He stood about five foot ten with blonde hair, a narrow build, and pale face. I looked around to see if I was missing a town or a house, a campground, any reason at all that a man might come straight out of a forest yelling to me. Teetering on that fence between wanting to be polite and the need to protect myself, I said hello while keeping one hand on my pepper spray. He came toward me, babbling in Greek. "English?" I asked.

He indicated no and moved in closer continuing to babble in Greek, louder now, again and again and again. He motioned for me to come with him, and I responded with my Greek no. He motioned again. With the realization that this conversation was going nowhere, I thought it best to say, "I'm sorry, I don't speak Greek." Then I turned around to walk away. He grabbed my arm from behind and tried to pull me into the forest.

Excuse me? *Excuse me!* Did this poor fool try to pull me?!

It was just like in Turkey, not even two months before, when rage boiled to the surface, raising a fury the likes of which Kefalonia had never seen. I struggled away from this five foot, ten inch punk, my arms launching into defense, hands clenched like claws, which confused even me. My right hand pointed my pepper spray straight at his face, and I verbally let loose on him. "What the hell is wrong with you, you crazy psycho lunatic! Get the hell away from me!"

He stood perfectly still, pepper spray inches from his face, looking at me like I was the crazy one. He was silent. I should've just nailed him in the eyes with my pepper spray and run, as I had always been instructed, but instead I carried on screaming a lecture that I knew he didn't understand. "You don't just go grabbing strange women in the forest, you psychotic maniac! Go! Get the hell away from me! I said GO! Or I'll kick your ass into tomorrow!!" He stared some more. I still had my pepper spray raised in attack mode as I backed away, yelling all sorts of things my mother wouldn't be proud of. He remained still while all five foot, two inches of me raged on with f-words, s-words, x-words. Anyone passing by would have felt sorry for the poor little blonde man getting blasted by the American girl.

Safely out of my fury, he slowly backed away, step by step returning back into the bush—eyes on me the entire time—until he disappeared altogether.

I stepped into the middle of the road and threw myself in front of the very next passing car—a couple of British girls in their mid-thirties on the way to a beach. I babbled fast and breathlessly, still wielding my pepper spray above my head. They asked what they could do and obliged when I asked if they could just stay with me while I ran for a couple of kilometers to make sure I was well ahead of him.

It was another episode to add to my ever-growing list of Mysteries That Will Never Be Solved, but this one bothered me. Here was a man who walked out of the bush without any aggression. It was only when I couldn't understand him and opted to walk away that he tried to grab me. Was he asking for help? But help with what? There were no houses, campsites, or businesses in the area. It was pure forest. Was someone hurt in the forest? Was that what he was trying to tell me?

But no, no, no, wait! I couldn't feel guilty. The bottom line was that emergency or not, you never ever grab a strange woman on the side of a rural road. Particularly one whose stress-ometer is tilting heavily into the red zone.

I walked another three hours to Argostoli, looking over my shoulder with pepper spray ready, eyes wide open all the way to the police station. I thought it was a good idea to report the incident to the island police, because, I thought, that's what a good citizen does.

The first policeman laughed when I explained why I was there, which was a bit disconcerting. The second policeman, a big man with a big office, yelled for me to come in. I sat down on the rickety wooden chair across from his desk and he asked, "Why you here?"

Minutes into my account, the big policeman sat up from his reclined position and ripped off a corner of the morning's newspaper to use as scratch paper, then scribbled the occasional note. When I finished, he leaned back in his chair and folded his hands on his belly. "What you want me to do?"

"I don't know…I guess I thought, er, maybe it should be reported, you know, if it happens again you'll have a description."

"Hmm," he said, apparently in deep thought as he rocked back and forth in his reclined chair. "Why aren't you married?"

And my hand rose up to tend to my eye that was twitching out of control.

I had been in Greece five weeks and my spirit was plummeting. The pervasive ill-temper I found blindsided me so completely that I hesitated to ask directions or even make conversation with anyone. I felt lonelier than ever. And lost. Aimless. No breast cancer work, no Lions Clubs, no fundraising, no particular route or schedule, no plan. My thought just five weeks before that it might be nice to have no plan, no commitments, I now saw as naive. What was I thinking? I had to have a plan, a blueprint of sorts for getting across Europe with an objective other than anger management.

First I had to get through Greece. It was tearing me down and I couldn't spare what little morale I had left. With a study of my map, I devised a plan to walk to Igoumenitsa ten days away. Once there, I could catch a boat for Italy. I highlighted my route and circled the towns that would be a perfect walking distance each day. Then I researched those towns to find either a campground or youth hostel so I wouldn't have to free camp off the side of the road.

With renewed determination I walked out of the campground the next morning, clear of mind and organized, a new mood, new attitude. Then I noted my camera was missing. Damn! In a controlled panic I called the campground. They searched everywhere while I frantically emptied Bob's contents on the side of the road— crackers, water bottles, maps, toiletries, but no camera. Damn! I'll bet that guy camping next to me went in my tent when I was off to the showers. A number of times I had caught him watching me, both last night and this morning. Full roll of film too! Double Damn!

I took a deep breath and tried to hold back the tears that had been welling up for weeks. Methodically, I repacked Bob on the side of the road and tried to shake it off, but the tears came, big heavy ones that plopped when they rolled off my cheeks and hit the tar. It was through the blur of my tears that I spotted the directional sign right above my head. One arrow indicated that Igoumenitsa was 119 kilometers straight ahead. But if I turned left, there was a boat to Italy.

CHAPTER 18

I'm No Gypsy!

Polly's Journal, August 1, 2002

Three years today I stood in front of the Gondola in Vail looking down an empty road wondering what the world might have in store for me. Three years later I find myself on the SuperLiner speeding out of Greece heading to Ancona, Italy, a place I had certainly never heard of that day in 1999. I sometimes try to recall what I knew before this trip and what I didn't. Does everyone else in the world know that Minoans were the ancient people who lived a sophisticated life three thousand years ago on Crete? Or that Kefalonia is the Greek Island where Nicholas Cage and Penelope Cruz filmed *Corelli's Mandolin*? Or that Gujarat is a state in India and home to the best food in the world? I suppose they do. It seems impossible that at one time, I didn't know these things.

It's been an education-packed three years. I've learned a lot about the world, about myself, and surprisingly, about America. It excites me and exhausts me. A walk around the world is a walking university with classes in everything from ancient history and foreign language to political science and anthropology. Of course, we can't forget debate!

Traveling in Europe as an American during this post 9-11/pre-Iraq War era is shaping me into a master debater! At a bookstore recently, I spent many apples' worth of budget to buy *The Complete Idiots Guide to the Middle East* to study for my nightly debates in European youth hostels.

Europe is turning out to be no picnic, but it's probably better than the alternative. Plan A had always been to walk north from Greece through Bulgaria, Serbia, Romania, Slovakia, etc., all the way to the North Sea and across to England, but the Eastern European guide books were warning me about the two-tiered price system for everything from groceries to hotel rooms, one rate for locals, and quite another if you're a white American. Sometimes five times the price. That injustice, along with the out-of-control crime would've sent me right over the edge. Consequently, for the sake of my sanity, I opted for the easiest route possible—Western Europe. I just want it to be less "passionate" than Greece.

Bob and I rolled off the boat into Italia and made our way toward the nearest campground, sixteen miles up the beach to Falcona. It was one long, constant beach, a parade of entertainment including vacationers on trampolines, caged ones so you couldn't bounce out and land on someone's sand castle.

There was also a carnival of ongoing lawn tennis, ping-pong, foosball, and inflatable oversized pink castles for the kids. Europeans really know how to vacation, and you can't help but envy their ability to take off for five weeks and romp through this beach wonderland. The other side of the boardwalk was an endless procession of pizzerias and trattorias, leaving my nose in the air inhaling the deliciousness of my new country.

A father and son from Holland struck up a conversation with me while I was resting on a bench overlooking the beach. The father was in his eighties and his son, Rene, was taking him on a camping trip through Italy. "Letofsky? Is that a Jewish name?" the father asked. When I said yes he said he marched with Hitler's army. "Nothin' I'm proud of, but I had to stay alive. If you didn't work for Hitler you wouldn't get any food, and starvation is a long slow death."

I've always held a fondness for Dutch people and looked forward to walking through The Netherlands. They're big on world travel, and have proven to be bright, inviting people. Rene and his father fit the mold, even if he did march with Hitler. I enthusiastically accepted their invitation to lunch.

When our pizza arrived the father gasped. "What?" I said, quickly putting my food down.

"You eat with your hands?" Rene asked.

"Of course. It's pizza."

They looked at each other and snickered. "No wonder the French call the Americans barbarians."

"The French call us barbarians?" I looked around the pizzeria. Sure enough, everyone was eating pizza with a knife and fork.

I admit that we Americans are an informal bunch; it's all we can do to take a comb to our head. Europeans can nap in the middle of the day, blow smoke in your face, and routinely butt in line, but they wouldn't dream of going to a pasticceria with a wrinkle in their shirt.

"Are you going through France?"

"I'm not sure," I said with maybe a hint of sarcasm. "Would they let me eat cookies with my hands?"

"If you eat a cookie in a restaurant it is expected you would eat it with a knife and a fork."

In New Zealand I remember sitting around the dinner table with a family near Kaitaia waiting for someone to take the first serving. After a few silent minutes the mother of the house leaned over and whispered, "In this house we always wait for our guests to serve themselves first."

So while staying with an older couple near Turangi after a long hot day, I dove in as fast as the food hit the table. The lady of the house interrupted me with a gentle tap on the arm. "In this house we always pray before we eat."

In Australia I sat around a table with a family near Walla Walla and didn't dare make the first move. When I finally asked, "Do you pray first?" the woman of the house responded, "Oh, what a lovely idea! I've always thought it would be nice to pray before our meal. Would you like to pray?"

"Well, I was just…"

"Oh, don't be shy. Please, lead us in prayer. Honey, she's going to say a prayer before dinner! Isn't that lovely?"

"Okay…well, ahem…Our Father, who art in heaven… umm…thank you for the lovely food. Your friend, Polly…I mean, er, Amen."

In Singapore they use chopsticks. They also supply bibs for foreigners.

In Malaysia they use the fork and spoon together in one hand like chopsticks and sit twelve people around a table built for six. They supplied a bib for me and everyone in my immediate vicinity.

In Thailand it's customary for the host to put the food on your plate; as a guest you never put food on your own plate. They also never take no for an answer, which results in one big bottomless plate of pad tai.

In India you only eat with your right hand. You scoop up the food with the tips of your fingers and it is a no-no to let your fingers touch your mouth. The rule is that the food should catch air between fingers and mouth. No one in India cared if I wore a bib.

By the time I got to Turkey I was so used to eating with my hands that when dinner arrived on my first night, I thought nothing of diving in with my fingers. "Miss Polly," someone whispered after my third scoop, "The utensils will be here in just a moment if you care to wait."

My first night in Greece, my new friend George asked me what I'd like for dinner. I told him it was ten o'clock and I had eaten already. "You've already eaten dinner? It's only ten o'clock!"

Now in Italy I ate pizza with a knife and fork. And it's a small price to pay. Up the Adriatic coast of Italy a constant flow of pizzerias, trattorias and pasticcerias waited. It was like a noodle-crawl from town to town and I was in my gastronomic glory. Whenever the noodle mood struck it wasn't a matter of finding a *ristorante* but rather of choosing one. Mama Mia's Casa del

Tortellini? Papa Leo's Trattoria? Nor did it stop at spaghetti and tortellini—that's rookie class pasta eating. I was now in the big league—passatelli, cappelletti, fagottini.

The good news was that while thumbing through my trusty guidebook I happened upon this advice: "When eating pasta, don't be afraid to shovel it in. It's a welcomed sign you're really enjoying your meal."

So *buon giorno, Italia,* and *buon appetito!* They can serve me pasta with chopsticks, pasta by fingertips, pasta at midnight, or pasta with a prayer. And they best not forget the bib. Dare I say the French are probably right. This American was going to be a barbarian.

The receptionist at the Falcona campground said I was lucky because there was one space left and what a deal, it was only €19. I said good grief, €19! He said €19 very, very good price; you get free shower.

Campgrounds in Italy, I discovered my first night, are not where you pitch a tent and sit around a campfire roasting marsh-mallows and telling ghost stories. Their campgrounds are resorts with populations larger than many American towns. There are restaurants, tennis courts, grocery stores, even banks. And what kind of campground would it be without a disco?

The man at reception told me there were eight hundred people at this campground and ten showers. "You want hot shower, you must hurry. From 2:00 p.m. to 6:00 p.m. people are showering from their day at the beach, and 7:00 p.m. to 10:00 p.m. they are primping for the disco."

The man led me to my assigned spot for the night.

The streets from north to south were named after countries; east to west streets were named after months of the year. He led me three blocks up Francia Street, took a left on Novembre, two blocks up to Yemen, and pointed me to my home for the night, the corner of Yemen and Febbraio—a nice neighborhood, he said.

I unzipped Bob and methodically started setting up camp—popped up the tent, tossed in the flashlight and *The Complete Idiots Guide to the Middle East Conflict*, then made my way to the ladies room to take advantage of that free shower.

At the showers there were ten people waiting patiently in line—except the Italian women who came in and pushed right past everyone. In southern Europe the concept of standing in line waiting your turn was as foreign as Burundi. A British girl I'd met earlier had warned me about the line-butting in Italy; it's like a birthright, "You must be tough. If you're shy or passive, you'll be in line until Christmas." But I was reluctant to start a brawl at the showers, so I leaned across the doorway to protect my place in line. The Italian girls ducked under me. Then I got real tough and mustered, "Excuse me." It was no use. Finally, two older German women shamed the Italians to the back of the line, and we all clapped at the successful coup at the showers.

Back home on Yemen Street my neighbors to the left were a group of French schoolboys practicing for their choir competition—while their voices were changing. My neighbors on the right were a Dutch couple without a tent—just two sleeping bags zipped together. Occasionally their heads would pop out to shoot me a look as if to say, "Vill you giff us a leetle privacy, pleeze?"

The neighbors across Yemen Street were an Italian couple with a talking parakeet who—as they insisted on showing every passing camper—could perfectly imitate a crying baby.

Marshmallows and ghost stories be damned. Where else could I get this kind of entertainment—plus a shower—for only €19?

During the last vacation month of August I plugged along up the Adriatic coast through beach towns Fano, Ravenna, Sottomarina, right through Venice and over the Austrian border. Youth hostels and campgrounds sat all along the road, but at high season they were full. I begged and groveled until they said okay, okay, for €19 you can stay in the dirt pit behind the dumpsters, but clean up after yourself.

I asked a fellow camper for help translating the sentence, "I am walking around the world; can I camp on your farm?" But even while free camping on farms I had to increase my budget. I needed more maps. All the countries I'd walked through so far only had one or two road options. Across Europe the number of roads and routes numbered in the thousands. A single frame on my map contained an estimated twenty possible routes. Essentially I needed four maps at any one time: one that covered most of Europe so I could choose a general route up to the English Channel, a regional one so I could plan a few weeks in advance, one for a few days in advance and one for the day. Even a detailed map for the day was loaded with multiple roads, and I had to keep the map in my hand at all times so I didn't inadvertently wander off eastbound into a fifth map.

The rising value of the euro caused an even harder economic hit than in Greece, and the stress on my finances was becoming dire. I toyed with the idea of stopping to work, but simple math proved it just wouldn't be worth it. Let's say I stopped and picked olives or any similar transient job; it would take two years to earn the money I needed to finish. I had to figure out a way to cut in other areas.

A pizza with mushrooms cost €7. A pizza with no mushrooms costs €5.50. That meant if I got mushrooms on my pizza every day in Italy, it would cost an extra €45 a month. Mushrooms would be cut out of the budget.

A load of laundry jumped from €2 to €8 a load, which sent me into a series of trials and errors trying to master the art of washing clothes by hand.

In Italy and Greece restaurants charged €1.50 per person just to sit down. I said I would take it to go, and they tacked on a €1.50 takeaway charge.

In Treviso the Visitors Center wanted €2.50 for my day map. I decided to just ask directions to Belluno. The man told me, "Turn right at the next corner and go. Just go and go. Keep going. Go through the light and go. You just go. Keep going. And you go and you go…" I paid the €2.50.

At €3.80 a shot I had to forego the daily newspaper in English. To stay caught up on the fiery world news, I'd hover around the newsstand reading Britain's *Independent* until I was kicked out. "…Saddam has tried to procure uranium from Africa…" *Snatch!* "This is not a library!" Then I'd walk to the next newsstand to carry on.

I couldn't afford a cappuccino with my pizza with no mushrooms, so at the campground cafe on a cold night in Corvara I asked for a hot water. The lady said they didn't have hot water.

"No hot water?"

"No hot water. But I could bring you a hot tea with no tea, but we would have to charge you for the tea."

But Venice topped them all when they asked for €2 to use the toilet.

I tried to refinance my little condo back in Vail, but the bank said no way, silly lady, you've got to have a job.

So for the time being I settled on pizza with no mushrooms, no hot tea without tea, and decidedly there would be no peeing in Venice.

The autumn months came and went as I trudged my way up and over the Austrian Alps and headed due west along the north shore of Lake Bodensee in Bavaria, Germany. It was a picture postcard of Europe, but not easy for free camping as one village rolled right into the next with nary a cornfield, riverbed or farm between. Luck was on my side one night when I saw a sign for a youth hostel only two blocks out of the way.

The man at the youth hostel told me it was sixteen euros a night, but he was sorry, they only accept youth. I turned around to see who he was talking to.

He said, "They're not my rules, I just work here. None of the youth hostels in Bavaria take people over the age of 26. It's nothing personal. We have to turn away old people like you every day."

I said "How do you know I'm not twenty-six?"

He laughed and laughed, so I threw myself on his mercy. I gave him my best pathetic look and he gave in. "Okay, okay, just this once." Then he put me and all my oldness in a room in the corner in the basement far, far away from all his precious young Bavarians. "That'll be twenty-eight euros, please."

"Twenty-eight euros? It was sixteen a minute ago; do you charge by the wrinkle?"

"You are very funny. That's sixteen euros, plus personal tax, plus environmental tax..."

"Environmental tax?"

"And an additional €3.50 for sheets."

"I have my own sheets."

"We charge for sheets even if you have your own. Then there's the additional €2 for the one-night surcharge, which we'll forego if you stay two nights, but then we have to add resort tax. Then there's the €3 for being...well, old."

"An old tax?"

He reminded me that they were not his rules, he just worked there. "If you want a shower that'll be fifty cents, which gives you three minutes of water, but if you want hot water that's an additional fifty cents. Do you need any change?"

All that gouging was hurting my old bones, so I asked where the nearest campground was. He said he didn't know, he just worked there.

The light was disappearing, and all I wanted was a campground with a warm cafe where I could get a hot frothy cappuccino and eat a pizza piled high with mushrooms and onions and pineapple, too. But it was after eight so nothing would be open, and even if they were they'd probably tack on an "after eight tax." I started to talk to myself, venting out loud about stupid Europe and all their stupid taxes and the stupid weather getting cold. People crossed the street to steer clear of me; mothers pulled their children close. God help me, I was grumpy. Maybe I should go live in Greece.

Then I noticed a boat yard, a dozen or so boats parked for the season up on a grassy knoll where cars had no access. Yet I found just enough room in the fence for me to squeeze through with Bob.

After a good scout of the land I found a dream spot to camp for the night. Trees formed a boundary on two sides, boats on the third, while straight ahead was a front row view of the tranquil Lake Bodensee. Even with the light fading fast I caught a goodnight glimpse of the Swiss Alps peeking out south across the water. Lakeside real estate with no additional charge for the view, the sheets or wrinkles.

The very next day, after walking what I'm certain was close to a thousand kilometers, I finally found a campground. Given that it was October the grounds were nearly empty, and I had to go search for the receptionist. I finally found her in the pub next door. She was a big woman, as round as she was tall, dressed in brown polyester with a yellow daisy print and arms folded across her chest. "Are you the manager of the campground?" I asked.

She nodded.

"Oh, good," I said, digging for my wallet. "I would like to camp for one night please."

She didn't move her arms from across her chest, "We don't take tents."

I assumed there must be a language barrier. "I don't understand."

"No tents."

"No tents?" What could that mean?

"No."

Well, it goes without saying that I had absolutely no problem begging. "Please, please," I groveled, "I've just walked a thousand kilometers. I'm soaking wet, now it's dark outside, and rainy. Can't I please just pitch my tent behind that garbage bin behind the toilets? You'll never know I was here, I swear."

But she didn't budge. "No tents." She turned and walked away, arms still folded tightly across her bosom.

My shoulders slumped, along with my spirit, and I headed out into the rainy dark night. Where was the Europe I had looked forward to for so long? I had expected India to be tough, but Europe? I had expected it to be one of the highlights of my five years. Decidedly, it was not. Maybe it was a matter of failed expectations. I missed the Lions, missed meeting them as new friends. I hadn't realized it before, but meeting new people every day at specific times really helped me stay focused—focused on breast cancer and focused on the reason I had wanted to do this in the first place. In Europe I felt as if I were wandering aimlessly, losing the desire, the motivation, the excitement of discovery.

I enjoyed meeting people in the youth hostels and campgrounds, but with the world's headlines dominated by the impending war in Iraq, people would hear my accent and launch into the harsh politics of the day—a conversation I tried to avoid. I soon found myself avoiding conversations altogether and began to feel more isolated than ever.

However, while the anti-American sentiment was undoubtedly at an all-time high, I refused to believe my being American had anything to do with my surprisingly cantankerous reception in Europe. Heck, no one even stopped to talk to me long enough to know I was American. No, something else was going on in this culture that didn't welcome strangers as did other cultures; I just could never put my finger on it. There were theories of course. The day I entered Austria, two policemen stopped me in the village of Steinach and said I couldn't walk through their town. Because of the language barrier I tried to show them newspaper articles on my Walk, as well as my passport, trying to illustrate I meant no trouble. But they didn't look at them; instead one of them grabbed Bob by the handlebars and escorted me to the train station two blocks away. I didn't argue, but the scene did raise the questions another notch.

The receptionist that night at the Innsbruck Youth Hostel explained that the eastern part of Western Europe was having a dreadful time with the influx of Eastern European gypsies. She said they caused havoc in local villages and roamed the roads with their big carts bulging with tattered belongings. "With that buggy of yours piled high with camping gear and food, it wouldn't surprise me if people think you're an Eastern European gypsy."

People think I'm an Eastern European gypsy?

The next day I rode the train back to Steinach and walked to Innsbruck without Bob, allowing plenty of time to think about the receptionist's theory. She had a point. My slovenly look created a touchy situation walking across Europe. No one took kindly to my gray-tinted tee shirts and baggie shorts, not to mention the hat-head and occasional stains from trying to eat pasta on the run. It was something I'd grown self-conscious about and did make a concerted effort to change. Before entering a trattoria or pizzeria I'd first hide around the corner and attempt to comb out my hat-head or smooth out any clothing wrinkles. That, however, was usually an ill-fated attempt.

Let me make my point in numbers. Over the years, I kept an informal tally of useless trivia—for example, to date I'd found the equivalent of $36.36 on the side of the road, and thus far I'd used 546 maps. Another bit of useless trivia I recorded was how many people on a daily basis stopped and offered me a ride. People driving by saw me pushing Bob and automatically thought my car must've broken down and I was pushing my baby to the nearest town for help. The count was:

- Western USA – average twelve times a day
- New Zealand/Australia – average thirteen times a day
- Asia – seven times a day
- Europe – 0

I'd been in Europe for three months, and not a single person driving by ever stopped to see if my baby and I needed help. That's why I say it had nothing to do with my being an American. I could be their neighbor for all they knew. I can't analyze what that means, but it obviously means something more as a culture than simply not letting me pitch my tent in a campground.

During my months traveling in Europe, no one ever came up to my big teal buggy and me to ask what on earth I was up to. When I walked into a cafe people stared and I wondered if I had a boogie hanging off my face. It was not like in India; I looked like all these people, yet entire families stared. Mothers hovered over their babies, and fathers hid behind their menus following me with their eyes until I was a safe distance away. So after a few months of staring eyes, I decided to get some entertainment value out of it.

While I knew they were watching I would sit down, spread out my maps, plunk down my (new) camera, cell phone, order a plate of spaghetti, then maybe type on my little computer. No bum in the world can type faster than I can. Knowing they were still peeking over their menus, I would stop typing, put my hand to my chin like I was thinking long and hard about the words, then "ah-ha!" and I would type like the wind looking satisfied. I'd swirl up a bite of spaghetti on my fork and launch into the keyboard again. Afterward, I would pay my bill, say thank you in four languages, walk outside into the rain, and push Bob down the road leaving them mystified.

Years from now I'll bet you could still hear the mother spew off yet another possible scenario. "Honey, maybe she was a travel writer working incognito." He'd puff on his cigar and insist, "Come on, honey, maps, computer, camera? She was a spy."

It's dusk at the end of a fifteen-mile day and I'm walking into a new town. An uneasy feeling sweeps over me. There doesn't seem to be anyone here. Not a soul. No birds tweeting, no cars cruising Main Street, no kids playing kickball in the yards. Houses look empty, stores and cafes are locked up tight, no campgrounds, motels or even city parks to sleep in.

I'm standing alone at an intersection, my mind racing. Where is everyone? Should I call 911? Should I hide? Should I run? In which direction? I stand in the middle of an empty intersection as the last light of day disappears, surrounded by vacant houses and desolate streets. Turning around and around looking for someone, something, any sign of life. I'm spinning now, faster, faster, faster.

Then I woke up.

Not exactly a nightmare of monster proportions, but haunting nonetheless, particularly in the middle of the night when all logic seems to vanish. For a year prior to leaving on this walk, I periodically bolted out of sleep from that dream.

Three years later I was walking into the tiny town of Ortenberg, Germany, a lovely Bavarian village nestled into the edge of the Black Forest. Fellow travelers had told me about the youth hostel there that takes old people over twenty-six and the village with its warm cozy cafes and chalk menus, displaying the day's special hot German suppe (soup). I was desperately in need of a dawdle day, a youth hostel and a warm, cozy cafe with hot German suppe.

On the edge of town I saw the IYHA (International Youth Hostel Association) symbol, the one-dimensional blue house and pine tree, which marked the end of my day. The vacancy sign indicated availability—the bad news was that the directional arrow pointed up. Not left, right or ahead. Up. I looked up, the kind of look up where your back arches. There stood the youth hostel in a castle perched on top of a very substantial mountain. I took a deep breath, grabbed Bob by the handlebars and put one foot in front of the other, three steps at a time.

Two-thousand feet in elevation, grunting, pushing, "…breathe, two, three, four…" wait for the car to pass, look up, brace your quads, honk, honk, oh, bite me, visualize, cozy castle at the top, hot German suppe, hot shower, easy night, "…breathe two, three, four."

In an hour the summit flattened out and I flopped over Bob for support, exhausted but exhilarated. We had done it, I thought, knocking on the door, breathing heavily.

No one came.

"Guttentag!" I yelled through a screen.

The sign on the door listed the hours, which were pretty standard for Europe: "Open: 8-9am, 3-5pm and 8-9pm." It was a mystery how they got anything done in Europe with their doors open four hours a day, but the irony was that I was there at 4:00 p.m., smack in the middle of those limited hours.

Having nowhere to go, Bob and I found a patch of green and waited. And waited.

"We're sold out tonight," were the first words out of his mouth as he started opening the door to the castle. A chubby man of average height, he wore one of those mustaches that curls up on both ends, like Geraldo Rivera's.

I raced off the green patch to greet him. "Your sign down at the bottom of the hill says you have a vacancy. Are you sure?"

"Quite sure. We're sold out. We've been sold out. The sign is wrong," he said, avoiding my eyes as he opened the door and started inside.

I followed behind him. "I happen to be on foot and I don't need to tell you it was a heckuva jaunt up that mountain ha ha. Would you mind if I just camp out in your backyard?"

He turned around and took a step towards me. "We don't allow campers in our backyard. There's a campground down the mountain and across town." His speech was slow and terse, "We're sold out. We've been sold out. The sign is wrong."

He walked into his office and shut the door, leaving the sign that read "Sorry we missed you" swinging on the doorknob.

The campground across town said, "So sorry, we're full."

The Bed & Breakfast said, "We don't take a one-night stay."

Ten more kilometers in the next town of Offenberg, their only accommodation was a Bed & Breakfast that was closed on Wednesdays and a campground that claimed they only took RV's. "I'm so sorry, but we don't take tents. They're bad for our soil."

Now it was 8:00 p.m., and my dream of a short lazy day in a quaint little Bavarian village with hot German suppe vanished in the darkness. The next town, thirty-one kilometers away, was too far to make before nightfall.

Standing alone in the middle of an empty intersection at dusk, I had nowhere to go. But this time I was not waking up.

A drunken homeless man asked if I had any change; I said buddy, I should be asking you for change. Surprisingly, he knew English, officially supporting the fact that every German knows at least two languages. I'm not sure why I was going to trust the word of a drunk, homeless man but I'd run out of choices. "Would you happen to know a good place to camp out around here? A riverbed, a forest, a farm?"

He hiccupped, which sent him into a stumble, "Vich vay ya travelin'?"

"I'm heading for Strasbourg, France."

He told me about a bike trail from Offenberg to Strasbourg. "A backcountry road...hic...across da farmland. It's vell signed vit a big blue triangle...hic...ya should be able to camp anyvere along da vay."

While the idea of a bike trail all the way to Strasbourg sounded like heaven, it was clearly a gamble. First, I was taking the word of a man who obviously wasn't quite in charge of his mental faculties. Secondly, there would be no streetlights or even moonlight on a rural farm road, which meant I would be walking like a blind person.

Why not?

I clipped the pepper spray to my hip, thanked my drunken friend and headed west into the dark.

The light disappeared completely as I drifted down the empty farm trail. My little yellow radio was my only source of entertainment, even though I didn't understand a word. During commercials I scrolled through the frequency knob until...*hello, what's this*? English! Actual English words! Simple, glorious words that I understood! It was American Armed Forces Radio playing...Dr. Laura!

It had its share of static, but if I tilted my head just right, it came in loud and clear enough. While I'm no fan of Dr. Laura, I was thrilled to hear her voice, to hear English and understand a language, to be entertained. Oddly, I found comfort out on this dark lonely farm road hearing about the underbelly of American life ticking along as usual.

A woman named Gina called in to say that she's thirty-two and dating a thirty-nine-year-old man who still lives with his mother. He has a decent job as an engineer, she says, but he's never lived on his own. His mother still cooks him breakfast, prepares him a bag lunch, does his laundry and he doesn't pay rent. Is that normal? I really love him, Dr. Laura.

Dr. Laura's response: "You're an idiot."

Maybe I did like Dr. Laura.

Total darkness blanketed my path. I couldn't see a single step in front of me, but Dr. Laura made me laugh out loud. I talked back to the radio as loudly as I pleased, reasoning that it was a nifty strategy that pre-empted any would-be lunatics from approaching me on this dark, lonely road. It also made me homesick. Oh sure, America is far from perfect (as Dr. Laura was clearly proving), but the more I learned about my own country while traveling, the more I loved it, warts and all.

While you hear a lot about how American culture has affected the rest of the world with its fast food and Britney Spears, the reverse is also true. It was fascinating to walk through other countries at a snail's pace and realize that it was the people of these countries that found their way across the Atlantic, and over the last two centuries incrementally built America. We all know America is a melting pot that sprang from the social experiment of self government consisting of immigrant cultures from all over the world. I saw firsthand how these cultures contributed to that pot in every way from fashion to music to dance.

In particular, I loved discovering the roots of our unique American English. In each country I could spot a word in a road sign or cafe menu that had made its way overseas to help form our crazy but lovable blended language. The simplest examples are "delicatessen" or "loaf" from Germany; "cafe" from France. The

Dutch give us "waffle," but more importantly they exported the word "cookie." It's no wonder I have a fondness for the Dutch.

European immigrants also brought with them a whole slew of traditions that we as Americans are free to cherry pick and build new family traditions around, traditions that are more than likely entirely different from our neighbors'. The more I learned about the world, the more I learned about my own country, my own roots, and felt downright blessed that I am able to be a part of that great social experiment. Hearing Dr. Laura took me home for an hour, and it made me feel cozy, even when she was yelling at women with pathetic love lives.

My little yellow radio stayed tuned to Armed Forces Radio, bringing me an almost custom made program lineup of Paul Harvey news, followed by NPR's *All Things Considered*, followed by the Minnesota Twins game. Fancy hearing my hometown baseball team play a game out here in Where-Am-I, Germany.

Sometimes my little yellow radio would lose reception, but if I tilted my head two ticks to the right and a couple inches back, the signal would catch and I carried on walking crooked down the bike path.

I walked and walked and walked, thrilled to be hearing from home for the first time in two years, entertained to the point that I didn't even realize I was walking. I just kept plugging along as if my legs had a mind of their own, completely detached from my head. My short dawdle of a day was now stretching into fifty kilometers, the longest day of my entire GlobalWalk. I was sure that I could walk all night. The last bit of light in my headlamp was flickering to nothing, so I had to budget conservatively. If I felt a sudden change in terrain under my feet, into, say, a puddle/river/fence post, I flashed my headlight just long enough to get back on track.

It was 1:00 a.m. when I noticed the city lights of Strasbourg, France, stretched out ahead of me. It was beautiful from my dark perch. My legs could've carried on and probably right through, but I had to stop. The reality was that I had to cross a border, then wind my way through a city to which I had no map. Surely no affordable place was going to allow me a room at this hour. No, it was best to pitch my tent out here in the safety of a rural farm road, wild animals, drunks and Dr. Laura.

My headlamp was barely surviving at a sputter, so in order to find a spot to pitch my tent, I patted the dirt path with my foot until I was off the road onto a grassy area. I took ten cautionary steps in each direction. The ground was lumpy, but there didn't seem to be a muddy ditch or a dead animal. I unzipped Bob and pitched camp by touch.

Safely tucked inside my sleeping bag, I put on my little yellow radio, tilted my head two tics to the right, a couple tics back and…*Car Talk*!

The noise of a car driving down the dirt road woke me. It was 6:30 a.m. A chill in the air left mist on the tent. Even Bob was misty sitting alone outside the tent. In October as I got further north into Europe, it was only going to get chillier. Luckily, Dad slipped some gloves into my last package because taking down a cold, misty tent in a thirty-eight degree chill is miserable with bare hands. Great stuff those titanium poles, but I defy anyone to fold up more than one pole without howling through a few choice expletives.

I poked my head out of the tent to get my bearings. Tall corn stalks surrounded me, and I congratulated myself at finding the perfect camping spot. Safely off the road and, better still, underneath a blue bike sign assuring me I had stayed on the right path.

I bundled up, wearing nearly everything I had, and resumed walking down the dirt road with the blue signs toward France. Within one mile the trail crossed a main road and there, shining above me, was the sign that put a flutter in my heart on chilly mornings: The Golden Arches.

"I'll have, umm, zwei Egg McMuffins, bitte."

"Two?" the clerk said, saving herself from trying to understand my German.

"Yes, two please—ja, zwei, bitte." My German translation book didn't have the entire "I just walked a million miles and spent the

night in a cornfield warranting four if it were socially acceptable."
So I left it at zwei.

While they filled my order I went to the bathroom to wash my
face and brush my teeth. I tried to make my hair presentable but
finally gave up and sat down to write in my journal. I wrote about
the previous night—how I tried to find a place to stay in Ortenberg,
Offenburg, Willstatt, Kehl and how at dusk the drunken homeless
man pointed me in the direction of the great bike trail—when it
occurred to me: the dream. The dream that made me sweat and
wake up with my heart pounding those many nights three years
ago had pretty much come true. I had entered a strange town at
dusk with nowhere to go and no one to turn to, not so much as a
spot to pitch my tent. How interesting, I wrote, that our comfort
levels increase at such an incremental pace through the years that
day-by-day you don't notice any change at all. Then one day you
look behind you and realize you're in a whole new world. That night
I was comfortable—not cozy, mind you, but at ease—walking into
the darkness down a strange road with no flashlight, no moonlight,
and pitching a tent blind. "Incremental steps," I wrote. "So little yet
so powerful."

Then I walked up to the counter to fetch my seconds—a Big
Bacon & Eggs with a cappuccino splurge.

The season changed rapidly into a late autumn. Days were wet and
windy as I made my way north through France and Luxembourg,
free camping along the side of the road most nights. Walking,
camping, spending all day in the rain—I never got dry. I couldn't
sit down to have a picnic or dawdle to enjoy a view; I just kept my
head down and plowed through the horizontal rain, trying to dodge
the nuts and apples falling on my head. I promised never to whine
about the heat again.

In November most campgrounds had closed, which was great
because although the campground gates were locked, there was always a gap just wide enough for me to squeeze through with Bob.
Inside the grounds I usually found a covered picnic area or, better

yet, a bathroom to sleep in. Campground bathrooms in November are dry and clean for the winter, and safe from nuts and apples falling on my head. The only minor inconvenience was that every time I rolled over in the middle of the night the automatic lights flipped on. Not quite the Marriott, but as close to heaven as a tired, wet, grumpy walker could get.

Those nights when I was lucky enough to find a closed campground with an open bathroom, I spread my wet gear under the hand dryers and re-hit the start buttons every thirty seconds for hours trying to dry out my life for at least one night.

Even when I hit the bonanza of a clean bathroom with hot hand dryers, my left eye continued to twitch. I was struggling. The language barrier, inaccurate maps, deficient road signage, freezing weather, businesses closed midday, afternoon, and anytime in between—all were wearing me down. Tourist Information Center signs read, "Out for Siesta." "We don't take one night stays." "Closed on Mondays." "We only take youths." "We don't take tents." "Dead end." "We charge €3.50 for sheets." "There's an Old Tax for you, Ma'am." I started to feel like those ultra-runners who, after the fiftieth mile, need a pacer to help keep them focused and motivated.

One night in a campground bathroom outside Leige, I sat on the floor shivering under the hand dryer wondering again if I was doing permanent damage to my psyche by putting myself through this day after day. I worried about spending so much time alone. Would I ever readjust to being social again, or would I become one of those bitter people who sit in dark houses where the neighborhood kids ring the doorbell and run?

In three weeks I would arrive in England where I had a stepsister, to say nothing of a familiar language that would make things exponentially easier. That thought cheered me up considerably. So right there on the bathroom floor I decided, for the sake of my sanity, I needed to get to England as fast as possible. I spread out my maps and circled all the youth hostels between me and a boat to England. Because of my perpetual fondness for the Dutch my plan had always been to go through The Netherlands, but my circles clearly indicated that the Netherlands had virtually no youth hostels across the country, as opposed to Belgium which had them conveniently staggered every fourteen miles along a footpath on traffic-free canals! Going through Belgium was not only seven days shorter, but it would get me out of the rain, the traffic, and officially-closed-for-the-season bathrooms with automatic light triggers.

The next morning I walked out of that campground bathroom and made a beeline for England.

CHAPTER 19

Can We Talk?

It was a simple question from the passport control officer in Dover: What 'tis it yer doin' here in the U.K.?

It had been five long, wet, miserable months walking through Europe, and eighteen months since I had been in an English speaking country. I was ready to talk!

I told him I was walking around the world for breast cancer and I've been on the road for three and a half years now and it's been great except for maybe a spell in India, and Europe was surprisingly tough, oh I know, I know, it's not the best time to be walking through England either because it's the rainy season, but at least I'll have the Lions Clubs involved again, and they're so great because they make sure I have a warm dry place to stay every night with food and help with my laundry and the breast cancer work, which is a whole different story than in Europe where no one would give me a glass of water if my head was on fire, but I'm so excited to be in England where I'll be able to ask directions in English and understand warning signs and even get caught up on the news by stepping up to any newsstand in the entire nation to see if we're at war yet, and who the heck are Posh and Becks?"

I paused to catch a breath and he quickly stamped my passport and waved me through. "Best a leuck to ye, Luv."

Giles and Geoff from the Dover Lions Club met me off the Dover dock and with little more ado took me out to celebrate my arrival at a good ol' English pub.

Pubs are a way of life in the U.K. Nearly every street corner in every village has a pub named The Owl's Arms, The Jolly Butcher, or some such mysterious cuteness. They tell me the pub culture evolved somewhat from England's dreadful weather. If not for a pub to duck into when it rained the British would never have left their homes at all. So pubs became neighborhood gathering places. Business people hold meetings, kids have birthday parties, and sweeties have anniversaries. Most Brits have a pub that they affectionately called "The Pub" and everyone knows which one they're talking about.

The Lydden Bell was about two hundred years old and the sort of place where you have to crouch down to get through the door. I'm only five foot two, so the English must've been really teeny people two hundred years ago. It was cozy inside with purple walls and a fire roaring in the ancient fireplace surrounded by historic photos of the pub.

Hallways were single-file. If you happened to meet with someone, say, coming back from the loo, it would be like meeting another car in the mountains and the downhill car—in this case the person on the way to the loo—would have to back up until they found a cul-de-sac.

One of the Lions warned me in a paternal sort of way that women don't much frequent English pubs, and if you popped in for even a single pint you would likely walk out smelling like an ashtray. But that was changing. With no-smoking laws sweeping across the nation, many pubs were becoming family friendly with kid menus and salads for Mum. Pub owners welcomed the new trend as it was good for business, but it tended to leave the old-timers a wee cranky.

Giles invited me to have a pint. "Perhaps a Bishop's Finger, or maybe ye'd fancy a Speckled Hen?" Then the man on my left leaned over and opened his silver cigarette case. "'ullo, Luv. Fancy a fag?"

I held up my hand to motion a no thank you, at which point he clamped up his silver box and asked where I was heading from Dover. I told him after spending a day doing errands, I would carry on to Canterbury.

"Ahh, yes, Canterbury," he said. "Goin' ta walk up the Old Crabble through Nackered on Wooly to Boughton under Splean are ye?"

Someone interjected, "Blimey, Ian, are ye mad? Ye tryin' to kill 'er, mate? Lorry drivers fly 'round Old Crabble. Why, some German lorry took out a Tescoes just last week!"

Then he turned to me with clear authority. "Ye got to stick to the A256, Luv. That'll take ye up the dual carriage through Bumpkindoodlyshire to the small ring. Then ye round the ring where ye half-left down the hedge road to the Belles Ousley. Carry on up the single carriage to the high street where ye cross the zebra. When you spot Marks and Spencer there's yer Canterbury."

I looked over to the first guy as if to say, "Hold me. Tell me everything will be okay."

"Ye know, Graham," he said putting his hand up to his chin as though in deep thought. "The old Roman Road 'as a footpath, dunnit?"

"Ahh, good thinkin', mate. Those Romans, now they knew how te build a road. Tha's much bette' innit?"

He then turned to me and spoke slowly as if that might help me understand him. "The Old Roman Road is the same as the Old London Road, which is the same as the New Dover Road, which is the same as the A2. Ye take 'er through te Clapper Junction. Then ye catch the big ring and carry on over the humped pelican to the Tescoes. Tha's yer Canterbury."

He paused for a minute to see if anything registered. I wanted to ask, among a host of other things, what's a Tescoes, but was afraid of a new can of worms.

"So what is it ye goin' 'ta do in Canterbury?"

I told him I was going to run as fast as I could to the bookstore to buy a dictionary; clearly it would be a few more months until I could actually speak English.

Waking up in a British guesthouse was like waking up in a dollhouse. There was exactly an arm's length between the bed and any one of the four walls. The door itself was only two feet wide, and for the life of me I couldn't figure out how they got anything in the room—lamps, telly, even the Bible, let alone that queen-sized bed.

But it worked. Words like *quaint, cozy* and *cute* were no doubt coined by someone lying in bed at an English guesthouse with her legs propped against the wall.

Bob couldn't make it upstairs to the room the previous night. I asked if they had an elevator, which undoubtedly will keep the proprietors entertained for a lifetime. I unpacked Bob and left him folded up under a table downstairs, the only ounce of spare room they had. Then I grabbed my bathroom bag, a towel and a tee shirt and took them through the bedroom door one at a time.

Thrilled to have a TV for the first time in four months, I turned it on before my eyes were even open in the morning. The only thing on besides gardening shows was Trisha, Britain's version of *Jerry Springer*, with the day's episode, "My Boy Toy Treats Me Like a Mum." I quickly decided that four months without television was a great gift.

I spent my first day wandering through town to get my bearings in this new country. I walked from the Hubert House Guest House into Market Square, noting cafes quaintly named Dickens Corner and The Cabin. I was in my glory walking up and down Market Square understanding everything people were saying.

I shamelessly enjoyed eavesdropping, a priceless perk to knowing the language. From now on if I needed directions, I simply had to ask, I didn't have to walk four kilometers out of my way until I hit a dead end then backtrack and wave someone down. Therefore, just because I could, I asked where the bookstore was.

The woman at the bookstore asked how she could help. I said I was looking for an atlas of Britain, but it had to be very detailed because I was walking and I had no sense of direction.

"Yer walking through Britain?"

"Yes. Actually I'm walking around the world and just entered Britain last night. Boy am I thrilled to be here!"

"Yer walking 'round the *world*?"

"Yeah."

"Fancy that!"

She then turned to her workmates, "Fiona! Philipa! Come 'ere! You won't believe! This woman is *walking* 'round the world!"

"Blimey!"

After the usual, how many pairs of shoes, the why's, how longs, and where-ya-been's, the three of them launched into the atlas section comparing notes as to the best map for me. They settled on the big one, and because I was able to ship my camping gear home again, Bob had room for the extra large atlas.

Moseying through the bookstore, I stocked up on a few necessary items to start my British trek—a phone card and the Sustrans book of cycle trails to lead me out of the path of those lorries that were trying to kill me. When I started flipping through *The History of the Crop Circles*, I knew it was time to check out.

The nice woman at the checkout counter said, "Thanks, Luv. Tha's smashin'." Holding back my giggle I thanked her and swung my book bag quite happily out of the bookstore and back into Market Square.

"Fancy?" "Blimey?" "Smashin'?" It may not be any English I knew, but something told me I was going to have a good time in England. I swung my book bag over to the Dickens Corner for lunch, spread my new atlas across the table and ordered a jacket and bap, whatever the heck those were.

Nearly a year before, when I arrived in India, I had temporarily suspended the fundraising portion of the breast cancer campaign. I simply continued with the awareness effort, understanding that a white person walking the streets of Kolkata asking for money was really pushing it.

The awareness campaign continued in full force throughout India and Turkey via press and Lions help with educational forums. In continental Europe there was nothing. Additionally, the difficulty in getting online across Europe washed out any hopes of making plans for fundraising across Britain.

The Dover Lions Clubs would hear none of it.

My first day in Dover I went to a Lions Club meeting where I stood up to tell my story—how I had been on the road for three-and-a-half years working with breast cancer organizations and Lions Clubs all over the world—except Europe—to get breast cancer in the press, and that GlobalWalk had been the catalyst for breast cancer awareness campaigns in some Asian countries. When I finished and took my seat, President Keith asked me to stand again. To my surprise, he announced that they had agreed to donate a hundred pounds ($150) to my cause.

I struggled for words, "That's really very generous, but the thing is I don't have a beneficiary here in the U.K. I'm just doing awareness work through press, forums, and brochures no fundraising."

"Why not?"

I explained that while in Europe I had been in no position to research, contact and nurture relationships with possible benefactors of a fundraising campaign in Great Britain. "So I really had no choice but to continue awareness work without fundraising."

The Lions in Dover said no. "You've got to fundraise in the U.K. We'll help you find a good, reputable organization and get you on your feet."

What a welcome turn of events! I embraced their help enthusiastically. After the meeting we sat down and talked about the criteria for a beneficiary. I explained that it had to be a national organization that would utilize the funds for education and awareness, not research. Research, I continued, was necessary, but one project costs the kind of money raised in big walks with tens of thousands of people. Educational funds might not sound as romantic as research, but it was essential. I pointed out that with the awareness campaign that had been going on in the western world for the past fifteen years, the mortality rate had dropped by nearly thirty percent.

The Dover Lions were on the case. Their first call was to a Lions Club member in London, Elliot Shubert, coincidentally an American from a small town in Minnesota. Thanks to his broad connections, he immediately got on board, researched the issue and settled on an organization called The Breast Cancer Campaign based in London. As a result, I walked up the Old Roman Road toward London, occasionally ducking behind a hedgerow to find a quiet spot away from the lorries to talk to Fiona at The Breast Cancer Campaign. She told me that The Breast Cancer Campaign, an organization primarily involved with sponsoring research programs, was coincidentally just starting to look for a sponsor to fund their Guardian Angel Bookmark program, an education campaign focused on early detection. For the first time in months I felt as if my stars were aligned again, and I bounded up the Old Roman Road, the bounce back in my step.

The days are short during a British November; light rose at 8:30 a.m., fell at 3:45 p.m., and in between it drizzled. The villages along the Old Roman Road blended together as one through Canterbury, Faversham, Gillingham, Rochester, Dartford—all featuring towering cathedrals and pubs conveniently located every seven miles for a rest and hot tea in front of the fire.

It was six o'clock on a Thursday night when I strolled into bustling nighttime London. Nine-to-fivers were hustling through the streets lugging briefcases, talking on their mobile phones, racing for the tube, living busy lives. I stood in the middle of the bustle hovering over my map, studying the maze of streets to Trafalgar Square, where I was meeting a man from the London Lions Club. The map indicated that to get into city center I had my choice of crossing the London Bridge, Waterloo Bridge, Southwark Bridge or Westminster Bridge. Since I didn't know one from another I took a stab in the dark—Westminster Bridge, just because.

I strolled over the bridge, pushing Bob slowly amid the grandeur of the historic Thames glowing in a nighttime London. The lights of the city surrounded me. I felt swept up in the energy of millions of people scurrying to friends and pubs and parties and families. Suddenly I was hit with a moment—the kind of moment you can't explain when people ask about your favorite moments—

when the light is just right; when there's a magic, an energy in the air, that hits you suddenly, centers you in the here and now and swallows you whole. A moment I'd thought about years ago when I had maps spread all over the floor and wondered about the day I'd walk into London after years on the road. Now here I was, walking over the Westminster Bridge into London with Big Ben greeting me in all his glory. Towering over the Thames sat the Parliament Building where the Tories were barking at the Labour Party MP's and maybe Tony Blair was on the phone at this very minute with George Bush shaping the future of the world as the war in Iraq looked inevitable. And they were all oblivious to the girl outside their window pushing her three-wheeled buggy Bob over the Westminster Bridge having a moment.

My stepsister Kathy landed in London virtually right out of college, eventually met Nick, and settled down in Windsor, just west of the city. Walking up the Thames River toe-path, I was awed at the fact that she lived virtually one kilometer off my route walking around the world. Would I have come this way if she hadn't been here? I suspect I would have; it's where the Thames River toe-path leads you.

Kathy and Nick have two boys, Robert and Joe, aged five and six. As though I had planned it, Kathy's niece Abby was in town from Minnesota. The fact that I was coming through Windsor into the arms of extended family at Thanksgiving provided an exceptional bonus. It had been four years since I had celebrated my favorite holiday. I always loved the idea of a holiday that celebrates the gathering and breaking bread with your loved ones to honor the things you're grateful for, so there could hardly have been a better place to be than Windsor with the first familiar faces I'd seen in years.

Mapquest map in hand, I walked right up to their house on College Crescent and saw two little boys in the window. They raced to the front door to greet me—or so I thought. Robert, the older one, seemed much more intrigued by Bob, offering to take over the burden of pushing him through the back door. Joe shrugged his shoulders at the sight of me and leapt back into the living room in his Superman pajamas.

"Two boys, huh?" were my first words to Kathy.

"Two boys is nothing; I've volunteered you to talk at their school—that's 100 five- and six-year-olds. You're on tomorrow."

Polly's Journal

Mrs. Hujack is the headmaster at Joe and Robert's school, and she is no nonsense. You never ever want to be sent to Mrs. Hujack.

I sat on a chair in the back of the assembly on my very best behavior—hands on my lap, back straight up, waiting my turn like a good girl.

Mrs. Hujack stepped up in front of the hushed crowd of children at St. Francis Primary School and said in her no nonsense tone, "Good afternoon, children."

A hundred children responded on cue and only slightly in unison, "Goooood aaaafteernooooon Miiiissssissss HuuuuujaaAAAACK."

Mrs. Hujack grimaced. "We'll have to work on that. But first we have a very special guest. We have a woman with us today who is walking, yes, walking, around the world. Doesn't that sound exciting, children? She is going to tell us all about her adventures, so let's show Miss Polly how we're on our best behavior. Would you please say good afternoon to Miss Polly?"

"Goooood aaaafteernooooon, Miss Poooooolllllyyyy."

I walked up to the front of the class with my hands folded neatly in front of me and said good afternoon, everyone, and thank you for having me, Mrs. Hujack.

My speech is very different when I speak to children. Breast Cancer plays no part. They're much more interested in if I've ever seen a monkey. Their eyes turned into giant saucers when I told them about the snakes I saw in Australia as big as tree trunks, how kangaroos bounced across highways, and the baby kangaroos, the joeys, jump into their Mummy's pouch headfirst.

"And as a matter of fact, yes, I did see monkeys! Lots of them! In Thailand a monkey actually jumped on my head!" That grabbed their full attention. "There I was, minding my own business when a monkey jumped out of a tree and plopped right onto my head!

"Well, good golly gosh, it took the breath right out of me! I started dancing around in circles like a crazy person with my arms flailing over my head, screaming 'Help! Help! There's a monkey on my head!' But that cheeky little monkey just grabbed hold of my ears and rode me like a cowboy. A crowd raced toward me, trying to shoo the monkey off my head—by throwing rocks!

"I shouted, 'Don't throw rocks! You're going to hit me in the head!' But no one understood English, so I went racing around trying to dodge hurling rocks yelling, 'Help! Help! There's a monkey on my head!' Then that silly monkey slid right down my head and over my eyes!

"A good Samaritan finally came running to my rescue and shooed the monkey off my head with a harmless broom, and that cheeky little monkey ran right up the tree and ate his banana."

The children laughed so hard they rolled around on the floor yelling, "Tell it again! Tell it again!"

Mrs. Hujack smiled.

I taught them how to say thank you in Mandarin and hello in Thai with a bow and their hands held together like a prayer.

I told them how people eat differently—like in Malaysia where they use the fork and spoon in one hand like chopsticks and that in India you eat with your right hand only. If Mrs. Hujack hadn't been there, I would've told them to try this at the dinner table tonight, but I was a good girl and said, "Please don't try this at home."

When I was finished, I asked if there were any questions and one hundred hands shot up in the air.

"How many houses have you stayed in?"

"How many times have you thrown up?"

"What songs do you sing when you walk?"

"Do you ever get lost?"

"Do you get stinky?"

"I know my daddy's phone number."

"What is your favorite country?"

That is a good question that I get often and still find hard to answer. "I think if we take the nice bike trails of Germany, the pasta of Italy, the lack of spiders and snakes in New Zealand, the scenery of Austria, the generosity of Australians, the smiles of the Thais, the cleanliness of Singapore, the weather of Turkey, the prices of India, the product and service of America," I paused, "and the kids of England, then we might have the perfect world."

Mrs. Hujack gave a nod of approval at my political correctness. "Class, now wasn't that interesting? Maybe one day you too can walk around the world. Now please say thank you to Miss Polly."

Thaaaaaaankkkkkyyooooouuuu Miiiissss Pooooolllllyyyy

And so I pootled along the Thames River toe-path through Henley-on-Thames, Whitchurch-on-Thames, Sandford-on-Thames and Slough. Every day I met my new hosts from the Lions club, and before I knew it I was using words like "codswallop," "bugger" and "sod off," and with the rest of Britain I could be found racing for the telly every night for a daily dose of Coronation Street to see if Gail was onto Richard's stalking yet. Each night my hosts would greet me at the front door and say, "Come'n, come'n. We do apologize for the weather; it's dreadful really. Ye 'aven't picked the best time te visit us in England, now have ye? Shame really, 'tis lovely when it's not rainin'. Oh, never mind anyway, I'll go put the kettle on." And off they'd scurry to tinker about the kitchen.

You don't have to be in Britain long before discovering that if you order a tea in a pub they look at you like you're speaking Chinese. If, on the other hand, you say no to a tea in someone's home, a hush falls across the table. "You don't want a tea? Are you sure you don't want a tea? Who is it that doesn't want a tea?" There's an uncomfortable silence until someone notes, "Oh, she's American. They don't drink tea over there." A collective sigh ensues and everyone bursts to life again over the tea.

The Lions Clubs took great care of me. Spoiled me silly, really. For dinner my new hosts went out of their way to cook great meals like lamb and potatoes and topped it off with a choice of mousse with cream or pie with cream or ice cream with cream. In England everything had to have cream on top or I got the same look as when I turned down a tea and that's just not on.

As the winds grew chillier and sprinkles of snow began to fall across the dainty green dales of the English countryside, I felt grateful that I didn't have to camp out in cornfields the way I did in continental Europe. It was my first winter walking and Dad sent my winter gear. Now every morning I put on an insulated layer of long underwear, ski pants, a puffy North-Face down jacket, hat and gloves and a thermos for a tea on the go.

It wasn't so bad. Sure, it rains in England, but it was just a sprinkle, albeit a constant one. The toughest part of walking in the rain was coming upon a High Street (Main Street), where hundreds of umbrellas threatened to take out an eye. When the weather shifted into a hefty sprinkle I would duck into a pub like The Fox and Hop and order a tea. They'd say "A tea? I'll bet you want some water too, with that ice; you Americans just love your ice. No? No ice? Just a tea? Are you quite sure? You could have water with that ice. It's no trouble."

The Thames River toe-path wound into the city of Oxford, where I stopped for a few days of fundraising and rest. I had organized my route through England with the fantasy of hanging out in Oxford and cavorting amongst the educated elite. I would frequent the Eagle and Child Pub where C.S. Lewis and J.R.R. Tolkien regularly shared a pint and a chinwag. I would sit there with my little laptop, take an occasional sip of my cappuccino and talk about Medieval English Law and feel like one of them. Maybe Chelsea Clinton would come by and ask, "Is this seat taken?" and I would say, "Please," then together we would sip, read, type, and talk about Kierkegaard and Dostoevsky. But after admitting that I couldn't understand so much as the first paragraph of either, everyone in the Eagle and Child Pub would know I was a fake, but Chelsea would stick up for me; she'd say, "Let her stay, she has a nice personality."

None of that happened of course. Truth is I sat in the Starbucks with an overpriced toffee nut latte, much too busy people watching to do any tapping on my little keyboard or reading J.R.R. Tolkien. I was able to eavesdrop on a number of conversations, but they turned out to be mostly Americans over here for post-grad work.

Roaming the labyrinth of Oxford's majestic twelfth and thirteenth century buildings, I wondered about the endless supply of mischievous gossip that had gone on in these buildings and helped shape our world. I wanted to know a little inside scoop about world leaders who were sculpted here: William Penn, Sir Walter Raleigh, Dudley Moore, etc., to say nothing of a few Bill Clinton anecdotes (I think it's safe to assume there are some).

In complete wonder I slowly made my way back to work. The Lions Club of Oxford had organized a couple of interviews on the BBC, two newspaper interviews and a fundraiser out at Templars Shopping Center. My biggest honor though, was a civic reception at the Town Hall, hosted by Oxford's Lord Mayor Gillian Sanders. A wonderfully warm woman, she gave me a personalized tour of the Town Hall's historic treasures, something only a few are privy to see. I wondered if anyone passing by at that very moment was looking through the windows into this six-hundred year old Town Hall, hoping they too could one day be an Oxfordian like that girl smiling, taking photos and hooting it up with the Lord Mayor.

I was having a great time in the U.K. Strangers kept me fat and fine, and every day I enjoyed the wild and fabulous personalities that make up the British Isles. To entertain myself through the daily rain, I snapped photos of the enchanting pub and town names that are such a rich source of amusement in England. According to the map if I were to follow Honeybottom Road to Old Butt Lane it would take me to Little Piddle via Studley.

I loved meeting the Lions members in village pubs, the meet-n-greets by town mayors and walking country lanes peppered with red letter boxes, red phone boxes, red buses. Everything was perfect.

Except the world news.

CHAPTER 20

Count Down
to Doomsday

The fervor across the airwaves was heating up. Every day I expected my little yellow radio to announce the invasion of Iraq that would set the world on fire.

The main topic of conversation, it blanketed newspapers, radio chat shows and television news, as well as pubs and people's homes. I was growing more uncomfortable each night as I was introduced to my hosts. I was a guest in their home, and in my position as fundraiser and advocate, it certainly was not proper to talk about the politics of the day—but it was the elephant in the room.

Who knew four years prior that this wouldn't be the best time to walk around this crazy world? It all seemed so pleasant, even welcoming, through New Zealand, Australia and Southeast Asia. But times had changed. Just like the days in Malaysia after 9/11, the world was on the brink of war and I couldn't talk about it with anyone.

The majority of people were most respectful, applying the unspoken rule: "Don't Ask, Don't Tell." But that big fat elephant was difficult to avoid. I knew people itched to know how, as an American, I felt about the impending war. But they didn't ask. I didn't tell. Indeed, what could I say? I'd been away from my own country for three and a half years and had no real idea how the war news was playing at home. Some nights I would sit with my hosts in their living room watching the news. Out of the corner of my eye I could see them squirming in their seats, itching to yell back at the telly, but they felt they couldn't with an American in their home.

Then again, some of my hosts didn't give a toss how I felt one way or another and would yell at the telly, the wife and the walls around them. We would sit around the dinner table sharing stories of breast cancer, jobs, kids and Coronation Street, but if someone were to ask me about the politics of the day I mumbled something generic like, "Oh, those crazy kids," or "Women should rule the world." Occasionally one would shock me with a greeting at the door like, "Why are Americans so arrogant? So stupid? So naive?" What could I say? I soon reached the point that before I knocked on the door I closed my eyes for a brief moment, took a deep breath and visualized patience.

The weather grew nastier, an ill-timed combination of marching north while sliding into winter. It was the sort of weather that's noisy, with winds howling so loudly I couldn't hear the news updates on my radio. The last three miles to the Scottish border offered no option other than to walk along the major A74 motorway, fighting a double whammy of nature's fifty-mile-per-hour wind and the blowback from the lorries that tossed me back four steps each time one of them passed.

Struggling through the gusts I finally spotted a small crowd, complete with a genuine Scottish bagpiper and a "Welcome to Scotland" sign flapping in the wind. I ran through the wind, recognizing a number of new friends even though we'd never met—particularly Jim Hamilton, a rosy-cheeked, white-haired man from the Stranraer Lions Club, with whom I'd been in touch for months. He had been assigned Polly duty for my entire journey around Scotland; together we prepared a route, which he followed up on by contacting everyone along the way. Lions Clubs around the country responded eagerly, offering assistance that included fundraising events and advice on a route.

My plan had always been to head all the way north to John o'Groats, then come down through Ireland, but the Lions unanimously advised otherwise. My experience with advice had been that people, albeit well intentioned, give it based on their own comfort levels, which usually aren't the same as mine. Like the man in New Zealand who insisted, "You can't possibly walk to Wellington! That's five kilometers!" Nevertheless, after the Lions unanimously warned me about the dangers of walking in the desolate Scottish highlands during winter with no Lions Clubs, towns, B&B's or even campgrounds, I decided it was a good opportunity to not be stupid. They advised, instead, I walk all the way along the southwest coast, carry on through Glasgow, and finish up at the top of Edinburgh Castle on the east coast. Scotland promised to be one of the easiest, most well-planned stretches of my journey, despite the lousy weather.

George and Jill were my hosts for the first couple of nights while I carried on through Gretna, Kirtlebridge and Ecclefechan. On the third morning I walked out of their house for the last time, yawning and stretching, seeking the motivation to walk twelve cold miles to Lockerbie.

Seven hours later, with the light fading fast, I reached the "Welcome to Lockerbie" sign. Such a nice quiet little village, I thought, what a pity that it will forever be associated with that awful day back in December 1988. Imagine ambling about the village doing some Christmas shopping, stopping off at the family butcher to get your dinner goose, when BOOM! a plane literally drops out of the sky taking the roofs off a couple of High Street shops and obliterating an entire neighborhood.

Like thousands before me who drive—or walk—into town, I looked up to the sky trying to picture the scene from that afternoon—fuselage, luggage, tray tables, little whisky bottles sprinkling the town and countryside. Eleven people on the ground died, as well as all 196 people on the plane. In that one moment, the tiny village of Lockerbie had lost its innocence forever.

I snapped back to Earth when a woman crossed the street with a smile. "You must be Polly."

It had to be Rebecca, my host for the night.

Rebecca lived ten miles away on a farmhouse in Dalton, a true-blue Scottish hamlet in the back of the beyonds. Along the windy dirt road she pointed out the one pub tucked among the hills and pronounced it to have the best Thai food west of Bangkok.

"Thai food in the back dales of Dalton?"

"Great Thai food at that! The real authentic stuff from a Thai woman named Orna. Can ye 'magine? One day ye wake up in your wee Thai village and decide yer goin te make a move to Dalton, Scotland, of all godforsaken places. Ye say te yerself yer goin' te make a go of it cookin' your mum's pad tai for these farmer blokes who only have the ache for a pint and a meat pie. Aye! She's brilliant, she is. People come from miles 'round down these very dirt roads to this nowheresville pub for a good feed of the Thai curry in front of the footy."

"I hope we're going there tonight!"

"Havin' ye here is a great excuse to go."

Rebecca at forty-ish had been married twice and now lived with Geoff. Or did she say she was married once then had two different live-ins? Oh, I'm not sure; it was all very difficult to follow. There were three children in the story, but I couldn't figure out if they were with husband number one or two. She no longer knew the whereabouts of husband number one, no longer spoke with husband number two, "But trust me," she punctuated, "that's a good thing." Number three lived with her now and had two grown children of his own. He had osteoarthritis, she had chronic fatigue syndrome and they'd just got a new Jack Russell puppy that couldn't be in the same room as the cat or whiskers would fly.

Number Three delivered the Thai food, and while we piled our plates with pad tai and a little chicken curry with rice, I made small talk. "So, Rebecca, what do you do for work?"

"I do Tarot reading."

"Tarot reading?"

"Yes," she said. "I do it at parties and for Lions fundraising events. I'm a witch."

Slight pause. "What exactly do you mean…a witch?"

"I'm a witch. I worship gods and goddesses and the balance of nature. It's my belief system, my religion, like paganism in that I am one within the cycle of earth and nature."

It had been three and a half years on the road, and I'd seen a hearty mosaic of cultures, foods, hobbies and religions. But this was the best. I sat down with a plate of pad tai, spread my napkin across my lap and prepared to be suitably blown away.

She explained that while all witches are pagans, not all pagans would be described as witches. Kind of like Christianity in that all Catholics are Christians, but not all Christians are Catholics.

"So being a witch is a religion? I think of a witch, and I think of poor Dorothy and Toto."

"Yes, people do. They hear the "W" word and think devil worshiper, but that's not what it is. As witches we see divinity in nature, and it's becoming quite a popular religion. Right now there are about 10,000 witches in the U.K., two million in the U.S. Web sites galore are popping up every day."

"Well, I'll be."

"The Goddess of Bast is my favorite Goddess because she's a great protector of women. One of her great forms is the big black cat."

Enter Charlie. Charlie is a black cat who leapt through the window on cue.

Rebecca admitted Salem would've been a great name, but they didn't name her. They had decided they wanted a cat and found Charlie hovering alone in the back of a haystack.

"What a coincidence."

"There are no coincidences."

Of course. "Do witches cast spells and mix potions?"

"I have cast spells on people, but you have to remember what you give out in the world is what you get back, so one spell that you cast in harm will get you back at least three times. For example, if I were to cast a spell to give you a broken leg, I would get two broken legs and two broken arms in return."

"So what was the spell you cast?"

"The last spell I cast was with a pagan group on Samhain—the pagan word for Halloween. We love Halloween; it's the witch's New Year. We celebrate by standing in a circle and passing a hazel rod around. The hazel rod accepts all the year's bad feelings and events that you want to get rid of—debt, illness, anger, and the like—and they all get thrown into the fire. The fire takes them away for us."

"The spell?"

"Right. So we then went back to the garden and planted the bulbs that manifest the good for the coming year. Out with the bad, in with the good. So I cast a spell of goodness for the new year."

"That's it?"

"Well, yes, but don't forget, what you give out in the world is what you get back, so if I cast one bad spell…"

That was a bit of a letdown.

"I have a little altar, my sacred space. Come, I'll show you."

We walked through the living room—I shook the puppy off my leg—and into a little room down the hall. She called it simply "The Room," a special room that holds her altar. "I visit The Room twice a day; first thing in the morning to say hello to the day and last thing at night, like a Christian would say a prayer. If there are special people on my healing list then I'll light the candle and send healing energy their way, but only with their permission."

"Do you believe in the afterlife?"

"Oh, yes," she said matter-of-factly. "While I was redecorating this room, in fact, there was a woman present who wasn't happy at all about my being here."

"Wait, wait," I said, trying to backpedal. "Never mind. I don't want to hear it." I didn't know if I should be thinking about spirits floating about the place if I should have to get up in the middle of the night to find the loo in that big ol' spooky farmhouse full of wands and candles and hazel rods with a dog clamped to my leg. That was way over my emotional cap.

Rebecca laughed, "Don't worry. The woman and I have made peace. She likes what I've done with The Room, so we're in a good place."

I asked how she got introduced to paganism, because I could live to the end of the century and never know it's an option. She told me that friends introduced her to it when she was seventeen and she was immediately hooked.

"What do your parents think?"

"My father is a Christian extremist living in Salisbury. Mum thinks I became a witch just te rile up Daddy."

Hmm.

"Would you give me permission to wish you all the luck I can gather from the Gods and Goddesses of the fire and earth?"

"That would be very nice, thank you."

Dear Editor,

My name is Polly Letofsky. I am an American walking around the world in an effort to raise awareness of breast cancer.

The Galloway Gazette has kindly been tracking my progress as I've inched my way through Wigtownshire. What has ensued is a welcome here in southwest Scotland that has undoubtedly surpassed all others in my three and a half years on the road. Sometimes it's a tough slog to get out into this winter weather and trudge along another sixteen miles up the road, but the encouragement has been uplifting at every turn.

At a break in little Creetown I was offered a complimentary lunch from the folks at the little Lido café. The townsfolk gathered, gave donations, had a chinwag and a laugh, then waved me goodbye down the A75.

The next day on a detour through Kirkcowen, a young man gave me the bad news that there were no cafés in town but insisted—insisted—that he pound on the door to wake up Stuart and Avril over at the Craighlaw Arms Pub. He was sure they'd be happy to make me some soup.

As I stood outside blushing with embarrassment a car drove up and asked if I was that girl walking around the world. I said I was. He then handed me a £20 donation for my cause and another £20 to go buy myself a nice meal.

Of course I didn't have to, Stuart and Avril at the Craigh-law Arms were indeed happy to open their doors and make me some soup and refused any money for it.

The council members of Newton Stewart came out to greet me in the dark cold night. Safeway offered their store for a fundraising venue; M&R Heating Services gave a £50 donation.

With the help of the Lions Clubs of Machars and Stranraer, we have raised well over £1,000 to go toward the Breast Cancer Campaign. The money will be used to sponsor their Guardian Angel project, an education campaign for early detection.

An extra thank you to Jim and Ann Hamilton, Eddie and Alice McWhir and David and Ann Hirst for all your time and energy. Wigtownshire is lucky to have you.

To sum it up in your own language, "Wigtownshire is a grand wee toon!"

Polly Letofsky
GlobalWalk for Breast Cancer

Scotland was undoubtedly one of the best legs of my entire five-year journey. Having Jim contacting the string of Lions along my route meant that I got to take a much needed break from the 24/7 planning, researching and calling strangers over the whistling winds of passing lorries. Jim pretty much handed me a new map every day, pointed me in the right direction and said, "I'll come find you at four o'clock. Go." Jim and his wife Anne shuttled me back and forth for so many days that one night when I came "home" they had put a sign up on my bedroom door that said "Polly's room." When I asked if we could get a cat, it was time to hand me off to the next county.

But by the time I reached Edinburgh, headlines regarding the looming war were becoming dire, complete with a countdown implemented by the U.S. and allies. Students at the University of

Edinburgh were waging a protest of the war, led in large part by American undergrads here for a semester. At every turn, every pub, every dinner table, the topic of conversation was inevitable and uncomfortable. I hung on patiently with my broad shrugs and generic replies to the barrage of rude comments at front doors and pubs.

Until poor George.

The day after my big finish at Edinburgh Castle, George, one of two Lions members in Edinburgh assigned to Polly duty, invited me to lunch. We were having a perfectly lovely conversation about Scottish history, when, with no lead in, he said, "With the exception of the woman sitting across from me, I find Americans to be entirely arrogant."

I was startled. Not that I hadn't heard it before, but it was so brazen, so out of the blue that it left no prep time for the deep breath, the visualization, the shrug. His remark was the last straw on this fragile camel's back. "Really? What do you mean?"

"Well, they're loud."

"Am I loud? Have I been loud?" I said trying to control the terseness in my voice.

"No, I said that you're an exception."

"I'm sorry, I don't understand then. All Americans are loud?"

"Well, maybe not everyone."

"Have you been to America?"

"No."

"So you're prepared to make a sweeping statement about a people you've never met?

"Well…I've seen a lot of Americans, and they seem arrogant."

"Give me an example."

He hemmed and hawed and said he's heard some Americans that were loud on the bus.

"Right, so loud people on buses are arrogant?" I said, rather clipped, feeling the impatience making my whole head turn red.

"Are loud Italians on buses arrogant? Greeks? Or is it just Americans?" I took a few shallow breaths, "Do you think it's okay to be prejudiced against Americans? If you, a grown educated man, are so prejudiced and refuse to acknowledge it, how will the world move forward?"

He sat across the table stunned. "I'm so sorry; I didn't mean to offend you."

My voice was thin and quivering (but not loud), "You did offend me. Your comment was bigoted and small-minded. You should be embarrassed."

"I'm entitled to my opinion."

"If you want an example of arrogance, it's not, for the record, loud people on buses. It would be your outlandish comment." My whole head was on fire, and while I knew I was completely over-reacting, I had reached the boiling point and couldn't get back to simmer. Poor George had no idea his flippant comment, which would usually receive a shrug, was the culmination of months of bigoted comments towards me, my family, friends, and country— my world.

Being a white girl from a nice progressive Midwest American city, I'd never had to face prejudice, certainly never been the victim of such a thing, until now. For eight months in Europe, seeing and hearing firsthand how people talk about immigrants and other nationalities, and of course Americans, it had been my observation that Europe was just then dealing with the problems of immigration, racism and asylum seekers that America had grown up with. It was inevitable that they would go through these growing pains. In America I grew up with the belief that everyone had the same rights and we should be judged by our individual behavior. In Europe it seemed there was still the assumption of class distinctions and a tradition of entitlement and subservience.

I methodically collected my belongings and got up from the table. "I'm leaving now. Thank you for lunch."

He caught me outside the pub and apologized—but only that he upset me, not that he had carelessly spewed bigoted remarks.

After an awkward goodbye I marched right over to the Internet cafe and barreled off a Letter to the Editor that was long overdue. With no one to talk to about the historic world events happening, or for that matter the nasty side of the reception I had received throughout Europe, it was like the perfect storm flew from my fingers onto the keyboard with hardly a pause. I ranted on about European prejudice until two thousand words later my blood pressure had receded. And under an alias, I ceremoniously hit the send button to *The Times*, and dashed to catch the boat to Ireland.

"Welcome to Belfast, let's go for a Guinness!" was the first thing I heard off the boat ramp. Jimmy and his designated party from Newtonbreda Lions Club met me off the ferry and led me straight to the nearest pub. "First timers 'ave trouble with the Guinness," Jimmy told me as a forewarning. "It's what ye might call, 'an acquired taste.'" That made everyone fall over themselves laughing, evidently remembering foreigners recoiling at a sip.

"I'm not crazy about beer, but I'll try one."

"Aye, but ye 'ave to try at least two. There's no such thing as one drink in Ireland."

Belfast hadn't been on my route until one day in Turkey when I saw a story on the BBC World News. The report revealed Belfast's dazzling rise as the hippest new European city. Its regenerated Cathedral Quarter attracted a young, worldly culture of boutiques and art galleries amid outdoor cafes with chic menus. It got me so excited I pulled out my map and rearranged my itinerary.

"There's one thing ye need te understand. We're not *Ireland*, we're *Northern Ireland*, and ye should never confuse the two. We don't like te be 'ssociated with each other. We're British. We're still in miles and the British pound currency. We've nothin' te do with Ireland 'cept we're on the same island."

"Got it."

"Another thing. If ye want a whiskey, ye should never order a Scotch. Instead ye order a true Irish distilled whiskey—that's whiskey with an 'e', as opposed to the Scotch whisky with no 'e'." A black beer slid in front of me. "Cheers! May ye 'ave a safe trip through our land!" With two hands I lifted the pint of Guinness to my lips. With a mere sip my whole face pursed, and before it even slid down my throat I shelved it alongside the Australian's vegemite and the Scot's haggis in the category of 'acquired tastes.'

When I told Jimmy that I had rerouted through Belfast because I had heard it's the hippest city in Europe right now, he agreed. He told me that ever since the Troubles ceased back in 1997, Belfast had been booming. I decided that *booming* wasn't the best adjective to use for a city with past Troubles. But The BBC was right; Belfast offered a spirited vibrant urban culture set amidst their oldest buildings. Their renewal reflected a new, peaceful era. For five days the Lions kept me busy doing interviews, late night fundraisers and enjoying the cafes on Royal Avenue.

Shirley Russo from Rochester, Minnesota, flew over to walk with me for a few days out of Belfast. We had been emailing for a number of years after she saw a newspaper story about my walk in the *Minneapolis Star & Tribune*. Shirley was a "professional volunteer," having traveled extensively as a member of Global Volunteers. She'd taught English and reading in Poland, the Cook Islands, China and Scotland; laid cement for a community center in Western Samoa and worked for an orphanage in Romania—to name only a handful. She had always expressed interest in joining me at some point, and recently I emailed saying that if she was serious she had better hurry as I was nearly back on U.S. shores. She hopped a plane to come and meet me in Belfast. Shirley and I were spoiled rotten for a week by every Lions Club from Belfast through Lisburn, Banbridge and Newry. Every morning we enjoyed a send-off by the mayor at Town Center. We were treated to dinners at night and given gifts by city councils and the Ulster Cancer Foundation. Northern Ireland was only a short dash—forty eight miles—but we raised a great deal of money for the Breast Cancer Campaign and got an enormous amount of press for breast cancer. I felt sure Shirley got back on the plane thinking that a walk around the world was one big hoot. In fact it was a near perfect leg, except for the terminal case of foot in mouth disease—like the time the High Sheriff in Belfast gave me a wonderful send off and I complimented her on her lovely green suit and how I found it just so charming when the Irish wore green. I was promptly pulled aside and reminded, "We're not Irish, we're British. Green is the color of Catholics, but this High Sheriff is Protestant whose color is orange, but no one looks good in orange."

Forty-eight miles south of Belfast there was no "Welcome to Ireland" sign—something about it being shot down every time they put one up—but there were some solid clues that I was nearing the border of another country. There were signs for money change offices and a number of political billboards that screamed FREE THE COLUMBIA THREE! With a single step over the invisible border, the highway turned from the British A1 to the Irish N1 and was marked with yellow lanes instead of white ones. Miles were out, kilometers were back in, road signs were in Gaelic. My U.K. mobile phone service went out of range, and I found myself back to the euro currency. Crossing the border also meant I was representing a new breast cancer beneficiary.

In Ireland I contacted Linda Keating with The Marie Keating Foundation. It was Linda's mother, Marie, who got Paget's disease and, due to a misdiagnosis, died unnecessarily. In her honor the entire family launched the Breast Cancer Mobile Information Center that traveled from town to town throughout rural Ireland to educate families about the disease.

Within steps of my new country the radio frequencies changed as well, and I scanned the dial to find a good talk show. Over the miles I'd discovered nothing better to educate me about a culture and its people than a good dose of talk radio. I settled on 2FM and a host named Gerry Ryan, who, unbeknownst to him, was giving me an introduction to the Republic of Ireland. I walked down the N1 passing cows, churches, the odd castle and listened as he took calls from women voting on favorite male butts. Americans might be pleased to note that Sly Stallone and Bill Clinton rated tops. Then two priests called in singing religious songs for a half hour.

The next topic was about a dating Web site called UsedBoyfriend.com where women try to flog off their exes, like the guy whose dream date would be to spend a day on a rock face in Thailand, followed by hours of monkey sex. Clearly I had entered one diverse country.

Ireland's relationship with America over the centuries could be best described as close siblings. It's estimated that the number of U.S. residents with Irish ancestry is over thirty-five million, almost nine times the population of Ireland itself. It's such a close relationship that on St. Patrick's Day the prime minister and many cabinet members head to New York City for the celebration. Proponents say it's a great opportunity to promote Irish culture overseas; opponents say it's a national holiday and they should be home leading the celebrations. Either way the Irish have unquestionably made their presence known around the world. It's always been a source of amazement how this tiny island has produced well beyond its share of artists: consider your Yeats, Keating, Wilde, U2, Richard Harris, and their latest, Colin (I'm Yummy) Farrell. In comparison, my home state of Minnesota, an area roughly the same size, has always been quite chuffed about creating the corndog. Really, I don't think the Irish brag nearly enough about their national exports.

After Shirley left I inched my way toward Dublin along the coastal route, admiring the village shops and pubs painted bright shades of red, shamrock green, a dash of yellow. If you were from, say, Namibia, and for some reason you had been dropped into one of these villages, there would be no doubt you were in Ireland particularly with place names like O'Connell's and O'Malley's and kegs of Guinness piled high in pub fronts.

The infamous Irish rainy weather considerably subsided as I marched down the east coast toward Dublin with nothing but sunny March days. On the world front, though, it was not as sunny. The deadline for the war in Iraq was closing in.

With just days until the deadline my little yellow radio was rarely out of my ears. Naval ships were piling into the Persian Gulf with 150,000-plus troops deployed to support them. Black Hawk Helicopters moved into Iraq, and Kuwait looked like an armed desert.

My host in Dublin, Sean, welcomed me into his house and handed me an article from the *L.A. Times*. "Look at this! The world is on the verge of war, and American headlines have nothing bette' te flaunt than how it rained an inch in L.A. Why are Americans so stupid?" I took the article and faked interest as he raved on. "I mean, good God above, Saddam Hussein could destroy Washington and New York too, but Americans would rather watch a car chase. I understand there are actually Americans graduating from college who can't read or write. Why are they such morons?"

My days were full of contradiction—sunny walks past colorful villages with war in my ears, or meet-n-greets raising funds for the Marie Keating Foundation where someone would corner me in a hallway and poke at my chest compelled to tell me their views on American Foreign Policy. To quote Charles Dickens, "It was the best of times, it was the worst of times; it was the age of wisdom, it was the age of foolishness." And after my explosive episode with George in Edinburgh, all I could do was resolutely return to the shrug.

The Gerry Ryan show had newsbreaks and a consistent string of guests calling in with opinions. Sometimes I was so tuned in to my little yellow radio that I walked obliviously, paying no mind to the road. But in my defense, it wasn't always my lack of directional skills that got me lost. Road signs in Ireland, while nowhere near as bad as in continental Europe, could leave a tourist ripe for aggravation. So when I couldn't find any signs coming out of Naas I asked the clerk at the petrol station which way to Newbridge. He said he didn't know, but pointed up the road and said that up that way just a tootle there was a shop that might have a map.

"How far is a tootle?"

"Oh, ye know—a tootle. Not even a tootle, just a might tippet. They'll put ye right with a map o' the land."

So I walked and walked and walked, and now I see a sign that tells me I'm on the N9 heading south towards Carlow. I couldn't imagine I had to head south in order to head west, and quite sure I'd gone well past a tootle. So I steamed and festered and had visions of going back to that petrol station and telling that young tippet what I think of him and his tootley directions.

In Ireland the signage wouldn't have been much of a problem until they started changing from the imperial system to metric. They didn't always take the old mileage signs down when putting up the new signs in kilometers. So when I saw a sign that said "Kildare to Monesterevin 12," I didn't know if it was going to take me two hours in kilometers or four hours in miles.

I'd felt the same frustration in continental Europe when I came upon a directional sign that was pivoted at an angle pointing toward the cows in the field, and I couldn't tell if I was supposed to veer to the right or the left. So I'd sit at the intersection in a fury over the injustice of bad directions and all the evil sign makers who were out to destroy me. Then I would wave someone down to ask directions and they would tell me, zat is ze vay to Saarbrucken, so I went right as they directed only to come to another fork within two hundred yards that had no signage whatsoever.

I swore up and down every day that I was going to march right into Paris and into those Michelin Map offices, go cubicle to cubicle until I hunted down the person responsible for omitting the fork in the road that left me stranded south of Zweibrucken, Immenstaad, Oberammergau, Saarlouis, Villingen. My fists would be pounding the air when I would say to him, "It's no wonder the French had to surrender to the Germans so quickly when here you've got an army standing at the foot of a three-pronged fork in the road tiffing over which way to Stuttgart! The French have no business in combat and should be internationally banned from cartography! And by the way," I would say on the way out, "I'm from Canada."

The upshot was that Europe would be a hotbed for my new business as Directional Consultant.

I remembered the moment I came up with the idea that was sure to turn my fortune around. I was in the Dubai airport on layover from India to Turkey (remember that I'd skipped over Pakistan and Iran under the American Embassy's directive, "They've closed the welcome for you."). I moved with the crowd off the airplane, down the corridors, up the escalator and that's when the crowd split up.

One group followed the arrows to stay in Dubai. Another group had to collect luggage from one airline and drag it through the airport to re-check it on another airline. I was a transit passenger. My sign told me to go left—easy enough except there was no left. If I were to go left I would have to go through a brick wall.

I read it again. "Transit Passengers" and an arrow indicating left. Was it some bizarre language barrier? It was so silly I was tempted to take a photo but white Americans in the Middle East shouldn't take photos in airports.

That's when I decided that my directional impairment had valuable marketability. An airport could hire me to analyze their flow and signage.

As a Directional Consultant I could spend the rest of my days roaming the hamlets of Europe hammering in signage at road forks and yanking out the ones that pointed towards cows. I would consult department stores, hospitals, underground parking lots. My first client would undoubtedly be Michelin Maps in Paris.

So walking out of Naas toward Newbridge, I ventured down a side road only to find myself heading south for a mile (or a kilometer) past a tootle. I walked back into town and asked a young man which way to Newbridge. He told me to just carry on up this road. But up the road a couple hundred yards I detected a fork so I asked, "Do I veer to the right or the left?" He pointed with a sweep of his arm and said, "Just carry on up that road."

He was not pointing to the left or the right, he was pointing to the cows in the middle, so I physically took hold of his arm and shifted it to the right, "That way?" Then I shifted it to the left, "Or that way?" He said matter-of-factly, "Just carry on a tootle."

I sighed and tuned back in to my little yellow radio where the Middle East seemed to be less frustrating, and went for a bowl of soup at The Chat and Chew.

I was savoring my carrot and coriander soup when a woman popped in to ask the hostess directions. "Excuse me," she said, "Could you tell me how to get to Newbridge?" My ears perked up. The hostess told her to just carry on up the road; it's hardly a tootle. The woman smiled and thanked her; she seemed perfectly satisfied with that.

The deadline to war reached the twenty-four hour mark, and the suspense kept me awake all night. I was staying with a Lions Club family just north of Limerick and had a TV in my room. At one o'clock in the morning I turned on the telly very quietly to hear the inevitable. Five minutes in I couldn't bear to watch the Sky News commentators anymore and flipped through the channels looking for anything to distract me from the bad news, to hide from the world. From channel to channel—close to 200 it looked to be—all the talk was war. War. War. War. War. War. War. Snooker.

Snooker? Out of dumb curiosity, I paused for a moment on channel 143. Who was the producer that didn't get fired for this idea? Who watches this stuff the night before the world goes to war? Or ever? Perhaps other people like me who want to hide our eyes as though we were watching a scary movie. A hushed voice droned on giving the snooker play-by-play. "He's aiming straight now. He's got to rule the shot, control his cue, take a wood advantage. Here he goes, number seven is heading for the bag...it's in!" Clap, clap, clap. I sighed and made a mental note for the next time someone from the U.K. mentioned how bad TV was in America.

Flipping through the channels again, I found a documentary called "Hairy Women." Fancy having an entire documentary devoted to women with unwanted body hair. They documented a woman's struggle with excessive chin and neck hair who, before her wedding wanted a face/neck/chin wax, but in order for the wax to get all the hair follicles she had to grow it out for ten days. So she went into hiding a week before her wedding. She says she would give anything to not have a hairy problem, and with all the problems in the world unhairy people just don't know how lucky they are: how they don't have to get up early and pluck for an hour and hide your hairiness from friends and family, how you can't go on overnights and camping trips, or the panic that would strike if you lost your tweezers. Unhairy people just don't think about things like that.

When the hairy show was over I was out of options and had to take my hands off my eyes. I switched back to Sky News and watched the countdown to war.

Sixteen hours 'til Doomsday. I was walking toward Limerick down the N7. On talk radio they were discussing how awful Tony Blair looked. Someone called in to say over the past couple weeks he'd lost his boyish good looks. He appeared drawn and tired, his groggy voice sounded like he hadn't had a good lie-down in weeks.

Another caller noted that in the photo of Tony Blair in the *Irish Times* today his collar no longer fit and his cheeks were hollowed. He said, "What Tony Blair needs is a good tipple o' whiskey. Look at Margaret Thatcher: during the Falklands War Maggie'd take a double shot o' Bells straight down the throat every night." He added, "Whiskey is good for ye, relieves anxiety, tension, social inhibitions. It's in the antioxidants. A good stiff tipple o' whiskey every night'll save you from stroke, cataracts and the devil himself. What Tony Blair needs is a few more jars o' the drink and the world will be safe for democracy."

Eleven hours from the deadline I'd made my way to Finnigan's Pub just north of Limerick. It was a big pub, crowded at lunchtime with a mix of businessmen, truckers and families. Sky News blared at full volume across the big screen that hung above the bar. A red ticker scrolled across the bottom "Breaking News…U.S. led forces enter Iraq/Kuwait demilitarized zone."

Finnigan's Pub was packed, but all you could hear were forks and knives clanging against plates, and Sky News commentators reporting what we all knew was coming. The atmosphere was somber: watching, listening, eating, clanging.

Polly's Journal March 20, 2003

The world woke up to the news that U.S. and U.K. troops were making their way into Iraq. My little yellow radio was glued to my ear as I made just a short walk today into the heart of Limerick.

The Lions Club of Castletroy in Limerick has put me up in the fanciest hotel I've ever laid my eyes on. It's the kind of place where the bathrobe and slippers are wrapped with a thick gold bow and sit in a basket with a note saying "Welcome, Miss Letofsky." The coffee table holds a fruit basket with melon, pineapple and strawberries—already cut into bite size pieces so I won't have to squander an ounce of energy cutting them myself. There's a box of chocolates too and a little bottle of wine with wine glasses. I hardly recognize myself in all this luxury, and although this beats the heck out of those cornfields and riverbeds of continental Europe, I'm laden with guilt at the extravagance of it all, particularly on this day, the day the world goes to war.

I rolled Bob into the room, gave him a nice corner view in front of the window, then unwrapped—well, tore open, really—the chocolates, and watched Sky News. The soldiers are hot out there in the desert, sandstorms blowing sand into their boots, their helmets, their mouths. My guilt trip lounging here in the luxury of the Castletroy Park Hotel was too much and I turned off the TV. The good news is that Iraqi troops are already surrendering, so I'm sure when I get back from the steam room and Jacuzzi the war will be all over.

The war had begun, and as I headed south toward my finish line in County Cork I tried to stay on top of the progress through my little yellow radio.

For months I had pictured my final steps in Ireland to be a big puddle of emotion. Walking into Crosshaven south of Cork was not just the finish line for Ireland but also Europe, as well as my last miles overseas. My next steps would be back on American soil, coming around full circle for the home stretch.

I had been spoiled beyond recognition in Ireland, even experiencing their sunniest March in seventy years. The Lions embarrassed me with the luxury of four-star hotels with steam rooms, Jacuzzis and heated floors. Doormen dressed in top hats and tails would swing open those grand doors to let Bob and me roll through like royalty. The breast cancer work was productive, raising thousands of euros for the Marie Keating Foundation to assist them in continuing their education campaign throughout Ireland. Even the food was great. I could get a meal without a potato these days—something virtually unheard of in Ireland even five years before.

The Lions Club from Carigaline was at the finish line to greet me, along with a handful of Lions from Cork City and the Crosshaven Yacht Club. They joined me for the last ten yards and presented a sizeable check of €500 to the Marie Keating Foundation. It could hardly have been a better reception.

So where then was the emotion? The tears? The sadness at leaving Ireland and all its sunshine and steam rooms and tasty soup in cozy pubs? Where was the happiness because I'd come 10,500 miles and was still healthy?

I recognized my unique perspective in walking through Europe during this unprecedented turn in world history, and I appreciated the value of the priceless education. But there were other days, as the war was upon us, when I just wanted to get back to U.S. shores. I loved my time in the U.K. and Ireland. I loved the colorful language, like when the Irish go to the pub for some good crack, but they're really saying *craic*, which means good conversation. I loved the nightly soapie *Coronation Street* and how the night Richard confessed to Gail that he was the serial killer there was an electric surge across Great Britain due to an extra 450,000 teakettles being plugged in.

But with the war upon us and an anti-American tide riding high, I was running on empty. I was tired. Lost. Emotionally drained.

I wanted to go home.

CHAPTER 21

Hallelujah, I'm Home!

I'm home! America! U.S. of A.! The country that brought the world the Internet, Oprah, a man on the moon—where you can shop all day and well into the night and be anything you want to be—anything. *I'm home!* Where Puerto Ricans, Russians and Chinese mingle in sushi bars, Irish pubs and Jewish delis. Home of ranch dressing, pink lemonade, free refills! Home of the great American diner, where you sit in a red vinyl booth and order a chocolate malt in a tall tin cup. *I'm home!*

A big fat lump got stuck in my throat as I looked out over the Manhattan skyline minus two skyscrapers. A reminder that it was a different America than the one I left four years before. An America bruised and scarred—but, hallelujah, baby, she's home!

My eyes grew wide as the bus from JFK neared Manhattan. New York City! The Big Apple! NYC! And when we turned into Times Square into the lights of 42nd Street a surge of electricity bolted up my spine and down my legs. God bless America, I had to get off that bus. I wanted to throw my arms up, twirl around a lamppost, kick up my heels, break into song. I wanted to be a part of it, New York, New York.

American flags waved Uptown, Downtown, Midtown; New Yorkers were dressed in starred-n'-striped ties and shirts with jackets to match. A construction worker near Ground Zero had "9/11—Don't Forget" tattooed on his bicep.

The display of patriotism overwhelmed me after the pounding I'd taken for the past couple of years overseas. People from Croatia, Zimbabwe, Burundi, Peru would get a pat on the back and a "nice to meet you." But if you were an American overseas after 9/11, you whispered, you lied, you said, "G'day, I'm from A'stralia." You would never dream of sewing the stars and stripes on your clothes or your backpack, or tattooing a bicep.

I eased into the idea that it was okay now to be American and started to draw out of the isolation that had weighed me down across Europe. I started to feel liberated, walking around the Big Apple surrounded by stars and stripes, feeling the spirit of the city, the nation pulling together after the traumas of 9/11, the war in Afghanistan and now the war in Iraq.

The thousand-pound gorilla that had taken residence on my shoulders since 9/11 overseas just fell off walking the streets of The Big Apple, and I felt an overwhelming sense of freedom—free to call myself an American, free to go mad with myself buying a sweater with a USA flag across the chest, an Old Glory cell phone and a green foam Statue of Liberty crown for my head.

The CBS *Early Show* invited Bob and me for an interview that was broadcast live across the nation—the perfect start to my home stretch. On the way back to my Greenwich Village apartment, the CBS van driver said, "Welcome home. I am from Brazil, and this is the best country in the whole world, the whooole world! My whole life I want to come to America. I apply four times to come to America, and they tell me no every time. So I apply again and again and again. The consul general say to me, 'Why you come apply again the very day after I turn you down fourth time?' I say to him, 'Because, Sir, I want to go to America. I want to live in America, and I will keep applying and keep talking to you until I get to America.' So he smile to me and say, 'Congratulations, anyone with that much want to go to America must go.'"

His enthusiasm was so infectious I couldn't help but be inspired. "I am here eight years now," he continued. "I learn English. I drive CBS van. I go to school. Anything is possible in America. Look at me, I will be accountant."

I was tempted to give him a big fat kiss for keeping immigration so alive and healthy. But I didn't want to send him screaming back to Brazil so I kept my lips to myself. Yet he was saying what I felt. Arriving back on U.S. shores after three and a half years left me unexpectedly overjoyed to be part of this country where I had grown up but had only recently been discovering through different eyes. Now I saw America through the eyes of the world, through the eyes of history. Emigrants from the nations I walked through in Asia and Europe came here to build this country. I loved the very idea that a country like this exists, a country in which people from every culture come together to be whoever they want to be. I felt lucky, blessed to be a part of this great social experiment.

So now, back on U.S. shores, despite all the bruises—to both me and America—or more likely because of them, I was moved more than ever before to ride that boat out to Lady Liberty, throw myself at her feet, and thank God I was born in this country. And if she could talk, I'm sure she'd say something like, "All right, all right, stop with all the dramatics. We've taken in your tired, your poor, your huddled masses, and clearly you qualify for all of the above. Welcome home. Now get up off my feet, dust yourself off and get a move on. You've got a long way to go yet. And nice hat."

Way back in Australia, a shy twelve-year-old boy had asked me, "What's it like living in America?"

I dropped everything I was doing to give him some serious attention. I told him that while most of the TV shows and movies take place in big cities, America is actually a country of thousands of small towns and neighborhoods. I told him when I was his age we played baseball or Frisbee in the park or got a game of kickball going with neighborhood buddies. There were all kinds of ball games happening in our neighborhood: dodge ball, stickball, football, SPUD, and when we heard a screen door slam, that was the cue that someone was up and ready to play. I told him that all over the country on a hot summer night, the local Dairy Queen had a line of people around the block waiting their turn for a Dilly Bar or a Mister Misty.

I lost him after Dilly Bars, but it was then I decided that when I walked across America I would, for the most part, avoid big cities.

I'd lived half my adult life overseas and I wanted to hear screen doors slam again. I wanted to weave through a mosaic of small town American life.

On my sprawling map of the United States I drew big red circles around towns, historic sites or theme parks representing the very best tapestry of this country that I had not yet experienced. The choices were endless, and with breast cancer everywhere, I could campaign anywhere I wanted to go.

Consulting my red circles after I'd finished, I concluded that if I headed to the South, I would be there in the peak summer heat and in turn, Minnesota during midwinter. I gave up that idea and reckoned I'd save a trip to the South—and therefore the use of words like *reckoned*—for an air-conditioned road trip by car. My route cross-country would start at Ground Zero in Manhattan. I'd catch the Staten Island Ferry past the Statue of Liberty and carry on across the north—including a smidgeon of Canada—en route to Minnesota.

With recognizable faces, a familiar culture and a blossoming spring, the very best days of my walk were about to begin.

My friend Jeff Shrager called to say he would like to walk with me from Elizabeth to Plainfield, New Jersey, on my second day of walking. I giggled and said, "That's great for the first mile, but what about the other sixteen?" reminding him of how, when we were housemates back in Vail, he would drive to the Safeway two hundred yards away.

He said he'd already thought of that and had rallied his mother Bonnie to stand by and wait for his rescue call. "If I can't take one more step I'll just sit on the curb and wait for her to come scoop me up."

On my second day of walking home across America, Bonnie dropped Jeff, Bob and me off at the Goethals Bridge across from Staten Island where I had stopped the night before. Bonnie pulled out a local map and reviewed the directions to Plainfield.

"Don't forget to pay attention at *this* circle, because if you miss this circle and take a wrong turn we'll never find you again. You want to take Front to South to Railway Road. Don't miss it. Pay attention. I know you'll get chatting, getting all caught up after four years, and you'll walk right by Front and South and Railway Road, and we'll have to come hunt you down in Hoboken or some godforsaken place.

"You have sunglasses?" she continued to both of us. "You want a bigger hat? Don't forget the map. Got your phone? All charged up? Need more Chewy Bars? How about sunscreen? You should have 30-spf. It's going to get hot today, up to eighty degrees. You don't want to get burnt. That's the last thing you need. Can you imagine walking for breast cancer and dropping dead from skin cancer? Slather that stuff on good. Don't forget the back of your ears. Call me if you need anything. Front to South to Railway Road. Pay attention at the circle."

"Jewish mothers," Jeff smirked. And we started walking, talking, getting all caught up after four years, weren't paying attention and walked right past the circle.

I was on my way, thrilled to be home, to have friends with Jewish mothers, hopping and skipping through Plainfield and Griggstown, down the toe path to Princeton. Through Pennsylvania, too, friends and friends of friends always knew someone nearby who would be "more than happy" to come pick me up, feed me and drop me off the next morning. Lions Clubs regularly came to pluck me off the road and take me to dinners where I would speak and continue the breast cancer fundraising.

Funds raised across the United States went to either the Breast Cancer Fund based in San Francisco or stayed with a local organization if that's what the club wanted.

The great mosaic that made up America unfolded at my feet through the Amish country of Lancaster County, where I detoured through the towns of Intercourse and Blue Balls just to send postcards to my friends. In Hershey, Pennsylvania, I rode the free Chocolate History Tour four times because they give you a free

Hershey bar at the exit. I walked through small Pennsylvanian towns with their tree-lined Main Streets, past patriarchal town halls and whopping clocks keeping time above the villages. Every old colonial house had an American flag waving because these little towns had neighbors in Iraq, and they were going to wave those stars and stripes until GI Joe and Jane came home in their American army uniforms and walked down Main Street safe and sound. Grandmas and grandpas waved at Bob and me from their front porches and yelled, "Where are you going with that little buggy?" I'd say I was walking to Colorado, and they'd say, "Oh, good heavens, dear. Would you like some water? How about some Bundt cake?"

I enjoyed sunny spring days walking through New Jersey and Pennsylvania, reveling in my re-discovery of all things American as if seeing them for the first time. I snapped photos of the cute yellow school bus picking up kids at a street corner, and the Dunkin' Donuts—with all the police inside taking a coffee break. My heart fluttered when I got to sit for a rest in one of those great American diners.

If some Hungarian were to ask me where to go to get a feeling for the real America, I would tell him to sit in a diner. On the outside they look like grungy old railroad cars buzzing along under neon signs, but inside old men flirt with sassy waitresses named Flo or Bev, who pour coffee into big thick cups and scream short orders to the hash slinger in the back. Grandpas sit in red vinyl booths sipping bottomless cups, trash talkin' 'bout the weekend's Troutarama Fishing Derby.

On Highway 283 just outside Highspire, Pennsylvania, I spotted the big word "Diner." It was a neon light with a splash of aqua flashing above the old stainless steel train car, looking perfect with its aged imperfections.

The waitress Bev, complete with a pencil tucked in her hair, leaned over the yellow Formica counter and said, "We saw you out there taking photos of our sign. Why on earth would you want to do such a thing?"

"I just love these old diners, and this one is as good as they get."

"*This* place? It's a dump! Hey, Sheila! This girl likes our sign. Can you believe it?"

"No kiddin'! We haven't changed that sign since Gus built the place in 1952."

I tried to explain to Bev that these original diners are like those old worthless paintings at a flea market that someone buys for five dollars and later discovers it's a Picasso. The old original diners had seen a resurgence in the past few years and were finally being recognized as priceless pieces of Americana.

"Are you doing a picture book?" Bev asked.

"No, but, hey, that's a good idea."

When I told them I was walking around the world for breast cancer they oohed.

"Hey, you're that girl that was in the paper yesterday," said Bev. "You and that little buggy of yours. Bob? Isn't that his name?

"Bob is out on the patio."

"Well, I'll be, there he is! Wow. Congratulations, that's just great. You are a piece of work. Hey, Sheila! We got a celebrity in the house!" Then she turned to me. "Lunch is on me." She handed me the twelve-page menu, pulled the pencil out of her hair and scribbled my order on her green pad. I settled in with my Caesar salad and a chocolate malt in a tall tin cup, and my soul was happy sitting in red vinyl.

By mid-May 2003, Bob and I had made our way through Pennsylvania and across the border into upstate New York. The war in Iraq that many had predicted would wrap up in just a few days raged on, the news dominated by war updates and America's plunging reputation. People around the world had passionate feelings about America, for and against, so as I walked across the U.S., I felt privileged to be in a position to realize that Americans are among the friendliest, most generous and hospitable people anywhere in the world.

After the *Sunbury Daily Item* featured a front-page article on my walk, people cheered me on along the banks of the Susquehanna River for days, stopping to share their stories of breast cancer and shower me with gifts. A couple pulled over in the middle of an intersection and sprang out of their car.

"We saw you and Bob in the newspaper and, well, that's just unbelievable that you walked through all those strange places like France and California. Good heavens, you must have all sorts of stories to tell about the strange foods you've had to eat!" They gave me $20 and told me to have lunch on them.

A man named Albert brought me a rock. "It's a special rock from the quarry right up the road near Shamokin Dam. I want you to have it."

A slight woman hotfooted down the block after me in Lewisburg. "I saw you walking down the road and said to myself, 'I'll bet that's that girl doing that big walk,'" she panted, "so I did a u-turn and just had to say hello. You're doing this for breast cancer I understand. I just had a lump removed. Biopsy shows it's benign, though. I'm so relieved. Early detection, you know, but I suppose you know that. My goodness, I'm just so proud of you." She gave me a bear hug. "I've just gotten divorced after thirty-eight years. Yep, just like that—*snap*—he comes home and says he's got a 'friend' that happens to be fifteen years younger. Can you believe it? But don't you worry about me, I'm a survivor. It's his loss. I'm going to go out and live the high life! My name is Coral, and if you need anything, anything at all—say you're walking down the street and get a craving for some Tic Tacs—you just call and I'll be there in five minutes."

On the road locals showered me with five jars of homemade apricot jam, four bottles of wine and three Bibles—pocket size, large print and The New Testament in Modern English. I spoke at the Ovid Chamber of Commerce Wine and Cheese do, attended fifteen Lions Club dinners, had twenty newspaper and radio interviews, and spoke at four breast cancer groups, all helping to raise $2,500 for the Ithaca Breast Cancer Alliance.

My spring days were filled gloriously with drive-by friends in small-town America. At night, I would tune in to the 6 o'clock news to hear how awful people were.

Crossing the border into Canada took me back to a youth hostel in Europe when I had been talking with a group of people. Someone asked where I was from. Tired of taking abuse for being an American, I lied and said I was from Canada, eh. Much to my mortification, someone said, "Wow, me too!" And with that one wee white lie, I found myself in the middle of a mighty snowball.

In front of the crowd, he asked, "Don't you miss Tim Hortons?"

I had no idea what that meant. But I was under pressure; the snowball was rolling downhill and picking up speed. I took the gamble. "Yes," I said. "Yes, I do." I then excused myself and swore I'd go back to being an abused American, which was at least predictable.

When I crossed into Canada what was the first thing I saw? Tim Hortons! Mystery solved. It's a sandwich and coffee shop. And they were everywhere. Tim Hortons is what happens when Starbucks and McDonalds interbreed. To satisfy my curiosity, I went in for a bowl of chicken noodle soup to see what it was all about.

Tim Hortons—or Timmys as the locals call it—is Canada's answer to England's pubs or America's diners. It's the place where the locals go for a cup of joe and conversation with neighbors and strangers. I immediately felt at home.

Across Ontario Tim Hortons coffee shops became my roaming office. I spotted their red sign on the road ahead and knew it was time for a rest and a bowl of chili. I'd make some phone calls and plan ahead or have a good read of the *Toronto Star*. A nice perk at Timmy's was that you never had to buy your own *Toronto Star* because the *six-a.m.-ers* always left them behind for the *ten-a.m.-ers*. I loved arriving at a Tim Hortons and grabbing a discarded Toronto Star off an empty table to see what Canadians had on their minds. The news across Canada was rough in the summer of 2003: SARS in Toronto, Mad Cow in Alberta, coyotes running amok at people's heels in Ottawa. Yet the rest of the world knew nothing of Canada's troubles.

Even Canada's version of *Time Magazine* ran a cover story recently entitled "Would anyone notice if Canada disappeared?"

Savoring my Timmy's chili, I saw a story regarding the latest survey on the relationship between Canada and the United States. Sixty-five percent of Americans had a favorable view of Canada, while sixty-three percent of Canadians had a favorable view of the U.S. Seventy-seven percent of Canadians said they liked individual Americans, it was just the politics they didn't like. The article went on to say that Canadians didn't like their own politics either and admired Americans' spirit and tenacity. It was all terribly confusing, so I left it behind for the next person who came into Tim Hortons and continued west toward London…Ontario, that is.

Remember my friends Debi and Jim Linker from Lake City, Colorado, whom I met two weeks into my walk? Back then, Debi was a one-year breast-cancer survivor and had just finished chemo. Despite her energy being zapped by chemo, she wanted to have a go at the 12,600-foot climb over Cinnamon Pass with my friend Randi and me, and who was I to discourage a woman with a plan? Since that day we made the climb, Debi and I kept in touch as I made my way around the world.

Now four years later Debi was stronger and healthier than she'd ever been, and she wanted to come and walk with me for two whole months. That's *two whole months* in her big ol' fancy RV!
I would have a place to stay, a microwave, satellite TV, a fridge for fresh veggies! Moreover, her personal experience with breast cancer would bring a bonding element to our evening fundraisers with survivors—something that had always eluded me despite my intentions.

Debi and Jim were on their way to meet me along Highway 402 near Warwick, Ontario, so I had just one more night to fend for myself.

The twenty-five miles from London to Strathroy was long and painful. My legs were stiff and throbbing with no Timmy's en route to rest. I decided to treat myself to a cheap ma-and-pa motel, a night with no strings or entertaining obligations attached. A teenage boy working at the convenience store in goth garb told me about the Garby Hotel.

"You might not feel very comfortable there, though," he said. "It's not very nice."

"I've just walked twenty-five miles. I don't care about nice."

He shrugged, which is the international language for *okay, it's your life*, and pointed to the right. "Two blocks that way."

I dragged myself two more blocks to the Garby Hotel and oh, good heavens. From a full hundred yards away I could see what the goth boy meant. The building on the corner was black with black trim, no windows and a crumbling roof. The sign dangling from a rope off the front door said *Welcome to the Garby Hotel.*

I paused. Could I pitch my tent in the town park? But it was supposed to rain that night. No, the Garby was better than a night in the rain to be sure. I took a deep breath and approached the crumbling building.

Cutting my way through smoke, past a pool table and blinking beer signs, I asked the lady with her bosoms tumbling out if… ahem…there might be any accommodation available in her… *cough, cough*…fine establishment?

In a voice that sounded like a martini she said, "No, we used to. Yah, we used to—but that was before the big fire last month. Fuckin' smokers, we'll prob'ly never have no 'ccommodation again, can't trust nobody." She turned her back to me and pointed to the door. "Nearest motel for you now is three miles up the road."

I'd pushed twenty-five miles already and should've grimaced at the thought of three more, but I thanked her and bounded over chairs with a new energy on my way out the door.

I couldn't wait until Debi and Jim arrived! For two whole months I wouldn't have to worry about where I was going to stay. Debi said there'd be a fridge for Timmy Hortons chili leftovers and a blender for blueberry smoothies. When we needed groceries, we'd just drive to a store and stock up on salmon, salad and sweet potatoes with chutney sauce.

But that was tomorrow. Tonight I made my way to the ma and pa motel, scrounged through the crevices of Bob, and went to bed after a meal of stale rice cakes and peanut butter.

Debi called bright and early the next morning to say they'd just passed Port Huron, Michigan, and would find me on Canada's Highway 22 about noon. I got off the phone bubbling. How fun it would be to see them after all these years—and stay in an RV with the TV, the microwave. I wouldn't have to pack and repack Bob every day. Maybe Debi would join me in an occasional game of Boggle!

But that was still five hours away and I had no food left. Ma, who ran the motel, said the road I would be on had no food until Warwick, eighteen miles away, and "We're due for the big weekly trip to London to stock up—but lemme see if we have anything for ye."

She went in the back to try and dig up some spare nibbles for me. Pots banged and cupboards slammed. In a few minutes she came out with an apple and a bag of popcorn. Not Timmy Hortons, but it would keep my belly from rumbling. I thanked her profusely and headed west out of the ma-and-pa motel toward Highway 22.

The Ontario countryside turned into vast farmland—cafe-less, service-less, Timmy-less farmland. What good is a picturesque red barn with a white picket fence, I groused, when your eyes are fixed on the horizon searching for any hint of a restaurant or a grocery store?

Debi and Jim said they'd find me about noon, so I rationed my popcorn and apple accordingly. Noon came and went. One o'clock, two o'clock, three o'clock. The popcorn and apple were far gone and I sat on the roadside for a grumble, assuring myself that no one had ever starved to death in a matter of hours.

It was three-thirty when Debi and Jim found me lumbering along Highway 22. They were in their truck, so after enthusiastic greetings—which included scarfing abandoned granola bars—we marked my spot and drove to the RV park for an introduction to my new life: America's RV culture.

CHAPTER 22

The Heartland According to Walmart

For months crossing the eastern U.S. I'd been watching RVs pass by in a whiz. Americans and Canadians take to summer vacations with the ferocity of a constitutional duty. They tow boats and trucks that tow bikes and scooters, and satellite dishes cling to the roofs. After three hundred miles, they might take a break at a handy rest area, make some pasta primavera in the microwave and enjoy the view while catching up on the minute-to-minute goings-on in Iraq on the flat screen. What an amazing time we live in.

RVing is an American subculture I'd never known. RVers have their own secret language, trade magazines and clubs you swap blood to be sworn into.

Jim said a lot of RVers stay in Walmart parking lots.

"Walmarts?"

"Yep. Walmarts are a great stop when you're hauling across the country and need a quick stop for the night. They don't advertise it, but they don't discourage it either. Heck, think about it, they've got groceries, goods for cooking and cleaning and fuel to BBQ. While you're at it, you can even get your eyes checked."

Jim pulled up behind the biggest RV in the whole campground and said, "Welcome home."

"This?" I screamed. "*This* is yours? It could hold a family of six! Seriously, which one is yours?"

They assured me it was theirs. "Come on," said Jim. "I'll take you for a tour of your new home."

Theirs wasn't an RV, but rather a "coach." The Safari Zanzibar was forty feet long with a bedroom, bathroom and Jacuzzi tub.

There was a storage compartment underneath, like on a Greyhound bus—where you could sleep another ten people if the humor struck you.

In the bathroom, Jim slid out a drawer. "This is for you. Your very own drawer."

"Thank you! Wow, my own drawer." I hadn't had a drawer for four years. My first step back into a "normal" world: a drawer. Should I make it a clothes drawer? A junk drawer? A paperwork drawer?

Debi hollered to Jim from the bedroom, "Honey, why don't you empty out that sock drawer of yours and give her two drawers."

Two drawers. What a day!

All that luxury made me think that, in the grand scheme of things, I'd been pretty spoiled during my GlobalWalk, largely if not entirely, due to the Lions Clubs and hotels that had been so generous.

The down side of staying with people is that it comes with the responsibility of being entertaining when all I wanted to do was shower and sleep. Night after night answering the same questions, being *on* wears down the best intentions after a while.

But being with Debi and Jim, being able to unpack and not worry about where I was going to stay for two whole months—what a gift!

The bonus was the opportunity to learn about yet another piece of the American mosaic—camping out in Walmart parking lots.

Debi, Jim and I seamlessly etched ourselves into a groove through the latter half of Ontario and back across the border into Michigan. I slept on the "living room" floor where Debi woke me at five-thirty every morning. She made each of us a two egg-white omelet with fruit for breakfast, then packed up our lunch. My job was to plan the route and push Bob with our daily food and water. Jim's job was to pack up the coach and get us settled in the next Walmart parking lot.

Jim said it's proper Walmart etiquette to park on the far perimeters of the lot so as not to block parking spots for shoppers.

Moreover, the far edges have nice grassy areas for barbecuing, just like real campgrounds. If you're camping to get back to nature, maybe Walmart isn't your best bet, but if you're looking for a glimpse of the real America, you can't beat a Walmart parking lot in the American Midwest. You meet truckers and fellow RVers, or like Jim and I did, sit on the bench in front of the store for a front-row look at our country. We regularly made ourselves a bowl of popcorn and watched people flooding in and out of Walmart, wearing baggie shorts and hairdos that never knew a comb. I felt so at home.

Europeans wouldn't dream of being seen in a wrinkly shirt or heading into public with their hair muffed. The merchants in Europe never took kindly to my "casual" look, and it was all I could do to get a croissant out of them. Americans, on the other hand, are—well, casual.

Folks in the Midwest are simple and unassuming. They're nice, wholesome people who wear flip-flops to the IHOP and always say hi. "Hi, where ya from?" "Hi, nice Chevy."

Debi, Jim and I went Walmart hopping west across Michigan's Highway 10, through Bay City, Midland and Clare. Debi is the only person who walked with me long enough to get a real taste of what this long-distance experience was truly like. At least one other person in the world could now understand that you get up and check the weather every day, not to determine whether you're going to go out, but to decide what to wear.

Debi also came to understand that when the press met us after we walked eighteen miles, we didn't have the option of saying, "Could we do this later. I'm a bit tired" or "I'd really like to take a shower and clean up this hat head before I'm on TV." She learned the aggravation of rotten directions and bad signage and the excitement of seeing a cafe or a convenience store for respite from the heat.

She also became skilled at telling people I was walking around the world.

"You can't just say, 'I'm walking around the world,'" I coached. "That's too much to grasp in one shot. First, you say, 'I'm walking across Michigan.' Once they have their head around that, you say, 'Actually, I'm walking across the country.' If they're still with you, you move forward with, 'Well, truth be known, I'm walking around the world.' Finally, they understand the whole story. Then they ask, 'Where are you going next?' And you say, 'On our way to Bay City. It should take four days.' And they cry, 'you're **walking** to Bay City? Impossible!'"

Too often people wanted to associate me with Forrest Gump, endlessly criss-crossing the roads of America, choosing a direction as the wind blows. But we had a route and a schedule. This was a fundraising and awareness effort for breast cancer. The people we depended on to help us from town to town needed to depend on my keeping to my schedule. The trick was to make it flexible enough that, were I to fall ill, I could make up mileage in a few days and stay on schedule.

Debi also experienced how strangers were excited to help—like the guys in the Lexington Cafe who treated us to lunch. Or when we took refuge from the 100-degree heat inside a General Store near Port Sanilac and the owner said, "Hey, didn't I see you two girls on the news the other night? Drinks are on me! Anything else you need? A beer? A game of pool? Fishing bait?"

We popped into the police department in Caro for directions, and they gave us a $20 donation. Near Clare, when we stopped to refill our water bottles at the corner bar, the bartenders dropped $10 in our donation can. Debi was awed at how supportive every-one was—and I was delighted to have at least one witness to the daily generosity.

My days with Debi and Jim were the best of my whole journey. Across Michigan and Wisconsin, Debi and I walked leisurely down quiet country farm roads, rarely having to dodge traffic except for the occasional tractor. We loped through the sloping hills of Wisconsin dotted with faded red barns and corn stalks that grew over our heads. We passed Cheese Road and Creamery Avenue in the town of Colby, the birthplace of Colby Cheese.

While we walked, Jim would rouse everyone at the next Walmart to gather 'round the entrance at four o'clock to cheer us in. He also contacted the local press and the Lions Club, so every night we engaged in an agenda of interviews, dinners, speeches and kissing babies.

On rest days we attended craft fairs, where church ladies sold crocheted doilies and homemade peanut butter cookies. We visited small-town festivals celebrating the produce of their local county from the Brussel Sprout Festival to the Bologna Fair. Bands played in town square gazebos. It was *Rockwellian,* the picture of small town America that made my heart swell. After four years of discovering the world, discovering different countries with their unique histories, cultures and heritage, I was now discovering my own.

Then we got a phone call.

In Chippewa Falls, Wisconsin, Debi, Jim, and I were camping in the town park, entertaining Mayor Doug who had come by for a cook-out, when they got a call from their son. His wife was in the hospital with emergency premature labor. Debi and Jim had to get to San Luis Obispo ASAP.

With no time to spare, they helped me empty my two drawers I had so enthusiastically filled six weeks before. The next morning they bolted to the nearest airport, leaving me alone in the park with Bob. On a dime, I was back to living off food that could take a beating being bounced around inside Bob. That meant bananas were out. Apples were in. Salmon was out. Canned tuna was in. Two egg-white omelets were out. Stale rice cakes were back in.

Minneapolis, my hometown, is just a hundred miles west of Chippewa Falls, but I had an alternative route. My plan was to turn north a hundred-and-fifty miles and cross into Minnesota at Duluth, then walk clear across the state. Two reasons: My grandma lived in Detroit Lakes in the northwest of the state, and at ninety-seven years old she could no longer travel to Minneapolis to join me. Grandma had faithfully followed the progress of my walk, sharing my journals with her friends. Every birthday and Christmas, or on no occasion at all, she sent me American Express gift cards, which I could use anywhere to spoil myself with a special meal. So it was a very big deal that I go through Detroit Lakes, even if that meant a three-hundred-mile detour. In addition, this was a once-in-a-lifetime opportunity to experience my own state, my own culture, to come full circle from the birth of my dream at the breakfast table in 1974 when I read the *Minneapolis Tribune* article about David Kunst.

So outside Chippewa Falls I sat in a cozy red-vinyl booth getting excited looking at my map of Minnesota. Quite possibly more excited than anyone has ever been while looking at a map of Minnesota.

Over the Bong Bridge into Duluth, Minnesota, a reporter from the *Duluth Herald* joined me and asked about the special moments I'd had during the past four years. At that instant, I spotted the "Welcome to Minnesota" sign and said, "I'm about to have one."

Crossing into Minnesota, I thought back to those tough days plodding across central India when I had to mentally psyche myself up every morning to face another day. I reminded myself then that someday I'd be walking into Minnesota where I understood the language and had friends who went way back to playing kickball on First Avenue.

Now here I was, back to *my* Minnesota, with its canoes and carp, pine and oak. It was like walking back into the womb, into a culture I understood. I'd learned by now that walleye is not on every cafe menu across the country, and people outside Minnesota borders have hardly ever heard of root beer. Mississippi is not the first word everyone learns how to spell.

It was the perfect summer day to enter northern Minnesota. Half-a-dozen women dressed in pink met me, all breast cancer survivors from the Duluth area. At the far end of the bridge, I spotted my friend Stephanie with her two boys, Daniel, eleven, and Jack, seven. They were carrying a colorful handmade welcome sign with green and blue balloons bobbing overhead. I'd known

Stephanie since the seventh grade, and I couldn't have asked for a better friend to welcome me into my home state. Consider:

When we were seniors in high school, we'd taken a creative writing class together. One day our assignment was to write about a day in our life ten years into the future. Everyone in class wrote about their wedding day—except Steph and me. She wrote about how she was going to be a pilot at United Airlines. I wrote that I was going to travel around the world, and on this day in ten years, I would be back in Minnesota for a visit.

Cut to the future—albeit more than ten years later—Stephanie was indeed a pilot for United Airlines, and I was coming home from traveling around the world.

I broke from the pink ladies and greeted Stephanie with a bear hug reserved only for friends who go back to age thirteen.

"I've walked nearly 12,000 miles to see you!"

"Well, I could point out a little short cut!" and we laughed and laughed like it was funny.

It took a full hour laughing and crying to cross the two hundred yard Bong Bridge into my home turf. I sent a mental message to "India Polly:" *It was well worth the slog.* I'd come full circle back to the land of the loons, home of Scotch tape, bundt cake and the office stapler, where the summers are short, the o's are long and the hot dish is always a surprise. That's *my* Minnesota.

Stephanie wanted to walk the seventy-five miles to Grand Rapids with me, at which point she would pass me on to another high school friend, Dawn. That gave us five days to get caught up on our respective lives. We reminisced while walking fifteen miles along Highway 2; at night, we poured over dusty high school memorabilia.

"Hey! Here's a note you wrote me," I said. "It says, 'I love Joe. I'll always love Joe. It will always be Joe.' Who's Joe?"

"I have no idea."

Steph went beyond the beyonds taking care of me, including a haircut, laundry and—upon noting I only had a long-sleeved shirt and one pair of pants—whisked me off to a WalMart.

"Have you forgotten how cold it can be in September? With good conscience, I couldn't possibly cut you loose without getting you some warmer clothes. Get in the car."

By the time we made it to Grand Rapids, I was coifed and warmly dressed, ready for the seasons to change in Northern Minnesota. Dawn fed, freshened, and fawned then pointed me toward Bemidji where I would cross through the Ojibwa (Chippewa) Indian reservation.

Highway 2 west of Grand Rapids was nothing but rows of pine and birch sprouting high on each side of the road. People waved enthusiastically, and I waved back as if I knew them. One man in a dumpy red truck, dressed in overalls and a John Deere cap, pulled over. "Hey there, didn't I see you in the *Minneapolis Star* and *Tribune* last week?"

"Yes, that's right."

"Well, that there's amazing what you're doing. God bless ya." He handed me a wad of bills. "Here's a hundred dollars. Do something nice for yourself."

"A hundred dollars!"

"It's the least I can do. You're doing a great thing, and I can't imagine you have much money left if you've been on the road all these years."

He was right, of course. Fact was, I'd just sold my condo in Vail to finance the last year of my walk. But he didn't know that.

"Wow, I don't know what to say."

"You don't need to say anything. It's my pleasure. By the way, keep your eyes open through these roads. There's a yeti out there somewhere."

"A yeti?"

"Yes, ma'am. A Sasquatch. People have been spotting him in these parts for years. They say he looks like a big ape man, huge and hairy."

My eyes darted down the tree-lined terrain. "Out there? So how often has this…er…yeti …beast…been sighted?"

"Not too long ago some folks looked out their back window and saw him playing with their clothesline, fiddling with the pins. They both saw it, said he was huge, like an ape, but he ran off and they haven't seen him since. Lot of folks say they hear things, grunting and the breaking of big branches, big tree trunks snapping in two. No bear can do that. You better pull out that pepper spray of yours."

"You bet!" I said and secured it to my hip, perhaps a little too confident that my four-inch yellow canister of pepper spray would keep me safe from a huge, hairy yeti man.

A few miles later, I came upon a store in the reservation town of Bena. I popped in to get a Gatorade.

"Where did you come from?" asked the bewildered young Ojibwa man at the front desk. "I didn't see you drive up."

I told him what I was doing, then changed the subject to something far more interesting. "So what do you know about a yeti man in this area?"

"Oh, yeah. Lots of people 'round 'ere have spotted him. People come by the store all the time to tell us of their sightings 'cause this 'ere store is kind of central patrol for Sasquatch sightings."

"What should I do if I see him?" I asked.

"He won't hurt you. Just take a photo and report back here to the Bena store for our records."

Easy enough. My pepper spray was secure on my right hip, my camera was unlocked, and I headed west out the door toward Bemidji wide-eyed and on the lookout for Yeti Man.

The fall temperatures remained above average. I trotted down quiet roads filled with lush red maples and golden oaks at their peak. Scenic lakes surrounded my every view. Minnesota is known as the Land of 10,000 Lakes, but everyone knows there are at least 15,000 and I'd been warned that if I was walking I'd better pay close attention or I'd likely fall into one.

My walk through Minnesota was perfect—an idyllic blend of friends, family and personal discovery of my own heritage. Every day I unearthed something new about my Minnesota. I was born and raised here, but until I walked through it I knew nothing of the Ojibwa, the Sasquatch man, or that Minnesota is the lutefisk capital of the United States.

It was late September when I walked into Detroit Lakes. Just seeing the welcome sign brought back fond memories of family vacations at the lake with my cousins when we were little. We would drive up to the cabin, tumble out of the car, and spend all day jumping off the dock and nights cramped around the table playing raucous games of Spoons.

The last time I saw Grandma was at her ninetieth birthday party when she was still bounding up stairs and playing piano like a pro. Now at ninety-seven she was frail, but still chatty and playing piano like a pro. She had a nice tidy apartment at the assisted-living home. It contained few belongings outside her beloved piano, which sat in the living room as if on display. After giving me a tour of her digs, she sat on the bench and played for me. Her fingers effortlessly tinkled across the ivories, and I wondered about the century of memories that had shaped her. She'd seen it all and lived it hard.

Grandma grew up in the rocky hills of North Dakota at the beginning of the twentieth century. She was six when the *Titanic* sank, and her mother told her more people died in that disaster than lived in all of Kidder County. After attending enough college to teach school for a few years and buy her own piano, she married a local boy and settled in the tiny town of Pettibone, where she'd grown up. They raised five kids (including my mom) through the Depression and dustbowl years and World War II. She taught piano lessons to practically everyone in Kidder County who wanted to learn and made enough money to help all her girls go to college.

Grandma was always a woman ahead of her time. I never heard her get on a soap box and declare that women could do whatever they wanted; she just did it. Watching her play the piano at ninety-seven and knowing how she'd handled her life with such grace, I only hoped I had a few of her tough genes in me.

Uncle Wally and Aunt Lue still lived in Detroit Lakes and took loving care of Grandma. They visited several times a week, took her to doctors, out to lunch, played Bridge and Pinochle with her. They also spoiled me on my walk through.

We made a mini family reunion out of my walk into Detroit Lakes. Mom and her husband John drove up from Tucson; my sisters Cara and Laurie came up from Minneapolis. All four generations joined together for a ceremonial walk into the heart of town—from Grandma walking with assistance, to the youngest, my eleven-month-old nephew Eamon, taking his first steps with assistance.

That night, after all the fanfare was over, we gathered back around Uncle Wally and Aunt Lue's kitchen table, and like the summer days all those years ago, played rousing card games until we couldn't see straight. After four years, I reveled in it all, surrounded by the people who had known me all my life. What better reason to make a meager 300-mile detour?

It was a mid-October day when I walked into Minneapolis. A dozen old friends joined me down the Mississippi River trail lined with autumn colors.

All biases aside, of course, Minneapolis has got to be one of the most beautiful cities in the world. The way Hennepin Bridge beams over the Mississippi with the city's perky skyline sparkling in the background. I wanted to take a bite out of it.

It's where I was born and raised, where I have friends going back to childhood, high school, college. I hadn't lived there for two decades, but it will always be *my* town, *my* Twin Cities, if only because we speak a common language that embraces words like "Uffduh."

At five o'clock, my friends and I closed in on downtown and a welcome party at Nye's Polonaise Bar right off the river road. My eyes squinted as they adjusted from a day in the afternoon sun, but I entered to a chorus of clapping, congratulations and welcome homes, and when my eyes came to I saw familiar faces that spanned forty years. My head started to spin.

"Julie! Haven't seen you in twenty years!...Mike, you haven't changed a bit!...Skip, thank you for all the emails of support!... Charlie, thanks for coming from Arizona!...Connie...Lois!... Michelle!...John!...Nicole!...Katie!...Jaci!...Mike!...Laurie!... Tami!...Diane!...Karen!...Bucky!...Gagstetter! My high-school track coach! And you thought the two-mile was a long race! Winnie! I'd recognize you anywhere, even if I haven't seen you since I was six....Andrea and John, your baby girl is gorgeous!...Lisa and Ann! Next-door neighbors from the seventies!...My eternal buddy, Jackie, with her mother Joanie and her boys, Timmy and Joe. They look just like you, only cuter!"

The evening sped by, exciting and chaotic with fragments of news from everyone—the new job in Wayzata, new house in Minnetonka, a snippet about a new love life. Then someone else would poke me on the shoulder and I'd squeal with delight at another face from long, long ago.

City councilman, Gary Schiff of Minneapolis took the stage to announce they'd passed a proclamation naming *this* day, October 16, 2003, GlobalWalk for Breast Cancer Day in Minneapolis. And that's how you walk back into your hometown after 12,000 miles.

CHAPTER 23

Iowa/Missouri: The Mother Lode of Nice

The weatherman promised it would be warm, up to forty degrees. He was wrong. It was sixteen degrees, with gusting winds and moist air. The prairies around me were foggy and beige; an endless sprawl of harvested cornfields warning that winter was imminent.

I pressed on down Highway 52 closing in on the Iowa border. Naked trees lined the Mississippi, quietly outlining the misty skies that spread a quiet mood across the river, like it was getting tucked in for the winter. Their golden leaves had fallen. I spent my days in a Huck Finn zone, imagining I was a great river adventurer trekking up and down the bluffs. Old Victorian houses with sprawling porches and big bay windows filled the historic river towns.

Each step I took in Iowa was a lovely surprise. I must ask about the statute of limitations on apologies as being a Minnesotan it's been my natural-born duty to make fun of Iowa. But I'm more mature now and discovering all the excitement coming from our neighbor to the south. For example, did you know that Iowa invented the tractor? Yes, I suppose you did, but there's more. My handy Iowa Pocket Guide informed me that Iowa is also the washing-machine capital of the world. Then you turn the page and discover that that's because Fred Maytag was born there, not because their clothes are dirtier than in other states'.

For the princely sum of $6.95 I splurged on the Iowa Pocket Guide in the hopes of learning everything there was to know about Iowa. What better way to spend twenty minutes? (Ba da boom.) Seriously though, Iowa is like a hidden secret everyone is trying to keep to themselves. Too bad I couldn't slow down and enjoy it. November days were short, and winter was due any minute. That meant my dawdling days were over; no more reading magazines at the Kwikky Mart or sharing chili with the farmers at the Food and Fuel.

But Iowans disagreed. They didn't give two hoots if they stopped their John Deere tractor right in the middle of the highway for a chat, rain or shine. "That's quite a load ye got there," they'd say, pointing to Bob. "I saw you working hard down Highway 52 pushing that buggy. Whadaya say you stop at the Pump and Munch a mile up the road and I'll treat you to a bowl of chili?"

When I had to say, "I'm sorry. I gotta keep moving. I have to hit Decorah by nightfall," I felt like the meanest person in Iowa.

Main Streets in Iowa towns buzzed amidst charming renovated nineteenth-century buildings. A woman at the post office said, "I haven't seen you in these parts before. Welcome to Iowa." College kids at the Magpie Cafe said, "Hey, aren't you that girl walking around the world? Let us treat you to that mochaccino." A lady at a card shop waved from the window. The librarian, bank teller and hotel clerk said, "Hi there. Where you from? You new in town?" The lady at the Qwikky Tripp asked if I needed any help—and she didn't even work there. It was like hitting the mother lode of nice.

My Iowa Pocket Guide said that the first microwave oven was introduced in Iowa—the Radarange, back in 1965. Even the first digital computer came out of Iowa! The biggest tourist attraction is Kevin Costner's Field of Dreams baseball field that was carved into a cornfield in Dyersville. And next time you drop change into a soda machine remember that it was Iowan F.A. Wittern who invented the change-giving vending machine.

There, I just saved you $6.95. Aren't I nice?

I carried on down the Mississippi where occasional commerce signs entertained me, like "Mrs. Ippi's Café" and "Mr. Sippi's Yacht Club." As I huffed and puffed my way up and down the bluffs, I grumbled under my breath that Iowa being flat is the big bluff.

Then one afternoon my Huck Finn zone was broken. Suddenly I heard a dog racing out of the trees toward me, and he didn't sound happy. I was on the other side of the road, so I acknowledged the dog and let him protect his territory. Granted, I'm a self-professed cat person, but I respect a dog protecting his turf. My problem is slack dog owners who don't train their dogs to leave globe walkers alone when they're minding their own business enjoying the mood and the river and being Huckleberry Finn.

Then a second dog came springing out of the trees. Wait. Three, four. Geez, five! Holy cow, six! Oh, for chrissakes, seven! Auuughhh, *eight* dogs bounded down the embankment from the farm and onto the road, snarling and barking, forming a circle around me. Trying to keep an eye on all of the dogs, I rummaged through Bob's front pouch for my pepper spray while my elbows wheeled the buggy in circles like a knight's shield, protecting me from the lunging canines.

My new pepper spray was a police force turbo-powered ten-foot spray. I'd been trained that if I found myself in a position when I needed to use it, shoot fast and aim for the forehead so it drips down into the eyes and paralyzes the guy long enough to get away. "Never pull out your pepper spray and threaten to use it," said the cop. "Just go for it. Otherwise, you've lost the element of surprise and you're doomed."

But I chickened out and just aimed my pepper spray at the eight dogs. They backed off. It surprised me. *When I'm out of pepper spray,* I noted, *I could frighten them equally with a stick of lip balm.*

But if my pepper spray frightened them, they quickly got over it. They surrounded me again, growling, seething, clearly trained to attack passersby.

The police officer was right. I should've just sprayed; now I had lost the element of surprise, and I was dancing around the middle of the road wondering if this was what Custer felt like at Little Bighorn.

The dogs surrounded me. Two of them lunged. I sprayed. One spray, two sprays. I barked back. All without effect.

A car came around the bend then, sending the dogs leaping to the opposite side of the road. This was my chance! I threw myself out in front of the car and waved it down, flailing my arms over my head with urgency to the young couple inside.

"Hi! Listen, this pile of dogs has just run off that farm and are getting aggressive! Could you stay with me for a mile or so and serve as a buffer between me and these %$*# dogs?"

He nodded. She stared. I hightailed it down the road with a car between me and my would-be killers. I imagined their conversation inside the car. "Honey, what did she say?"

"I don't know, but do what she says; she looks threatening with that lip balm."

After a half-mile, with no dogs in sight, I thanked the couple profusely and waved them on.

Over the next two hours, the Great River Road led me to the quaint town of Marquette and the Frontier Hotel. Todd, the owner who had donated a room, greeted me at the front door. Immediately, I spotted a fluffy black-and-white kitty in the front window.

"Oooh," I cooed. "You have a kitty cat!" I went to give her a cootchie coo behind the ear. She lifted her chin, inviting more. No barking, no lunging, no teeth. Just a purring bundle of fuzzy love. I scooped her up in my arms to give her a tickle on the belly. "What's her name?"

"We call her Sweetie."

Sweetie? Seriously. Where is the cat-versus-dog debate here?

Early on the morning of December 14, 2003, news shot around the world that U.S. soldiers had captured Saddam Hussein. He was found in a six-foot rat hole south of his hometown in Tikrit. Uttering one of the great lines in history, he crawled out of his spider hole and said, "Okay, I'm ready to negotiate."

At the Best Western's free, hot breakfast buffet in Muscatine, Iowa, sleepyheads came in one at a time and addressed everyone as if we were all friends. "Have you heard?" Strangers sat together, talking about the news from halfway around the world that bonded us all over the free hot breakfast buffet.

The morning Saddam Hussein's bedraggled butt was hauled out of a rat hole, the local weatherman—whose name was Joe Winter, isn't that great?—forecast winds up to forty miles per hour, with sleet expected. The weather gods had been on my side thus far, but my luck had indisputably run out.

Lions members in Muscatine, Helen and Richard, called to check on my sanity. "Are you sure you want to go?" they asked. "This would be a great day to relax inside the Best Western listening to CNN eternally loop 'Okay, I'm ready to negotiate.' We could come over and watch with you. It would be fun."

"That is tempting, but Joe Winter said it might reach ten degrees. I'll be okay."

They questioned my stubbornness, but alternatively offered to transport Bob so I wouldn't have to walk him along the icy roads. I then piled on five layers and charged head on into the Iowa winter I always knew would catch up to me.

There was another guy walking around the world at the same time as I, and we'd been in touch occasionally. When I was walking down the icy roads of Iowa, he was in Alaska, preparing to cross the frozen Bering Strait into Russia.

Big deal. Sure he had only one hour of daylight each day and was dependent on airdrops for food, but he didn't have to deal with semi-trucks threatening to jackknife into him from hidden patches of black ice.

So I started thinking. My better judgment told me to get off the icy roads and hibernate for the rest of the winter. For the next two months I could go back to Minnesota, play with my new young niece and nephew, Rosie and Eamon, bug my sisters, and get reacquainted with old friends. My friend Shirley even set up a deal with the nuns in Rochester, where I would help them with their house-sitting business for a month. House-sitting for nuns would be decidedly safer than walking the icy roads of Iowa.

Wind-burned and frostbitten, I walked into Keokuk, Iowa, just days before Christmas. The President of the local Lions Club offered to store Bob in the basement of his workplace and lent me a suitcase. I then caught a train back up to Minneapolis to start my hiatus. When the ice melted, I would come back to Keokuk to kick off the beginning of the end, the last 1,200 miles. With any luck, the weatherman's name would be Sonny Daily.

By early March the ice had thawed, and it was time to hit the road again. But the nomadic life was beginning to weigh heavily. After four-and-a-half years I was nearing the end of my rope, weary of never knowing where I was going or where I would stay, the constant adapting, packing, unpacking, unable to control what food I could eat. Even with the end in sight, it was wearing me down.

In a year I'd probably be settled in a career, whining about how life is so boring. Someone please remind me then how nice it is to not have to figure out where I'm going to stay every night, someone slap me upside the head and point out how nice it is to just get up and move about my day without stuffing all my clothes into a sack, wrinkles, dirt and all. I looked forward to having a laundry basket, to being able to sort the dirty clothes from the clean ones.

And so on a Saturday morning in March, I rescued Bob from his toasty hideaway in Keokuk, Iowa, and forced him out on the road again. My route would continue down the Mississippi River into Missouri, where I would turn west toward Kansas and Colorado.

But just because it was the home stretch didn't mean that it was going to be easy. The last 1,200 miles were taking me through the open prairies of tornado alley, the natural disaster capital of the world—during high season. The year before, news of three hundred tornadoes crisscrossing Missouri and Kansas had dominated the headlines.

The Lions Club of Keokuk walked a hundred yards with Bob and me, then waved goodbye, pointing us toward Missouri and into the heart of Tornado Alley.

My first stop was Canton, a town still reeling from last year's tornado. Lions member Sam told me there had been a tornado warning from 9 a.m. to 6:30 p.m. on that fateful day, so everyone in town took cover in their cellars with a good stock of food, board games and battery-operated radios. Sam and his wife watched their neighbor across the street as he went around his house collecting all his photographs, methodically taking them off the walls—weddings, graduations, softball games, anniversaries—and carrying them into the cellar. They thought he was a bit crazy. After all, tornado warnings were a part of the culture in Canton.

At 6:30 p.m. Sam came out of the basement and looked out his kitchen window. Skies were sunny and blue, and they all praised the weatherman for having his fingers on the pulse. But at 6:33 he saw things spiraling through the sky.

"What do you mean, *things*?" I asked.

"You know, *things*—fences, cars, Subway Sandwich shops."

For ten minutes the funnel roared through the small town of Canton, randomly ripping up some people's homes while sparing others by the lucky stroke of settling their property a hundred yards to the south. When the roaring stopped, Sam came out of his basement again. The first thing he saw was his neighbor across the street, climbing out of his cellar gripping his box of photos. His house no longer existed.

A year later, you could still see the devastation. Every other house was under construction. Stairways led to nowhere. Driveways entered empty lots. But the college had reopened, so had the Comfort Inn and grocery store. The Subway shop was probably somewhere near Topeka. Don't know if it reopened.

Between the Lions Club members and the friendly people of northwest Missouri, I became comfortable with the idea that if a tornado were to whip down Highway 24, someone would stop and take Bob and me to the safety of a Walmart storage cooler.

People in northeastern Missouri could not have been friendlier. I stopped at neighborhood gathering spots called Jimmy's or Mama's, where locals invited me to their tables and told me all about Missouri, from Mark Twain to the local gossip of Clark County.

It was my very favorite part of walking across America— hanging out at a good ol' rural cafe. Not for the food, mind you. Nooo. Food there knows only the grill and the deep fat fryer. Rather, I loved it for the great display of local character.

Outside of La Grange, I popped into the 18 Wheeler, a truck stop open 24/7 with black stools lined up at the red Formica lunch counter. Local farmers gathered early every morning to solve the world's problems and order the Farmers' Special: three-egg omelet, hash browns, bacon strips, two sausages and a biscuit with gravy, "With a heart attack on the side," they joked.

When I walked into the 18 Wheeler, I recognized Roger, the Lions Club member I'd met a few days before. He introduced me to his buddies, "Howdy, ma'am. Take a seat 'ere. You Republican?"

They all laughed and said, "Knock it off, Roy. You shouldn't be askin' no visitin' lady what her political orientation is."

But I flirted back. "I'm too young to vote yet. Anyway, I'm going to sit over there with Roger, 'cuz he's the best lookin'."

They all hooted and hollered and slapped their knees. "Order anything you want; it's on us!"

Being back on the road after my winter hiatus meant struggling to find something edible on truck-stop menus. Oatmeal was always a safe bet, but you had to remember to order everything on the side or they topped it off with a half a cup of sugar and whole milk. Chicken salad and tuna salad were doused in mayonnaise between two slabs of Wonder Bread. There was usually a side order option, like cottage cheese or salad, but not at the 18 Wheeler.

The waitress, Lois, pulled the pencil out of her hair and said, "Hey there, little Missy, what kin I gitcha?" I asked Lois for two scrambled egg whites, with an English muffin, which seemed a safe bet. But no, I got egg whites marinated in grease and an English muffin swimming toward me on a raft of butter.

For two hours that morning the gang at the 18 Wheeler shared a laugh, and I patted my egg whites with a napkin to soak up the grease.

Two days later in Monroe City I had breakfast at Tilly's Cafe. Tilly's had the twirly stools and Formica lunch counter that I like and plastic displays flaunting pie—boysenberry, raspberry, huckleberry, elderberry. I never ordered the pie, but I liked the homey pie atmosphere. What made Tilly's special was The Big Table. You didn't have to be invited; it was just a big square table that sat eight people who would come and go, giving a howdy to anyone who cared to order a Farmer's Special and discuss the news of the day.

All the men at Tilly's wore overalls, and hats advertising something like the National Horse Barrel Racing Association. The women wore sweatshirts that said World's Best Grandma. The folks at The Big Table waved me over to join them, and I quickly took a seat, ready to find out the goings-on in Monroe City, population 2,500.

One of their very own Monroe City boys had recently been killed in Iraq, a nice young man just nineteen-years-old, a leader at school and on the cusp of a grown-up life. Pictures of him and his family flanked the walls of Tilly's, surrounded by American flags. I'd seen his picture at the Monroe City Inn, too, where Lions had put me up the night before and at the local Kwikky Mart where I got my cappuccino. The whole town was in mourning.

One of the great lessons of my walk was the respect I gained for the people in these small towns. I hate to admit it, but I used to make fun of small town people. They weren't well traveled, most have probably never been out of the county. I'm now so ashamed that I ever thought of them like that. These are people filled with peace and honor. They chose to build families and communities. It's these people who laid the foundation of this great country. What would we, or our world, be like without them? They were the ones to be respected.

The people of Monroe County, Clark County and throughout small town America are the kindest people in the world. They live a slower life; hardly in sight as the rest of us race down their highways in our hurry. But they're far more attached to each other, they take care of each other; they have fundraisers for their neighbors when they get diagnosed with breast cancer.

There's no doubt that traveling and discovering other cultures is eye opening, but I was inspired, indeed comforted, by the people who met every morning at the Big Table—and relieved that I learned that lesson again and again.

CHAPTER 24

The Long Unwinding Road

All right, who's the wise guy that said Kansas was flat? Holy criminy. Up, down, up, down, all bloody day long. Oh, I knew Kansas was flat, somewhere. *Time* magazine had just reported that if 1.000 is the mathematical value of perfect flatness and .957 is the flatness of a pancake, then Kansas at .9997 is scientifically proven to be flatter than a pancake. I just didn't experience it on my first half of Kansas.

I settled into the Lenexa Days Inn and on my way out for dinner, grabbed the *Kansas Getaway Guide*. I told the front desk clerks I was going to learn everything there was to learn about Kansas. They laughed. "All you need to know is that it's flat and boring."

"Well, I *know* it's not flat, and I doubt very much it is boring. I'm sure Kansas is great."

They were still laughing as I tucked the *Kansas Getaway Guide* under my arm and headed out to find a salad.

At Panera's Cafe, I spread out the map of Kansas. I had decided to follow the old Santa Fe Trail, the historic route that opened trade between Missouri and Mexico. Today, Highway 50 is the road that follows the old Santa Fe Trail. It cuts right across the middle of Kansas into Colorado, and that's the road I would walk. It's also the last coast-to-coast highway that had not been transformed into an Interstate, therefore still had character with old motels and cafes and historical markers pointing out original Santa Fe Trail wagon wheel ruts. For that reason it's a very popular route for anyone traveling cross country—bicycle tours, motorcyclists and car tourists who like to dawdle through antique shops and marvel at old wagon wheel ruts.

I continued to thumb through the *Kansas Getaway Guide*, and I couldn't figure out what those boys at the Days Inn were talking about. You can stand in the town of Osborne and be in the geodetic center of the U.S., then go forty miles north to Lebanon and be in the geographic center of the forty-eight states. In Liberal you can go to the Land of Oz Museum and see the flying house used in the *Wizard of Oz* film. And right along my route through the Kansas prairie was a whole museum dedicated to the history of prairies. God bless America.

Then there was Dodge City, which, in keeping with the cowboys-on-the-trail tradition, promised to dish me up a big plate of Butt Bustin' Beans. Dodge City also took the honor as windiest city in the USA. I hoped the two weren't related.

Call me crazy, I'd always looked forward to crossing Kansas. I liked the idea of seeing the old West meet twenty-first century modernity. The first couple of days were full of warm welcomes. Kansans stopped to give donations and best wishes of support, yelling out their windows as they passed, "Hey there, we saw you on the TV news! Welcome to Kansas. You'll love it! It's flat!"

This was the next-to-the-last state in the last country, the last four months of my walk. The cottonwoods plumped up and leafed out, an announcement that spring had arrived. Seventy-degree temperatures allowed me to ditch my winter layers. These were the twilight miles of my global walk, and I enjoyed the longer sunny days and a sky that grew bigger and bigger, stretching out over undulating hills that everyone swears don't exist in Kansas.

I passed itty-bitty Kansas towns like Baldwin City, Ottawa and Lebo, where the locals picked up my tab at the diner and breast cancer survivors walked with me long enough to get me in the right direction. I officially entered the West when I met my first cowboy, a real live one with spurs on his boots and a swagger in his step. At the Kwikky Mart he tipped his hat and said, "Howdy, ma'am."

As I moved farther west the hills subsided. The roads got straighter and trees disappeared—prime conditions for forty and fifty-mile-per-hour winds. "Hang onto your hat today," the weather-man regularly warned. "Even by Kansas standards, it's going to be a gusty day!"

Kansas is famous for wind, and as a walker there's no getting used to it. Wind sucks. And blows. It pushes and pushes and all I could do was plow through it like I was trying to run a sprint in a swimming pool. Then, like Mother Nature is having a good laugh at your expense, it let up for a second, just a split second, and sent me tumbling down Highway 50. But windy as it was, I was grateful to be dodging the tornadoes that regularly thundered across the southern portions of the state.

Western Kansas, like much of middle America, has its share of towns that have crumbled into ghostliness, leaving little behind but grain elevators that poke out of the horizon on otherwise empty plains. Old farmers told me that grain elevators were located every six miles so the farmers of horse-and-wagon days were never more than three miles away to load, unload and make the trip home in a day.

Fighting my way down Highway 50, I regularly listened to the Western Kansas Farm Report above the wind whistling through my earphones. One morning they were promoting the upcoming Beef Empire Days, the annual celebration of the region's history with beef. The guest of the morning was the festival's Carcass Evaluation Contest judge. I was intrigued that anyone could build an expertise on cattle carcasses, but more surprised that it held my attention.

Walking between the grain elevators of Offerle and Bellefont —that's six miles if you're paying attention—it dawned on me how flat Kansas had become. I turned a full 360-degrees and saw nothing but wheat growing all around me as far as I could see. In every direction, green wheat met the wide-open sky. The wind put a wave in the green sea, and a single ray of sun poked out of the clouds providing a sparkle that rippled across the tips. Dumbstruck by the simplicity, I twirled around in the middle of barren Highway 50 having a moment.

This is Kansas! All of it, right here, wrapped up in a single moment: the grain, the waving, the sparkling, the horizon with the flatness, the cattle carcass report, the grain elevators three miles ahead, three miles behind. This was Kansas!

I took out my camera and sought the best shot, but shortly snapped it shut. There was no way I could capture the scene in a photo. Instead, I took a moment to wrap the whole feeling around me and freeze it as a photo inside my head.

When the local Lions Kathy and Bill met me outside the Bellefont grain elevator, I told them about my moment with the grain and the waving and the sparkling and the horizon with the flatness.

"Oh, yeah, the amber waves of grain."

I retreated back a step. "*That's* the amber waves of grain? You mean the amber waves of grain I've been singing about since elementary school?"

"Well they ain't really amber right now. They'll turn amber 'bout mid-June for first harvest."

I never even realized that I didn't know what *the amber waves of grain* meant. But now I understood the magic.

What a country. Fruited plains? We got 'em. Purple mountains' majesty? They take your breath away. Sea to shining sea? Check. Amber waves of grain? Been there, done that. Can't possibly take the photo.

The skies turned a deeper, darker blue as I stepped over the Colorado border. Those rich blue skies are unmatched anywhere, a blue so shocking that you have to stop and stare and wonder if Crayola could ever create a color so brilliant.

But southeastern Colorado is decidedly not what that John Denver was yodeling on about. Still hundreds of miles from the Front Range cities, or even a peek of a peak, the wheat fields and cattle feed lots of southeastern Colorado looked more like Kansas than a Rocky Mountain high.

The finish line in Vail lay two months away. Part of me was so ready to just sit down in one place and get settled. I was done with shoestring travel, being broke, dressing in the same two shirts and dragging my sorry butt through whatever Mother Nature felt free to throw at me. On the other hand I was nervous about the up-coming re-assimilation process.

Last year a stranger in a London, Ontario, cafe congratulated me on doing so well on my walk, but cautioned me to beware of the "afterward." Years before he'd taken a five-month bike trip across America and getting settled afterwards was the toughest period of his life. He had plugged himself right back into the life that he had had, but he was different. It took him years to get through the depression of resettling. A woman named Lisa, who rode her bike around the world for breast cancer, emailed to tell me that getting settled afterwards was the toughest part. She wasn't satisfied with her town anymore, her job, her own mind. She said, "You know how it takes a few days to bounce back after a vacation? Multiply that by a year." It took her a good part of a year digging deep into a spiritual journey to climb out of her depression. Lisa said she was worried about me, and if I slipped into depression after my finish I could email her for consultation.

Entering Colorado and watching the last miles spread out before me, I felt like an airplane coming in for a landing. I saw the runway, now I just needed to get lined up and release the landing gear. I had to find a place to live, get a job, buy some new clothes—something suitable for job interviews and looking snappy in my corporate American cubicle.

I'd have to get back to paying monthly bills, cleaning house, driving a car, caring about the cost of gas. It was about adapting—and that was something I'd become very good at over the years. The irony was that I'd have to adapt to not adapting. But I looked forward to routine, to walking around town without a map. I looked forward to spending a Saturday morning with friends over a cappuccino, knowing my neighbors, to having a closet with hangers and a dresser with drawers.

What job could be as satisfying? Maybe I could do some freelance writing. Under the guise that you write what you know, maybe I could pen a few magazine articles like:

How to Eat Healthy at Gas Stations and Truck Stops; Skin Care for the Outdoor Life; Top Ten Snappy Comebacks for Americans Traveling in Europe; How to Get a Haircut Overseas.

Or maybe I could become a documentary filmmaker and rebut that bozo that made zillions off *Super Size Me*, the documentary that proved yes, you too can eat like a pig four times a day and become a fat cow. Give me zillions and I'll document how I walked around the world without a single sick day, and McDonald's was my savior. How I survived on McDonald's Grilled Chicken Cobb through New Zealand, Australia, Europe and Midwest America because they were the only ones who offered a salad that's not deep-fried. In my documentary, which I'd call, *I'm Lovin' It!*, I'd tell the story of whenever I would near a town in Europe and see a billboard for the Golden Arches my heart would flutter knowing that at least something would be open in the next town while the rest of Europe was napping off their four hour work day.[2] Whatever I ended up doing, I knew I'd stay involved with breast cancer. But until then I had to wait for the right time to put down my landing gear and hope for a smooth landing.

Temperatures climbed over a hundred degrees through the flat plains of Southeastern Colorado, and I dripped sweat through Lamar, Las Animas, La Junta, towns that John Denver never sang about. The heat wasn't the problem, though. It was gnats!

Killer gnats. Relentless. Millions of them gnawing and clawing right through my clothes to get my legs, behind my neck. Two months from the finish line, on my very own turf, and gnats set out to get me. They descended so suddenly that I assumed they must be temporary, like a swarm of killer bees. But this went on for miles. I looked around for a swamp, a cattle feed lot, any reason for this battering. But there was none.

---

[2] Whew. I got on a bit of a rampage there. Apparently there's still a little angst left from my experience in Europe. And no, McDonald's was not a sponsor.

Colorado gnats are like grains of sand with fangs, so small they can sneak through anything, including the scarf I put over my face to block them from going up my nose. I couldn't wave in front of my face fast enough to keep them away. By the time I reached safety inside the Mid-Town Motel in La Junta, my neck and ears were swollen and throbbing red. "Hi, I'm Polly, checking in," I announced, still leaping around and slapping myself.

The manager, PJ, looked at me curiously, wondering if she'd donated a room to a lunatic. "You okay?"

"Yeah, it's these darn gnats. Where on earth did they come from?"

"Oh, yes. They're awful this year. It's the dry spell we're having. Vanilla extract is good for it."

Vanilla extract? I had no idea what that meant and assumed I'd heard her wrong. I thanked her and made a run for a tub.

The next morning at McDonald's, I met eight women who worked with breast cancer or had had breast cancer. We exchanged stories, and I asked advice on the gnats. "They're trying to kill me!" I lifted the back of my shirt to show them my red puffy battle wounds. They oohed.

"Vanilla extract is good for that," one said with a grimace.

So I had heard right. "You mean the vanilla extract you use for cooking?"

"My husband swears by it, something about the smell. Just dab a little behind your ears and below your eyes. You won't see a gnat for miles."

Another woman chimed, "My husband swears by fabric softener. Just stick a sheet of Bounce in your belt loop. All the cowboys use it."

I didn't recall ever seeing a cowboy with a sheet of Bounce hanging from his holster, but perhaps I hadn't been paying attention.

Another lady said, "You really should have some Deet. The West Nile virus took sixty-three lives here last year, and you're walking along the Arkansas River clear to Pueblo. You'd sure hate to walk around the world for breast cancer and drop dead from the West Nile."

The La Junta breast cancer ladies drove me to Walmart and outfitted me with Deet, vanilla extract and lightweight cotton pants so the gnats and mosquitoes couldn't nip on my legs. Unfortunately the only long pants we could find were the bright pink ones on clearance.

In the Walmart parking lot the women prepped me for my day's walk. First we spread on aloe lotion for the dry Colorado air. Next came forty-spf sweat-proof sunscreen for the high altitude sun. A pinch of vanilla extract behind the ears, below the eyes, near the nose. Then I stood with my arms out and face covered while they sprayed me head to toe with Deet. Finally, they tucked a sheet of Bounce under my watch. The bright pink pants didn't have belt loops.

Appropriately outfitted to take on an insect no bigger than a sesame seed, I waved goodbye to the La Junta breast cancer ladies, looking snappy in my bright pink pants and smelling like a lab experiment.

For the first few miles there wasn't a bug in sight. I rejoiced and broke into spontaneous whistling. I was listening to Denver radio and keeping a sharp eye on the horizon for the first glimpse of my Colorado, the one with the mountains But at mile six the gnats reappeared. I reapplied vanilla extract to my wrists, eyes, back of my ears. But they got thicker. I hung Bounce fabric softener off my sunglasses.

The gnats came on stronger, more relentless, up my nose. I rubbed vanilla extract clear up my nose. But those little buggers still snuck in and nibbled and I was outnumbered a zillion to one. All I could do was start running. Maybe I could outrun them.

My left hand pushed Bob, and my right hand waved frantically in front of my face to keep the gnats from flying up my nose. It didn't work. A dozen shot up my nose, and I screamed bloody murder, now waving with both hands while pushing Bob with my belly.

The welts swelled, but I had to stop running. With the scarf over my face and the long sleeves and long pants, my body wasn't getting any ventilation in the 105-degree heat. I felt lightheaded, so dizzy.

Oh, God, I'm going to faint and roll out into the traffic. Lean over onto Bob! Quick!

I slumped over Bob.

I stood perfectly still, flopped over Bob's handlebars, my head thick and stuffy. I couldn't think straight, but I knew I had to move off the side of the road. But I *couldn't* move or the dizziness would plunge me into the traffic where the trucks could squish me. But I *had* to move. I had to get out of the sun. But I *couldn't* move, my head felt like it was going to explode. But I *had* to move, the bugs were relentless. But I couldn't move. And for the first time in five years I toyed with the idea of waving down a car and begging for a ride to safety. But I couldn't move.

I recognized what was happening. It was an inner-ear infection. My first bout with this was one morning in Belgium when I got out of bed with a dizziness that dropped me right to the floor. I couldn't move my head or the dizziness would send me tumbling over again. I just had to lie down perfectly still for a couple hours until it ran its course. The doctor said it was an ear infection, nothing a little Benadryl couldn't clear up. Same thing happened a year and a half later in Keokuk, Iowa, and I had to crawl on my hands and knees down the hallway to the front desk of the Motel 6 and ask for a Benadryl.

On Highway 50 near La Junta, I'd been hit by the perfect storm: 105-degree heat, swarms of voracious gnats, no ventilation with all the protective clothing, and a blinding concoction of vanilla extract, Deet and Bounce. Toss in bright pink pants and something had to give.

I felt like I was on a sailboat during a tidal wave. If I moved, I'd toss my cookies and/or faint. I squatted behind Bob for a little shade and didn't move even a single hair on my head. I slowly removed my hat and bandana to let my body breathe. I had no energy left to fight. The gnats had at me.

Up the road the nearest piece of shade looked about a mile away—that may as well have been a thousand. It looked to be a building, but from this far away I couldn't be sure. Slowly I pulled myself up and leaned over Bob for support and took one ... slow ... step ... at ... a ... time ... my ... slowest ... mile ... ever.

The promising piece of shade turned out to be the Big Animal Veterinarian Clinic. It was closed, but it had an inviting shady porch. I made my way to the shade like a ship-wrecked sailor who had just spotted land. Gingerly lowering myself down, I leaned my head back to guzzle some electrolytes. Then I spread out my tarp and curled up in the fetal position.

My radio played in the background, a Denver station talking about the Colorado I knew—*my* Colorado. It was my native tongue, and it gave me great comfort while I fell asleep on the shady porch of the Big Animal Veterinarian Clinic.

My flatland bones schlepped west toward the Rocky Mountains. At Pueblo, I turned north through Colorado Springs and on toward Denver.

Just south of the Denver metro area, I spotted a sign for a dirt road called Daniel's Parkway. My map indicated it was a shortcut-but-you're-gonna-have-to-earn-it road, but I took the gamble. It was a tough climb pushing seventy-pound Bob up the side of a mountain, but it was worth the effort. After two hours I reached the peak, and there—poking out from the flat plains—was my Colorado. The Rocky Mountains, her purple mountains' majesty, peeking across the sky, jagged and layered, serene and powerful, the sky as blue as I remembered.

I pushed Bob up to the rim of Lookout Point and stared at my long lost Colorado without a thought in my head. To the north, the Denver skyline popped out of the Front Range like a jack-in-the-box. My new city, the city I had decided to call home after wrapping up this global circle in one more month.

I peered at the Denver skyline wondering if I'd be working in one of those big fancy buildings. From way up on this summit it looked easy to rejoin that society, but I knew once I reached the hustle bustle of those tall buildings I'd see the true life of corporate Americans walking briskly with important destinations. I wondered if I would ever fit into their world. I had that craving for routine, but if I were to belong to that crowd walking down Denver's 16th Street Mall with a latte-grande-skinny-no-whip and a hands-free cell phone dangling down my pressed suit for more than, say, a week, would the walls close in?

I wished you could try on a new job and a new lifestyle the same way you test-drive a car. Maybe I could start with a part-time gig where I could ease my way into a new life. In a couple weeks I could trade in my t-shirt for a pressed blouse, and slowly, maybe within a few months I'd be decked to the nines in Anne Klein striding down the 16th Street Mall in pumps and a flip-phone. Or maybe I'd just stay up on this peak and enjoy the view and the fantasy.

They're back! One month to go and Debi and Jim Linker came bounding into Denver like the cavalry to save the day. For my last month on the road, I would have a place to stay in the welcome familiarity of their forty-foot coach, friends to walk with, talk with and share with. To say nothing of having that fridge back! The golden miles of my GlobalWalk were at hand.

Vail sits a hundred miles from Denver, but I had decided to detour through Rocky Mountain National Park, an additional hundred miles out of my way. One might think I'm a wee crazy adding a hundred miles after already walking fourteen thousand, but hear me out. First, for friends and family to join me for my last mile, I had to set a finishing date months beforehand. Therefore, in planning my schedule I always had to plan for extra days in the case I got sick or injured. Happily, I never got sick or injured (minus the ear infection, but that only took an afternoon on a shady porch.) So because I never got sick I had an extra two weeks to play with.

Moreover, I'd never been to Rocky Mountain National Park before, which should be illegal for a Coloradoan—or even as an

American—and July is the single greatest time to go, with the wildlife and wildflowers in peak season. Besides, what better welcome home to my Colorado than to climb right through a John Denver song?

So while the sign to Vail pointed west from Denver, Debi and I got back into our groove and marched due north. Estes Park is sixty miles north of Denver. It's the gateway town to Rocky Mountain National Park, where the elk feel comfortable roaming down Elkhorn Avenue saying hello like good neighbors.

Rocky Mountain National Park is a 416-square mile protected wonderland. They say the area is so well protected that chances are good you can spot rarely seen mountain sheep, moose and eagles.

There are 355 miles of hiking trails, but the vast majority of visitors opt to see it through their windshields on Trail Ridge Road. It's the only road that crosses the park and is considered a national marvel to all who travel it. Affectionately called the "highway to the sky" it's the nation's highest continuous highway (Highway 34), peaking at 12,183 feet. When you enter Trail Ridge Road, you leave your hurry at the gate.

Debi and I planned to walk the forty-eight miles over Trail Ridge Road to the town of Grand Lake at the southwest corner of the national park. We figured four days would be ample.

The ranger said no.

"What do you mean, no?" I asked.

"Trail Ridge Road is a recipe for disaster for walkers," he explained. "It's very narrow and full of looky-loos taking photos of big horn sheep from their windshields. If a ranger catches you walking on Trail Ridge Road, he'll pluck you up by the scruff of the neck and drop you right back in Estes Park."

"Well, poop," I grumbled as my shoulders slumped. "Then how can we walk to Grand Lake?"

"There's a hiking trail straight up and over the spine of Rocky Mountain National Park—but it's not for sissies. It's four-and-a-half miles up, and fourteen down on the other side. You've gotta leave early to avoid the noon-time lightning storms that can kill you, and you'd better be prepared to carry up to two gallons of water."

Debi didn't show me any sympathy. "This was your idea."

I sighed and grudgingly accepted Plan B. Jim would drive our 40-foot home the 144 miles around the park with Bob and meet us on the other side in Grand Lake.

The next day at 4:30 a.m. we started our charge up to Flat Top Mountain. We were both nervous about the difficulty, but soon felt like mountain goats marching 4.4 miles to the summit.

We giggled at the irony that it was nearly five years to the day that we climbed over Cinnamon Pass near Lake City in a similar fashion. Although this time Debi wasn't falling behind due to chemo. She nearly ran to the top—a peak at 12,324 feet, even higher than Cinnamon Pass.

When we reached the summit, Debi and I took a seat on a big flat rock and enjoyed our lunch in front of the world's greatest theater. Elk and big horn sheep put on a show strutting across the tundra like models on the runway. They held their heads high with attitude, moving their long legs with style and grace, giving us a rare chance to admire their beauty. The summer tundra exploded with alpine flowers in yellows, reds and purples. I wanted to lick the whole scene right out of the sky, a sky that reached beyond forever. "It was my idea." I said, with maybe a bit of a smirk.

"You smirked too soon, smarty pants. Look behind you."

I turned around and saw a very different sky. Coming in from the west was that darn Rocky Mountain weather with the angry noontime clouds ready to unleash.

"Colorado hasn't changed a bit," I said. "Let's go!"

For the next ten days Jim, Debi and I moved right back into our roles. Jim contacted the press and moved our house from town to town. Debi made egg-white omelets in the morning, and I pushed Bob—full of water, lunch and rain gear—all day. We climbed over Berthoud Pass, through Georgetown and up Highway 6, closing in on Vail.

When we descended off Loveland Pass into Summit County, I found myself in familiar surroundings—the mountain peaks I had climbed every weekend to build my strength for this undertaking. For the first time in years I had my bearings. I recognized the roads, the towns, the Butterhorn Cafe in Frisco.

The last miles felt like a victory lap. Reporters from around the country called every few hours for interviews. "How many pairs of shoes have you walked through?" "What was your favorite country?" "Do you have any blisters?" "Will you ever walk again?" "What will you do when you finish?" "What is Bob going to do upon retirement?"

Friends and family were calling, getting on planes, trains and automobiles, making their way to Vail for the last mile. A group of friends in Vail was organizing a final celebration and regularly called with updated plans. The momentum was building.

Shrine Mountain is located along a dirt road high above Vail Pass. There are three cabins at the top nestled among the pines at 11,200-feet in elevation, surrounded by some of the Rockies' most beautiful mountain peaks. It was the end of July and the colorful wildflowers were at their peak.

Shrine Mountain was where I'd always envisioned my last night. Friends and family would gather at this Rocky Mountain treasure, stay in the cabins, hike among the wild flowers during the day and whoop it up late into the night without complaint from the neighbors.

I reserved the cabins for two nights and one full day, and with essentially no further plan I emailed friends and family with simple instructions: "There are thirty beds and room on the floor. Bring your sleeping bags, drinks and food to BBQ."

And they made their way. Throughout the afternoon and into the evening, a medley of people from various chapters of my life converged on the cabins of Shrine Mountain.

Dad flew in from Los Angeles with new shoes to help him tackle the last mile. My sister Laurie drove from Minneapolis and my brother PJ showed up with his movie camera to get crucial footage for the documentary of my walk he was planning. Mom and John drove up from Tucson; my sister Cara and her family flew in from Minneapolis.

Shirley Russo from Rochester, Minnesota, drove out in a six-seater van with five members of the Mayo Clinic's breast cancer department, who had hosted a monster fundraiser when I walked through their town. My college friend Charlie Chapman flew in from Phoenix, insisting he could make the whole seventeen-mile walk on the last day. Old-boy-friend-turned-good-friend, Mike Agnew, flew in from West Palm Beach, Florida. Gene and Joanie, Lions from Lake City, Minnesota, were vacationing nearby and joined us.

Uncle Wally and Aunt Lue from Detroit Lakes, Minnesota, made their way to the top of Shrine Mountain in their RV, along with Uncle Vern and Aunt Keeny from Florida. Friends from Vail arrived, introducing new loves and extended families. Frances, a previous roommate from Vail, flew in from Miami; friends Carol and Jim drove from Las Vegas; Vicki and Linda came from Denver; and my best high school girlfriends, Steph, Dawn and Julie, arrived together from Minnesota.

I had warned everyone there was no grocery store for twenty miles, so the food multiplied with every arrival, piling in like a food mart had exploded. Without a plan, everyone assumed a natural role. Breakfast, lunch and dinner ran seamlessly into one another. Those who, just hours before, didn't know one another puttered together in the kitchen, cooking a big pot of chili from which people filled bowls at their own pace. Mom rallied hikers during the day. Jim started a barbeque. Charlie decided it was chilly enough that we should light a roaring bon fire.

I looked around the bon fire at the Shrine Mountain cabins that last night and saw all my favorite people drinking and laughing, huddling together sharing jokes, and felt this single event was worth the 14,000-plus miles on the road. I watched Vicki and Frances chat all night like they'd known each other forever. Charlie and Julie teased each other as if they'd earned the right after years. Charlie told me how great Jim and Debi were and that they were already planning a golf outing together in Palm Springs. Carol and Debi hunched together on the porch swing discussing my future. Dad and John stood in the corner talking, and I wondered what kind of conversation they were having since John can barely hear and Dad's dry sense of humor is frequently indecipherable.

I went to bed at eleven. Woke at midnight. Fell asleep about two. Woke up at three. For the fifth night in a row, I couldn't sleep. The lack of oxygen at 11,000-foot didn't help, but I suspect it had more to do with the enormity of the moment, the culmination of five years of walking. The day I always knew would come, the day I never *really* knew would come.

So now what? I fretted in the dark of night where fret thrives. *What happens the day after I finish when I have no route, no plan? Where will I live? Can I get a job? Who will hire someone whose resumé says she'd been walking for five years? How will I assimilate back into a normal life?* Toss, turn. Flip, flop. I felt anxious about how the last day would play out, anxious that I'd faint just miles before the finish line if I didn't get some sleep, but all the anxiety over not being able to sleep was keeping me awake.

At 5:00 a.m., I finally gave up.

It was July 30, 2004. At the top of Vail Pass I stood seventeen miles from Lionshead Village where I had begun one day shy of five years before. Not everyone at the cabins was up for a walk that long, so we mapped out a number of locations where they could join me through the day. But four tough pals opted to hike the whole seventeen miles—Charlie, Linda, Randi, and, of course, Debi. We started at the crack of 6:30 a.m.

The party started in Uncle Wally's RV, where Debi made me her famed egg-white spinach omelettes for the last time, and we were sent off with cheers and photos into the crisp mountain air down Vail Pass toward the finish line.

The five of us walked and talked and skipped toward East Vail, six miles away at the bottom of Vail Pass. Reporters called from the *Minneapolis Star & Tribune*, from CNN, The CBS *Early Show*. They asked the regular questions about the shoes, the miles, the toughest, the favorite.

But one reporter asked something new: "What sort of characteristics does it take to walk around the world?" I broke from my early bird walkers to spend time with this question. It might not be a characteristic, but I knew that to do this walk, anyone would need a healthy support system. I remembered Gulab, the woman in Kolkata who so wanted to walk around the world, but her husband, mother, culture didn't allow even a second day of walking with me. While going through the toughest times, I would log on to my Yahoo! email to find notes from friends and strangers cheering me on. It gave me strength, as if people around the world were pulling me forward, assuring me I wasn't alone.

Another characteristic you'd need is a healthy dose of reality. You better get your head out of the clouds and realize that walking around the world is not romantic. It's hard work. It's frustrating. It will tick you off and take you down. You'll need patience for disruptive aggravations, unruly surprises and constant adapting. Many people on the road said to me, "I would love to do that, sounds fun, but how do you find the time?" as if I had five years to kill so I thought I'd just saunter out the door and down the block, and, oh, what the heck, I don't have anything better to do, I'll just keep going.

But I told the reporter that a key characteristic you need is a hefty dose of naivete. I say that because you can plan and plan and keep planning, but at some point you've got to hold your nose and jump. You've got to trust that things will go your way. And when they don't go your way, as they invariably will not, you've got to trust that you have harvested the skills through life to navigate through the obstacles.

"Naivete?" The reporter sounded baffled.

"Call it hope, call it faith—there has to be a raw confidence that you can handle whatever is thrown at you."

The reporter didn't sound convinced.

I ran to catch up with my friends, who were now approaching the base of Vail Pass. Twenty more people joined us. It was mile eleven and counting down.

Local Vail radio station KZYR called once an hour for a live update, at which point passing cars honked to show their enthusiasm.

The crowd grew. Friends I hadn't seen since August 1, 1999, made their way. Local breast cancer survivors came to walk along with locals I'd never met but who had followed my articles in the *Vail Daily*. We paraded along the shoulders of Bighorn Road weaving through Bighorn Park, waving at passing cars. A homeless person joined us, although he didn't seem to understand why. "What are we walking for?" It was mile eight.

Another batch from the Shrine Mountain Cabins dropped in at mile six. The whole gang from the Mayo Clinic Breast Cancer Department joined in. My cousins Ruth, Mary, Shelley, Jane and Steven drove up from Denver. We walked past the Vail Racquet Club, where old friends stood on the side of the road waving Welcome Home signs. A local reporter came to walk, and I told her how odd it was to think it took me five years to walk from Vail to East Vail taking the scenic route.

It was mile four. I started to feel dizzy. *Oh God, please don't be an ear infection again. Please don't let me faint. Come on, just four more miles.* I imagined the awkward news stories if I were to topple over so close to the finish line. "Like the Olympic athlete who trained her whole life only to lose by a tenth of a second, Letofsky almost made it!"

The better explanation was a combination of lack of sleep and too little food, putting an end to the theory that one can survive on adrenaline alone. I sat down on a curb and downed a sandwich to fuel up while people streamed by.

The two-mile mark was the Betty Ford Gardens. My friend Bob Moroney had organized a picnic and it was a welcome relief to rest and greet more people who were joining our walk. Excitement was building.

At the Betty Ford Gardens Vicki presented me with my last pair of New Balance shoes. "Under the theme 'There's no place like home,'" she announced, "I'd like to present you with your twenty-ninth and final pair of shoes swathed in ruby sparkles. Dorothy's ruby slippers took her back to Kansas. In Colorado, Polly has her ruby New Balance walkers."

"They're gorgeous! And what better way to finish off the last two miles than to have sparkly ruby feet? Let's go!"

All my best buddies surrounded me as I walked Bob through Vail's Covered Bridge into the heart of town. It felt so normal, as though I were just here yesterday and that the past five years were all a dream. Then the flashbacks started—the overwhelming support in Australia, the 9/11 events when I was in Malaysia, the glorious walk through Thailand, the chaos of India, a simmering Europe and the great re-discovery of America. Yes, it really had been five years.

At the International Bridge we were greeted by a gaggle of Vail school kids who had made flags of all the countries I walked through, and they held them high over their heads. A crowd had formed; some I knew, some I didn't, some were breast cancer survivors. They all wanted to walk the last mile. I mingled through the group, thrilled to have them there. They were asking me how I felt, and I wasn't sure what to tell them. Anxious, nervous, excited—a host of feelings churned around and came out like *auubluugugughwgh!* but I didn't know how to pronounce that.

At 3:30 on July 30, 2004, it was time to start the last mile. I moved Bob to the front of the crowd and gathered those who had helped me the most on this journey to converge at my side. I yelled for Mom to get right near me. Dad was there in his new walking shoes. Debi was on my left, Vicki on the right and a hundred people reaching for my hand in support as I headed for the finish line.

Walking the last mile I caught a glimpse in the crowd of my friend, Jean McGuey, who was going through cancer treatment but was still determined to walk with me. Seeing her so brave, as well as Vicki and Debi, who had survived and prevailed over their own breast cancer bouts, made me think of the similarities between this walk and women going through breast cancer. If I were to meet a woman who was diagnosed with breast cancer on August 1, 1999—the same day I left—I'm sure we'd have parallel stories. We both looked down an unfamiliar road with the end unclear and unnerving. We were both overwhelmed those beginning days as we began our first steps. We both asked questions when we were in unfamiliar territory, and sometimes we took wrong turns and had to backtrack. In our respective journeys there were days when we wondered if we could even get out of bed and other days when we were so mentally worn down we felt ourselves sinking. But we both continued taking one step at a time. Now, five years down the road, we were standing healthy and strong, with a much better understanding of ourselves and the world around us.

Of course the biggest difference between a breast cancer survivor and me is that mine was entirely my choice.

Approaching Lionshead Village I spotted the Welcome Back Polly banner a hundred yards ahead. The adrenaline swept in like an emotional tsunami and my legs took on a life of their own. The crowd broke into a cheer as I broke away with Bob, trotted toward the finish line and pushed him right through the Welcome Back banner, officially bringing this GlobalWalk full circle at 14,124 miles, 22 countries, 4 continents, 29 pairs of shoes, and over $200,000 USD raised for thirteen breast cancer organizations around the world.

CHAPTER 25

Lessons From the Road

During the first few months of my walk, I wondered and dreamed of the day I would walk through the finish line in Lionshead Village, how after five years on the road I would be a worldly wise woman and know everything about everything, and how nice that would be in just five years.

Now I want to tell the Polly of 1999, *Don't get your hopes up. You can walk around the world a hundred times, along every latitude and longitude, and you'll still stumble over a newly discovered cultural no-no that will embarrass you and, worse, inadvertently insult someone.*

I'd tell 1999 Polly, *you'll never feel worldly and wise, because every time you learn one thing, you'll turn a corner and there will be a dozen more things you don't understand. Every day you'll walk into a new culture that holds a uniquely blended history of politics, language, climate and religion that have helped to shape that national character, and you can't possibly get your head around it in the one to three days you walk through it.*

But, *1999 Polly, the upshot is that you'll learn how to get over whatever hurdle gets in your path. You might not receive any awards for grace, but you'll always find a way.*

I always knew this journey would be an education, but I was thinking more along the lines of languages, geography and history—which naturally there was plenty of—but who would have guessed I'd learn so much about the trials of sugar farming or the idiosyncrasies of the international trucking industry? My brain is stuffed with useless information. (Once in a while it pays off, like when the *NY Times Crossword Puzzle* recently had the clue "Smelly fruit in

Malaysia" and without missing a beat I filled in D-U-R-I-A-N. Though it would hardly get me a job.)

There were lessons well beyond the trivial, of course; chief among them that cultures don't just happen from border to border but rather in each household. It was all very exciting to see how people lived their lives. Each night I'd walk through the front door into a new culture with a distinctive diet, a different family dynamic, and a variety of tastes and rules. For me, as a guest, I had to adapt to their culture from the doorway. Would they like me to take my shoes off when I enter their house or are they offended if I walk around in my socks? Some people were offended if I asked to help with the dishes, some were offended if I didn't. Some families grunted with disapproval if I didn't pray before I ate, others wouldn't dream of it.

Personally, I would like to see every political science, journalism and business major ditch their college thesis and instead, spend their senior year walking across a country, any country. Their assignment would be to talk to local farmers and businessmen, talk to locals at ma-and-pa cafes, talk to local developers and mayors and school administrators. When you're taking a seat at dinner tables village to village, you learn how various policies affect them that might not be the case in the village down the road. And incrementally you become a more critical thinker.

People often ask would I do it again. If they're asking, would I do it a second time, the answer is no. One lap around the world is plenty, thank you.

On the other hand, if they're really asking, if I had looked into a crystal ball on August 1, 1999, and known the trials and aggravations I would endure, would I still go? then the answer is an emphatic yes. There is no greater education, or means to personal growth than a walk around the world.

I'm sure those five years affected me in ways I'll never fully comprehend. There are obvious changes, like the way I bond with strangers instantly or how I compartmentalize difficult situations and just keep putting that proverbial foot in front of the other until I'm past them. But I've also noticed some changes full of contra-dictions. I'm undoubtedly more patient. You can hardly walk around the world one step at a time and not embrace the art of going slow. Oddly, though, I've also become less patient, adopting the one-strike-you're-out rule. I'm sure it stems from the dramas of my first seven months of this walk, and fair enough. I've put the kibosh on the niceties of giving people a fourth, fifth, tenth chance and alternatively adopted one of my biggest lessons, "People show you who they are—if you let them." And it kept me safe.

My biggest education by far, though, was my discovery of America. My patriotism surprises me, because I don't recall ever giving two hoots about America or being an American prior to leaving. But having traveled through this turbulent crossroads in world history I've discovered the priceless gift we've been given with our freedom of religion, freedom of speech, free to be whoever we want to be, and how those basic freedoms are at the core of my very own heritage. Those are my GlobalWalk's greatest lessons.

Only days after crossing the finish line in Vail, I got a ride down the mountain to Denver and started creating a new life for myself. To the surprise of everyone, including myself, I fell into my new life seamlessly. With the money left over from selling my little condo in Vail, I bought a small place at the edge of the city in the village of Glendale.

I've continued working with breast cancer through Sense of Security; a non-profit organization that my friend Vicki founded. They provide financial assistance to Colorado breast cancer patients in treatment to assist with basic necessities such as housing, food and groceries, transportation and health insurance premiums and utilities. I am regularly hired to speak to groups and conventions about my journey in a program I've affectionately entitled, "Little Steps, Big Feat." I joined a local Lions Club in the suburb of High-lands Ranch; and just as Alan MacKenzie and I had discussed all those years before, we became sister clubs with my club in Mackay

North, Queensland, Australia. I also secured a job in the hotel industry in sales and marketing, where much to the chagrin of management, whenever a charitable organization requested a donated room, I was a little too quick to say, "Sure! Do you want two nights?"

I went to an animal shelter and found the two furry loves of my life, Penelope and Maddie, two old lady kitties I've wanted for years. They waddle out on the balcony to curl up on top of Bob who has retired there. I settled in quickly and happily, as if the mystery I'd felt so compelled to go solve about how the world ticks had been resolved. Enough anyway, that I feel at peace, secure, happy. I *love* having a fridge, and a Whole Foods four blocks away. I love having a blender for the blueberry smoothies and a laundry basket for the dirty clothes. I revel in having friends to while away Saturday mornings with a laugh over a toffee-nut-latte-soy-no-whip, and who, with a hint that maybe it's time to start delving into that strangest culture of all, gave me a copy of *The Complete Idiot's Guide to Dating*. (Stand by for what could be a sequel!)

A few times a year I get an email from someone who is toying with the idea of walking across their state, their country, or around the world, and they ask if I could give them any advice.

I politely respond, "I got nothin'. If a thousand people go on a walk around the world there are going to be a thousand different journeys. You'll adlib every day, which is part of the discovery. So go out and put one foot in front of the other and be prepared to be unprepared. There will be difficult times, and that's okay; the bumps in the road are the fabric of the journey. But in the darkest times, when you don't know where to turn, just take one more step," I philosophized. "Sometimes the next step is the only one that counts."

In July 1999, when I sat to write my first journal entry, *Pre-walk Thoughts*, I stared at my blank computer screen wondering what story would develop on those empty pages. The story that did unfold was a story in which I took on the world by myself but was never alone. Thousands of strangers came to my aid in many small ways and in record numbers. Doing the math, an average of ten people a day times five years equals nearly 20,000 people who formed a human chain around the world to help me get safely back to Colorado where I belong.

Because it took me 22 years of dreaming, 3 years of planning and 5 years of walking simply to discover that Dorothy was right—there's no place like home.

Acknowledgements

There are thousands of good Samaritans around the world to whom I am indebted, a handful of which I would like to single out. First, Alan MacKenzie of the Mackay North Lions Club in Queensland, Australia, who changed the course of this walk. His belief in me and his subsequent passion to get Lions Clubs involved gave this walk its chain of support from village to village around the world, and, in turn, raised the awareness of breast cancer ten levels from what I could've done on my own.

To Dr. Joel Dekanich, who put me through a painful ten-month treatment prior to my walk, but fixed my plantar fasciitis when other doctors told me it was incurable. That million dollar check I promised you is in the mail.

Phil Novotny of B.O.B and John Cutter of Cutter Designs, for conceiving my special little guy, my companion, my pal, my buggy, Bob. He was a star around the world and did you proud.

To Randy Gaudet with All Thailand Experiences, who donated his tour services by way of van and driver Prayoon for the four month trek through Thailand. Thank you to Elliot Shubert in England, who took me under his wing and made contacts throughout the British Isles. Sincere gratitude to the late Jim Hamilton of the Stranraer Lions Club in Scotland, who was so overprotective of me through his country it's a wonder he didn't hold my hand through the back roads to Edinburgh.

Shirley Russo of Rochester, Minnesota, who tirelessly organized fundraising events for the Mayo Clinic's breast cancer department and fielded calls from me through America's wheat belt when I asked for MapQuest directions.

Endless gratitude to the entire Shrager family, who spoiled me rotten from Elizabeth, New Jersey, to Hershey, Pennsylvania; Bonnie and Jim, who fed me and fed me and fed me, and Jeff, who served as my bodyguard walking into Trenton (family members, insert joke here). An extra special note of thanks goes to Jen and Ely (Shrager) Lourie for that very generous box of hot chocolate. I promise to pay it forward to some penniless, exhausted nomad one day.

To Curtis Wheaton, a onetime stranger on the side of the road in Ontario, Canada, who offered 300,000 priceless Marriott Reward Points to a tired soul.

Debi and Jim Linker, I thank you eternally for the miles of laughter camping out in Walmart parking lots across Midwest America. My life is so much richer because of our time together.

To Linda Murphy, my "Re-assimilation Officer," my heartiest thanks for letting me stay with you in Denver while I got reacquainted with the real world after five years.

Vicki Tosher, two-time breast cancer survivor and master advocate, it's hard to believe I didn't know you before I embarked on this journey. Having you as a friend was worth walking the 14,124 miles.

My sisters, Cara Letofsky and Laurie Letofsky, for their unwavering support through the miles, and brother, PJ, for believing this story was worth three years of his life producing a documentary, *Polly's GlobalWalk*, a 104 minute HD DVD available for $24.95 online at www.PollysGlobalwalk.com.

To the thousands of breast cancer survivors who came to walk with me, whether it was one mile through their town or four days down the road, the thought of your courage and grit always nudged me out of my darkest times, realizing they were a mere discomfort compared to what you face. You are my heroes.

If I were to sit here until the end of this century, I would never be able to thank the Lions Clubs International adequately. You took this stranger and passed her town to town around the world, making sure she got home to Colorado safe and sound. The smallest village with three members served as important a role as did the clubs in the largest cities. So to Lions Clubs up the east coast of Australia, through Singapore, Malaysia, Thailand, India, Turkey, England, Scotland, Northern Ireland, Republic of Ireland and across the United States, please accept my eternal gratitude.

Above all, if my most profound gratefulness were able to reach across every line of latitude, it wouldn't be enough to thank my mom and dad. Not a day goes by when I don't thank God I was born to the two of you—two parents who would be supportive if I announced I was going to walk to the moon. To Rosemary Rawson and Irv Letofsky, due to your unconditional love and unselfish support, I owe you all the happiness that has filled my life.

P.S. Oh, and my fuzziest thanks to Penelope and Maddie, whose catnaps kept my keyboard warm, albeit furry, while I wrote this.

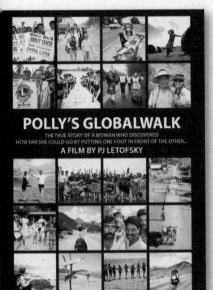

Polly Letofsky's story of courage and determination is both entertaining and inspiring.
There's no better way to hear it than from Polly herself.

Your audiences will walk away with a renewed commitment to achieve the seemingly unachievable, determined to move past unexpected obstacles and endless challenges, and embrace a new spirit toward their lives and work.

Polly's GlobalWalk has been featured in over 2,000 newspapers, magazines, radio and television stations around the world including *Good Housekeeping, CNN International, The CBS Early Show, NBC's Your Total Health,* and *Fine Living Channel's Radical Sabbatical.*

A natural storyteller, since her return Polly has been speaking to a variety of groups around the country. To rapt audiences, she richly details her journey with humor and honest reflection, the good times and the hardships. She tells of how she took on the challenge of a life-long dream and learned quickly how to adapt to a swiftly changing world.

Sometimes serious, sometimes funny, always inspirational, Polly's inspirational keynote personifies the spirit of commitment and perseverance that will compel your audience to take on life's biggest challenges – one step at a time.

To book Polly for your event please contact:
Ashley Andrus
303-722-1947
Ashley.andrus@zoetraining.com
Or contact Polly directly at www.PollyLetofsky.com

SENSE of SECURITY

Providing peace of mind... when you need it most.

Sense of Security was incorporated in March 2000 to fill a much needed niche for breast cancer patients living in Colorado. **Sense of Security's** strategy focuses on meeting basic financial needs that do not disappear during treatment and often cause anxiety when steep medical expenses move to the forefront of a patient's mind; housing, food and groceries, utilities, transportation, health insurance premiums, household goods. **Sense of Security's** mission is meant to ease that burden:

We seek to provide a sense of security from financial hardship and enhance the quality of life for breast cancer patients in treatment

Please visit us at
www.senseofsecurity.org
303-669-3113